EMPIRES IN THE WILDERNESS

Foreign Colonization and Development
in Guatemala, 1834-1844

THE UNIVERSITY OF NORTH CAROLINA PRESS

CHAPEL HILL

EMPIRES IN THE WILDERNESS

---

*FOREIGN COLONIZATION
AND DEVELOPMENT
IN GUATEMALA, 1834-1844*

BY WILLIAM J. GRIFFITH

PREFACE

Happily, this study is concerned with no rival in duration to the Hundred Years' War, for the time elapsed in its preparation exactly coincides with that of the period covered. It was conceived as an inquiry of modest scope into an ostensibly uncomplicated arrangement for massive foreign colonization of Guatemala, but only slight investigation disclosed that the plan was neither so simple nor so localized as supposed. As the complexity of the subject became evident and the search for relevant material broadened in consequence, the project enlarged to several times its anticipated size, and the period of investigation lengthened in proportion.

The topic was selected as a contribution to one of the themes chosen for investigation in the Tulane faculty-student interdisciplinary Latin American area seminar. It was suggested by a few tantalizing sentences in Chester Lloyd Jones's *Guatemala, Past and Present* and the third volume of Hubert Howe Bancroft's *History of Central America*. These terse passages record an extraordinary transaction in which the government of Guatemala in 1834 granted to a London colonization company (the Eastern Coast of Central America Commercial and Agricultural Company) some fifteen million acres of public lands. Few other historical works accord this arresting action by the government of Dr. Mariano Gálvez more than passing remark, and fewer still note that almost simultaneous companion grants virtually completed the transfer of the state's unclaimed lands to *empresarios* who agreed to colonize them with foreign immigrants. The only extensive treatment of the topic, that of Pedro Pérez Valenzuela in his *Santo Tomás de Castilla: Apuntes para la historia de las colonizaciones en la costa atlántica* (1956), largely misconstrues the effort for want of relevant documentation and makes it principally a test in patriotism on which low marks are assigned to the Liberal Chief of State. Jorge Luis Arriola gives some attention to the subject in one chapter of his *Gálvez en la encrucijada* (1961), but with much the same emphasis. This study examines the colonization projects as a part of the grand design formed by Gálvez for the development of his state.

It has been impossible to bring to fruition the most ambitious hopes raised as the project took form. The relationship between the Guatemalan government and the London company suggested the possibility of attempting an integrated case study of a Latin American effort to achieve economic development and of European capital employed in speculative New World enterprise during the first decades of independence. Materials appropriate to such treatment, however, could not always be discovered.

To establish a solidly documented record of operations by the Eastern Coast of Central America Commercial and Agricultural Company proved impossible. The frivolous character of the enterprise, at least in its early years, apparently determined that by default if not by deliberate intent of the directors it would leave, even in the public realm, the scantest possible evidence of its existence. The administrations that succeeded the first adventurers produced a more informative public record of their transactions, but the Company's papers seem not to have survived, and by coincidence the void in the archives of Glyn's, the prestigious banking house it employed, includes the years during which the directors maintained their account. The Company's activities, therefore, could be reconstructed only in such areas and with such degree of completeness as were made possible by its own publications, occasional newspaper notices, and documents relating to its affairs that found their way into official archives in Great Britain, Belgium, British Honduras, and Guatemala. These materials were sufficient to form a circumstantial sketch of Company operations, but they did not afford an adequate basis for an exhaustive examination of its role as a gatherer and investor abroad of European capital.

The absence of certain desirable evidence impaired less drastically the study of the colonization projects as devices for achieving development. No personal papers came to light, either for Gálvez or for any other important figure of his time, which might have recorded the intimate details of formulation, adoption, and attempted execution of the colonization scheme. The evidence on these subjects, therefore, came principally from official documents. These sources, fortunately, supplied abundant material for exposition of the official plan formulated by Gálvez for achieving development by means of foreign colonization and of controversies produced by specific features of the contracts he approved. Authorship of ideas, evolution of thought and of attitudes by individuals and by groups, conflicts of interest and of principle, and the source of contrary opinions, among other topics, might have been more clearly illuminated had personal papers been available; their absence, however, does not rob of merit the synthesis made from public documents. Although more generalized and less precise than might be desired, it still is valid.

The attempt to assess the colonization projects as instruments of national development is in no way intended to assert *expertise* on that complex subject. For that matter, no claim is laid even to mastery of the technical literature in the development field. It seemed sufficient for the purposes of this work to accept as a basis for comparison and comment a popular synthesis of some of the views generally accepted by contemporary students of the process.

Fidelity to contemporary purport required use of some relatively unfamiliar and specialized terms. Rather than to insert definitions and explanations of these words at the scattered points in the text where they first appear, it seemed preferable for easy reference to bring them together in a glossary.

Note should perhaps be taken in passing of special circumstances that resulted in deviations from the usual form of citation for two collections now found in the Archivo Nacional of Guatemala. The records of the Guatemalan Congress were opened for my use immediately after they had been deposited in the Archivo Nacional and before they could be reclassified. My citations therefore identify the documents by the categories and symbols assigned while they were in the possession of Congress, followed by the word "unclassified." A similar observation applies to the archives of the Department of Baja Verapaz consulted in Salamá during the summer of 1956 several years before they were transferred to Guatemala City. A hasty recheck of the documents on the day they were delivered to the Archivo Nacional revealed much deterioration during the interval: some were half mouldered away with dampness, and others were entirely missing. My citations are to documents and to classifications as they existed at Salamá in 1956.

The research abroad was made possible by assistance from several sources. I gratefully acknowledge grants from the Middle American Research Institute of Tulane University for several summers of work in Central America and from the Tulane Council on Research and the Social Science Research Council for a semester of investigation in Europe. While its cruise ships were still in operation, the United

Fruit Company twice provided summer transportation to and from Guatemala.

During the course of the investigation in widely scattered places I incurred obligations to many persons who assisted me in various ways. I am grateful to them all, but to some I owe particular thanks.

My most pervasive debts are to the staff members of libraries and archives in this country and abroad who helped me to locate in their collections the materials relevant to the study. My domestic obligations of this order are due principally at the Library of Congress, the Yale University Library, and the Latin American Library (formerly the Middle American Research Institute Library) of Tulane University.

In Central America I am beholden chiefly to the late Dr. J. Joaquín Pardo for assistance both in working through the monumental holdings of the Archivo Nacional of Guatemala and in securing access to the valuable but smaller collections in the archives of the Ministerio de Gobernación in Guatemala City, and of the Department of Baja Verapaz in Salamá. Benjamín Godoy and the late Ricardo Castañeda Paganini, successive directors of the Biblioteca Nacional of Guatemala, and Francisco de León, Rigoberto Bran Azmitia, and Albertina Gálvez, the current *directora,* facilitated use of that institution's early Central American newspapers, pamphlets, and *hojas sueltas,* especially those contained in the Gilberto Valenzuela Collection. Baudilio Torres, Director of the Biblioteca Nacional of El Salvador, granted permission to consult the small store of federal records in his care that survived the disastrous fire of the last century.

To Alastair Maitland, then British Consul General in New Orleans, and to Michael S. Porcher, Chief Secretary of British Honduras, and Hamilton Anderson, Archaeological Commissioner and Curator of the archives, I owe the opportunity to examine the records in the Registry in Belize. The full contribution of that archive, however, I was not able to extract during a single short stay.

The personnel of the Public Record Office and of the British Museum in London gave the prompt, efficient, and cheerful service for which they are justly renowned. Muriel Hicks, Assistant Librarian of the Society of Friends Library, and L. M. Payne, Assistant Librarian at the Royal College of Physicians, most generously checked through their collections for material. Irene Shrigley, Secretary of the Business Archives Council, helped to establish with near certainty that no records of the Eastern Coast Company survive. At the University of London, A. T. Milne opened the facilities of the Institute of Historical Research, and Robin A. Humphreys, among other courtesies, aided in obtaining photocopies of several of the Hume Tracts from the magnificent collection owned by University College. In Brussels, P. H. Desneux, Director of the Archives du Ministère des Affaires Ètrangères et du Commerce Extérieur, and his staff were gracious and helpful with advice, and at some inconvenience to themselves arranged emergency work space.

Several especially valuable personal contributions to the work I acknowledge with particular appreciation. My wife, Connie G. Griffith, has been my language expert, indefatigable collaborator in research, and patient bearer of summer exile in sundry archives and libraries. The note file burgeons with the tangible product of her labor, but similar identification of her written and her oral contributions in the text has been impossible.

Colleagues in the Department of History have helped in special ways to advance the work. William R. Hogan, Chairman, with skill born of extensive practice has warded off any number of encroaching responsibilities that might have postponed the publication date. Thomas L. Karnes has shared in the running discussions that accompanied the progress of the book with wit, wisdom, and broad knowledge of Central America; he has read parts of the manuscript, and has given helpful advice on a variety of problems. Charles P. Roland on several occasions has suggested from his own very recent experience tested paths through the maze of last minute emergencies. Hugh Franklin Rankin has suggested sources of information on subjects close to his own specialty, has read and criticized several chapters, and has helped to find the manuscript a congenial publisher.

Several individuals provided material of different kinds for use in the book. A former colleague at Tulane, Mario Rodríguez, took time during his first summer of research in Guatemala to make typescripts of several contemporary pamphlets on the colonization issue. Two graduate students, Ralph Lee Woodward, Jr., and Ora-Westley Schwemmer, contributed from Guatemala and Belgium, respectively, typescripts of several *Memorias* published by the Consulado de Comercio de Guatemala, and copies of letters from the dossier of Colonel Remy de Puydt in the Musée Royale de l'Armée et d'Histoire Militaire. John Lochhead, Librarian of the Mariners Museum of Newport News, Virginia, furnished from Lloyd's *Register of Shipping* data on each of the immigrant ships sent out by the Company. Mrs. Mary V. Johnston drew the three original maps that accompany the text.

Finally, I must acknowledge my debt to two exceptional secretaries. Mrs. Reba Herman kept the wheels turning on several occasions when office emergencies threatened to mire down the work, and Mrs. Shirley Lucas McAfee typed every word of the book for me—at least three times.

CONTENTS

Preface   v

I   PROSPECT   3

II   WANTED: DEVELOPMENT   8

III   CHOSEN INSTRUMENTALITY: THE COLONIZATION CONTRACTS   32

IV   BRITISH SETTLEMENTS, OLD AND NEW   53

V   DEVELOPMENT OR EXPLOITATION?   74

VI   FOREIGNERS OR NATIVE SONS?   93

VII   WILDERNESS SETTLEMENTS: NEW LIVERPOOL AND
       SANTA CRUZ   120

VIII   DISASTER SURMOUNTED   157

IX   COMMERCIAL TOWNS: ABBOTTSVILLE AND SANTO TOMÁS   188

X   BRITISH COLONY OR BELGIAN?   224

XI   INFRASTRUCTURE OR ANACHRONISM?   253

XII   RETROSPECT   282

Abbreviations   311

Glossary   313

Bibliography   315

Index   323

MAPS

AREA OF COLONIZATION GRANTS   62

COLONIZATION GRANTS OF 1834   124

POYAIS AND THE MOSQUITO SHORE   192

DISTRICT OF SANTO TOMÁS   258

EMPIRES IN THE WILDERNESS

---

*Foreign Colonization and Development
in Guatemala, 1834-1844*

I

PROSPECT

High expectation was the dominant mood in America as the nineteenth century neared its first-quarter mark. Political independence of Europe recently achieved by large portions of both continents, north and south, seemed to promise the fortunate residents of the new nations opportunity to demonstrate that proper institutions, functioning in the pristine environment of the New World, could achieve the perfection of man, dreamed of but unattained under the regimes of old Europe. To this idealistic feeling of political separateness, this intent to maintain the New World in unblemished isolation from the Old, President James Monroe gave expression in his message to the United States Congress on December 2, 1823. His declaration that "the American continents, by the free and independent condition which they have assumed and maintained, are henceforth not to be considered as subjects for further colonization by any European powers" spoke the mind of the Hemisphere.

The New World repudiated the political auspices of Europe, but it did not renounce the European components—men, money, and matériel—with which the new societies of America had been built. Indeed, the leaders of the young nations recognized that, unless they were able to draw immigrants and capital from Europe to continue the subjugation of New World wildernesses, their utopian expectations would remain a fantasy. Juan Bautista Alberdi, the Argentine political philosopher, stated the equation in three words: *gobernar es poblar*.

The republic of Central America anticipated Alberdi's dictum by at least a generation. Indeed, the idea of colonization as a means of development far antedated independence in the Captaincy-General (or Kingdom) of Guatemala. The colonial authorities several times considered such projects, particularly in relation to their desire to create a port on the Bay of Santo Tomás and to open the Motagua River to navigation, but their efforts produced no tangible results. The Consulado de Comercio, the merchant guild established in 1793 and charged with responsibility for executing public works projects within the Kingdom, was no more successful. Independence nurtured the belief that an enlightened government, energetically pursuing the national interest, could quickly attain economic growth that lethargic or ill-disposed Spanish administrators had not achieved during three centuries of misrule. When five provinces of the former Captaincy-General, after a brief union with Mexico under Agustín Iturbide, declared for a separate national existence as the United Provinces of Central America in July 1823, they were able for the first time to install officials who could be presumed to foster local development.

The Liberal-dominated National Constituent Assembly, which served as both legislature and constitutional convention for the nascent Central American republic, acted in the belief that economic growth required scarcely more than removal of the artificial shackles placed by Spanish colonial restrictions. Convinced that a larger and more highly skilled population would speed the process of development, the Assembly during the first few months of its deliberations enacted two measures intended to foster immigration. In December 1823, acting on a motion of which Dr. Mariano Gálvez was a co-sponsor, it declared the territory of the republic an inviolable asylum for foreigners who might seek sanctuary within its borders. The following January it adopted a general colonization law that established conditions under which the five states of the new union were authorized individually to contract with national or foreign *empresarios,* singly or in associations not exceeding three persons, for the settlement of immigrant colonists on public lands within their frontiers. The federal law empowered the states to confer certain special privileges and land grants, duplicating the total of the individual allotments of one million square varas (about 180 acres) specified for each married couple established, upon any entrepreneur who founded a new settlement and populated it with a minimum of fifteen immigrant families.

The states of El Salvador, Honduras, Nicaragua, and Costa Rica took little advantage of the federal legislation, but Guatemala attempted at once to put it to use. Between 1824 and 1826 Liberal governments of that state accepted several colonization offers, but the proponents were able to carry none to completion. During the next several years civil strife deterred virtually all constructive initiative. A feud between the President of the republic, Manuel José Arce, and Liberals in the federal Congress and at the head of the state government of Guatemala erupted into civil war in 1826. The fall of Guatemala City in April 1829 to Liberal invaders from El Salvador commanded by Francisco Morazán sent Arce into exile and restored Liberal control over the governments of both the nation and the state of Guatemala. Successful military operations against Arce, conspiring in Soconusco, and suffocation of rebellions led by Vicente Domínguez and Ramón Guzmán at Trujillo and Omoa finally restored some measure of domestic quiet to the federation.

Dr. Mariano Gálvez, elected Chief of State of Guatemala in August 1831, made use of the opportunity afforded by relative internal peace to undertake a complete Liberal reform of his native province. Doctrinaire and magisterial in his enlightenment, the new executive was determined to restructure Guatemalan life in harmony with what he conceived to be "the spirit of the century." To this end he projected a variety of developmental activities that he believed necessary to establish the foundations of a modern state. Conspicuous among his plans were projects for rapid settlement of immigrant families in the relatively uninhabited north of Guatemala.

Gálvez was not beguiled by the distant harvest and the puny fruit promised by the federal colonization law; his impatience to achieve national growth required plantings of "giant-sized," "quick-maturing" varieties. When local promoters proved incapable of meeting his demands he turned to foreigners. In 1834 he signed with several British-born promoters a succession of colonization agreements framed in what he believed to be mutually advantageous terms. By these instruments he ceded to foreign entrepreneurs enormous areas of Guatemalan public lands on condition that they be immediately settled and developed. As a result of his largesse, the Eastern Coast of Central America Commercial and Agricultural Company in contemplation of its grants could exult: "Fifteen millions of acres are a kingdom in extent." With only somewhat reduced justification the other concessionaires also could have made the same boast. In land area and in powers conferred upon them, each of the *empresarios* was made proprietor of a wilderness empire.

His pledging of Guatemalan resources Gálvez conceived as a frontal assault on the obstacles retarding national development. It is hardly to be supposed that to describe his program he would find terms identical with those a specialist would now employ, yet his appraisal of the local problem seems to have enabled him to grasp the essential elements of the development process. His projects display understanding, for example, of the basic functions recognized by contemporary students of the problem, which Barbara Ward sum-

marizes in *The Rich Nations and the Poor Nations* (New York, 1962).
The four "revolutions" which she asserts poor countries must experience if they are to achieve the major economic breakthrough prereq-
uisite to sustained material development involve the concept of
equality among men and nations, the idea that material progress is
attainable, the sudden increase of births, and the application of science and capital (saving) to all economic processes. All of these
movements, she observes, originated in the North Atlantic area, and
it is perhaps a further evidence of his clarity of vision that Gálvez
sought to draw his collaborators directly from that source.

Two of the four elements thus identified Gálvez clearly recognized
as essential; indeed, his projects were shaped by his belief in the
necessity of obtaining them abroad. A sudden major increase in the
laboring population he expected to achieve, not as a result of a
higher domestic birth rate, but by attraction of Europeans to take
up residence in the Guatemalan wilderness. Capital and scientific
knowledge, both to be applied to development of resources, he expected foreign entrepreneurs and colonists to provide until nationals
had attained the sophistication necessary to achieve mastery over
their environment and until the enhanced productivity of the country could supply an accumulation of domestic capital sufficient for
its developmental requirements.

Overt recognition of the relevance of the two remaining "revolutions" is less clearly evident in the plans of Gálvez, possibly because
he believed them already accomplished in Guatemala. The spirit of
equality he considered established by independence and guaranteed
by law, but he intended the colonization enterprises to undergird it,
notwithstanding that expediency required him temporarily to trans-
gress the principle in the contracts themselves by guaranteeing privileged position to immigrant settlers. Ultimately he expected equality
to acquire substance from the projects as a result of a generally dif-
fused prosperity, derived from more efficient exploitation of resources,
and a higher level of competence among nationals, attained as a
consequence of tutelage by more advanced foreign colonists. Finally,
the idea of progress—concern with direction of material change in
such fashion as to create a better contemporary world—was a tenet
of Liberal belief to which Gálvez fully subscribed and to the realization of which his program was directed.

If Gálvez acquired some intellectual mastery over the problems
of development by objective assessment of Guatemalan requirements,
he failed to appraise with equal realism both the efficacy of the means

he employed to achieve his ends and the adequacy to his purpose of the instruments to which he confided the execution of the enterprises. The almost total failure in performance, however, robs neither the plan nor the effort of interest and significance, for the Gálvez program was more than a single incident of short duration confined within the borders of a small and remote country. It was in fact one among many similar ventures sponsored with like objectives after independence by a variety of Latin American states. The Guatemalan experiment may not be entirely representative of these enterprises, for some of the features devised by Gálvez in recognition of peculiar circumstances were possibly unique and some of his measures produced consequences that were perhaps without counterpart elsewhere. As an example of a widespread phenomenon, however, the Guatemalan experience has relevance, not only to the peculiar complex of local problems it was devised to solve, but to the general Latin American desire for immediate development after independence and to the large-scale activities of various sorts undertaken then and since by foreigners with the collaboration of nationals in recurring attempts to reach that fugitive goal.

This investigation treats the Gálvez projects as a case study in this context. Beyond the contribution it may make to the history of Guatemala and its relationships abroad during the period covered, it may throw some incidental light on the role that mass settlements of Europeans were expected to play in the early national life of Latin American countries and, perhaps, on the first large-scale efforts after independence to attain national development. Such a study and other similar or more general ones that may follow should give some better perspective, at least in time, on the search for national development in Latin America.

II

WANTED: DEVELOPMENT

"Colonizations are the first interest of the State and to accomplish them we should before now have made an extraordinary effort."[1] This declaration Dr. Mariano Gálvez made to the Legislative Assembly of Guatemala only a few weeks after he took office in August 1831. The immediate purpose of the Chief of State was to persuade the legislators to approve a minor colonization proposal, but his words could well have been emblazoned as the motto of his administration. They stated a policy to the execution of which he committed the full power and prestige of his office.

The operation which Gálvez envisioned was far more comprehensive than the simple location of immigrant settlers on uncultivated land in Central America. His overt purpose was to develop the empty northern reaches of his state in order to increase the productivity, wealth, and power of the Federation. He hoped, however, that internal development would accomplish unobtrusively certain external objectives. He expected increased economic activity and improved communications on the north coast to free Central American commerce from its tributary status to the merchants resident in the port of Belize, and he believed that settlement of the unclaimed lands bordering on the Gulf of Honduras would confine the woodcutters of the British Settlement within the territorial limits set by the Anglo-Spanish treaties of 1783 and 1786 that the Central American authorities held still to govern British tenure in the area.

The major facets of this developmental program Gálvez had sketched the year before when, as federal Minister of Finance, he had addressed the national Congress. "We find ourselves today," he told the deputies, "separated from commercial contact with the great European markets by difficult roads, by wild mountains and forests, and by deadly climate; our cultivation and population are situated on the coasts of the Pacific to which we were confined by the policy of the Cabinet of Madrid. Our civilization and prosperity depend

1. A los Diputados S[ecreta]rios de la Asamblea Legislativa, Oct. 24, 1831, ANG, leg. 1395, exp. 32331, n.f.

on our drawing closer to the Atlantic."[2] He had discussed the external aspects of the problem with particular reference to British Honduras in an earlier report to the same body. "Belize," he observed, "is today . . . the warehouse for Central America from which all our merchants and the contraband traders supply themselves. This circumstance forces our commerce to accept prices set by four suppliers who consistently undervalue our products. This situation requires preferential consideration, as does the state of our coasts, ports, and frontiers, our roads and our internal navigations." In the same message he made explicit his concern for the security of the frontier: "The advances made in all directions and for such distances [from Belize] that the axe blows of the woodcutters resound in the Petén and at the mouth of the River of Izabal [Río Dulce] have been, and should be, opposed. . . ."[3]

As chief executive of Guatemala, Gálvez had fresh opportunity of "drawing closer to the Atlantic." The dream was an old and cherished one, but neither the colony nor the republic had found the means to accomplish it. In the last decade of the eighteenth century the Spanish crown tried to give impetus to works of this nature by chartering in Guatemala a guild of merchants, the Consulado de Comercio, and charging it, among other functions, with responsibility for stimulating economic development in the Captaincy-General. After independence this association was allowed to continue with much the same powers, but its jurisdiction was restricted to the state of Guatemala. The Liberals, however, opposed both the monopolistic character of the Consulado and its operation in a field that they believed to belong properly to the government. During their initial period of control over the state government of Guatemala, therefore, they curbed the activities of the merchant body, and when at the end of the civil war in April 1829 they regained power, one of their first acts was to suppress the guild. Thereafter the powers that had been conferred upon the Consulado were exercised directly by the state government.[4]

2. *Informe que presentó al Congreso federal, el Secretario de Estado y del despacho de Hacienda . . . en la sesión pública ordinaria del sábado 24 de julio de 1830* ([Guatemala], n.d.), p. 5.

3. *Exposición que al comenzar la actual Legislatura ordinaria, hizo al Congreso federal de esta República el S[ecreta]rio de Estado y del despacho de Hacienda . . . leida . . . en . . . los días 20 y 23 de abril y 4 de mayo . . . de 1830 . . .* (Guatemala, 1830), p. 7.

4. Ralph Lee Woodward, Jr., "The Consulado de Comercio of Guatemala, 1793-1871" (Unpubl. Diss., Tulane, 1962), pp. 6, 9-10.

Gálvez proposed to use these new powers of the state to initiate a program of development more broadly conceived than any attempted by the Consulado and to make his projects an arm of public policy. He intended to sprinkle the northern wilderness with populous and productive communities, to connect them with the interior by adequate facilities for land and water transport, and to provide direct outlet for the resulting foreign commerce through deep-water ports established on the Gulf of Honduras within the territory of the state. Obviously, settlers were the first requisite to the success of his plans.

Gálvez attempted to secure agricultural settlements in the northern wastes by both direct and oblique means. In October 1831 he recommended favorable action by the Guatemalan Assembly on a proposal submitted to the government by José Sacasa for colonizing the north and south coasts with Europeans.[5] During the same month he opened the stands of timber along the northern waterways of the state to exploitation by foreigners, subject only to a declaration of intent before the military commander of the district in question and to an agreement to live in consonance with the laws of the state. The immediate stimulus for this action Gálvez found in the report that the authorities at Belize were issuing to all applicants grants for woodcutting operations within the boundaries claimed by Guatemala. His own measure would produce no greater immediate benefits to the state than did the grants made in Belize, but he hoped that foreigners permitted to cut wood on Guatemalan soil would ultimately turn to agriculture as a means of livelihood.[6] His offer of protection by the Guatemalan government was intended to attract settlers rather than trespassers.

In accord with this policy the government of Guatemala made a succession of woodcutting concessions in the northern part of the state during the years immediately following 1831. Among other grants, concessions were issued to several individuals subsequently prominent in colonization projects. The most important of these were the associates Carlos Antonio Meany and Juan Manuel Rodríguez of Guatemala and Marshal Bennett of Belize, and the firm of Ignacio Zerón, Juan José Balcarzel, and Cándido Pulleiro, all of Guatemala.[7]

5. A los Diputados S[ecreta]rios de la Asamblea Legislativa, Oct. 24, 1831, n.f.

6. Al C[iudadano] Secret[ari]o del Consejo Repres[entativ]o, Oct. 24, 1831, ANG, leg. 477, exp. 7718, n.f.

7. The grants are recorded in ANG, leg. 1151, exp. 26611, n.f., and leg. 1152, exps. 26625, 26645, n.f.

For his attack on deficient transport Gálvez found authorization under a law passed by the Legislative Assembly of Guatemala on April 20, 1831, which he amplified by an order of October 1 of the same year. This measure empowered the government to contract with private capitalists for widening the major thoroughfares of the state into cart roads and for establishing steam navigation on its rivers and lakes. If private capital could not be found to undertake these tasks, the government itself could make the necessary improvements.[8] During the next few years the Gálvez government tried to carry out such projects under both private and public auspices.

The principal road that demanded attention was the route over which the major share of the commerce of the republic passed. It was a mule track that led from Guatemala City to the Motagua River near Zacapa, along that stream past Gualán to Los Encuentros, and then over the towering bulk of Mico Mountain to the port of Izabal situated on the southern shore of the inland lake of the same name (or Golfo Dulce). Access to Lake Izabal from the Gulf of Honduras was afforded by the waters of Amatique Bay, the Río Dulce, and the Golfete, but the bar at the mouth of the Río Dulce denied entrance to most oceangoing ships. Coasting vessels of shallow draft plying between Izabal and Belize, however, made the lake port the principal national entrepôt of both import and export trade. In the interest of equipping the town better to serve this function, the government of Guatemala forwarded to the federal authorities in November 1832 a merchants' petition that the lake village be habilitated as a national port[9] and itself undertook there an extensive program of construction that was reported in the late spring of 1833 to be nearing completion.[10] Concurrently the Assembly ordered that repairs be made on the segment of the road between Izabal and Gualán and that the cost be defrayed from the proceeds of a toll to be collected at the port on all cargo and from mounted travelers using the thoroughfare.[11]

The obvious deficiences of Izabal as a port led to a search for a more satisfactory site elsewhere on the north coast. The Carib village situated on the right bank of the estuary formed by the Río Dulce where it discharged into Amatique Bay offered some hope for development as a deepwater anchorage. To this settlement the state govern-

8. Alejandro Marure and Andrés Fuentes Franco (comps.), *Catálogo razonado de las leyes de Guatemala* (Guatemala, 1856), pp. 11, 16.

9. Acuerdo ejecutivo, Nov. 21, 1832, ANG, leg. 177, exp. 3788, fol. 3.

10. *Boletín Oficial* (Guatemala), Núm. 34, Segunda parte (May 26, 1833), p. 375.

11. Marure, *Catálogo*, p. 12.

ment in November 1831 gave the name of Livingston, in honor of
the Louisiana jurist whose legal codes Guatemala was in the process
of adopting, and made it the capital of the district of the same name
within the territory of the Department of Chiquimula.[12] By the
creation of the district Gálvez hoped unostentatiously to reassert
Central American authority over the coastal area to the north,
threatened by the Belize woodcutters, and over the Carib residents of
the area who, scattered as a result of the rebellion of Guzmán and
Domínguez at Trujillo and Omoa, were reported to be re-establishing
their settlements under the protection of the British authorities at
Belize. The new status of Livingston, he hoped, would attract the
former Carib inhabitants of the town to return to their homes.[13]
Early in 1833 the federal Congress habilitated Livingston as a major
port of registry for the republic,[14] but the site could not fulfill its
expected destiny. Its waters could accommodate seagoing vessels, but
its remote situation at the mouth of the outlet from Lake Izabal
made access from the capital difficult.

The only practicable alternative to the Izabal road was the land
route leading north from Guatemala City across the upper Motagua
River (Río Grande) to Telemán on the Polochic and then down
that river to the lake. The Polochic route was the shorter of the
two, but Carib canoemen supplied only erratic transport service of
limited capacity on the waterways, and the Motagua crossing was the
terror of travelers and muleteers alike. No bridge spanned the chasm,
and steep banks during time of drought and turbulent water during
the rainy season made fording extremely hazardous. Passengers, equipment, and cargo were drawn across the stream in a sling suspended
from cables that occasionally broke and plummeted the occupant to
a terrifying death, or property to oblivion, in the waters below. Pack
animals and mounts were driven into the torrent upstream from the
cable crossing, and their owners could count themselves fortunate
if they recovered them on the opposite shore. Farther along, between
Chamiquín and Telemán, the route crossed the deep and turbulent
Polochic at a point where the river was confined between banks
some sixty or seventy yards apart. Between two closely spaced trees
rooted in the fissures of a massive rock overhanging the south bank

12. El Siglo de Lafayette (Guatemala), Núm. 8 (Dec. 3, 1831), p. 29.

13. Mariano Gálvez to federal Minister of War, June 30, 1832, ANG, leg. 182,
exp. 3979, fol. 5; A los C[iudadano]s Dip[utado]s S[ecretarios] del C[uerpo] L[egis-
lativo], April 1, 1834, ANG, leg. 364, exp. 6404, n.f.

14. Federal Minister of Finance to Gálvez, Jan. 17, 1833, ANG, leg. 178, exp.
3790, fol. 11.

and two others similarly placed on the elevated slope opposite, the natives of the region had contrived some thirty feet above the flood level of the stream a footbridge of *bejuco* vines lashed together and handrails of the same material laced to form a "V" with the walkway beneath. The stability of the bridge under load is suggested by its popular name, *la hamaca*.[15]

The inescapable hazards to life and property at the river crossings and the sparse population along the Polochic route deprived it of any great commercial usefulness except to contraband traders. To surmount the barrier to transport imposed by the Motagua crossing, Gálvez proposed to the Assembly of Guatemala in 1833 that it authorize the government to contract with a private company for the construction of a wooden bridge across the river, the investment to be amortized and the interest paid from the proceeds of tolls assessed for use of the structure. Gálvez received the authorization he requested and decreed the formation of the company.[16] Apparently investors were not found to contribute the capital, however, for the government itself undertook the construction of the bridge in 1837. Some of the initial construction was completed, but by the following year the work had been suspended,[17] presumably for lack of funds.

A site offering greater promise as a port than either Izabal or Livingston was the Bay of Santo Tomás, which opened at the extreme southern tip of Amatique Bay. Santo Tomás afforded a sheltered and capacious anchorage for seagoing ships, and its proximity to the lower Motagua and to the Izabal road before it began the ascent of Mico Mountain gave hope that it could be approached from the interior both by land and by water over relatively easy routes. Although the site had been known for more than two centuries, the dream of developing it as a major harbor had never been realized. Indeed, there was no road to the bay, nor was there a settlement on or near the site.

In 1833 the government of Guatemala initiated the attempt to open a deepwater port at Santo Tomás. On May 29 the Assembly

15. George W. Montgomery, *Narrative of a Journey to Guatemala, in Central America, in 1838* (New York, 1839), pp. 165-89; Frederick Crowe, *The Gospel in Central America* (London, 1850), pp. 547, 549 n.

16. Orden legislativo No. 36, May 11, 1833, ANG, Congreso, 1833, No. 43, unclassified; Marure, *Catálogo*, p. 12; *Boletín Oficial*, Núm. 34, Segunda parte (May 26, 1833), p. 375.

17. *Memoria de la Secretaría Jeneral de Estado del supremo gobierno de Guatemala . . . presentada a la Legislatura de 1837 . . .* (Guatemala, [1837]), p. 16; *La Verdad* (Guatemala), Núm. 8 (Nov. 29, 1837), p. 40; Proposition of Diéguez, March 5, 1838, ANG, Congreso, 1838, No. 22, unclassified.

voted to request the federal government to habilitate Santo Tomás as a major port, reduce Izabal and Livingston to the rank of minor ports, and authorize the state government to contract for the construction of necessary buildings and fortifications on the bay.[18] On the same day, Gálvez requested the national government to assign Lieutenant Colonel Angel Floripes to the state for the purpose of exploring a practicable route from Gualán to Santo Tomás. The request was granted, but apparently Floripes was unable to do more than organize the expedition, for in July the state government requested the assignment of Felipe Molina for the same purpose.[19] The federal authorities had designated Santo Tomás as a major port of the nation, but there seemed to be no immediate way to get a road built to it or to have the necessary buildings constructed.

Gálvez was beginning to realize that chronic penury, which incapacitated the treasury for even ordinary maintenance and repair of existing facilities, put the inauguration of new projects beyond any hope of accomplishment from public funds. Local contractors offered no solution to his problem, for their proposals often fell below the minimum standards set by the federal colonization law. The first of these facts was demonstrated to Gálvez almost daily; the second was called to his attention, if he had not thought of it earlier, by the proposal made by the firm of José Croskey of Izabal early in 1833.

The practiced hand of the Chief of State could scarcely have wrapped so many diverse elements into so neat a package as that presented by Croskey. The firm proposed to begin woodcutting operations on the shores of Lake Izabal and, to facilitate the work, to put a steamer in operation on those waters. The vessel would require a crew, and these individuals Croskey proposed to settle at Santa Cruz, on the north shore of the lake, where British penetration already menaced Guatemalan possession. As a prospective colonizer Croskey asked, under the terms of the federal colonization law, that he be granted title to the lands on which he expected to cut wood.

Gálvez was intrigued by the Croskey proposal, but he observed to the Assembly that it did not fulfill the conditions set by the federal statute. Before it could approve the project the legislative body would have to repeal several provisions of the national law, one of which was the requirement that a colony consist of at least fifteen families.

18. Orden legislativo No. 45, May 29, 1833, ANG, Congreso, 1833, No. 38, unclassified; Marure, *Catálogo*, p. 12.

19. The events are recorded in ANG, leg. 183, exp. 3989, fols. 15-35; leg. 168, exp. 3545, fol. 11.

The Assembly recognized that the standards imposed by federal legislation required resources greater than those commanded by most prospective contractors and in this sense hindered the states in their colonization efforts. It was not eager, however, to provoke a controversy by state revision of a federal law, and it hesitated to grant woodcutting concessions as a subsidy to colonization because it did not share with Gálvez the belief that woodcutters could become settlers. In the end it chose to temporize by deferring decision on the Croskey proposal.[20]

A year of frustrated hopes convinced Gálvez that speedy realization of developmental projects of the magnitude he envisioned called for "extraordinary effort" of another type. If neither the state nor individual nationals could provide the capital required for development, he would turn to foreign companies whose shareholders could be expected to command greater resources. By offering as inducements such concessions as were already authorized by law or established by precedent he believed that he might attract foreign capital to undertake the public improvements the country so desperately needed. With this objective in view he proposed to the Assembly on February 6, 1834, the formation of a "Company of Colonization, Industry, Commerce, and Agriculture of Verapaz, Livingston, and Santo Tomás."[21] Some six weeks later he asked the legislative body to establish general bases upon which the government might contract with private enterprises to undertake necessary public works.[22]

The Assembly began work immediately on the proposal to authorize a Verapaz colonization company, but twice it suspended its deliberations to resolve related questions. It first set aside the measure intended ultimately to attract a colonization offer to act on one already at hand. The proposal came from Colonel Juan Galindo, a British-born immigrant who had arrived in Central America in 1827, obtained a commission in the federal army, became a naturalized citizen, and held a number of state and federal positions of importance, one of them the post of Commandant in the Petén. He had explored the northern reaches of Central America with some thoroughness and, it may be assumed, had acquainted himself with the areas

20. The *expedientes* detailing the Assembly's actions are in ANG, Congreso, 1833, No. 54 and No. 89, fol. 19, unclassified.

21. A los C[iudadanos] Diput[ado]s S[ecreta]rios de la A[samblea] L[egislativa], Feb. 6, 1834, ANG, Congreso, 1834, No. 1, fol. 4, unclassified. A draft of this letter of transmittal, dated Feb. 4, 1834, is to be found in ANG, leg. 1395, exp. 32334, n.f.

22. A los C[iudada]nos Diput[ado]s Secret[ario]s de la A[samblea] L[egislativa], March 17, 1834, ANG, leg. 362, exp. 6397, n.f.

in which British woodcutters were already working and those into which they were likely soon to expand. His observations confirmed the popular assumption that mahogany cutters from Belize had extended their activities beyond the boundaries set for such operations by the Anglo-Spanish treaties of 1783 and 1786. Galindo had excellent reason to believe that the British government would not support these encroachments; indeed, he had heard former British Consul John O'Reilly state what he assumed to be the official view that British tenure in Belize was a permissive occupancy of Central American territory allowed by the government of the new republic within the limits set by the last Anglo-Spanish treaty.[23]

These circumstances suggested to Galindo that without risk of collision with Great Britain he could successfully challenge the Belize mahogany cutters on the frontiers of the republic, not only to the enhancement of his reputation for patriotism, but to his personal profit as well. To this end he asked the Guatemalan government to cede to him for purposes of colonization a tract of land in the Petén lying immediately adjacent to the western boundary of Belize as defined in the last European treaties. When the British authorities had recognized his title, as he was certain they would, he could require British mahogany cutters to buy from him the land they expected to log, and he could claim credit in Guatemala for having saved national territory from encroachment. If he could also succeed in establishing settlers upon the land, all parties in Central America would be satisfied, and the British woodcutters would have borne the cost. The Assembly reacted to his proposal as Galindo had hoped, and on March 8 it approved by legislative order the concession he requested.[24]

The Assembly also postponed action on the proposed Verapaz colonization company law to set the general conditions requested by Gálvez under which the government could employ private capital to

23. Frederick Chatfield, British consul in Central America, to Lieutenant Colonel Francis Cockburn, Superintendent of Belize, Oct. 11, 1834, ABH, Letters Inwards, 1826-1848, Records 10, fols. 24-25; Chatfield to Lord Palmerston, No. 23, Nov. 13, 1834, FO 15/14, fols. 318-19; *ibid.*, No. 2, Jan. 30, 1836, FO 15/18, fols. 46-47; William J. Griffith, "Juan Galindo, Central American Chauvinist," *Hispanic American Historical Review*, XL, No. 1 (Feb., 1960), pp. 25-29; Ian Graham, "Juan Galindo, Enthusiast," *Estudios de Cultura Maya*, III (Mexico, 1963), 13-16.

24. Orden legislativo No. 20, March 8, 1834, ANG, leg. 360, exp. 6315, n.f.; Chatfield to Palmerston, No. 15, Sept. 17, 1834, Enclosure 5, FO 15/14, fols. 226-27; Certification of Galindo's title, March 24, 1834, FO 252/3, n.f. Mary Wilhelmine Williams errs in locating the grant between the Sibún and Sarstoon Rivers (*Anglo-American Isthmian Diplomacy, 1815-1915* [Washington and London, 1916], pp. 33-34).

undertake public works. On April 21 it authorized the executive, during recesses of the legislative body, to contract under certain conditions with private companies without the necessity of legislative ratification. He could sign agreements for rebuilding existing roads, provided the interest allowed on the investment did not exceed twenty-five per cent and the tolls imposed in any year for the use of the improved facilities did not exceed the amount actually necessary to cover the cost of repairs, interest, and a twentieth part of the principal. The government could contract for new roads, the use of which would be optional to traffic, under any terms it might consider expedient. Works on ports habilitated by the national government could be undertaken and paid for, subject to reimbursement from federal funds, by utilizing two per cent of the import duties destined to the treasury of the state. The executive could also contract for public works of other types, but the Assembly limited to five years the period of any special concessions he might find it necessary to make to reach an agreement.[25]

These actions taken, the Assembly gave its attention to the Gálvez proposal for a Verapaz colonization company. The bases suggested by the Chief of State made it clear that he hoped to persuade foreigners to attempt for profit what native sons had been unable to accomplish either for patriotism or for the promise of individual gain. He proposed to entrust to foreign *empresarios* the whole complex problem of developing the northern area of Guatemala and to induce foreign settlers to occupy the uncomfortable and pestilential lowlands that residents of the agreeable highlands had shunned for centuries. There he expected the imported skills, capital, and labor to transform the erstwhile wilderness into flourishing communities. The tasks he set were monumental, and the rewards he offered were scaled in proportion.

To undertake this work of development Gálvez proposed creation of a foreign company capitalized at two million pesos, divided into ten to twenty thousand shares. This company would establish a minimum of one thousand families in northern Guatemala, one-fourth of the total to be settled at Santo Tomás, an equal number at Livingston, and the remaining half distributed among the most advantageous points along the Polochic route to the interior. It was to attempt to open a channel through the bar at the mouth of the Río Dulce to accommodate seagoing vessels and to construct new roads or to im-

25 Decreto No. 15, April 21, 1834, ANG, leg. 361, exp. 6374, n.f.

prove existing trails leading from Santo Tomás, Lake Izabal, and the Polochic River to the towns of the interior.

In compensation for the public services it performed the company was to be given a variety of monopolies, concessions, and special privileges that it could turn to profit. Gálvez proposed that it be allowed for twenty years to monopolize woodcutting and extraction of other forest products on public lands (excluding private property and the *ejidos* of existing towns, such as Cajabón) bordering the sea and the Polochic and Pasión Rivers and stretching in the interior from the settlements of Verapaz to the province of Yucatán. He offered twelve-year monopolies of steam navigation on the Polochic and Pasión Rivers and their tributaries and of turtle and tortoise fishing on all rivers from the Polochic to the sea and along the coast of the Gulf of Honduras to Belize and eight-year monopolies of iron founding and of such other new industries as might be introduced into the country, subject only to the obligation to teach the arts to nationals who might care to learn them.

For public works accomplished the company was to receive special rewards. If it succeeded in opening a channel through the bar of the Río Dulce, it was to be allowed to collect a two per cent toll on the value of imports carried by all ships previously unable to enter the lake. If it built new roads or improved existing ones, it was to be allowed to collect tolls for their use for a period of time to be stipulated in each case.

On the basis of equality with native inhabitants, and without prejudice to the special concessions made in the contract, the company could exploit mineral deposits found within its concessions, grow and export crops without payment of export duties, import and export commodities, and contract for necessary labor. In like manner the colonists were guaranteed religious toleration, protection in the free and public exercise of any religion or faith, and the right to erect churches, altars, or other symbols of devotion.

Individual colonists were to receive land grants of the size specified by the federal colonization law. They were to be exempted for twenty years from all monopolies and from payment of all taxes and contributions, export duties on the products of their labor and industry, and import duties on tools for agriculture and the crafts and on machines for the development of industry. Neither the company nor its colonists would be required for twenty years to pay the Guatemalan land tax. Colonists, shareholders who chose to live in the colonies, and all employees and functionaries of the company were excused from military service. Colonists were to have complete liberty to bequeath their property to heirs within the country and abroad and were guaranteed the absolute and inviolable enjoyment of their lands and properties. They were to be governed within the colony only by municipal authorities chosen by themselves, but they would be required to live under the laws and guarantees of the federal constitution and the laws of the state. The government of Guatemala would establish a court of original jurisdiction in the colonies to hear differences between colonists and agents of the company and other cases that could not otherwise be settled, and appeals to higher courts were to be allowed.

The Assembly accepted the project essentially as it was proposed by Gálvez, yet made some significant amendments, deletions, and additions. It reduced the land area to be granted to each family from one million square varas (about 180 acres) to one *caballería* (about 112 acres). It reduced from twenty years to ten the period for which the colonists were to enjoy enumerated special privileges and to be exempted from payment of the land tax, and it limited to eight years the unrestricted exemption from military service and military contributions. It restricted the monopoly of woodcutting given to the company by the addition of the phrase "as against other foreigners," and it expressly prohibited the export by the company of crude mineral ore which would deprive natives of opportunity to learn the art of smelting. It omitted mention of the establishment of a Guatemalan court in the colonies and, except for the guarantee of religious liberty, of privileges to be enjoyed by colonists on an equal basis with the native born. Presumably it believed that these constitutional guarantees applicable to all residents of Central America required no restatement as assurance to immigrant settlers. In this modified form the Assembly approved the law on April 29, 1834.[26]

Gálvez informed the Assembly at the time he submitted his proposals for a colonization company that he intended to seek English capital to carry out his purpose. His hopes for success rested on the report that the British Parliament had just abolished the privileges of the East India Company and the assumption that some owners of capital formerly employed in that enterprise might find opportunities for investment in the empty wilderness of Guatemala no less appealing than those afforded by the fabulous kingdoms of the maharajas. Gálvez therefore requested authorization to send an agent to England

26. Bases para una compañía de colonización, industria, comercio, y agricultura de Verapaz, Livingston, y Santo Tomás, ANG, Congreso, 1834, No. 156, unclassified.

and, failing there, to France to solicit backing for a colonization company. When the legislative body did not respond promptly to the suggestion, he repeated his proposal, and during the last week of April he appears to have received from the Assembly the authorization he sought.[27]

Circumstances spared Gálvez the trouble and expense of sending an agent to England: an emissary from London came to him. In July of 1834 Thomas Gould arrived in Guatemala in company with Marshal Bennett of Belize. Bennett was well-known in the capital as owner of a variety of business interests in that area. Gould was unknown, but he was reported to carry credentials from a group of London associates called the Eastern Coast of Central America Commercial and Agricultural Company which authorized him to discuss colonization projects with the government. To Gálvez the casual similarity between the name of the London company and the title he had given to his own recent creation may have suggested that a providentially devised instrument was at hand for the accomplishment of his purpose. The jubilant Chief of State, modestly crediting the energy of his administration for the happy turn of events, announced to the Assembly the presence of the agent from London. Eager to take advantage of the opportunity to conclude an agreement for colonization of the Verapaz, he requested the legislative body to authorize the government to negotiate a contract under terms somewhat more liberal than those approved in the recent law.[28]

Gálvez described Gould to the Assembly as the commissioner of "English houses much respected for their capital and credit." This ostensibly authoritative evaluation was given by Marshal Bennett for an enterprise that he either did not know or chose cynically to misrepresent. The fact was that Gould came to Guatemala as the emissary, not of the wealthy and prestigious former lords of the India trade, but of an association of obscure London speculators whose assets and plan of operation had been acquired from Gregor MacGregor, the Scottish adventurer whose unprincipled manipulations during the 1820's of a colonization project based on a concession he had obtained from the native "King" of the Mosquito Shore in Hon-

27. Memoria presentada a la Asamblea por el M[inis]tro G[ene]ral de Gob[ier]no, Feb. 14, 1834, ANG, leg. 369, exp. 6425, fol. 13; A los Diputados S[ecreta]rios de la Asamblea, April 21, 1834, ANG, leg. 364, exp. 6408, n.f.; Dictamen of Committee on Agriculture, April 26, 1834, ANG, Congreso, 1834, No. 18, unclassified.

28. A los Ciud[ada]nos Diputados S[ecreta]rios de la Asamblea, July 19, 1834, ANG, Congreso, 1834, No. 156, fols. 16-17, unclassified.

duras had made the name "Poyais" a by-word and a synonym for fraud.[29]

The London company had its origins about 1828 when MacGregor, after serving a term in a French prison for fraud, returned to England "to start afresh." He approached James Day who recognized in him "a very shrewd man . . . [of] rather high notions" whose title to the land in the Mosquito Kingdom appeared to be valid. Day with some eight or nine associates he recruited bought from the adventurer about two million acres of land at prices of one shilling sixpence an acre or less. They also bought up the securities of the first loan negotiated by MacGregor amounting in total face value to about £800,000. They "tried to form a commercial and agricultural society," apparently the Río Tinto Commercial and Agricultural Company, and "thought to begin operations." They hoped the land to which they had acquired title would give the appearance of a legitimate colonization project to a scheme which had as its real object the sale at artificially inflated prices of the bonds they had purchased. The disrepute of Poyais, however, and the discredit into which Mac-Gregor had fallen embarrassed their operation. In an effort to dissociate themselves from the evil reputation earned by the original enterprise and from interference by its founder, they appealed to the Colonial Office for help in finding some way to carry on their operations without association with MacGregor, but they "could not

29. In 1820 Gregor MacGregor obtained from the Mosquito "King" George Frederick August a land grant, comprising some 70,000 square miles of territory and including the Río Tinto (or Black River), which corresponded roughly to the present department of Olancho in Honduras. The cession was called Poyais after the Poyer Indians who inhabited the mountains in which the Río Tinto rose.

The grant was of the sort commonly made by the Mosquito "Kings" in exchange for liquor or other trival favors. MacGregor, however, chose to represent it as a legitimate and singular cession and to use it to promote an extensive and imaginative fraud. He styled himself "Prince of Poyais" (or "Cacique of Poyais"), installed a "Poyaisian Legation" in London, commissioned entourages of uni-formed civil and military officers, issued banknotes, floated loans through ex-perienced and reputable bankers, sold land in his "kingdom," and recruited and sent to the barren and inhospitable Mosquito Shore several ship loads of deluded colonists, many of whom perished. The survivors and the remaining property of the first colony were taken off to Belize by Marshal Bennett, an event which was later interpreted, according to the purposes of the declarant, as an act of mercy or as deliberate sabotage to destroy a potential rival. For fraudulent activi-ties carried on in Great Britain and France, MacGregor served brief prison terms in both countries (Alfred Hasbrouck, "Gregor MacGregor and the Colonization of Poyais Between 1820 and 1824," *Hispanic American Historical Review*, VII [1927], 438-59; Victor Allen, "The Prince of Poyais," *History Today*, II [1952], 53-58; James Hastie, *Narrative of a Voyage in the Ship Kennersley Castle, from Leith Roads to Poyais* [Edinburgh, 1823]).

get a clear line marked out." For some time, therefore, they were forced by fear of hostile public opinion to hold their plans in abeyance,[30] although one of the associates apparently tried to keep interest in Poyaisian securities alive in connection with his regular business.

In the summer of 1833 the speculators seized what appeared to be a favorable opportunity to relaunch their enterprise. The abolition of Negro slavery throughout the British colonies by act of Parliament on August 28 allowed them to link their offer of lands in Central America with the entirely new prospect of attracting former bondsmen from the British West Indies to work them. About the middle of September they announced the formation of the Eastern Coast of Central America Commercial and Agricultural Company. Over the name of Thomas Bugden, Secretary, they invited interested persons to obtain from the Company offices at No. 7 Tokenhouse-yard, Lothbury, copies of the "Prospectus and Plan of a Company for Promoting Free Labour and Commerce on the Eastern Coast of Central America" and application forms for shares in the enterprise.[31] Announcement of a new prospectus and of a new directorate for the Río Tinto Company, published briefly during September and October, and the appearance of a new Poyaisian Trust Office at 147 Fenchurch Street somewhat later suggest that the functions of the parent society were divided between two new entities whose relationship to the earlier speculation the directors hoped to conceal.[32]

30. James Day to Lord John Russell, June 8, 1840, CO 123/58, n.f. This statement of land and securities held in the Poyaisian enterprise does not coincide exactly with the Company's claims in 1837. At that time its holdings were listed at 1,600,000 acres of land, and £800,000 and £82,000, face value, in stock certificates.

31. Chatfield to Palmerston, No. 12, Aug. 25, 1834, FO 15/14, fol. 155. The advertisement was first carried by the *Morning Herald*, No. 15,943 (Sept. 18, 1833), p. 1. The actual prospectus has not been found.

32. The *Morning Herald* assumed the Rio Tinto Company to be a new facade erected by the Eastern Coast Company to conceal its identity (No. 15,984 [Nov. 7, 1833], p. 2). The advertisements of the Rio Tinto Company in the *Times* (No. 15,284 [Oct. 2, 1833], p. [1], and No. 15,309 [Oct. 30, 1833], p. [2]), however, reveal it to have been an existing company undergoing a mysterious reorganization, understandable only to the initiated, that altered its structure and changed its purpose. My surmise is that the Rio Tinto Company was the original society formed by the speculators, that the Eastern Coast Company replaced it as a front organization, and that the Poyaisian Trust Office took over the management of its Poyaisian interests. Prior to 1834 the address of the Poyaisian office was identical with that of Daniel Mocatta, the Company director most closely associated with manipulations of Poyaisian securities. The new office cannot be directly identified with the Company, but its advertisements (*Morning Herald*, No. 16,274 [Oct. 14, 1834], p. 1; No. 16,481 [June 12, 1835], p. 1; and No. 17,205 [Oct. 25,

The prospectus of the Eastern Coast Company set its capitalization at £212,500.[33] Its shares were to be issued "open," and each purchaser was to be provided, as proof of ownership, a properly signed list of serial numbers and a notation of the amount invested. Registration of subscribers continued until October 15. On that date all prospective purchasers were notified to cover within a week the first installment on the securities they had contracted to buy. With some wonderment the *Morning Herald* observed that speculators had been found "to pay the first instalments for 300 shares, at a very respectable banking firm, in the names of the three Nobody Directors." Assuming that the financial status of the Company was unaltered between that date and the reorganization undertaken in February of the following year when 3,327 shares were reported outstanding, it would appear that the original speculators held some 3,000 shares obtained largely or entirely in exchange for Poyaisian securities and carried on the books as with £20 paid on them. New investors seem to have paid up about 300 additional shares to the same level. Some part of the capital acquired in this fashion appears to have been Poyaisian bonds and land certificates accepted in order that the Company, through control of the major proportion of the MacGregor securities, could force minor holders to acquiesce in its manipulation of the issues. The payments made in cash provided the liquid resources from which the Company intended to defray its meager expenses.

The prospectus announced that the Company's affairs were to be managed by five directors. The members of the provisional board were not named, but the *Morning Herald*, at least, professed to have learned their identity. "One or two," that journal observed, "we know to be men of some property, and the rest may be; but of this we are assured, that not any of them are of sufficient weight in society to conduct a concern of such magnitude, or to induce any but the inexperienced and the unwary to risk their money in the bubble." When the new investors had regularized their status, a general meeting of shareholders was held which selected proprietary directors and authorized them to proceed with execution of the Company's plans. If, as appears certain, the members of the board elected at the shareholders' meeting continued in office during the ensuing

1837], p. 1, for example), reveal activity that coincides precisely with the rise and fall of the Company's speculations in Poyaisian securities.

33. The information on Company organization in this and the following paragraph was given in the regular column headed "City" on page 2 of the *Morning Herald*, Nos. 15,967 (Oct. 18, 1833), 15,970 (Oct. 22, 1833), 15,976 (Oct. 29, 1833).

nine months, the directors, "whose names," the *Morning Herald* avowed, "would not look well in print," were Jeremiah Barrett, Daniel Mocatta, William Crozier, and Robert Sears. The evidence suggests that these men were chosen for their positions largely because each had the capacity to perform some special service important to the Company's projected operation.

Barrett was an engineer and small manufacturer who lived at 41 Wilmington Square, Clerkenwell, Middlesex. In partnership with his brothers, Richard and Jonathan, he operated an inherited iron and brass foundry at 25 King's Head Court, Beech Street, Cripplegate. He and Jonathan also maintained an engineering office at 14 New North Street, Finsbury. He belonged to the Society of Friends and was an active and respected member of the Peel Monthly Meeting. He appears, therefore, to have been a man of moderate wealth and standing in London and, by his own statement, perhaps the largest single investor in Company shares.[34] He may have been chosen for the board because of the importance of his holdings, because of his relative respectability among associates to whom that attribute was something of a novelty, or, supposing that the irresponsibility of the enterprise permitted his colleagues to indulge themselves in an organizational pun, because the nature of his foundry business kept him constantly supplied with large amounts of the commodity most needed to transact the business of the Company.

Mocatta was a member of a prominent Anglo-Jewish banking family who early in MacGregor's career became involved in his financial manipulations. He made an offer to market one of the £200,000 Poyaisian bond issues which the Scottish adventurer refused, but when the successful bidder was unable to execute his agreement, Mocatta took over the sale of some £160,000 worth of the fallen securities and briefly revived them. His interest in the Poyais speculation apparently drew him into the Company. Although his occupation listed in the London directories changed from "stock broker" to "merchant" about 1830, he appears to have been managing the Company's Poyaisian interests from his office at 23 Threadneedle

---

34. *The Register of Persons Entitled to Vote in the Election of Members of Parliament for the City of London* (London, 1833), pp. 18, 337; *Post Office London Directory for 1833* (London, 1833), p. 24; A List of the Members of Peel Monthly Meeting in the County of Middlesex from 1st. March 1837 to ——, and Luke Howard Collection, MS. vol. 150, case 57, fols. 50, 52, both in Library of the Society of Friends, Friends' House, London; *Brief Statement, Supported by Original Documents, of the Important Grants Conceded to the Eastern Coast of Central America Commercial and Agricultural Company by the State of Guatemala* (London, 1839), p. 61.

Street when the prospectus was issued in 1833, and, presumably, he continued to serve as the specialist in Poyaisian securities on the board of directors.[35]

Crozier and Sears were apparently less distinguished but still useful members of the board. Crozier was a shipowner[36] whose position as a director might help to establish the appearance of serious intent to send out colonists even though the Company's operations actually might never require his vessels to perform that function. Sears was a brass founder and typecutter turned printer and engraver. In 1833 he appears to have been a partner in the firm of Sears and Trapp, printers, at 11 Bridge Row, but by 1834 he maintained his own printing and engraving establishment at 53 Paternoster Row.[37] He probably printed the prospectus of 1833, although the document did not reveal its source. It can hardly be doubted, however, that Sears's presses were the major reason he sat among the directors.

The hostile reaction the Company had anticipated and feared early in its career almost immediately greeted its new public announcement. The press pointed out the relationship between the ostensibly new enterprise and the infamous Poyais bubble and openly branded the promoters as swindlers. Frederick Chatfield, preparing to take up the post of British Consul in Central America to which he had recently been appointed, inquired into Company affairs "lest an inability hereafter to fulfil any engagements it might make with Persons whom it had induced to emigrate on the faith of its promises, should occasion disappointment, and consequently oblige the Poor Emigrants to seek my Protection, and even my assistance to return home."[38] James Hyde, agent in London for the Settlement of British Honduras, was informed of the project by the government secretary in Belize and likewise began to investigate.

The *Morning Herald,* the first London newspaper to carry the Company's advertisement, exposed the operation in the public press. It ridiculed the enterprise as a "perfect humbug" devised by the "celebrated Poyais concocters" to deceive "the unfortunate holders of the real and forged securities, as well as other parties, by inducing

35. Herman Hendriks, *A Plain Narrative of Facts* (London, 1824), pp. 6-7; Paul H. Emden, "The Brothers Goldsmid and the Financing of the Napoleonic Wars," *Transactions* (1935-1939) of the Jewish Historical Society of England, XIV (London, 1940), 229-30; *Robson's London Directory for 1833* (London, 1832), p. 272, and Part II, n.p.

36. Certificate of British registry [of the "Vera Paz"], No. 415, CO 123/56, n.f.

37. *Pigot and Co.'s London & Provincial New Commercial Directory for 1828-29* (London, 1829), pp. 78, 193; *Post Office London Directory for 1833*, p. 358.

38. Chatfield to Palmerston, Aug. 25, 1834, fol. 156.

them to enter into a colonisation scheme in Central America ('God
bless the mark!') with the faint hope" of recuperating their earlier
losses. The editors promised that just as "this Journal exposed some
of the infamous schemes which were concocted by the needy adventurers during the bubble mania of 1825 . . . we shall not flinch
from our duty to the public in the year 1833." In a succession of
notices appearing in the column headed "City" they fulfilled their
threat. Assuming the Company's interest in colonization to be
genuine, the column pointed out that the climate of the tropical
paradise described in the Company prospectus in reality "assimilates
in the best part to our West Indian Islands; in the low part to the
marshy lands of Demerara, and of course there it is very unhealthy."
The prospectus, however, "clearly shows that it is concocted only
to get rid of 100,000 l [£] worth of Poyais bonds at a much higher
rate than their market value." Unless the speculators "wish to push
the subject further, and make them[selves] the whip-tops of society,
we recommend them to burn their prospectuses, close their office, and
turn their mind to the pursuit of honest trades or professions."

This exposé of their guilty plans provoked the directors of the
Eastern Coast Company to attempt a rebuttal. They issued a paper
in which, by "reiteration of their late flattering but highly coloured
and false statement of the nature of the soil and climate of the independent State of Guatemala [read republic of Central America], and
the blessed Mosquito shore," they thought to repair the damage done
to their interests by the newspaper's revelations. The *Morning
Herald,* however, did not give up the attack. It repeated its earlier
charges and alleged that the directors were "pursuing a line of deceit
more disgraceful than that of many other schemes, because its affected plausibility will entrap only the unwary. . . . They know their
grant is not worth a farthing . . . and we state . . . the opinion of
unbiased and honest men of business that this concern will end as
all other bubbles do."[39]

Chatfield's investigation led him to an equally adverse opinion
of the Company and its proposed operations. When Gould called
on him in December "to gain what information I might be disposed
to afford him," the Consul gave him a lesson in Central American
geography. The language of the prospectus, he pointed out, "spoke,
either in ignorance or in conscious misrepresentation, of territory to
be colonized as situate on the eastern coast of Central America in

39. Nos. 15,965 (Oct. 16); 15,970 (Oct. 22); 15,976 (Oct. 29); 15,984 (Nov. 7);
Chatfield to Palmerston, Aug. 25, 1834, fols. 155-56.

Honduras," a country that possessed no eastern coast. He expressed to the Company agent his candid opinion that the operation "was evidently a revival of the Poyaisian scheme, and that it appeared to me a delusion as concerned the publick, in order to procure to the Poyaisian Securities a temporary value, for the benefit of the present holders of those Bonds." Moreover, he pointed out that "Central American sovereignty over a considerable extension of the coast was challenged by Colombia and by a 'possessory right' of the Mosquito Indians," and he proved the first point a few days later by sending to the Company offices a copy of the Colombian decree that asserted a sovereign right to the territory between the Chagres River and Cape Gracias á Dios, and forbade foreign establishments upon it.[40]

James Hyde's investigations of the Company likewise led him to the conclusion that it harbored no honest intent. His emissary sent to the Company offices found Bugden singularly reluctant to discuss the plans of the directors, indisposed to answer questions, and unwilling to surrender a prospectus. Hyde reported, however, that such information as was gleaned from the secretary left the impression that the promoters hoped to attract investors by holding out to them the prospect of transferring to the mainland the slave labor system now outlawed in the British colonies. The device was utterly simple. Free Negroes would be inveigled to leave Jamaica after they had completed their period of apprenticeship and to take up residence on the Mosquito Coast where, beyond the protection of the British government, they could be exploited under a regime of slavery in everything but name. This information Hyde passed on to the government secretary in Belize with the suggestion that Chatfield be informed so he could keep Gould under scrutiny, and he promised, should circumstances warrant, to call the operations of the Company to the attention of government ministries in London.[41]

Unabashed by the evidence of hostile sentiment manifested toward it in both private and public circles, the Company proceeded with its plans. Uncertain of the posture the government of the new republic of Central America might adopt should a gesture be made toward occupying the lands they had purchased from MacGregor, the directors determined to send an agent to Guatemala to secure confirmation of their title from the federal government,[42] which disputed the pretension of the Mosquito "King" to sovereignty over the

40. Chatfield to Palmerston, Aug. 25, 1834, fols. 156-57.
41. Extract of a letter from Mr. Hyde to Mr. Dickinson, enclosed with Cockburn to Chatfield, Nov. 22, 1834, FO 252/8, n.f.
42. Day to Russell, June 8, 1840, n.f.

Mosquito Coast and, hence, his assumed right to make land grants. For this mission they selected Thomas Gould who, because of a former connection with the Dorsetshire militia, affected the title of "captain." A general meeting of shareholders was called for March 3, 1834, which approved the step, and on March 23 Gould was dispatched to Guatemala.[43] The directors were not well enough informed on Central American events to know that the federal capital had been transferred from Guatemala to El Salvador.

By coincidence, Gould and Chatfield both sailed as passengers aboard H.M.S. "Belvidera," bound from Portsmouth for the West India station. The Consul was much discomfited lest "the Passage of this Person on board the Ship which conveyed me from England, would be made a matter of undue importance with the authorities here [Guatemala], and would seem to give indirectly a sanction by His Majesty's Govern^t. to Mr. Gould's enterprise."[44] After a hazardous voyage the pair eventually reached Belize, from where Chatfield continued his journey to Guatemala. Gould remained some time in the Settlement, where he met Marshal Bennett.

Bennett had just returned to British Honduras after six years of nearly continuous residence in Central America, which must have eroded considerably his position as the most prominent citizen of the Settlement. Prior to his departure he had been the veteran among the inhabitants of Belize, the most important mahogany operator, the principal merchant, and the wealthiest resident. He was a perennial choice of the Public Meeting for local Magistrate, and he was also the senior judge of the Supreme Court and colonel commander of the local militia. He was a recognized leader of the merchant oligarchy that had traditionally dominated the affairs of the Settlement but that steadily lost power after 1829 to the local representatives of British branch houses set up in competition with the old independent importers and to the new crown-appointed superintendent. Perhaps because he saw the old order changing in Belize, Bennett determined to explore the opportunities offered by Central America.

Bennett involved himself directly in Central American affairs in 1826 when he established a branch of his commercial house in Guatemala. For this purpose he formed a partnership with Carlos Antonio Meany of Guatemala and with William Hall of Belize, whom he

43. Chatfield to Palmerston, Aug. 25, 1834, fol. 158; *Morning Herald*, No. 16,079 (Feb. 28, 1834), p. 1, and No. 16,099 (March 24, 1834), p. [2].

44. Chatfield to Palmerston, Aug. 25, 1834, fol. 158.

took to Central America to head the business. The firm of Hall, Meany, and Bennett was the sole branch house maintained in Central America by a Belize mercantile establishment and, hence, the only concern based on the Settlement that operated in direct contact with the Central American environment.[45] The partners were sometimes subjected to assessment of forced loans or confiscation of some part of their goods during the recurrent political and military crises in Central America, but they remained on relatively good terms with the authorities and on occasion performed a friendly service for the government or imported a shipment of rifles on its order.[46]

Beyond his partnership in the mercantile business, Bennett acquired holdings in mining, agricultural, and manufacturing properties in Central America. In 1826 he purchased and began successful operation of the Tabanco mine in El Salvador,[47] and some six years later he made an arrangement with Ramón Vigil, a relative of Francisco Morazán, to take charge of the Guayavillas gold mine near Tegucigalpa, Honduras, the production of which he sharply increased.[48] He may also have begun negotiations as early as 1829 to purchase for the partnership some of the properties of religious orders confiscated by the Liberal government of Guatemala, for in that year a native claimed preference over a foreign bidder for the estate of San Jerónimo, the famous hacienda and *ingenio* near Salamá that Bennett and Meany ultimately bought in 1834 or early 1835. At about the same time they also purchased the Convento Viejo, the new sugar factory of the Dominicans in Guatemala City, and placed bids on the convent of Recolección but withdrew from the auction because of public criticism.[49]

45. Robert Arthur Naylor, "British Commercial Relations with Central America, 1821-1851," (Unpubl. Diss., Tulane, 1958), pp. 161-64, 167, 183.

46. Some of the loans made by Bennett to the federal government and the state of Guatemala are detailed in Colonel Alexander Macdonald, Superintendent of Belize, to Lord John Russell, No. 14, March 24, 1841, Enclosure 2, FO 15/27, fols. 14-15; William Hall to Macdonald, Sept. 4, 1841, FO 15/28, fols. 71-73; and Carlos A. Meany, *Pocas razones de un lego . . . reclamando la nulidad de la venta de unas casas . . .* (Guatemala, 1842), p. [5]. His services in recruiting for Guatemala a director for training teachers in the Lancastrian system of instruction, and sailors acquainted with the north coast, for example, are recorded in ANG, leg. 3606, exp. 83745, fols. 27-28.

47. Naylor, p. 162 n.; George Alexander Thompson, *Narrative of an Official Visit to Guatemala from Mexico* (London, 1829), p. 216.

48. Chatfield to Palmerston, No. 14, March 6, 1839, FO 15/22, fol. 141.

49. Orden legislativo No. 81, Nov. 10, 1829, ANG, leg. 258, exp. 5593, n.f.; Chatfield to Cockburn, Oct. 31, 1834, ABH, Letters Inwards, 1826-1848, Records 10, fol. 33; Chatfield to Palmerston, Aug. 25, 1834, fol. 163; Certification of purchase

Although Bennett had acquired extensive holdings in Central America, his ambitions were not entirely satisfied. For several years he had considered ways and means of extending his mahogany-cutting empire in order to employ the crews that had been half-idled by the progressive depletion of the forest resources within the limits of British Honduras. The virgin stands of timber that lay to the south within the territory of Central America excited his avarice, but for some time he found no way to secure the monopolistic arrangement required by his designs.[50] In partnership with Meany and Juan Manuel Rodríguez he obtained woodcutting concessions on the north coast of Guatemala in 1833, but they afforded him no important competitive advantage over other cutters. Then, in rapid succession, the Verapaz colonization law provided him with the means he sought to acquire title to a large block of mahogany-producing territory, and the fortuitous appearance of Gould in Belize suggested ideal circumstances under which to make his overtures to the Guatemalan government. If he could interest the agent of the London speculators in negotiating a colonization contract with Guatemala, his own proposals would be made to appear a part of a comprehensive colonization effort. Bennett had good reason to interest himself in Gould.

In Belize Gould received information on recent developments in Guatemala that completely changed the objective of his mission. It seems that Bennett was the informant who brought the news that the Verapaz colonization law, passed by the Guatemalan Assembly while the Company agent was on the high seas, placed within the grasp of his sponsors an incredible windfall. It appears probable also that Bennett suggested to Gould the daring maneuvers of ignoring his instructions to treat with the federal authorities for confirmation of title to the Company's portion of the MacGregor grant on the Mosquito Shore and of negotiating instead with the state of Guatemala for an entirely new cession of land in the Verapaz. Such a course certainly might result in great potential advantage to the designs of both the Belize woodcutter and the London speculators.

Whatever may have been their relationship in Belize and their agreement before leaving the British Settlement, Gould and Bennett proceeded together, first to the Verapaz and then to Guatemala City. There they both made proposals to the government and, like Galindo,

---

of San Jerónimo, Jan. 21, 1835, FO 252/29, n.f.; Lorenzo Montúfar, *Reseña histórica de Centro-América* (Guatemala, 1878), II, 244.

50. Russell Ellice to Earl of Aberdeen, Feb. 13, 1835, CO 123/46, n.f.

were accepted as colonization *empresarios* entrusted with functions and powers vital to the future of the state. His mind filled with visions of mighty works soon to be performed, Gálvez gave his blessing to the contracts. He could scarcely have known that the fair promises of grand accomplishment they contained were made with guile appropriate to the surrogates of Gregor MacGregor.

III

CHOSEN INSTRUMENTALITY:

THE COLONIZATION CONTRACTS

Within a period of six months in 1834 the government of Guatemala approved a series of colonization agreements that stripped the state of virtually its entire public domain. The concessions granted away all the unoccupied public lands contained within the three great northern departments that comprised about three-fourths of the total area of the state. Each of the grants was itself a wilderness empire both in geographical extent and in powers conferred upon the entrepreneurs. The Guatemalan government expected the contracts, scrupulously administered by the concessionaires, to result in spectacular internal development. Misused, they were capable of destroying the state that made them.

This wholesale disposal of Guatemalan real estate was accomplished by five colonization agreements entered into by the government with three entrepreneurs of British origins. The Assembly of Guatemala in March approved the first concession of this nature to Juan Galindo, and then in rapid succession during the month of August it authorized the government to sign four more such contracts. Thomas Gould obtained for the Eastern Coast of Central America Commercial and Agricultural Company a cession of the Department of Verapaz, including most of the District of Petén, and the partnership of Marshal Bennett and Carlos Antonio Meany arranged three similar pacts covering the Departments of Chiquimula and Totonicapán and a strip of territory lying north of Lake Izabal.

The arrangements signed in March and August were of disparate character that reflected two levels of maturity in a developing colonization policy. The grant to Galindo was made while the Verapaz colonization law was under consideration in the Assembly, but before it reached final form. The rudimentary statement of conditions and obligations in the instrument of cession went little beyond the nebulous requirement that within a period of five years the *empresario* colonize certain lands that were ceded to him. The contracts with Gould and with Bennett and Meany were signed after the Verapaz colonization law had established a general formula for such projects. The provisions of that enactment, with some modifications, formed the basis of those agreements. The Gould contract was the pilot document, and those signed with Bennett and Meany for Chiquimula and Totonicapán were almost identical copies, except for appropriate changes in geographical descriptions and some provisions inserted in recognition of peculiar circumstances. The partners' agreement for colonization of the Lake Izabal region was regarded as a special contract. It was separately negotiated and was much simpler than the other three.

For transactions of such profound import to the state the contracts were consummated with incredible casualness. The government acted on the assumption that colonization projects of any sort would automatically contribute to national development and that concessions of any nature required to induce contractors to undertake such works were entirely compatible with the objectives sought by the state. The government's impetuous movement in accepting Galindo's proposal became a stampede when Gould and Bennett appeared in Guatemala.

The prodigal role that Guatemala could be expected to play in negotiation was presaged by the request made by Gálvez to the Assembly on July 19 for authorization to treat with Gould. "In order that obstacles shall not appear during the recess that will deprive us of the advantages of a laborious population situated in our present wilderness," the Executive asked the legislative body to approve four deviations from the standards set by the Verapaz colonization law. He requested power to accept as expediency required offers to settle any number of families, rather than the stipulated minimum of one thousand; to cede at once the public territory within specified geographical limits for colonization within a period not longer than twenty years, rather than to make progressive allotments of land in proportion to the number of colonists established; to extend the exemptions from military service and military contributions from eight to twenty years as a means of inspiring confidence and a sense of security among prospective colonists; and to give certain assurances to the prospective contractors. Specifically, he asked for authority to pledge that colonizers would enjoy all privileges and exemptions guaranteed to native-born citizens, that land grants would confer full proprietary rights, and that contractors would receive for themselves lands equal in extent to those granted to colonists.[1] Gálvez may have been motivated to some degree in making these requests by pique that the Assembly had seen fit to alter the bases he had originally suggested, but it seems clear that his principal objective was to obtain prior approval from the legislative body for concessions demanded by Bennett and Gould to which he thought it expedient to accede in order to assure an agreement. The Assembly gave its approval to the Executive's request, and most of the extraordinary concessions were included in the contracts.

Gould capitalized immediately on the atmosphere of delighted expectancy his arrival produced in Guatemalan government circles. The actions of the Chief of State and the Assembly must have assured him in advance that the gamble he had taken in forsaking negotiation with the federal government to treat with the state authorities would be rewarded with full success. He made his formal proposals for a colonization project in the Verapaz on July 30,[2] the Guatemalan government named Carlos Antonio Meany and Juan Manuel Rodríguez as its agents to negotiate the contract with him, and on August 5 the executive branch recommended as "most urgent business" that the Assembly ratify the resulting agreement. Gálvez recognized that the contract "altered the base and system established by the decree of April 29 because only in this way was it possible to reach agreement," but he argued that the changes favored, rather than prejudiced, achievement of the aspirations of the state.[3] The Committee on Legislation reported favorably on the contract on August 9, and on August 14 the Assembly ratified it. Five days later an executive order attached four "explanatory additions" to the contract, the first of which stipulated that, should Galindo fail to comply with his obligations, the territory in the Petén granted to him would be added to the holdings of the Company.[4]

During the negotiation of his contract Gould remained "a good deal aloof" from Chatfield. The Consul complained of the "unbecoming reserve used in this matter with me, to whom it would have been more judicious on every account freely to communicate the

1. A los ciud[ada]nos Diputados S[ecreta]rios de la Asamblea, July 19, 1834, ANG, Congreso, 1834, No. 156, fols. 16-17, unclassified.

2. What appears to be the final page of the proposal, containing only points 6 and 7, signed by Thomas Gould for himself and the other four directors of the Company, and dated July 30, 1834, is found in ANG, leg. 7555, no exp. number.

3. The record of the Assembly's action on the proposal is in ANG, Congreso, 1834, No. 156, fols. 22-24, unclassified. The letter of transmittal, signed by P. J. Valenzuela, the Secretary General, on Aug. 5, 1834, is the first folio.

4. Draft executive decree, Aug. 19, 1834, ANG, leg. 7555, no exp. number.

prospects of the Company," but Gould, probably remembering the unpleasant December interview in London, approached the British representative only when he had need of his official services. On August 12 he appealed to the Consul to substantiate his claim that the £300 allowed by the directors of the Company for the expenses of his mission were insufficient to cover his needs, and under the same date he received the equivocal assurance that Chatfield did not consider the agent's allotment "more than sufficient" to cover the cost of his travel and maintenance. Ten days later Gould took the ratified contract to the British Consulate where Chatfield attested to the authenticity of the official signatures on the document and, incidentally, gleaned information on the cession that he made the basis of a report to his superiors in London.[5]

The trail blazed by Gould showed the way to other eager adventurers who hastened to file their claims to a share in the wilderness bonanza. By virtue of copying the major part of its petition verbatim from the Verapaz colonization law the commercial firm of Klée, Skinner and Company of Guatemala outdistanced its competitors in the race to the land office. On August 3 they proposed that the government cede to them two thousand *caballerías* of land in the region north of Lake Izabal for what they described as a colonization project in return for cancellation of a portion of the debt owed to them by the state treasury. The following day Bennett and Meany submitted a somewhat more original document in which they offered to buy a much larger area in the same general vicinity "for wood-cutting or other purposes." On August 6 the executive branch sent the petitions to the Assembly for action, and when on the following day Bennett and Meany made a more elaborate but less candid proposal that the area they had offered to buy be ceded to them for purposes of colonization, that proposition also was sent to the legislative body for consideration. The Assembly declined to choose among the projects, and on August 14, the same day it ratified the Gould contract, it authorized the Chief of State "to choose the one that under the circumstances appears to him most advantageous." On August 19 Gálvez accepted the colonization proposal of Bennett and Meany but appended four clarifying declarations to which the proponents had already agreed.[6]

5. Frederick Chatfield to Lord Palmerston, No. 12, Aug. 25, 1834, FO 15/14, fols. 158-59; Gould to Chatfield, Aug. 12, 1834, FO 252/6, n.f.; Chatfield to Gould, Aug. 12, 1834, FO 252/9, n.f.

6. The entire transaction is recorded in ANG, Congreso, 1834, No. 145, fols. 1-6, and No. 151, fol. 31, unclassified; ANG, leg. 7555, no exp. number.

Emboldened by the favorable reception given their initial request the partners ventured a more daring proposal. On August 15 they requested the government to cede to them all the public lands within specified limits in the Department of Chiquimula with "twenty years of grace for enjoyment of the same privileges and exemptions that were conceded to the Verapaz company." Gálvez amended the petition by extending the eastern limit of the proposed grant to coincide with the boundary of Honduras and stipulated that "the conditions for the concession of lands shall be the same as those arranged with Captain Thomas Gould for the colonization of Verapaz." On this basis the contract was drawn up on August 19, and two days later the executive submitted it to the Assembly. During the next week, whether on the initiative of the partners or at the suggestion of the Chief of State, the scope of the cession was enlarged to include the unoccupied public lands in the Department of Totonicapán as well as those in Chiquimula. On August 29 the Committee on Legislation recommended that the Assembly approve the arrangement subject to the stipulations that separate contracts be drawn to govern the two transactions and that a declaration be attached requiring that the families settled in the state under these and the similar previous agreements be of foreign origin. The Assembly accepted the Commission's recommendations, and on August 30 it ratified the contracts.[7]

Considering the vital functions it delegated, the government of Guatemala concluded the contracts with imprudent haste. It gave no more than perfunctory consideration to the motives of the proponents and to their ability to discharge the obligations they offered to assume, and in Galindo's case it dispensed with this formality altogether. Bennett and Meany were perhaps too well known in Guatemala to require investigation, but that familiar knowledge could scarcely have recommended them as seriously interested in colonization. Gálvez made a ritualistic investigation to establish the legitimacy of Gould's representations, but whether because of deliberate purpose or naïveté, he reduced it to a travesty of its intended function. Indeed, Bennett's hand was more clearly discernible in the transaction than was that of the Chief of State, and the mahogany cutter contrived to have the interests of the petitioners better represented than were those of Guatemala. Gálvez allowed Bennett himself to vouch for the financial responsibility and personal integrity

7. Marcial Bennett and Carlos A. Meany al S[upremo] G[obierno] del E[stado], Aug. 15, 1834, AMG, Expedientes, Guatemala 1834, n.f.; Opinion of Committee on Legislation, Aug. 29, 1834, ANG, Congreso, 1834, No. 151, fols. 8-9, unclassified; Orden legislativo, No. 72, Aug. 30, 1834, ANG, leg. 1395, exp. 32343.

of the directors of the Eastern Coast Company, and he appointed Carlos Meany, Bennett's current partner, and Juan Manuel Rodríguez, his business associate and intendant of the Federation, to negotiate for the government the agreement with Gould. These circumstances, added to the almost simultaneous concessions made to the partners under conditions virtually identical with those that Meany helped to establish for Gould and the pointed omission from the London Company's grant of the territory north of Lake Izabal to which the partners shortly filed claim strongly suggest collusion among the applicants for grants and, perhaps, between them and the Chief of State. This impression is strengthened by the peculiar role played by Bennett and Meany in the subsequent operations of the Company and by its appointment the following year of both Galindo and Bennett as honorary directors.

The backgrounds of the contractors and the terms they insisted on in the agreements clearly revealed that their principal concern was for the resources, especially the mahogany, ceded to them. This incompatibility of interest between the *empresarios* and the state, however, Gálvez may have explained away on the basis of his earlier-expressed belief that woodcutters might ultimately abandon their transitory exploitation and take up the sedentary and productive occupation of agriculture.

That personal interests and even fraud may have influenced the grant of the concessions has been several times suggested, but the evidence is too fragile to provide any substantial base for a judgment. It was rumored in Belize that Klée, Skinner and Company helped to maneuver the grant to Galindo in the hope that the territorial dispute it could be expected to provoke would favor the firm's commercial projects.[8] Should the Beliceños maintain their pretensions so doggedly that a punitive duty on trade between the British Settlement and Central America became necessary to force recognition of the Guatemalan boundary claims, the measure would have the effect of subsidizing the direct trade with Europe that the firm was attempting to establish through the Pacific port of Iztapa. Gálvez, who himself was said to have some small interest in trade, was sympathetic to such action, and his government did in fact establish preferential duties on imports through Iztapa in the fall of 1834[9] and in 1835 threatened to interdict commerce with Belize. Petty intrigue may

8. Lieutenant Colonel Francis Cockburn, Superintendent of Belize, to Chatfield, Sept. 15, 1834, FO 252/8, n.f.

9. Chatfield to the Duke of Wellington, No. 7, June 1, 1835, FO 15/16, fols. 99-100.

indeed have brought some influence to bear on these decisions, but it seems hardly plausible that individual interest was any necessary catalyst to the adoption of measures so expressive of the major policies of the Gálvez administration.

Whether or not Galindo's grant was an unsullied transaction, some of the later concessions were tainted by suspicion of fraud. Cockburn believed that, as a blind, Bennett allowed incorporation into his contracts of certain conditions ostentatiously beneficial to Guatemala, such as the prices he agreed to pay for the land, but "that other means may have been used for gaining friends in his behalf."[10] Cockburn was no admirer of Bennett, but his was no idle opinion expressed in ignorance of the subject's character. Chatfield also implied, in another context, that judicious purchase of support was the common method of assuring acceptance of treaties in Central America, but he made no allusion to venality in his reports on the Gould and Bennett negotiations. He remarked only that attitudes toward the transactions were decided by the way in which individuals believed their personal interests to be affected.[11]

The conclusion of the Gould agreement and the continuing negotiations with other prospective colonizers were reported in the official newspaper of Guatemala,[12] but the contracts were not published. Residents of the state who considered themselves injured by the contracts later accused the government of ulterior motives in concealing the nature of the transactions, but Chatfield reported to his superiors that the secret was guarded for reasons of state. The Guatemalan government suspected Mexico of aggressive designs toward the Verapaz, and Gálvez anticipated a hostile reaction from the agents of that government then carrying on negotiations in Guatemala, should they discover the nature and extent of the grants. He may also have hoped that the residents of Belize could be kept in ignorance of the concessions until the contractors began actually to place colonists on the land. In neither quarter, however, was secrecy maintained. The Mexican agents learned of the grants and took no pains to conceal their displeasure with the arrangement.[13] The de-

10. Cockburn to Chatfield, Oct. 17, 1834, FO 252/8, n.f.

11. Chatfield to John Backhouse, April 4, 1835, FO 15/16, fols. 72-74; Chatfield to Palmerston, No. 22, Nov. 12, 1834, FO 15/14, fol. 297.

12. *Boletín Oficial,* Segunda parte, No. 63 (Aug. 26, 1834), pp. 519-20 [in error for 319-20].

13. Federal Minister of Internal Affairs to Mariano Gálvez, Feb. 21, 1832, ANG, leg. 161, exp. 3383; Chatfield to Cockburn, Aug. 25, 1834, ABH, Letters Inwards 1826-1848, Records 10, fols. 20-21; Chatfield to Wellington, No. 3, March 16, 1835, FO 15/16, fols. 40-41.

tails of both the Galindo and Bennett grants were soon generally known in the British Settlement, and Gálvez noted with mingled apprehension and delight that the news had "alarmed the residents of Belize who see their advances restrained."[14]

The government of Guatemala had not the slightest doubt that it possessed full authority to enter into binding colonization agreements, but because the contracts had aroused the fears of powerful neighbors, Gálvez sought the additional security of federal approbation. On October 22, therefore, he submitted the Verapaz, Chiquimula, and Totonicapán contracts for ratification by the federal Congress in accordance with procedures authorized by the national colonization law. A special Committee on Colonization, set up by the Congress to consider the agreements, reported on February 14, 1835. Discussion of the recommendation was deferred, however, when the presiding officer suggested as a matter of "greater urgency" that the body inquire into the legality with which Juan Manuel Rodríguez, by coincidence a negotiator of one of the contracts, occupied his seat. Eventually the Congress considered the colonization question, but it was unable to agree on any action, and the protests that the national government began shortly to receive against the Chiquimula grant to Bennett and Meany only heightened its indecision.[15]

Nearly a year after he had first submitted the agreements, Gálvez reminded the central government that the question of ratification was still pending. His prompting produced only the equivocal opinion relayed from the President of the republic that the failure of Congress to act on the contracts left the state "in a position to carry them out in the hope that they would accomplish their expected results" and his unconvincing promise that, "within the limits of its abilities," the federal government would give to the undertakings all possible aid.[16] Embarrassed at home and abroad by the want of positive federal sanction, Gálvez and the concessionaires had no option

14. Cockburn to Chatfield, Nov. 5, 1834, FO 252/8, n.f.; Minister General of Guatemala to federal Foreign Minister, Oct. 22, 1834, ANG, leg. 168, exp. 3556.

15. Minister General of Guatemala to federal Foreign Minister, Oct. 22, 1834; Libro de Actos del Congreso Federal, 1835, sesiones públicas ordinarias, Feb. 5, Feb. 14, April 28, May 11, June 8, 1835, San Salvador, El Salvador, Biblioteca Nacional.

16. Gálvez to federal Minister of Interior Relations, Sept. 9, 1835, and reply, Sept. 25, 1835, ANG, leg. 164, exp. 3425. At the request of Gálvez, Chatfield inquired and reported during the spring of 1836 on the status of the contracts in the federal Congress. On March 18, Gálvez acknowledged the news that the matter "had been sleeping in Congress, and sleeps still." The correspondence is in FO 252/12 and 13, n.f.

but to proceed with the colonization enterprises under the authority of the state alone.

The government of Guatemala had already taken some steps in the direction of independent administration of its colonization projects. Immediately after the Assembly ratified the contract with Gould, Gálvez named an official agent in London in the expectation that the government would need to maintain contact with the Company and to transact business in the British capital. Following the recommendation of Bennett and Meany, he appointed John Waldron Wright, a wealthy former member of the Belize oligarchy, to the position and dispatched to him a commission in the care of Gould. Somewhat earlier the government had begun to take measures intended to insure the orderly administration of concessions of all sorts involving temporary or permanent assignments of land. To determine the status of titles that might affect the large-scale colonization project made imminent by passage of the Verapaz colonization company law, the Executive revoked all woodcutting concessions currently in force and required the operators to revalidate their grants. A little more than a year later the government ordered a register opened in which all colonization contracts, land sales, and woodcutting concessions were to be recorded and their boundaries marked on a map of the Republic.[17]

If the cessions to Galindo, the Eastern Coast Company, and Bennett and Meany were entered in the new register and their boundaries charted on the map, it must have appeared to the clerks in charge that there was no further need for the book. Indeed, after the grants were made little territory remained within the gift of the government, for the composite holdings of the concessionaires occupied virtually the entire domain of the state. Unassigned public lands remained only in the southern tier of departments that formed a strip of territory bordering on the Pacific to an average width of perhaps seventy-five miles.

Within the ceded area Juan Galindo received title to about one million acres in the District of Petén that comprised the segment of territory between the Hondo and Belize Rivers not included within the treaty limits of Belize.[18] The Eastern Coast Company acquired

17. Gálvez to John Waldron Wright, Aug. 18, 1834, ANG, leg. 1395, exp. 32341; Acuerdo ejecutivo, June 24, 1834, and Acuerdo ejecutivo, Sept. 26, 1835; Alejandro Marure and Andrés Fuentes Franco (comps.), *Catálogo razonado de las leyes de Gautemala* (Guatemala, 1856), pp. 27-28.

18. Order No. 20 of the Guatemalan Assembly, March 8, 1834, approving Galindo's project is in ANG, leg. 360, exp. 6315; the title document, dated March

an estimated thirteen million acres of public lands in the Department of Verapaz and its subordinate district of Petén which together formed the largest single territorial unit of the state. Its flattened apex resting in the south on the segment of the Motagua River that served also as the northern boundary of the Departments of Sacatepéquez and Guatemala, the Company's cession formed a wide, irregular "V" opening to the north and east. The western limit angled generally west of north along the line of the Chixoy (Negro) and Pasión (Usumacinta) Rivers in the direction of an undefined frontier with Mexico. The eastern confines ran diagonally from the Motagua to Lake Izabal, then clockwise around the southern and western lakeshore to the mouth of the Polochic River. At that point the line fell back along the river some eight leagues and at that distance skirted the northern shores of the lake and the Río Dulce to the Gulf of Honduras; then, following the line of the coast, it ran to the Sibún River where it met and followed the treaty limits of Belize and the western boundary of Galindo's grant until it reached Mexican territory.[19]

The Bennett and Meany cessions flanked the lower portion of the Company's holdings on either side. On the southwest the Department of Totonicapán extended from the Chixoy and Pasión Rivers to the frontier of Mexico. To the southeast the Department of Chiquimula and the partners' grant north of Lake Izabal occupied the area between Company property and the boundary of Honduras. The Chiquimula grant contained the lower Motagua and its tributaries and a stretch of the coast of the Gulf of Honduras that included the Bay of Santo Tomás. The grant north of Lake Izabal consisted of a strip of land five leagues in width beginning at the mouth of the Polochic and extending around the lake to within a few miles of the mouth of the Río Dulce.[20] Between this band of territory and

---

24, 1834, is copied in Chatfield to Palmerston, No. 15, Sept. 17, 1834, FO 15/14, fols. 226-27. The summarized terms of the concession given in subsequent paragraphs are drawn from these sources.

19. The contract for cession of the Verapaz, dated Aug. 7, 1834, is in ANG, leg. 1395, exp. 32338; the explanatory additions are found in ANG, leg. 7555, no exp. number. The summarized terms of the concession given in subsequent paragraphs are drawn from these sources.

20. The boundaries of the territory ceded to Bennett and Meany north of Lake Izabal are given in their proposal to the government of Guatemala, dated Aug. 7, 1834, previously cited. The contract for cession of both the Departments of Chiquimula and Totonicapán is published in *Arbitraje de límites entre Guatemala y Honduras: Anexos del alegato presentado por Guatemala . . .* (Washington, 1932), pp. 420-27. The summarized terms of the concessions given in subsequent paragraphs are drawn from these sources.

the Company's holdings beyond, a neutral strip three leagues wide remained ungranted to either concessionaire.

The contracts excluded from the cessions to Bennett and Meany and to the Eastern Coast Company several general and specific categories of territory. Lands within a radius of two leagues of established towns and villages were withheld, as were those already granted as private property or in the process of being transferred to individual owners. A plot four leagues square between the town of Izabal and the mouth of the Polochic River was reserved from the Company's grant for the construction of a port at Refugio, and six *caballerías* were set aside from the Bennett and Meany concession in Chiquimula for the establishment of a settlement on the Bay of Santo Tomás. An area half a league in radius around the Castillo de San Felipe that guarded the passage from the Golfete into Lake Izabal was also reserved from the partners' grant north of the lake for the use of the fort and its garrison.

In a special sense two plots of territory that Bennett and Meany contracted to purchase were also excluded from the cessions and the conditions placed upon them. One of these parcels was to consist of fifteen hundred *caballerías* of land to be selected in the area north of Lake Izabal, and the other was an area of thirty-six square leagues to be chosen in parts or as a single plot, either in Chiquimula or Totonicapán. For each of these parcels of land Bennett and Meany agreed to deliver in Belize on account to the government of Guatemala one thousand first-quality rifles or to pay their equivalent value in goods or cash. These lands were to be transferred to the partners immediately "in absolute property" and, in contrast to the remainder of the cessions, were designated as sold.

The contracts gave the concessionaires title to the ceded lands in absolute and perpetual ownership. They were free to exploit them in any way they saw fit or to dispose of them "as their own property" to individuals or to other companies who would honor the obligation to colonize them. Ceded lands that remained unoccupied and undeveloped at the expiration of the period stipulated for their colonization were to revert to the government. Thus, any land within Galindo's grant that had not been surveyed, registered, and the property tax paid on it within five years returned to the domain of the state. Similarly, any of the lands ceded to the Eastern Coast Company and to Bennett and Meany reverted after twenty years, if they had not been fenced or cultivated, unless the concessionaires chose to retain them by paying the annual land tax of two pesos per *caballeria*.

The government ceded the territory to the *empresarios* under condition that it be colonized. The assumption seems clearly to have been that the colonists were to be foreign immigrants, but no such specific provision was included in any contract until the Assembly retroactively established the requirement as one of the conditions under which it approved the last agreement. No precise number of colonists was fixed for Galindo to locate in the Petén or for Bennett and Meany to establish in the area north of Lake Izabal, but the other three contracts required the concessionaires to settle stated numbers of families within specified time intervals. The Eastern Coast Company agreed to install one hundred families in the Verapaz within two years, one hundred more within four years, and a total of one thousand before the expiration of ten years. Bennett and Meany obligated themselves to establish the same numbers in each of the Departments of Chiquimula and Totonicapán, but the time intervals were set at three, five, and ten years.

In addition to the obligation to colonize, the contracts in some cases anticipated that the concessionaires would undertake public works projects of considerable magnitude. Neither Galindo's grant nor the cession to Bennett and Meany north of Lake Izabal envisaged such operations, but the other agreements made provision for a variety of developments. The Eastern Coast Company in the Verapaz and Bennett and Meany in Chiquimula acquired options to construct roads desired by the Guatemalan government with the understanding that, should they elect not to do so, the government might seek other contractors to whom it could cede from the territory granted to the concessionaires a strip of land a league in width on either side of the thoroughfares. The option of the Eastern Coast Company covered the construction of a road from the projected port of Refugio on Lake Izabal to connect with existing routes in Verapaz and Chiquimula; that of Bennett and Meany allowed them to link Santo Tomás by road with the Izabal highway. The partners also agreed, if possible, to open a canal to connect the Bay of Santo Tomás with the Motagua. Their contracts guaranteed to both entrepreneurs the exclusive privilege for eighteen months of submitting proposals for establishing steam navigation on the waterways within their concessions. The London company could thus enter noncompetitive bids for the monopoly of steam transport on the Río Dulce, Lake Izabal, and the Polochic River, and Bennett and Meany enjoyed the same privilege for the Motagua River in Chiquimula and for the Pasión River in Totonicapán. The government guaranteed to both contractors, under equal conditions, preference over all competitors for subsequent colonization and road-building contracts in their respective cessions after each had "proved up" on the initial obligation to establish one hundred families.

The Bennett and Meany contracts for Chiquimula and Totonicapán contained an arrangement for sharing with the government the proceeds from exploitation of the resources granted to them. The partners pledged to contribute to the state fund for public education a fourth-part of the profits earned by their enterprises. The stipulation that any attempt by the government to divert these funds to another use would automatically relieve the partners of their obligation gave the arrangement the appearance of serious purpose. The agreement to leave for later negotiation the method of calculating the amount of profit, however, suggests that the partners intended the collection of the money to be less rigorously supervised than was its expenditure.

As compensation for the public services they were expected to perform, the contracts granted the London company and Bennett and Meany a variety of special privileges. They could make free use of the lands, forests, and waterways within their concessions, and they held monopolies, as against all other foreigners, of commercial hunting and fishing within their grants and along the waterways and seacoasts assigned to them. Bennett and Meany also received the exclusive right to exploit for twenty years the unoccupied lands and the forests along the southeastern margin of Lake Izabal and the southern shore of its outlet to the Bay of Honduras, the entire seacoast from the mouth of the Río Dulce to five leagues beyond the mouth of the Motagua, and the lower course of that river including its tributary streams on both sides. Both the partners and the Company could acquire title to all mines they might discover within their domains simply by registering them under Guatemalan law. Finally, they enjoyed the right of free trade with the interior and with foreign countries as promised by the federal colonization law.

The contractors also obtained several guarantees significant to the operation of their enterprises. The government agreed to recognize and to sustain their contracts with colonists, to give full protection of their persons and property under local law, and to exempt their employees and other personnel for twenty years from civil and military service.

The government also guaranteed to prospective colonists a wide variety of special privileges and concessions. Galindo's contract contained no explicit statement on this point but, by implication, colonists settling on his tract would enjoy exemption for five years from payment of the land tax and for eight years from payment of all other state taxes. The Gould and the Bennett and Meany agreements promised even more extensive fiscal immunities. For twenty years colonists would pay no internal taxes or contributions except those levied by their own municipal governments for local purposes; no export duties on their own produce, on other national products, and on foreign merchandise that had been nationalized by legal importation; and no import taxes on tools, machinery, and other articles useful to agriculture, industry, and other arts. For a like period they were to be exempted from all monopolies operative within the state.

Colonists were guaranteed complete local autonomy subject only to the condition that they and their officials obey the laws of the state. For twenty years the internal government of the colonies was to be entirely a function of municipal authorities chosen by the settlers under local law. For the same length of time they were exempted from civil and military service, except for a local militia which could not be used outside the colony. Colonists were not required to foreswear their national allegiance, but they were obliged to swear fidelity to the constitutions of the state and of the republic. When each of the departments opened to colonization had achieved the minimum population required by law for the formation of a state, the government committed itself, should the majority of the inhabitants so desire, to request the federal Congress to enact the necessary legislation to give it separate political identity.

In addition to the special concessions, the government guaranteed to the colonists all the privileges and immunities enjoyed by the native born. Specifically, it assured them freedom of religious belief and practice, security of their persons and property, and the right to trial by jury should that system of judicial procedure be established within the state either by a general law of the republic or by a specific enactment of the Guatemalan legislative body. Slavery was prohibited within the colony, as it was elsewhere in the republic.

With concessions arranged that must have fulfilled their wildest hopes when they came to Central America, Gould and Bennett departed together from Guatemala for Salamá on August 22. At Izabal they took passage for Belize, and on September 11 they arrived in the British Settlement. By early November Gould was back in London where for several days he quietly "dabbled" in securities that could be expected to react when the results of his mission were known. Then he informed his sponsors of his return.[21]

The contract that Gould delivered to the directors opened to the Company the possibility of an entirely new existence. The Guatemalan concessions put at the disposal of the speculators resources that would enable them to make their operation in fact what previously they had only pretended it to be. By coincidence, the situation of the ceded lands even retrieved the egregious geographical blunder in the Company's title that had provoked Chatfield's withering scorn. The directors had, in short, experienced the miracle of having a palpably fraudulent undertaking turn suddenly legitimate in their hands.

Conversely, the cession afforded the directors an opportunity for speculation on a scale previously undreamed of. By only token compliance with the requirements for validating its title or by acting within the deadline set by the contract for performance of the first obligations, the Company could with complete legality exploit, sell, or barter away a tract of land seven times the size of the holdings it had acquired from MacGregor. But while speculation might yield a quick and sizable windfall, serious colonization offered the prospect of sustained profits from a progressively developing economic empire. The choice lay with the directors and the shareholders of the Company.

However desirable the directors might now consider industry and rectitude as standards for their future conduct, there was some reason to question their ability to achieve so abrupt a change. Integrity had been a stranger to their earlier transactions, and Gould had inaugurated the new era in the same tradition. As he framed the contract he had the presence of mind (and the absence of scruples) to include his own name among the directors to whom the government conveyed the ceded territory.[22] He thus made his appointment to the board virtually a contractual engagement with Guatemala. His clandestine dabbling in shares after his return suggested further that the talents and habits of manipulation might prove difficult to adapt to the standards of ethical enterprise. Furthermore, should the Company succeed in divesting itself of the attributes of irresponsible speculation, it was by no means certain that it could demonstrate the

21. Chatfield to Cockburn, Aug. 25, 1834; "Private," Oct. 13, 1834; and Feb. 16, 1835, all in ABH, Letters Inwards, 1826-1848, Records 10, fols. 20, 28, 47.

22. Chatfield to Palmerston, No. 12, Aug. 25, 1834, fol. 159, and No. 15, Sept. 17, 1834 (Enclosure No. 2), FO 15/14, fol. 196.

fact convincingly enough to gain the confidence of a skeptical government and public.

The directors made their decision almost immediately after Gould returned from Central America. Whether with serious purpose or only to replace the shabby façade behind which their business had failed to prosper, they accepted the role of colonizers in which the contract cast them. On this basis they prepared to submit new plans to the shareholders. They repeated with fresh purpose an earlier routine call for the second installment on shares and extended the deadline for payment to December 31, on which date all unpaid shares were to be annulled without further notice. A hint that the Company was setting a new course for itself was given when the directors invited the shareholders to examine a translation of the Guatemalan grant in the Company officers and shortly thereafter announced that from December 31 forward Poyaisian stock and land certificates would no longer be accepted in payment on new shares. The impression of impending change was heightened by a call for a general meeting of shareholders.[23]

The proprietors met at the London Tavern on February 9, 1835. The *Morning Herald* had detected an air of suppressed excitement in the Company announcements and, possibly thinking to find justification for resuming its role as the nemesis of fraud, sent an observer to report on the transactions of the assembly. When the newspaperman appeared at the tavern, however, he was informed that attendance at the meeting was restricted to shareholders, as announced, and he was turned away. Having declined the opportunity and the risk of free newspaper coverage of their session, the directors drew up a report on the meeting and had it inserted a week later as a paid advertisement in the *Herald*.[24] The secret proceedings undoubtedly contributed nothing to the Company's reputation for responsibility, but they allowed the proprietors in decent privacy to take their farewell of knavery and to prepare themselves to assume the obligations of probity.

The reorientation given to its affairs the Company explained in a new prospectus issued as of the date of the shareholder's meeting.

23. This information was given in Company advertisements appearing on the first page of the *Morning Herald*, No. 17,239 (Sept. 3, 1834); No. 16,309 (Nov. 21, 1834); No. 16,315 (Nov. 28, 1834); No. 16,321 (Dec. 5, 1834); No. 16,330 (Dec. 15, 1834); No. 16,366 (Jan. 27, 1835); No. 16,369 (Jan. 30, 1835); and No. 16,373 (Feb. 4, 1835).

24. *Morning Herald*, No. 16,378 (Feb. 10, 1835), p. [2]; No. 16,383 (Feb. 16, 1835), p. [1].

The Guatemalan grant, that document admitted, had totally changed the nature of the operation. "This Company," it explained, "was originally formed with the express object of protecting the Poyaisian Securities, so long and so unjustly neglected. The Directors have fulfilled their engagement in extending to them (even under very different and more beneficial circumstances than those originally contemplated) all possible support, by allowing them to be incorporated into the shares of the Company until the 31st of December last: at that period all connection with those Securities ceased," except that the directors promised that those held by the Company would "be made available to its resources when circumstances shall permit." The original prospectus thus became inoperative, and the Company was, in effect, reconstituting itself "on a basis suitable to its new character." The new organization made the Guatemalan colonization project absorb the Poyaisian securities scheme in the hope that the legitimate venture would carry the original speculation to success.

The prospectus outlined a financial structure for the Company altered to conform with its obligation to undertake extensive operations overseas. The original enterprise commanded few liquid assets, its capital apparently having been subscribed largely, or entirely, in Poyaisian securities and land documents. Two calls had been made on shares, one before Gould was sent to Central America and the other immediately after he returned. At that point, 3,327 shares were outstanding. The new regulations increased the number to 5,000 and set their unit value at £30. Outstanding shares were to be exchanged for an equal number of new shares as with £20 paid on them. The remaining 1,673 authorized units were to be issued as script shares and offered first to the old proprietors and then to the public. Subscribers were to pay £5 with their orders and an equal amount in each of three quarterly installments, or a 4 per cent discount could be taken for full payment with order. When the new shares had been paid up to £20, they were to take equal rank with the old. No call was to be made for any part of the remaining £10 per share, unless voted by a majority of shareholders at a meeting called expressly for that purpose.[25] Thus, of a nominal capital of £150,000, the Company might expect to have available for its operations a maximum of some £33,460 in cash within the course of the

25. *Eastern Coast of Central America Commercial and Agricultural Company, Department of Vera Paz. One of the Principal States of Guatemala. Prospectus* [London, 1835], enclosed in Thomas Miller to Mr. Under-Secretary Gladstone, Feb. 20, 1835, CO 123/47, n.f.

ensuing year. It seems, however, that the directors were disappointed in their expectations, for only 3,917 shares had been taken in 1837.

The Company apparently carried out the reorganization as planned. It notified old proprietors to exchange their original shares for the new issue and new subscribers to make their initial payment on the script shares which were promised for distribution on May 1.[26] It seems probable that the opportunities offered by the Guatemala contract attracted some of the more highly regarded investors who a short time later became prominent in the management of the Company's affairs.

Notwithstanding the apparent fundamental reorientation of its activity, the Company made no immediate change in its management. Whether as a reward for their fortuitous accomplishment or because the Guatemalan concession listed them by name, Jeremiah Barrett, Robert Sears, William Crozier, and Daniel Mocatta remained as directors, and Thomas Gould was confirmed in the position to which he had elevated himself by the terms of the contract. Indeed, Gould became chairman of the board, perhaps because a Guatemala expert was now essential and he was the only member who could speak firsthand of the territory on which the Company now staked its hopes. The new regulations authorized these five officials to add as many as four members to the board, perhaps in recognition of the need for a broader array of talents to carry on the new program and for representation of new proprietors who might invest in the venture. It seems certain, however, that the framers of the new regulations intended to keep control of the Company, for a time at least, in the hands of the original proprietors. The old directors constituted a majority of the authorized board, and this arrangement was to continue unchanged at least until May 1, 1840, when the annual procedure of replacing, or re-electing, two of the directors was to be inaugurated. The shareholding requirements for eligibility to office and for voting appear also to have favored the old proprietors. Directors could be chosen only from among the owners of twenty or more shares, and proprietors were allowed one, two, or three votes on the basis of their holding as many as five, ten, or twenty or more shares.[27] The financial arrangements make it clear, moreover, that the capital for the reoriented program was to be supplied principally by purchasers of the new shares.

26. *Morning Herald,* No. 16,388 (Feb. 21, 1835), p. [1]; No. 16,423 (April 4, 1835), p. [1]; and No. 16,431 (April 14, 1835), p. [1].
27. *Prospectus.*

Although its new status produced no alteration in management of the Company, it brought changes in lesser officials and in locale of its headquarters. Thomas Bugden remained as secretary for a month after the reorganization, then he was replaced *pro tem* by J. Hammond in April, who in turn gave way to Rest Fenner in November. Leonard S. Coxe took the position provisionally in early 1836, then accepted permanent appointment and held the office until 1839. The Company also moved its offices in March 1835 from No. 7 Token-house-yard to the Lombard Street Chambers, 33 Clement's Lane, that remained its headquarters until 1838 or early 1839. A proper office in the financial district of the City would perhaps convey to government officials and to prospective investors and colonists a sense of the serious purpose, responsibility, and respectability of the enterprise.

The Company might also lay some claim to an honorable reputation on the evidence of its activity during the spring and early summer of 1835. Concurrently with its new prospectus it published *A Compendium of the Leading Points of the Charter* . . .[28] it had obtained from the government of Guatemala as a means of informing the public on the situation of the Verapaz and some of its principal physical features. No publisher was shown, but it may be assumed to be the work of Robert Sears who engraved and published the same year a *Map of the Department of Vera-Paz, One of the States of Guatemala, Central America* on which the Company delineated the purported boundaries of its grant. The work was alleged to be taken "from an authorized Sketch of the Federal Government of Central America," but it was in fact based on the map Gould brought back with the contract. When copies were sent to Gálvez, however, he noted a number of errors in the limits as drawn and returned a marked copy to the Company through John Waldron Wright to guide the work of correction.[29] In early March the directors invited applications from experienced tropical agriculturalists qualified to direct the projected colony in the Verapaz, and by early summer they had employed a superintendent and dispatched him to Central America.

The Company's burst of activity carried over to the fall, but it lost momentum significantly. The price of its securities sagged over the

28. *A Compendium of the Leading Points of the Charter Granted by the Government and Chief of State of Guatemala, to the Central America Commercial and Agricultural Company of London* [London, 1835], 3 pp., enclosed in Thomas Miller to Mr. Under-Secretary Gladstone, Feb. 20, 1835, CO 123/47, n.f.

29. Leonard S. Coxe to Sir George Grey, Dec. 16, 1836, CO 123/49, n.f. See also p. 67 and note 25.

same period. On March 9, exactly one month after its new prospectus was issued, Company shares with £20 paid were quoted at 42; on July 1, they had dropped to 7, and on July 9, they stood at 8.[30] A number of circumstances undoubtedly contributed to the Company's decline, but the attitude taken by the Cabinet toward the enterprise must have been one of the most important.

At the same speed with which Gould carried the evidence of his Central American coup to the directors of the Company, the news of the colonization contracts traveled to officials of the British government. The vessel that landed Gould and Bennett at Belize also carried a letter from Galindo to Cockburn, in which the concessionaire announced the grant made to him in the Petén, and enclosed a copy of a public notice warning the woodcutters of the Settlement to respect his title. Two days earlier the Superintendent's office received a dispatch from Chatfield to Lord Palmerston that reported in full on the grants and called to the attention of the British government both the opportunities and the hazards created by the contracts. The secretary failed to notice that the document was mailed under flying seal to Cockburn and, hence, forwarded it to London in routine fashion without the Superintendent's knowledge. Chatfield interpreted the resulting silence of his colleague on the subject of the grants to mean that Gould and Bennett had somehow managed to purloin his dispatch in order to allow the Company agent to arrive in London before the British government learned of the transactions. While the Consul fulminated against the supposed conspirators and speculated on the possibility of resolving the entire issue by having the principal contractors transported, the dispatch in question reached its destination.[31] British officials both in London and in Belize thus learned of the cessions that might be interpreted either to favor, or to challenge, British interests on the Gulf of Honduras.

The attitude taken by the British authorities was of crucial importance to the concessionaires. Their titles to the lands granted to them by the government of Guatemala were only as valid as the authority of Central America over the ceded territory. Failure of the federal Congress to ratify the contracts left the state in the anomalous position of asserting the Central American claim against a foreign power without the sanction of the national government. Chatfield

30. "City," *Morning Herald*, No. 16,402 (March 10, 1835), p. [5]; No. 16,497 (July 1, 1835), p. [3]; No. 16,504 (July 9, 1835), p. [3].

31. Galindo to Cockburn, Aug. 2, 1834, FO 15/17, fol. 95; Chatfield to Cockburn, "Private," Oct. 13, 1834, fols. 28-29; Cockburn to Chatfield, Oct. 17, 1834, FO 252/8, n.f.

sensed the Guatemalan dilemma immediately. "The State government," he observed, in reality, has no voice in it, and even allowing that it had, this new arrangement virtually makes over the advocacy of the case to its successors to the territory in dispute, the Colonists from England."[32]

The Consul's assessment of the situation was essentially correct, but he was mistaken in his identification of personnel. The supporters of the Central American claim were not the colonists, but the *empresarios*. To these men Gálvez had pledged the resources of the state thinking to assure the prosperity and safety of his border provinces by binding them through personal interest to advocacy of the Central American interpretation of British tenure in the Belize settlement. Only an official challenge, however, could determine whether their intervention would aid or encumber their sponsor.

32. Chatfield to Palmerston, No. 12, Aug. 25, 1834, fol. 161.

IV

BRITISH SETTLEMENTS,

OLD AND NEW

The political objectives Gálvez set for the colonization projects challenged Great Britain to proof of sovereignty along the total length of the western and southern boundaries of her Honduras settlement. He calculated the Galindo and the London company grants to confine British subjects precisely within the limits set for the woodcutting establishment by the Anglo-Spanish treaties of 1783 and 1786. In this fashion he intended to reclaim for Central America the territory threatened by the recent activity of operators from Belize and to secure the frontiers of the state against further unauthorized incursions from that source. His action bid defiance to the mightiest military and naval power on earth.

It is probable, however, that Gálvez had no thought of committing his country to a decisive conflict with a major opponent. He apparently held the view propagated by Galindo on the authority of former Consul O'Reilly that the British government recognized its settlement in Honduras to exist at the sufferance of the Central American republic. This premise accepted, the issue was reduced to the conduct of a few errant subjects of the British crown in Belize whose persistent poaching on neighboring estates was unsuspected by their sovereign. If the misdeeds of these knaves were brought to the attention of the government, it certainly would reprehend them. Defined in these terms, the boundary dispute could be settled promptly if the issue were sharply raised, for the Baymen could only yield or risk the consequences of allowing their record of trespass to come to the attention of London.

Gálvez apparently was willing to resolve the controversy with Belize either through diplomatic channels or on the ground in the northern wilderness of Guatemala. He expected the colonization agreements to commit the *empresarios* as firmly as his own government to the exertion necessary to attain a result favorable to Central

America. He calculated that the loyalties of European colonists settled on the land would be won for the government under whose aegis they held their titles and that the property interests of the new residents would be incentive enough to induce them to resist the expansionist tendencies of their kinsmen on the other side of the border. He even found some grounds to believe that the inhabitants of Belize would assist the colonization projects to a successful conclusion and then, abjuring their British allegiance, would join the Federation in order to forestall the damaging consequences that might befall them should the boundary question cause the republic to interrupt their Central America commerce or to curtail their woodcutting privileges.[1] The Chief of State manifestly believed that the territorial question could be satisfactorily resolved by counter-colonization if not by diplomatic negotiations between equals.

Neither Gálvez nor the Guatemalan Assembly appears to have doubted that the projects could do other than yield the desired results. Neither seems to have considered seriously the possibility that the British government might resist the attempted coup of the disputed territory or that the concessions might afford a means for extending the identical conditions they were intended to restrain. Chatfield, however, was not so ingenuous. He recognized both the threat and the promise of the contracts for British interests, and in a series of ambivalent dispatches he painstakingly outlined possibilities in each category.

The official policy of the British government toward the colonization grants the Cabinet would of course decide, but Chatfield exerted his best effort to incline the choice in the direction of taking advantage of the opportunities the projects offered. The agreements, he pointed out, if "taken up in earnest by speculators in England, cannot but prove of the first political and commercial importance to Great Britain, as a means of extending her sway in America, and as offering a new source of advantage to her Industry." Should British nationals appropriate the province of Verapaz and the government of Central America acquire stability, "the whole country then becomes subservient to British influence without requiring on the part of England the trouble and expense of its direct government." Far from injuring Belize, he argued, such a development would make the settlement in Honduras "one of the most valuable and important of the British possessions upon this Continent." Practicable commercial

1. These views Gálvez was reported to have expressed to the federal government, Frederick Chatfield to John Backhouse, Feb. 1, 1835, FO 15/16, fol. 34

routes to Guatemala City opened by the English colonizers would eliminate the Pacific ports from maritime competition and leave Belize as the Central American entrepôt of European commerce. If the first settlements were made in the Petén at San Luis, near the western boundary of the British establishment, they "would be wholly dependent on Belise, and with such a neighbour as Peten, it would not be difficult whenever desirable to stretch into the interior." In short, with proper management of the colonization projects, the entire Verapaz and perhaps much of the country beyond could be made an extension of Belize.[2]

Such attractive opportunities would have to be exploited with some dispatch, Chatfield believed, or another nation might pre-empt the field. Mexico, for example, could be expected, as soon as its internal conditions permitted, to incorporate the territory lying south of Yucatán and between the state of Chiapas and Belize. Before citizens of another nation were permitted to acquire privileges such as those now held by British subjects "it is worth reflecting what embarrassments might arise should any people but the English prepare to avail themselves of the Project."[3]

Even though the colonization agreements offered great potential advantage to Great Britain, Chatfield recognized that they also brought to issue the overlapping territorial claims of Belize and Central America. The contracts, he noted, granted away a "Portion of Territory which the British now occupy in Honduras, beyond the Boundaries of the Settlement as they were laid down in the British Treaties with Spain of 1783, and 1786." The assumption by the government of Guatemala of the power to dispose of these lands was the only exceptionable feature he found in the boundaries described. Before the Cabinet took any irrevocable stand on the boundary issue, however, he counselled that it consider fully the opportunities opened to British subjects by the contracts. His idea of a practicable course of action he illustrated by his observations to Cockburn on Galindo's concession. The grant was invalid, he remarked, but Galindo was a British subject and there would be no need to dispossess him should the boundary question be brought to issue, because "he interferes with no ones property acquired under an anterior right, & may consequently be admitted as a settler within the limits of British Hond[uras]." The Consul patently believed that the British govern-

2. Chatfield to Lord Palmerston, No. 12, Aug. 25, 1834, No. 21, Nov. 7, 1834, and No. 28, Dec. 17, 1834, FO 15/14, fols. 161, 292-93, 355.

3. Chatfield to Palmerston, No. 21, Nov. 7, 1834, fol. 292, and No. 23, Nov. 13, 1834, FO 15/14, fol. 319.

ment might, for the moment, find it expedient to ignore the question of the current boundary in anticipation of achieving vastly expanded frontiers in the future. Until official policy toward the contracts had been decided in London, he hoped that the sovereignty issue could be held in abeyance.[4]

Chatfield's desire for deliberate and mature consideration of the alternatives presented by the colonization projects was frustrated by events in Belize before the British Cabinet learned of the contracts. Galindo's letter announcing to Cockburn his concession in the Petén and the Consul's dispatches apprising Palmerston of the negotiation of the other four grants arrived almost simultaneously in the Settlement, but by some miscarriage of Chatfield's intent, his reports were not delivered to the Superintendent for perusal before they were forwarded to London. Without knowledge of the broader context, therefore, Cockburn committed himself on the issues raised by Galindo's announcement under the impression that he was dealing with an isolated incident. He did, however, suspect that other, similar cessions would soon be made. When he learned a short time later of the grants made to the Eastern Coast Company and to Bennett and Meany, he was "rather inclined to view [them] in a favourable light as concerns this Settlement,"[5] but it was already too late.

Cockburn interpreted the cession to Galindo as "a decisive and certainly no friendly" move by the government of Guatemala on the boundary question. Like Chatfield, he could only refer the issue to the Cabinet for a policy decision, but unlike the Consul, he was the responsible administrator of a British dependency under instructions to maintain the inhabitants in possession of such territories and in exercise of such rights as they had hitherto actually held. He therefore reported the incident to the Colonial Office and asked for immediate instructions, and he dispatched Thomas Miller, the Keeper of the Records of Honduras, to London to present to the British government the claims of the local inhabitants. Meanwhile he took swift and thorough action to maintain the *status quo* within British Honduras. He obliged Galindo's agent in the Settlement to discontinue the publicity he had been giving to the grant, acknowledged Galindo's letter but warned him that the cession might "lead to official Representations between our Respective Governments," and requested his brother who commanded the West India Station to

4. Chatfield to Palmerston, No. 12, Aug. 25, 1834, fol. 161; Chatfield to Lieutenant Colonel Francis Cockburn, Superintendent of Belize, Sept. 30, 1834, ABH, Letters Inwards, 1826-1848, Records 10, fol. 26.

5. Cockburn to Chatfield, Oct. 17, 1834, FO 252/8, n.f.

place two armed vessels under his orders for defense of the disputed coastal area south of the Sibún River against any attempted occupation under Central American auspices.[6]

This sudden and unanticipated flaring of the boundary question disturbed Galindo's plans. He did not doubt the ultimately successful outcome of the controversy, but he feared that an issue affecting only a part of his grant might so delay recognition of his title to the uncontested portion that aggressive British cutters would have opportunity to log off the entire area before he could prevent it. To forestall any such occurrence, he requested Cockburn in mid-October 1834 to prohibit the operation of Belize cutters in the western part of his grant where "surely no claim whatever can arise." Cockburn did not comply precisely with this request, but he achieved the approximate result by another, more portentous means. He attempted to fix a line beyond which mahogany would be considered foreign timber for purposes of assessing duties at the port of Belize. Cockburn had already accepted and announced to the Colonial Office the commonly asserted boundaries of the Settlement, but he called a council of local judges and Magistrates and asked them, in view of the grants made by Guatemala, to define the limits of British occupation at the time of Central American independence. That body answered the inquiry on November 5, 1834, probably as Cockburn intended, by describing the popularly claimed frontiers. It declared that the occupied area in 1823 comprised the segment of territory between the Río Hondo on the north and the Sarstoon River on the south, extending inland from the coast to a line between the two streams drawn north and south through Garbutt's Falls on the upper Belize River. The Superintendent then had notices posted advising mahogany operators that all logs cut beyond these limits would henceforward be subject to payment of the local duty levied on foreign mahogany.[7]

The effect of this ostensible regulation of mahogany cutters was to state formally in Belize, if not officially in London, the extended boundaries for Belize that had been popularly claimed for years. News of the *de facto* limits thus established for the Settlement and of the

6. Cockburn to Chatfield, Sept. 13, 1834, CO 123/45, n.f.; Cockburn to Thomas Spring Rice, No. 46, Sept. 15, 1834, CO 123/45, n.f.; Cockburn to Juan Galindo, Sept. 15, 1834, ABH, Letters Outward, 1829-1838, Records 8, n.f.; Cockburn to Chatfield, Oct. 17, 1834, Nov. 22, 1834, FO 252/8, n.f. See also R. A. Humphreys, *The Diplomatic History of British Honduras, 1638-1901* (London, 1961), p. 25.

7. Cockburn to Spring Rice, No. 48, Nov. 6, 1834, and enclosures, CO 123/45, n.f.; Humphreys, *Diplomatic History*, p. 22.

aggressive posture Cockburn had assumed in their defense immediately reached Central America, where they produced an angry outcry against the British Settlement.[8]

Chatfield believed that the premature action in Belize and the unfortunate reaction to it in Central America could have been avoided had Cockburn received his dispatches as intended.[9] Once the steps had been taken, however, and the home government had acquiesced in them, all possibility of converting the anticipated adjacent colonies into extensions of Belize disappeared. Chatfield therefore proposed an alternative means to obtain essentially the same objective by taking advantage of one of the two concessions that were not directly affected by the boundary issue.

The Bennett and Meany grant in Chiquimula lay safely beyond the areas in dispute. It contained extensive stands of valuable timber, the Consul observed, "but its principal advantage is the possession of the Port of San Tomas de Castillo, with a most spacious and safe anchorage, and capable under proper management of forming a formidable rival to the Port of Belize." Chatfield did not share Cockburn's fear that if colonized the site might become an immediate threat to the commercial dominance of Belize, but when domestic conditions in Guatemala settled, he asserted, "there is no doubt considerable exertions will be made to open a Port at Saint Thomas, in a view to shake off a dependence on the British Possession in Honduras." To forestall any such maneuver he made the extraordinary proposal that "His Majesty's Government should authorize me to treat privately, as for a third Party, with Mrss. Bennett and Meany for the purchase of the ground in Chiquimula. . . . The object which such a purchase would encompass, is not merely the future absolute command of the passage of the river Dulce, but a perpetual right to lands in a state which would prevent Saint Thomas ever becoming a rival port to Belize."[10]

The British Cabinet gave Chatfield's proposal only routine consideration. The Colonial Office dismissed the idea with the curt observation to the Foreign Office that "it will be by no means expe-

8. See, for example, the *hoja suelta* without title beginning "Privado de titulos y aptitudes . . ." (Guatemala, Nov. 19, 1834), attributed to José Antonio Azmitia by Galindo in his note addressed to an unidentified "Dear Sir" [Palmerston?], n.d., FO 15/18, fol. 230.

9. Chatfield to Cockburn, Oct. 13, 1834, ABH, Letters Inwards, 1826-1848, fols. 29-30.

10. Chatfield to Palmerston, No. 15, Sept. 17, 1834, FO 15/14, fol. 182; Cockburn to Spring Rice, No. 48, Nov. 6, 1834, n.f.; Chatfield to Palmerston, No. 17, Sept. 12, 1835, FO 15/16, fols. 146-46A.

dient to adopt Mr. Consul Chatfield's proposal. . . ." Henry Taylor explained the ethical reason for the decision by his marginal comment that "Independently of other objections, I conceive that the trickery of the procedures proposed by Mr. Chatfield would be altogether out of the question on the part of the British Gov^t. & that if territory is to be alienated by one Country in favor of another it must necessarily be by direct negociation & compact." In language almost identical with that of the Colonial Office opinion the Foreign Office a few days later declined Chatfield's invitation to covert imperialism.[11]

Had the Central American government known of Taylor's ethical objections to Chatfield's Chiquimula proposal, it could hardly have been convinced that the same standard governed the Belize question. Rather, it appeared that the British policy on that issue was the exact reverse of the "direct negociation" principle stated by Taylor. Chatfield was enjoined by his instructions from discussing the question of limits with the Central American authorities, and hence, he refused to be drawn into negotiations on the subject. In his unofficial conversations, however, he departed from the letter of his instructions far enough to state the British arguments against the current validity of the Anglo-Spanish treaties of 1783 and 1786 and to express the concept that British tenure in Belize "depends upon circumstances with which this gov^t. has neither a right nor an interest to interfere. . . ."[12]

Galindo assumed, on the basis of the contrary views he had earlier heard expressed by O'Reilly and by some residents of Belize, that Chatfield stated only his personal views. He was convinced that both the Consul and Cockburn, without the knowledge or approval of the government in London, were attempting to frustrate the just claims of Central America as successor to Spain in the area and to deny him access to a part of the grant made to him by the government of Guatemala in exercise of a legitimate right. Chatfield tried to convince him that he was misinformed, but Galindo persistently maintained his opinions. He agitated the question of British tenure in Belize and the legal limits of the Settlement with the purpose of forcing them to an early decision, confident that the British government would reverse the stand of its representatives in Central America when the issue reached London. Chatfield's official silence on the

11. Draft letter, George Grey to John Backhouse, Jan. 7, 1836, and marginal note, CO 123/47, n.f.; draft FO dispatch No. 3 to Chatfield, Jan. 12, 1836, FO 15/18, fol. 5.

12. Chatfield to Cockburn, Aug. 25, 1834, ABH, Letters Inwards, 1826-1848, fol. 20.

subject he interpreted to confirm his belief that the views expressed unofficially by the Consul were contrary to those held by the Foreign Office.[13]

Galindo managed to have his personal campaign to establish the line of 1786 as the boundary of Belize progressively clothed with official authority. Late in November 1834 Gálvez appointed him to act for the state of Guatemala against the British mahogany cutters operating in the disputed territory and particularly those active in the area of his own grant. Perhaps because the Commandant of the Petén had recorded his opposition to any measures which would disturb the good relations between that remote outpost and Belize, he requested and received from the state government a few days later orders that the *jefe político* of the district was to give him all possible aid in his projected reconnaissance of the mahogany frontier and in his attempts to recover the value of trees illegally cut in the disputed area. He induced the Central American government to require agreement to the 1786 boundary for Belize as a *sine qua non* for negotiation with Chatfield on a treaty of amity and commerce with Great Britain, and even before the Consul's refusal to discuss the subject made it clear that no satisfactory arrangement could be achieved locally, he persuaded the Vice President of the Federation to send a special commissioner to London to negotiate directly with the Foreign Office and to name him for the mission.[14]

The appointment as special commissioner was a personal triumph for Galindo—of self-interest and vanity, Chatfield believed.[15] In soliciting the commission, however, he assumed a grave responsibility. On the correctness of his assumption, despite Chatfield's warning, that former Consul O'Reilly faithfully expressed the views of the Foreign Office, he hazarded the territorial claims of Central America on the frontiers of Belize, as well as his own personal fortunes and those of the other colonization enterprises affected by the boundary dispute.

Had he known the trend of recent events in London, he would perhaps have been less eager to obtain the commission. Consistent with the position Chatfield had reported in Central America, the Foreign Office denied that the questions of British tenure in Honduras

13. Chatfield to Palmerston, No. 23, Nov. 13, 1834, fols. 318-19, and No. 28, Dec. 17, 1834, fols. 349-50; Chatfield to Cockburn, Oct. 11, 1834, ABH, Letters Inwards, 1826-1848, fols. 24-25.

14. Acuerdo ejecutivo, and draft letter to Galindo, Nov. 22, 1834, ANG, leg. 3606, exp. 83743, fols. 1-2; Chatfield to Palmerston, No. 28, Dec. 17, 1834, fols. 350, 354.

15. Chatfield to Palmerston, No. 29, Dec. 29, 1834, FO 15/14, fol. 380; fragment of a letter Chatfield to Cockburn, n.d., ABH, Letters Inwards, 1826-1848, n.f.

and the boundaries ascribed to the Settlement were in any way a concern of the republic, for they were governed by covenants and by circumstances that antedated any declaration of independence in Central America. Hence, any right in the area which had not devolved upon Great Britain remained with Spain. The British took the position that events between 1786 and the establishment of Central American independence had in fact extinguished all Spanish rights and allowed them to devolve upon Great Britain. Recognizing what he believed to be a favorable opportunity to negotiate, Palmerston decided in September 1834, before news of the colonization grants had reached England, to invite Spain as a matter of courtesy formally to recognize British *de facto* succession to her former rights in the area. The Colonial Office had drawn up a statement of boundaries to be presented during the negotiation, but when Cockburn's report on the Galindo affair arrived, the boundaries declared by the council in the Settlement on November 6 were substituted for those suggested by the Colonial Office. It is of some interest that the Colonial Office was willing if necessary to accept the treaty line of 1783 north of the Belize River if Mexico could be shown to have clear title to it, but Central America was excluded from consideration.[16]

Galindo's instructions were to proceed to London by way of Washington where he was to discuss with the government of the United States the purpose of his mission. For his interviews with the Secretary of State, Miguel Alvarez, acting Minister of Foreign Affairs of the Federation, provided him with a memorandum which accused Great Britain of territorial usurpation in Central America and invoked the non-colonization principle stated by President Monroe to solicit the support of the United States government for Galindo's representations in London. Gálvez also addressed a letter to the Secretary of State on the same subject, presumably on the assumption, Chatfield acidly observed, that "having granted away the lands . . . he can be permitted to communicate with a foreign government."[17]

Chatfield surmised that Galindo would attempt in Washington to make great capital of the non-colonization principle. He expected him to argue it against the alleged extension of British dominion in Central America and, perhaps, against the cession to the Eastern Coast Company as a means of thwarting the incorporation of his

16. Humphreys, *Diplomatic History*, pp. 26, 37-38.

17. Miguel Alvarez to Secretary of State John Forsyth, Dec. 30, 1834, William Ray Manning (ed.), *Diplomatic Correspondence of the United States. Inter-American Affairs, 1831-1860*, III: *Central America, 1831-1850* (Washington, 1933), 85-86; Chatfield to Sir Charles R. Vaughan, Jan. 10, 1835, FO 252/10, n.f.

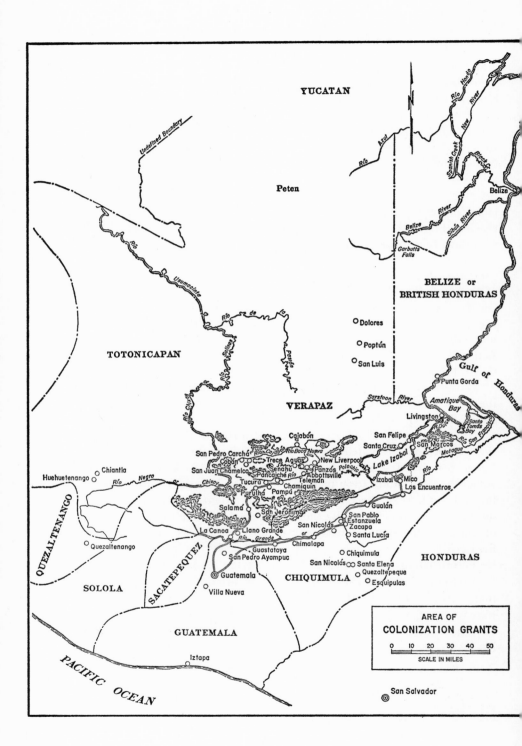

YUCATAN

N

Peten

Río Azul

Hondo

Río

New River

Santón Creek

Black R.

Belize

Belize River

Belize

Sibún River

Garbutts
Falls

BELIZE or
BRITISH HONDURAS

○ Dolores

○ Poptún

○ San Luis

Gulf of Honduras

● Punta Gorda

Sarstoon River

Amatique
Bay

Río Dulce

Santo
Tomás Bay

San Francisco

Livingston ○

San Felipe ●

Santa Cruz ○

Río

San Marcos

Motagua

Lake Izabal

Cajabón ●

Río Cahabón

Río Boca Nueva

San Pedro Carchá ○

Coban

Trece Aguas

New Liverpool

Senahú

Pancaiché

Río Polochic

Panzós

San Juan Chamelco

Río

Telemán

Abbottsville

Izabal ○

Mico ●

Tucurú

Chamiquin

Río

Los Encuentros

Purulhá

Pampú

Chiantla ○

Huehuetenango ○

Río Negro

Río Chixoy

Salamá ○

San Jerónimo ●

Gualán ●

Río

TOTONICAPAN

VERAPAZ

QUEZALTENANGO

La Canoa ○

Llano Grande

San Nicolás
or

San Pablo

Estanzuela

Zacapa ●

Quezaltenango ○

Río Grande

Chimalapa ●

Santa Lucía ○

SACATEPEQUEZ

SOLOLA

Guastatoya ●
San Pedro Ayampuc ○

San Nicolás ○○

Chiquimula ○

HONDURAS

◎ Guatemala

CHIQUIMULA

Santa Elena

Quezaltepeque ●

Villa Nueva ●

Esquipulas ○

GUATEMALA

Iztapa ●

PACIFIC OCEAN

AREA OF
COLONIZATION GRANTS

0   10   20   30   40   50

SCALE IN MILES

◎ San Salvador

own grant into that of the Company. The Consul warned Sir Charles R. Vaughan, the British Minister in Washington, of these possibilities and exacted a promise, which was apparently not honored, from Elijah Hise, the United States Chargé d'Affaires in Central America, to put his government on guard against the adventurer.[18]

Galindo departed from Guatemala in early January 1835 and made the first leg of his journey to Belize. There he remained for nearly three months attending to his personal interests and, incidentally, to those of Guatemala and the Federation. He attempted unsuccessfully to collect the value of the logs he alleged had been cut from his grant, he reconnoitered the Garbutt's Falls boundary and found that British woodcutters were already operating west of it, and he discovered that residents of the Settlement denied any intent to respect the new line. His reports on these "offenses against the national honor" further inflamed Central American opinion against Belize and supplied justification for proposals made by the government of Guatemala to the federal Congress for retaliatory measures against the commerce of the Settlement.[19]

From Belize Galindo sailed to New York where a "continuing indisposition" prevented him for a month from proceeding to Washington. He forwarded the Alvarez memorandum to Secretary of State John Forsyth, however, and during the latter part of June he went to Washington, where he had interviews with the Secretary of State and President Jackson. Although sympathetic to the Central American claims, "the President deemed it inexpedient to comply with the request of that government." Perhaps, as he reported to Palmerston, Vaughan had indeed convinced Forsyth "that the Government of the United States could not possibly listen to any such proposal from Colonel Galindo." What he may have feared to do openly, however, Forsyth attempted to accomplish obliquely, for even before he saw Galindo he instructed the United States Minister in Madrid to use "all prudent means" to forestall an Anglo-Spanish agreement on the Belize boundary "as being incompatible with the rights of the Republic of Central America." Whatever the circumstances, Galindo failed to enlist the diplomatic support he had hoped to obtain from Washington for his representations in London,[20] and, with failure

18. Chatfield to Vaughan, Dec. 26, 1834, FO 252/10, n.f.; Chatfield to Palmerston, No. 1, Jan. 10, 1835, FO 15/16, fol. 25. Galindo carried documents to Washington for Hise, but no comment on his mission appears.

19. William J. Griffith, "Juan Galindo, Central American Chauvinist," *Hispanic American Historical Review*, XL, No. 1 (Feb., 1960), p. 34.

20. Daniel Webster, Secretary of State, to William S. Murphy, Special Agent

in two capitals behind him, he sailed from New York in mid-July for the crucial negotiations with the Foreign Office.

While Galindo was crossing the Atlantic the Eastern Coast Company blundered headlong into the boundary controversy. The reorganization undertaken in the early months of 1835 completed and plans underway for sending out colonists later in the year, the directors, through their chairman, Thomas Gould, applied verbally to the Colonial Office in July for a charter of incorporation that would imply official sanction of the Company and validation of its grant in Central America. Whether or not the directors were aware of the decision, the Cabinet had already determined on the basis of reports received from Chatfield and Cockburn to prevent the grantees from occupying the disputed portions of their concessions south of the Sibún until the question of limits was resolved. Henry Taylor, who prepared the staff memorandum on the petition, therefore probably restated largely accepted views when he cited a number of reasons for rejecting the request.

The conflict of territorial claims was the major objection pointed out by Taylor to granting the charter requested by the Company. He noted that in making the grant "the Central American Govt. arrogates the sovereignty of a large tract of Country between the rivers Sibún and Sarstoon which is in British occupation & was so before Central America existed as an Independent State, & of which the sovereignty, if not devolving to Great Britain must necessarily rest with Spain." He argued further that the limits described in the grant assumed a prior delimitation of boundaries between Central America and Mexico within the province of Yucatán and that, in the absence of such an agreement, British recognition of the validity of the Company's title might "give just cause of complaint to Mexico" and encourage British subjects to enter territory where they would risk being "treated as intruders by Mexico."

James Stephen concurred in these objections. He rejected as invalid, however, Taylor's argument that the government could not countenance a project for colonizing with Englishmen "a territory not within the King's allegiance," because the legal impossibility of the colonists' divesting themselves of their obligations as British subjects could not be reconciled with the requirement that they swear

to Central America, Aug. 6, 1841, Manning, *Diplomatic Correspondence*, III, 29; Forsyth to W. T. Barry, Minister to Spain, June 30, 1835, Manning, *Diplomatic Correspondence*, XI: *Spain* (Washington, 1939), 13-14; Vaughan to Palmerston, No. 38, July 4, 1835, CO 123/47, n.f.

allegiance to the constitution of the state of Guatemala. Both officials agreed, however, that the charter was requested for the purpose of promoting a speculative enterprise. Taylor observed that the directors had been reported "to have used unfair means for raising the price of shares in the projected Company & that every word which is said to Mr. Gould will probably be perverted to the same purpose." Stephen held "the very strong suspicion that the whole affair will turn out to be a mere contrivance for creating a salable Commodity in the Form of Shares. What rational Man would seriously hazard his Property or his person in speculations in the Province of Vera Paz in the State of Guatemala unless his Fortunes or his Character were desperate? The scheme seems nearly allied to that of the Cacique of Poyais." Cockburn had correctly predicted that, regardless of the opportunities it might offer, the Company project would be opposed by the government "on account of the wildness of the Speculation, & the evident risks it will involve all those in who may be induced to join in it as Settlers."[21]

These Colonial Office memoranda stated the elements of the position that the British government consistently sustained on the Belize question. The Cabinet rejected the Central American claim to sovereignty over the lands in question and denied that the Federation was an interested party to the dispute on the grounds that any sovereign right not possessed by Great Britain must reside with Spain, it declined any discussion of the question of limits until a prior boundary agreement had been reached between Central America and Mexico on the basis of which Great Britain could determine with which country to negotiate a given segment of the frontier, and it enforced the British view of the matter by maintaining the residents of Belize in possession of the disputed territories and denying access to any agent of the Central American government. In accord with these principles Lord Glenelg informed Gould on August 18 that "on full consideration of the subject, it does not seem advisable to accede to your proposal."[22]

Two days before Glenelg denied the Company's petition for a charter, Galindo landed in Liverpool. He proceeded immediately to London and on his arrival there informed Palmerston of his mission. The Foreign Secretary decided to give him an unofficial audience, and in preparation for the interview he requested the advice of the

21. Memorandum "For Lord Glenelg: Colonization of Vera Paz," initialed "H. T.," July 30, 1835, and another with same heading, initialed "J. S.," Aug. 5, 1835, CO 123/47, n.f.; Cockburn to Chatfield, Oct. 17, 1834, n.f.
22. Glenelg to Thomas Gould, Aug. 18, 1835, CO 123/47, n.f.

Colonial Office on "the course it would be expedient to pursue" on the Belize issue. In reply Lord Glenelg answered that "the only proper course" was to refuse to negotiate with Central America on the question and to maintain the inhabitants of the Settlement in possession of the territory they actually occupied. In support of this position he repeated the arguments on the basis of which the Company had been denied the charter. These principles restated to him during his interview with Palmerston in mid-September brought Galindo to the shattering realization that Chatfield had in fact accurately stated the British position on the Belize question. Dazed to encounter a vigorous defender guarding the ramparts he had expected to find deserted, the Central American colonel fell back in confusion, and for several months he did not risk showing himself.[23]

As soon as he was able to reassess the situation, Galindo began to plan a new attack. If success was not to be won at the Foreign Office by a single brilliant stroke, he might force Palmerston to yield by massing opposition against him. If he could provoke the Central American government to take punitive action against the commerce of Belize to reinforce his diplomacy and if he could induce the Eastern Coast Company to join him in a common demand for recognition of territorial rights acquired under the colonization charters, the power balance might be shifted to his advantage.

With this objective in view Galindo abruptly discontinued the accounts of fictitious successes he had been writing to the Central American officials during his initial bewilderment and bluntly reported the incendiary evidence that the British government denied Central America status as an interested party in the Belize dispute. He had little expectation that the federal government would be moved to action, but he founded his hope on the possibility that Gálvez would be able to deliver the support he needed.[24]

Simultaneously, Galindo insinuated himself into the affairs of the Eastern Coast Company. The directors accepted his overtures without question, presumably because he appeared as the accredited agent of Gálvez and because Chatfield had recommended him to Gould. After the agent had concluded his negotiations in Guatemala, the Consul had pointed out to him "the advantages of securing Colonel Galindo's cooperation in the views of the company, for he has travelled much in the part of the country named in your Contract and possesses a greater local knowledge of it, than any other Person in the

23. Griffith, "Juan Galindo, Central American Chauvinist," pp. 35-36.
24. Galindo to [Gálvez], Dec. 31, 1835, AMG, Comunicaciones 1835, n.f.

Republick." Moreover, Galindo held title to a grant the directors hoped to incorporate into their own. They therefore appointed him an honorary member of their board and commissioned him to supervise the work of correcting the errors pointed out by Gálvez in the boundaries shown on the Company's map of its concession. In accord with the spirit of fraternity and consolidation Galindo appeared to promote, they offered to exchange with him shares in their enterprise for title to his grant in the Petén. Galindo had no desire, however, to push unity to any such unreasonable extreme, and he appealed to Gálvez to save him by specifically excluding his grant from that of the Company.[25]

In late October 1835, probably at Galindo's suggestion and using arguments and data he supplied, the directors initiated a correspondence with the British government in an attempt to secure recognition of their title to the disputed lands south of the Sibún. They addressed an undated memorial to the Privy Council, and apparently at the same time, Barrett directed a letter of similar tenor to Palmerston. The memorial described the grant of land and the concessions received from Guatemala, significantly omitting mention of the possible addition of Galindo's cession, and pointed out the "great importance to have so vast an extent of Coast possessed by British subjects, rather than Americans, French, or any other nation, as it commands the extensive commerce of the neighboring states of Central America & Mexico." The directors announced their intention "with your Lordships' assistance, [to] secure those possessions as an English colony." To that end they requested, in view of reports that British troops were ordered to halt all approaches to the coast south of the Sibún, that the Government "given immediate directions to the proper Authorities not to molest or otherwise impede the progress of Your Memorialists' Agents, or the Settlers under their charge in proceeding to occupy the Coast under the authority of their grant. . . ."[26]

Barrett's letter to Palmerston protested the encroachments by resi-

25. Chatfield to Gould, Sept. 30, 1834, FO 252/9, n.f.; J. Hammond, Secretary, to Gálvez, Oct. 9, 1835, ANG, leg. 3619, exp. 84739, n.f.; translation of R. Fenner, Secretary, to Galindo, Oct. 21, 1835, AMG, Comunicaciones, 1835, n.f.; and Galindo to [Gálvez], Dec. 31, 1835, n.f. Galindo claimed that the map of the Petén he drew incorporating the results of his own explorations was stolen by agents of the Company and used as the basis of its published map (Ian Graham, "Juan Galindo, Enthusiast," Estudios de Cultura Maya, III [Mexico, 1963], 29).

26. The Memorial of the undersigned Directors of the Eastern Coast of Central America Company to the Right Honorable the Lords of His Majesty's Privy Council, Oct. 1835, FO 15/17, fols. 249-50.

dents of Belize on lands assigned to the Company by the government of Guatemala. He alleged that "by nothing short of an infringement of the law of nations" British woodcutters had extended their operations south of the Sibún into territory that by the terms of the treaty of 1786 belonged to Spain and subsequently to Central America. He professed to believe that the British government would never knowingly sanction such incursions but suggested that, should the Cabinet now find it difficult to relinquish a footing thus acquired, the grant held by the Company afforded the opportunity "to do justice, at once, to the Republic of Central America and the British Company . . . and, yet, to sustain for England all that she has gotten, or could hope to get," at the cost only of transferring "to one portion of his Majesty's subjects (the Company to whom it justly belongs) a part of the profit now illegally engrossed by others."

The directors of the Company argued the opportunity for British expansion afforded by their concession with no greater success than had Chatfield. The Privy Council appears to have ignored their memorial after Glenelg expressed the opinion that protection of British interests required no new orders to the authorities in Belize, and Palmerston coldly informed Barrett in early November that his complaint should properly be addressed to the Colonial Office. The Foreign Secretary could not refrain, however, from observing "that if British subjects choose to take from a foreign Government a grant of land which is included within the limits of a British Settlement such persons must take the consequence of their connivance with the encroaching pretensions of such foreign Government."[27]

The charge of connivance Barrett used as justification for continuing the correspondence with the Foreign Secretary. He argued the innocence of the directors on grounds that the evidence of the Anglo-Spanish treaties supported the contention that Great Britain "had no right to Belize beyond that sanctioned by the Conventions of 1783 and 1786" and that the limits of the Settlement "were too well-defined to be obliterated by the encroachment" of the inhabitants on adjoining territory. He expressed the hope that "when your Lordship shall have duly considered all the Treaties and shall have weighed the pretension of the Belizians, you will not only exonerate me from an imputation which I feel to be unjust, but will accord in the opinion I firmly possess that the grant made to my Company is al-

27. The correspondence is in CO 123/47, n.f. Except for one missing letter, it was published in the *Brief Statement, Supported by Original Documents, of the Important Grants Conceded to the Eastern Coast of Central America Commercial and Agricultural Company by the State of Guatemala* (London, 1839), pp. 61-69.

together unimpeachable and that the honor and equity of Great Britain will ere long confirm it." To this argument of the Central American case on British tenure and boundaries in Belize, Palmerston gave curt acknowledgement devoid of comment.[28]

The menacing terms in which the Foreign Secretary disdained their appeal for his intervention apparently overawed the directors, and they abruptly desisted from their direct attempt to influence government policy. The results of the correspondence must have confirmed Galindo in his opinion that the directors possessed "neither wealth, nor knowledge, nor influence," for he undertook to see that the affairs of the Company were placed in the hands of more capable men. He reported to Gálvez on the last day of 1835 that he had succeeded in securing the election of a new board composed of Edward Blount, John Wright, Joshua Walker, and Peter Harris Abbott, men of position whose influence in the Colonial Office he expected to reinforce his own representations at the Foreign Office. To secure the support of the new directors for his negotiations on the Belize question, he held out the promise that, should their assistance enable him to secure British recognition of the Central American claims on the boundary issue, the government of Guatemala would grant the Company an extension of one year to the period set for the performance of its contractual obligations.[29] These more influential directors may have given verbal support to the arguments Galindo advanced, but they hazarded no expression of views in writing. The Central American commissioner was therefore left to make his way with the government as best he could.

28. Jeremiah Barrett to Palmerston, Nov. 6, 1835, and reply, FO 15/17, fols. 257-258. The Barrett letter does not appear in the published correspondence because "the copy is unfortunately lost."

29. Galindo to [Gálvez], Dec. 31, 1835, n.f. This letter is the only document encountered which links the names of Blount, Wright, and Walker with the Company. Abbott remained the dominant figure on the board until 1841. He was a brewer at 10-½ King's Arms Yard, Coleman Street (*The Register of Persons Entitled to Vote in the Elections of Members of Parliament for the City of London* [London, 1833], p. 4), an official assignee (*Post Office London Directory for 1834* [London, 1834], p. 1), and a professional mercantile accountant of "highest rank" who made a name for himself by his study and report on the books kept by various government departments (Henry Parnell, *On Financial Reform* [London, 1830], pp. 161-62, 192-93), and by publication of a pamphlet *On the Public Debt, with a Plan for its Final Extinction* (London, 1839). He was also Secretary of the Anglo-Chilean Mining Company (*Pigot & Co.'s London Directory for 1834* [London, 1834], p. 643), a member of the Committee of Management of the South-Western Railway (*Morning Herald*, No. 16,728 [April 1, 1836], p. [1]), and a director of the British and Colonial Trust and Assurance Company (*The Colonial Gazette*, No. 104 [Nov. 18, 1840], p. 776).

During the month of January 1836 Galindo had two more informal interviews with Palmerston that produced results no more satisfactory than had the first. During the second conference Palmerston destroyed Galindo's last hope for successful negotiation by informing him that, because he was a British subject, the British government could not recognize him as the representative of a foreign nation. Although he was denied recognition as an accredited diplomatic agent, Galindo nevertheless maintained contact with both Palmerston and Glenelg, and during the spring he appears to have been on the verge of signing with the British government a convention establishing the boundary of Belize at the line claimed by the council of the Settlement in 1834. The arrival of dispatches from Chatfield reporting the propaganda use that had been made in Central America of Galindo's accounts of his conversations in London made further contact with the Central American commissioner embarrassing to the Cabinet, however, and the relationship was broken off in May. Galindo busied himself with other projects until his return to Central America in the fall, and during the remainder of his stay in London he did not again venture to try to move Palmerston from the position he held on the boundary of Belize.[30]

Despite the unhappy result of its first encounter with the Cabinet, the Eastern Coast Company could not allow the boundary question to lie indefinitely in diplomatic limbo. The conditions of its contract required it before August 1836 to establish the first one hundred families of immigrant settlers somewhere in the Verapaz. During the spring and summer, therefore, it sent out the first colonists who were situated on the Polochic, deep in the interior of the province. The project was badly executed, and by fall a provisional committee composed of Peter Harris Abbott, Charles Bourjot, and W. Gordon Thomson had taken over direction of the Company,[31] committed to more energetic management of its affairs. The members recognized that until they knew the limits claimed by the British government for Belize they could not be certain that their settlement was safely beyond challenge. They therefore applied to the government to learn what part of their grant, now described as including Galindo's concession "should that individual (with whom the Company disclaim

30. Griffith, "Juan Galindo, Central American Chauvinist," pp. 37-43.

31. William Hall to Chatfield, Sept. 8, 1837, FO 252/18, n.f. Bourjot was a merchant with offices at 25 Coleman Street (*Post Office London Directory for 1834*, p. 51).

all conexion whatever) fail to fulfil certain conditions," they would be free to occupy without fear of governmental interference.[32]

On October 8 Leonard S. Coxe, the provisional secretary of the Company, requested an audience at the Colonial Office for "a deputation of shareholders and proprietors" consisting of R. F. Gower, W. G. Thomson, John MacDonnell, Charles Bourjot, and Peter Harris Abbott. In pursuance of a suggestion made by James Stephen during the interview, Coxe addressed a letter to Lord Glenelg in which he explained the reasons for which the Company required precise information on British territorial claims. He requested that the Colonial Secretary inform the Company whether negotiations reported to be in progress with Spain had resulted in any formal agreement to extend the boundaries of Belize beyond the Hondo River in the north or the Sibún in the south and, if not, what were the precise limits of the territory being claimed. Glenelg replied that the question should be put to the Foreign Office, but an inquiry there was not acknowledged. A reminder brought the response on October 29 that Palmerston did not "feel it consistent with his public duty to give a company of private individuals information on the status of negotiations pending between the British Government and foreign powers," but he felt it proper to remark "that there is some reason to believe that some portion of the lands" accepted by the Company from Guatemala was included within the limits claimed for Belize and to repeat his earlier admonition that the directors "consider the position in which, as British subjects, they may place themselves by acknowledging a foreign authority over lands which are claimed by the British Crown."

The Foreign Secretary's imputation that the directors were guilty of connivance with a foreign government again stung the Company to indiscreet rebuttal. The implied culpability of the directors, Coxe pointed out, was incurred by their having acted in ignorance of negotiations that were even yet kept secret by the Foreign Office and in accord with "the public acts, and published documents of this Government" which seemed to attest to "the inviolability of the Grant . . . ." Even had the fact of the negotiations with Spain been made public, "history and experience" gave the Company no more reason to suspect that Great Britain would treat with Spain for a cession of territory in Central America after 1821 than it would have

32. The correspondence summarized in subsequent paragraphs is published in *Brief Statement,* pp. 70-87. The names of the deputation listed in the October 8, 1836 application from Coxe to James Stephen are not given in the published letter. They appear, however, in the original CO 123/49, n.f.

expected a "foreign power [to] accept from Great Britain, in 1784, a Grant of a portion of the back settlements of the United States, from which the British flag had recently been driven."

The purpose of the interview requested for the deputation, however, was not to debate the justification for the negotiations in progress but to learn the location of the boundaries they were intended to attain. The Company representatives had no intention of inquiring into the state of pending negotiations; they hoped only to ascertain for "what portion of territory, 'believed to be,' within the limits of Belize," Great Britain was treating. They could discern no legitimate deterrent to confirmation of British claims to a part of the territory included within the Company grant and colonization and cultivation of the remainder by British subjects.

The deputation hoped to resolve the impasse so that "the Company may, without chance of collision or interference with the claims of Great Britain, locate the settlers already sent out, and those which are to follow." In reply, Palmerston stiffly cited to the Company his answer of October 29. He repeated his warning to British subjects who "think fit to accept from the government of a foreign state a grant of lands which are claimed by the British Crown," referred the committee again to the Colonial Office for an answer, and declined to meet the deputation on grounds that "he thinks it desirable that whatever communications that take place between them and his Lordship, on the subject, should be made in writing in order that they may remain on the record."

Frustrated at the enforced delay to its plans and exasperated at Palmerston's dark insinuations of trespass against frontiers that he refused to define, the Company again addressed the Colonial Office, where it had begun its inquiry. On November 23, 1836, George Grey supplied the information the directors had been seeking for more than a year. Great Britain, he stated, claimed boundaries identical with those set down by the council in Belize in 1834, but he warned "that the greater part of the territory in question has never been the subject of actual survey, and that parties, who should assume the topography of the remoter tracts, and especially the course of the rivers, upon the authority of maps, would, in all probability, be led into error."

Yielding nothing of its pretension in any part of its grant, the Company informed its superintendent in Central America of the extent of the British claims and instructed him to prevent any collision of interests between the Company and Belize. On its part, the British government gave instructions to the authorities in the Settlement to keep the residents within the new limits where, by inference, they could offer no obstruction to occupation of the remaining parts of the Company's property. Their inquiry at an end, the Company officials sent to Gálvez copies of their correspondence with the Cabinet,[33] in part to demonstrate the overwhelming odds that had prevented prompt discharge of their obligations and in part, it may be assumed, to claim from the Chief of State such consideration as gratitude might suggest was deserved by their audacious, if fruitless, espousal of the Central American territorial claims.

33. *Brief Statement,* pp. 88-91; Carlos A. Meany to Leonard S. Coxe, Sept. 1837, copy in FO 252/18, n.f.

V

DEVELOPMENT

OR EXPLOITATION?

The fundamental purpose of the colonization agreements was to accomplish the rapid development of the northern wilderness of Guatemala. As a means of fostering this end, the contracts afforded the concessionaires a wide variety of opportunities to exploit the natural resources of their grants, to develop industries, and to establish commercial monopolies. Ultimately, all these privileges might be made a source of profit, but most of them would become remunerative only after the contractors had established a relatively large population and had made heavy capital investments in equipment and internal improvement. Virtually the only resource that offered hope of profitable exploitation in the undeveloped state of the country was the mahogany that grew interspersed among the other forest trees of the region. Mahogany stands were believed to cover large areas of each of the concessions, and the operations of Belize woodcutters had long since demonstrated that trees of marketable size standing within dragging distance of a sufficient stream could be cut and exported at a profit. These circumstances made mahogany the resource of chief immediate interest to the contractors.

The privilege of cutting mahogany, like the other concessions it bestowed, the government of Guatemala conferred upon the colonization *empresarios* to facilitate the development they were pledged to achieve within their grants. The terms in which the contracts were drawn, however, by no means assured that the assets ventured would be applied toward the principal objective sought by the government. The right to exploit resources presumably became operative immediately, but the obligation to colonize was stated in relationship to time intervals that made it impossible to judge compliance in less than two years and that might defer the evaluation for five, ten, or even twenty years. Despite the conditional nature of all the concessions, the original agreements established no procedures for terminating the grants for non-performance of obligations at any of the stipulated intermediate time periods. It was therefore possible that, inadvertently or by deliberate choice, the contractors might for several years exploit the resources of their concessions without performing any part of the service in recompense for which the privileges were granted.

The hazard of linking woodcutting concessions with colonization had been drawn to the attention of the Assembly of Guatemala shortly before the colonization contracts were signed. The issue was raised when Gálvez sent to the legislative body in 1833 the proposal for woodcutting and colonization in the Lake Izabal region made by José Croskey under the federal colonization law. The committee of the Assembly that examined the project pointed out that the petitioner would probably take advantage of the woodcutting privilege for the period allowed by the federal statute and "would cut logs for this entire time, bringing in workmen, called colonists, who would plunder the forests without settling." The two functions were in fact incompatible, the commission believed, for "woodcutting does not make settlers of those who practice it." These objections were immediately withdrawn, however, in response to pressures exerted "in private," perhaps by Gálvez himself,[1] and the issue was not revived when the Assembly ratified the colonization contracts that embodied the same basic arrangement.

It is possible, despite the forecast of the Assembly, that the government of Guatemala recognized no need to relate the privilege of woodcutting directly to the obligation to colonize. The obvious intent of the contracts was to employ the concessionaires as intermediaries by means of whom the ceded land and resources could be exploited to finance colonization or held in trust for division among the actual settlers. The language of the agreements, however, made them the property of the contractors. The hazard of the arrangement lay in the assumption that entrepreneurs so thoroughly shared the government's commitment to development that they would invest in colonies the profits they extracted from exploitation of resources. The loosely articulated conditions of the contracts established no safeguards to prevent the concessionaires from accepting the obligation to colonize, with deliberate intent to default, as a means of securing the opportunity to engage in ungoverned exploitation of mahogany resources until such time as the Guatemalan government discovered

1. Opinions of the Committee, March 11, and March 13, 1833, ANG, Congreso, 1833, No. 54, unclassified.

the deception and revoked the concession. In justification of this apparent profligate disposal of resources Gálvez could argue that British woodcutters, operating under licenses issued by the officials of Belize in much of the territory included in the colonization grants, were already despoiling the timber stands without profit to the state. The colonization agreements at least offered some hope that identical exploitation would provide the means of achieving the internal development ardently desired by Central America.[2]

Whatever their motives for accepting the grants, all of the contractors expected immediately to capitalize on the mahogany reserves contained within their concessions. Each had a different plan of operation, but, with the possible exception of the Eastern Coast Company, all appear to have been concerned exclusively with profit from exploitation, with no thought given to development. Their astute choice of lands beyond the limits claimed for Belize allowed Bennett and Meany to carry out their designs without outside hindrance, but the plans of Galindo and the Eastern Coast Company immediately ran afoul of the Belize boundary issue.

Galindo was well aware when he applied for his grant that mahogany was "its only valuable production,"[3] but he did not propose to exploit the timber himself. Rather, he planned to use the trees to bait the trap his proprietorship of the territory would allow him to spring on the woodcutters of Belize. Residents of the Settlement were already active along the Belize River and its tributaries within the limits of his grant, and these loggers Galindo believed would be forced to accept his terms in order to save their established works or to extend their operations. His announcement in Belize of the regime he intended to impose within his concession notified cutters that they would be allowed to remove logs already felled on his grant, subject to payment of their fair value to Edward Shiel, his agent in the Settlement, but that further cutting was prohibited except by special permission signed by Galindo himself. The new owner announced his intent to survey as soon as possible the entire grant, to lay it out in square plots of 160 acres each, and to sell the tracts at public auction. Should a successful bidder acquire property on which another had erected houses or other improvements, the purchaser was to pay the dispossessed individual the value of the construction

2. Al C[iudadano] Secret[ari]o del Consejo repres[entativ]o, Oct. 24, 1831, ANG, leg. 477, exp. 7718, n.f.

3. Juan Galindo to Lieutenant Colonel Francis Cockburn, Superintendent of Belize, Oct. 17, 1834, CO 123/45, n.f.

as fixed by arbiters.[4] These dispositions clearly indicate that Galindo intended to force mahogany operators to buy from him the land beyond the old treaty line on which they expected to fell trees. They also suggest that despite his bitter criticism of British exploitation of Central American resources, he contemplated no basic change in the system. British woodcutters would be transformed into "colonists" by virtue of their proprietorship of the soil, but they would continue to cut mahogany in the area and to export it through Belize as before with profit to no one in Central America save Galindo himself.

Galindo's misconception of official British policy on the Belize boundary question foredoomed his carefully contrived plans to failure. The refusal of the authorities in Belize to recognize his title to territory lying within the limits claimed for the Settlement thwarted his intention to sell the land and frustrated his attempt to collect the value of the trees cut from it. Although he was authorized to act in the name of the State of Guatemala and was promised the support of the *jefe político* of the Petén in his efforts to collect his claims,[5] the position taken by the Belize authorities and supported by the home government allowed the cutters to ignore his pretensions. Even the *de facto* definition of the boundary gave him no security, for the Belize operators made no secret of their intention to continue to cut every marketable tree they could find standing within dragging distance of flowing water. His anguished protest in the spring of 1835 that he had been robbed of seven hundred mahogany trees brought a sympathetic response only in Central America.[6]

The assertion of the Garbutt's Falls line as the western boundary of Belize thus entirely shattered Galindo's hope for substantial profit from his grant. He lost entirely the eastern segment of his cession that he had expected to be most valuable to him, and the western part, to which his title was undisputed, was so remote from suitable watercourses that large-scale mahogany cutting was not economically feasible. Principally on this basis Cockburn disputed Galindo's assertion that the loss of a part of his grant deprived him also of a source of substantial revenue. "I do not imagine," the Superintendent observed to Chatfield in November 1834, "that between Garbutt's Falls & Belize there is a Mahogany Tree remaining on any part of

4. Galindo "To the Inhabitants of the Spanish Side," dated San Salvador, Aug. 2, 1834, CO 123/46, n.f.

5. Draft letter to Galindo, Nov. 22, 1834, ANG, leg. 3606, exp. 83743, fol. 2; draft letter to *jefe político* of the Petén, Nov. 28, 1834, ANG, leg. 3355, exp. 73940.

6. Galindo to Minister General of Guatemala, April 15, 1835, AMG, Comunicaciones, 1835; Galindo to Secretary of Belize, April 18, 1835, FO 15/17, fol. 274.

Galindo's grant within sufficient distance of Water to admit of its being brought out without the certainty of loss."[7] He had earlier remarked that, if Galindo hoped to export mahogany, "he will find very little if any to transport, every Tree worth cutting having already crossed the Atlantic."[8] The belief that he had been defrauded, however, was an important force behind Galindo's determination to carry the boundary issue to London for settlement.

The Eastern Coast Company, like Galindo, expected the mahogany resources of its grant to supply an immediate revenue. The directors assumed that their concession from the government of Guatemala would enable them to supplant at once the woodcutters from Belize who were working south of the Sibún and to exercise their option to cut timber in their own interest or to sell the privilege to operators already engaged in the business. The explosion of the boundary controversy brought all such plans to an abrupt halt. The disposition of the British government to prevent by force any approach south of the Sibún to an expanse of coast, the southern limit of which it refused to define pending the outcome of negotiations with Spain, prevented the Company from undertaking operations anywhere in the region.

During the first two years of their enforced inactivity, the directors alleged, woodcutters from Belize extracted from the Company's holdings timber valued at not less than £100,000.[9] "It is obvious," the exasperated officials wrote to Palmerston in November 1836, "that the timber, &c., now forcibly carried away by the Belizians, grows on land belonging to some power or other. The treaties of 1783 and 1786 declare it to have belonged to Spain; the constitution of Central America declares it to belong to that Republic: by that Republic it was granted, two years since, to this company; whilst Great Britain is still in treaty for the cession of it to her by Spain. Is it not then, my Lord, for the benefit of all parties, whether they be Belizians, or of the Company, to be made acquainted with what extent of land Great Britain claims, for what extent she negotiates, how far she wishes to go, and where she is willing to stop?"[10] Three weeks later the committee had its answer: Great Britain claimed the entire ocean

7. Cockburn to Frederick Chatfield, Oct. 17, 1834, FO 252/8, n.f.

8. Cockburn to Chatfield, Sept. 13, 1834, CO 123/45, n.f.

9. Jeremiah Barrett to Lord Palmerston, Oct. 28, 1835, *Brief Statement, Supported by Original Documents, of the Important Grants Conceded to the Eastern Coast of Central America Commercial and Agricultural Company by the State of Guatemala* (London, 1839), p. 65.

10. Leonard S. Coxe to Palmerston, Nov. 2, 1836, *Brief Statement*, p. 83.

frontage on the Bay of Honduras between the Sibún and the Sarstoon and the intervening territory westward to the Garbutt's Falls line. The Company reluctantly adjusted its plans to conform to the British territorial claims, but the directors refused to concede that they did not hold valid title to the land in question. Indeed, they alleged in 1839 that the policy of the British government had enabled residents of Belize to plunder the Company's rightful property of mahogany to the total value of £1,500,000 in the British market.[11]

The formal statement in 1836 of British claims as far south as the Sarstoon totally excluded the Company from mahogany cutting on the Bay of Honduras. The territory claimed for Belize included the entire ocean frontage granted to the Company, and the Bennett and Meany grants pre-empted the remainder of the coast along the Bay. If the Company was to cut mahogany from its own territory, therefore, it would have to do so in the interior of the Verapaz.

The conditions announced by the Company for sale of lands in the vicinity of the Polochic make clear that it expected there also to make the mahogany trade one of its principal sources of revenue. It withheld standing mahogany from all the lands it sold, and it prohibited settlers from cutting trees within its domain except on hire for the Company. Land purchasers who discharged their obligations in installments could receive credit on all payments after the first at a fixed (but unstipulated) rate per ton of wood, calculated at forty cubic feet per ton, for all reserved trees they felled on their lands and delivered to the Company. Should the installments be overpaid in this fashion, the Company agreed to repay the excess either in additional land or in cash, at the settler's option.[12]

Some of the colonists sent out to the Verapaz in 1836, and perhaps some of the local Indians hired by the Company's superintendent, may have been assigned to mahogany cutting, but if so, the accounts left by the participants in the enterprise failed to record it. It seems probable, however, that preoccupation with activities essential to survival, inaccessibility of timber stands from the rivers, and total absence of shipping of sufficient capacity on the Polochic and Lake Izabal, combined to frustrate any intent the Company may have entertained to reap a mahogany harvest in the interior of the Verapaz.

Until 1840 the Company expected to inaugurate large-scale mahogany cutting operations. The local agent in Guatemala warned

11. *Brief Statement*, p. 2.
12. Eastern Coast of Central America Commercial and Agricultural Company, *To Respectable Emigrants of Small or Large Capital* (London, [1836?]), p. 2, CO 123/51, n.f.

Belize cutters in March 1839 against trespassing on Company property, and plans for renewed activity in the Verapaz presented to the directors in the fall of that year envisaged a beginning of actual cutting. An exploration crew was to be established to seek out marketable trees, and income from the sale of timber was promised as a source of revenue from the venture. The directors continued the early restrictions on sale and cutting of standing mahogany through 1839, but in 1840 they abandoned them. They did not entirely give up hope of beginning operations, however, and instructed their superintendent in the Verapaz to withhold from sale and to reserve for Company exploitation any tracts of land "which shall contain mahogany of any quantity."[13]

Deprived of opportunity to exploit timber on its own holdings, the Company may have obtained mahogany for export by purchasing standing trees from local owners or logs cut by operators in the Bay of Honduras area. It was reported at Belize that at least some of the vessels sent out by the Company to transport emigrant settlers in 1836 loaded return cargoes of mahogany to which Major John Anderson, acting Superintendent of Belize, believed he would be obliged by existing laws to give clearance as lumber cut in the Bay of Honduras and transported in British ships manned by British sailors.[14] The loss of the Company's sloop "Turbot," off the Wanks River on the Mosquito Coast in the summer of 1838[15] suggests that the two voyages made by that vessel in the previous March and April may also have been for the purpose of lading mahogany for export. Although the evidence is scanty and inconclusive, it appears probable that the Company engaged on a small scale, not as an operator but as a middleman, in the mahogany trade. It seems clear, however, that, rather than playing the primary role in the Company's early operations originally planned by the directors, the exploitation of mahogany was of slight consequence either as an occupation for Company personnel in the Verapaz or as a source of revenue to the officials and stockholders in England.

In contrast to the difficulties encountered by their rivals, Bennett

13. "Public Notice," signed "Young Anderson," supplement to *The Belize Advertiser*, I, No. 21 (March 2, 1839), 108; *Brief Statement, Supported by Original Documents, of the Important Grants Conceded to the Eastern Coast of Central America Commercial & Agricultural Company by the State of Guatemala* (2nd ed.; London, 1840), pp. 118, 158.

14. Major John G. Anderson to Frederick Chatfield, Sept. 12, 1836, FO 252/8, n.f.

15. Colonel Alexander Macdonald, Superintendent of Belize, to Lord Glenelg, No. 11, May 6, 1839, CO 123/55, n.f.; Petition of Peter Harris Abbott and Charles Bourjot to Glenelg, Feb. 4, 1839, CO 123/56, n.f.

and Meany experienced no significant impediment to the exploitation of the mahogany stands on their concessions. The northeastern point of their grant north of Lake Izabal extended slightly beyond the lower reaches of the Sarstoon River,[16] but elsewhere their selection of lands beyond the limits they knew to be commonly asserted for Belize made it possible for the partners to escape involvement in the boundary controversy. Hence, they were able to avoid the obstacles placed by Great Britain to the operations of the other contractors.

Although the import of Bennett's projects was for a time concealed from the government of Guatemala, Chatfield and Cockburn immediately surmised his probable motives. Both officials admired the shrewdness of his arrangements, but neither doubted their cynical purpose. The Consul remarked that Bennett had exerted his influence in Guatemala to induce the government to make grants that as a Magistrate of Belize "he votes to be an unwarranted encroachment on the part of the very Persons he a few weeks before urged to make the cessions." This bit of double-dealing enabled Bennett "to acquire a temporary possession of the northern shore of this Republic in the Bay of Honduras, for the sake of the Mahogany and Logwood which grow there, and to secure a permanent right of property to such parts of the coast as he deems most suitable to his Trade."[17] Cockburn commented that "Mr. Bennett is playing a deep game & certainly for a huge stake. . . . [but] one thing seems pretty clear— that British or Belize interests in no way influence his speculations."[18]

Bennett was indeed working both sides of the frontier, and he was working strictly for himself. The concessions he obtained opened the vast, forest-covered territory lying south of the disputed boundary of Belize to exploitation by his mahogany gangs, and the rich triangle embracing the lower Motagua to Lake Izabal and the sea he held as an exclusive patrimony. Bennett thus placed himself in an incomparably advantageous position over his competitors, whether Guatemalan or British. He was still eligible on equal footing with other Belize cutters for such grants as the authorities of the Settlement could make within the territory claimed by Great Britain, and he held as a private monopoly the most accessible stands of mahogany in the adjacent territory of Central America.

Bennett and Meany chose their grants around the three principal

16. Chatfield to Palmerston, No. 15, Sept. 17, 1834, FO 15/14, fol. 181.
17. Chatfield to Palmerston, No. 17, Sept. 12, 1835, FO 15/16, fol. 146; Chatfield to Cockburn, Oct. 31, 1834, ABH, Letters Inwards, 1826-1848, Records 10, fol. 32.
18. Cockburn to Chatfield, Oct. 17, 1834, n.f.

watercourses of Guatemala that gave access to the most valuable timber resources of the state. The cession in Totonicapán included the southern banks of the Chixoy and Pasión Rivers; that in Chiquimula included the lower Motagua and its tributaries on both sides, the southern margins of Lake Izabal and the Río Dulce, and the seacoast extending from the mouth of that river to a point five leagues beyond the mouth of the Motagua. The cession north of Lake Izabal brought most of the remaining lakeshore and the greater part of the northern bank of the outlet to the Gulf of Honduras under the control of the partners. Bennett's monopoly of the Central American mahogany stands in the Bay of Honduras area become virtually complete in 1835 when Francisco Morazán placed under his administration the mahogany cutting concession on the north shore of Honduras that had just been granted to him by the government of that state.[19]

Bennett's hopes for profit from his concessions in Guatemala were founded in part on the provisions of the colonial tariff enacted by Great Britain in 1832. That regulation allowed all mahogany cut in the Bay of Honduras area and cleared out of Belize in British ships to be exported as a product of the Settlement under a preferential duty.[20] This arrangement would enable Bennett to market timber cut from his new acquisitions on the same favorable terms as wood cut in the Settlement itself. His rivals, fearing that their own product, obtainable only at relatively higher cost, would suffer if the choice production from Bennett's enormous holdings in Central America were shipped on equal terms through Belize, resolved to nullify his advantage by manipulating the local duty against him. In November 1834, therefore, they pushed through the Public Meeting a measure that established a discriminatory duty on logs cut by residents of the Settlement from land they owned in foreign territory and brought to Belize for clearance.[21] Whether or not it was aimed specifically at Bennett, this measure would operate to the disadvantage of all the colonization contractors who attempted to work their own holdings and ship the logs through Belize or who intended to sell the land rather than the timber that grew on it. This enactment the Colonial Office disallowed in 1836[22] as obviously discriminatory. It appears, however, that even while it was in effect the law did not

19. Chatfield to Palmerston, No. 20, Sept. 16, 1835, FO 15/16, fols. 176-77.
20. Robert Arthur Naylor, "British Commercial Relations with Central America, 1821-1851" (Unpubl. Diss., Tulane, 1958), p. 96.
21. Russell Ellice to the Earl of Aberdeen, Feb. 13, 1835, CO 123/46, n.f.
22. Naylor, "British Commercial Relations," p. 97.

seriously impede the activity of the operator it was expected principally to handicap.

Bennett began immediately to exploit the advantage he obtained from his Guatemalan concessions. He was able to move swiftly because he could begin operations simply by transferring to a new cutting area equipment and crews from one of his quiescent mahogany works in Belize. If the charges of the Municipality of Gualán were correct, he obtained capital for the venture—and shared the profits also—by selling shares in London and in Guatemala.[23] His intent seems to have been to log off the choice timber in those areas of his concessions where he expected his tenure to be temporary and to claim the most concentrated stands of mahogany and the areas he wanted for permanent installations as the purchased property the terms of his contract entitled him to select.

For the first few months Bennett gave the appearance of energetic execution of his contract. In September 1834, the Guatemalan authorities in the Verapaz authorized the partners to take possession of the tract of 1,500 *caballerías* they were to choose on the north shore of Lake Izabal, and the following month Bennett arrived in the port of Izabal to supervise the installation of a sawmill.[24] Within a short time the partners had mahogany gangs working on the shores of the lake and in the vicinity of the Motagua River in Chiquimula. During 1835 they selected at least a part of the land they had contracted to buy in Chiquimula, and when Gálvez elected to accept payment for the tract in money rather than in rifles, Bennett deposited £1,000 to the credit of the government with John Waldron Wright, the agent of Guatemala in London.[25] The partners also delivered to the government the rifles that would confirm their title to the land they selected on Lake Izabal.[26] Neither in the region of the lake nor in Chiquimula, however, were the purchased tracts measured and the limits precisely defined as required by the contracts. It appears that this omission was more deliberate than careless, for the imprecise boundaries allowed Bennett and Meany to avoid payment at Izabal of the proportion of their profits due to the government under the

23. Petition of the citizens of Gualán, April 24, 1835, ANG, Congreso, 1834, No. 151, fols. 16-17, unclassified.

24. Minister General of Guatemala to Jefe Departamental of Verapaz, Oct. 7, 1834, ANG, leg. 3355, exp. 73939; Cockburn to Chatfield, Oct. 17, 1834, n.f.; Chatfield to Cockburn, Oct. 31, 1834, fol. 34.

25. Marshal Bennett to Mariano Gálvez, Nov. 5, 1835, ANG, leg. 3633, exp. 85297, n.f.

26. This information is given in the unsigned informe to the Secretaries of the Constituent Congress, July 8, 1845, ANG, leg. 1395, exp. 32383.

terms of the contract on the plea that the timber they exported was cut from their own land.[27]

For a time Bennett was able to maintain the fiction that his operations were a legitimate preliminary to colonizing activities and that he was entitled to all privileges conceded to him as a colonizer. On this basis he obtained duty-free entry for the equipment, tools, supplies, and provisions he imported for his mahogany gangs and for some of his unrelated operations in Guatemala as well. By the time the deception had become clear the government of Guatemala calculated that Bennett's firm had evaded payment of duties aggregating more than 2,500 pesos on imports fraudulently entered at Izabal.[28]

Although the government of Guatemala did not at once suspect that it was being made the victim of guile, the residents of Chiquimula quickly recognized in the contract the earmarks of fraud. No sooner had the news of the grant reached Gualán than the municipal corporation drew up a protest. Other Municipalities and an occasional individual followed its example until the department spoke in a single voice of disapproval. The contract, the protests alleged, defrauded the citizens of their patrimony. They decried both the principle of colonization of the department by foreigners and the exclusive proprietorship of unclaimed lands conferred upon Bennett and Meany. Some residents reportedly considered their opportunities so irreparably prejudiced that they emigrated to Honduras. Before the department was entirely ruined, the Municipalities asked that the contract be rescinded or substantially modified.[29]

Rather than curtailing the operations of Bennett and Meany, Gálvez hoped to enlarge them. As the Belize boundary issue moved toward crisis during the last months of 1834, he sought to clear the way for the partners to develop an alternative deep-water port at Santo Tomás in their Chiquimula concession. This measure he believed would provide a means for taking reprisals against the commerce of the British Settlement in order to force recognition of the eighteenth-century treaty limits, reduce the tribute Central Americans were forced to pay to the merchants at Belize, and assist the *empresarios* to colonize their grant.

27. Mariano Trabanino, *jefe político* of Chiquimula, to Minister General of Guatemala, July 12, 1836, ANG, Congreso, 1836, No. 36, unclassified.

28. Miguel Alvarez to Gálvez, Dec. 31, 1834, leg. 1395, exp. 32344, n.f.; the calculation of duties and the record of attempts to collect them in 1840 are found in ANG, leg. 2401, exp. 50016.

29. The protests against the Bennett and Meany contract are treated in detail in Chapter VI.

To construct a national port within the state, Gálvez expected to make use of the authorization to contract with private companies for public works granted by the Guatemalan Assembly the previous April. On November 19 he asked the federal officials to co-operate with his plan by habilitating Santo Tomás as a port of the republic, and a few days later he solicited authorization to contract for the required facilities. Specifically, he requested permission to extend the provisions of the Chiquimula agreement with Bennett and Meany to include construction of the port. The federal executive granted the general powers Gálvez requested, and relative to the proposal to amplify the arrangement with Bennett and Meany he suggested, not realizing that the contract was already before the federal Congress, that a copy of the original agreement be sent for study.[30]

Gálvez immediately put to use such power as the federal government granted to him. In January 1835 he commissioned Bennett to reconnoiter the Bay of Santo Tomás to select the best site for the town, and he obtained from two of the individuals best informed on the area estimates of the cost of constructing on the site a temporary fortification, a customs house, a *comandancia*, a hospital, and houses for some six families of settlers.[31] He obviously intended to push the project to completion with vigor and dispatch, but it fell suddenly quiescent in the spring of 1835. The excitement the Bennett and Meany contract still evoked in the towns of the department probably forced him temporarily to desist from his design.

During the first months of 1835 the government tried to explain away the fears of the inhabitants of Chiquimula and to mitigate some of the objectionable features of the Bennett and Meany contract by explanatory modifications. It did not, however, act on the advice of the legislative branch that it separate the "work of colonization from the business of wood cutting." In consequence, its efforts to still the unrest bore no fruit. The Municipalities continued to charge the contractors with exploiting the resources of the department without making any corresponding effort to colonize and with failing to pay into the treasury the proportion of their profits called for by the agreement. These issues were seized upon and successfully agi-

30. Draft letter to federal Minister of Finance, Nov. 19, 1834, ANG, leg. 178, exp. 3809, fols. 2, 4-5, 7; draft letter to Alvarez, Nov. 25, 1834, ANG, leg. 168, exp. 3557, fol. 3; acuerdo ejecutivo, Dec. 30, 1834, ANG, leg. 178, exp. 3813, fols. 1, 3; Alvarez to Gálvez, Dec. 31, 1834, ANG, leg. 163, exp. 3416, fols. 35, 39.

31. Draft letter to Bennett, Jan. 15, 1835; Rafael Quiñones to Minister General, Jan. 18, 1835; and Trabanino to Minister General, Jan. 26, 1835; all in ANG, leg. 1398, exps. 32633-35.

tated to enlist support in the department for the short-lived revolt against the governments of Morazán and Gálvez launched in El Salvador during the fall of 1835 in the name of Nicolás Espinosa.

When the rebellion had been safely subdued Gálvez returned to the Santo Tomás project. In the spring of 1836 he obtained from the Assembly authority to contract for the necessary roads and buildings at the port. Almost immediately thereafter he sent out work parties under Manuel María Velís, a Spanish mariner resident in Zacapa, and Felipe Molló, *jefe político* of Livingston, to trace the route for a road between Santo Tomás and Gualán.[32]

The prospect of a port development in the department did not quiet the unrest in Chiquimula. The Municipalities continued to criticize the terms under which the concession had been made to Bennett and Meany. Some of the protests may have been motivated by legitimate concern for conservation of the state's resources, but the basic objection seems to have been that local mahogany cutters were excluded from the stands ceded to the contractors. Gálvez, at least, understood the controversy in these terms, for he remarked to Chatfield that "the outcry is not because of colonization but because of the mahogany trees, for although they say colonization they mean mahogany."[33] The discontent in Chiquimula finally forced the government in May 1836 to order that, until their obligation to colonize was honored, the contractors either desist from cutting wood or pay for all the trees they felled.

Faced with the probability of default by Bennett and Meany, the government of Guatemala undertook to open the port of Santo Tomás under its own auspices. On the same day that the executive approved the order placing Bennett and Meany on probation, the Guatemalan Assembly passed a measure offering to families who settled at Santo Tomás advantages similar to those conceded to immigrants under the colonization contracts. With the approval of the federal government the state then tried to raise the funds needed for the initial construction by soliciting among the citizens of the capital, Zacapa, Chiquimula, and Gualán advances of 100 pesos each to be redeemed with interest from the warehouse duties collected at the port after it was opened. This device apparently resembled the hated

32. Decreto legislativo, April 23, 1836, Alejandro Marure and Andrés Fuentes Franco (comps.), *Catálogo razonado de las leyes de Guatemala* (Guatemala, 1856), p. 13; *Semanario de Guatemala* (Guatemala), No. 1 (April 30, 1836), p. 4, and No. 27 (Nov. 3, 1836), p. 119; draft letter to federal Minister of War and Marine, Jan. 12, 1837, ANG, leg. 183, exp. 4024, n.f.

33. Gálvez to Chatfield, March 4, 1836, FO 252/12, n.f.

forced loans too closely to attract the necessary capital, however, and although the federal government habilitated Santo Tomás as a port in August the state could not command the resources to proceed with its development.[34] The government therefore turned again to private companies to accomplish this task.

In mid-January 1837 a Guatemalan woodcutting firm operating on the north coast offered terms for opening the port. Juan José Balcarzel and Ignacio Zerón proposed for themselves, Cándido Pulleiro, and the other members of their company to construct a customs house and a *comandancia* at Santo Tomás and to settle twenty Canary Island families there. They offered to submit plans and budgets within three months and to complete the buildings within one year under penalty of a fine of 5,000 pesos, should they fail for any cause other than fortuitous circumstance. They asked that the government defray the expense of clearing the site, but they offered to advance the cost of the two buildings, subject to reimbursement from public funds. Specifically, they proposed repayment from the contribution of a fourth-part of the value of the wood cut that they and other operators were required to make to the treasury, but which they had allowed to fall 2,500 pesos in arrears. The government was to confirm to the associates the free and exclusive exploitation of the six woodcutting concessions made to them within the preceding nine months, to cede to them as property a part of the former exclusive Bennett and Meany grant between the mouth of the Río Dulce and the Bay of Santo Tomás, to authorize duty-free import of the food and tools necessary for the workmen constructing the buildings, and to request the federal authorities to grant a like dispensation from duties it collected.[35]

The government of Guatemala formally accepted the proposals on January 19, 1837. It granted to the contractors the concession they requested and guaranteed to repay them at 40 per cent above invoice price the sums they invested in the buildings. It insisted, however, that they advance from their own funds the cost of clearing the site of the town. When Balcarzel represented that the associates could pay for clearing the land only from funds destined for erection

---

34. Orden legislativo No. 42, May 21, 1836, *Boletín Oficial* (Guatemala), No. 76 (May 21, 1836), 195-196; draft letter to federal Minister of Finance, July 29, 1836, ANG, leg. 179, exp. 3842, fol. 3; *Boletín Oficial*, Segunda parte, No. 4 (Aug. 23, 1836), pp. 54-56.

35. Petition of Ignacio Zerón and Juan José Balcarzel, n.d., ANG, leg. 1395, exp. 32350. The plans for the customhouse submitted by Pulleiro on January 5 are in ANG, leg. 3220, exp. 66288.

of the buildings, the government obligated itself to reimburse them as promptly as possible for this expense also. The agreement completed, the government submitted the contract on February 17 for approval by the federal authorities.[36]

The confusion of woodcutting grants and colonization projects on the north coast produced by these measures soon became manifest. The Pulleiro associates began immediately to log the mahogany from their concession, but their rights were challenged by several other operators. Angel Floripes protested that one of the earlier concessions made to Pulleiro and confirmed by the new agreement was illegal because the same tract had been assigned to him under a prior grant. This conflict of interest the government apparently attempted to reconcile by considering a new grant for Floripes. Marshal Bennett also tried to enforce his claims to a monopoly of mahogany cutting in the department. He circulated the report that only his own concession was valid and that all who recognized the Pulleiro-Balcarzel grant were taking an unwarranted risk. When the associates complained to the government, however, the authorities ruled against Bennett and confirmed the new contractors in full enjoyment of their concession. With this provocation, and in the absence of any evidence that the partners intended to heed the warning given the year before, the government of Guatemala rescinded the Bennett and Meany concession in Chiquimula in May 1837.[37]

Cancellation of the Bennett and Meany contract did not entirely close the issue, for the question of reciprocal claims was left to be resolved by subsequent negotiation. Gálvez and Meany, however, agreed upon a basis of settlement the following day. The government recognized and promised to pay in two installments at intervals of six months the 5,000 pesos due to the partners for the £1,000 they had deposited in London, less the amount of duty they owed on goods illegally introduced under the colonization agreement. The government withdrew its claim to a fourth-part of the value of wood

36. Acuerdo ejecutivo, Jan. 19, 1837, and certification of the agreement, Jan. 21, 1837, both in ANG, leg. 1395, exps. 32350, 32368; acuerdo ejecutivo, Feb. 17, 1837, ANG, leg. 179, exp. 3857, fol. 2.

37. Angel Floripes to J. Carmichael, July 1, 1837, ANG, leg. 1418, exp. 33203, fol. 1; *Documentos, El licenciado ciudadano José Antonio Azmitia . . .*, hoja suelta (Guatemala, Aug. 9, 1838); *Carlos Salazar Jeneral de la primera division, y Secretario del Supremo Gobierno del Estado . . .*, hoja suelta (Guatemala, Feb. 3, 1837), both in Valenzuela Collection, Biblioteca Nacional, Guatemala; *Memoria que el Secretario general . . . presenta a la novena Legislatura del estado, leida el 12 de febrero de 1836* (Guatemala, [1836]), p. 18; decreto ejecutivo, May 4, 1837, *Boletín Oficial*, Tercera parte, No. 16 (May 9, 1837), pp. 53-54.

cut by the partners from the thirty-six square leagues of land they had contracted to purchase in return for their agreement to charge no interest on the money advanced in London if it was repaid on schedule. No mention was made of a settlement for the trees cut elsewhere in the concession.[38]

The formula appeared simple, but it proved difficult to apply. The payment of import duties the partners had evaded during the period of their contract was still pending in 1840 when the government of Guatemala calculated that principal and interest at 2 per cent per month on arrears amounted to some 4,140 pesos.[39] This evidence suggests that the transaction had not been closed by 1840, and it is not clear that a settlement was ever reached.

Meanwhile, popular belief that Bennett had been allowed to exploit the resources of the state without corresponding benefit to the inhabitants contributed in 1837 to the outbreak of the insurrection of the *montaña* captained by Rafael Carrera. The dissidents pressed the charge that, had the partners paid into the treasury of Guatemala the part of their profits they were obligated by their contracts to contribute to the government, the financial stringency of the state would have been entirely relieved. This grievance, among others, held against the governments of Gálvez and Morazán, aligned the department of Chiquimula with the insurrection and contributed to the overthrow of Gálvez early in 1838.

Perhaps because the Lake Izabal region was more sparsely populated than Chiquimula and hence possessed fewer nationals who could observe and protest their operations, Bennett and Meany were able to defer for several years a reckoning with the government for the abuse of their privileges in that area. Indeed, the partner's manipulation of their contract almost permitted them to escape permanently the consequences of their failure to fulfill their obligations.

It appears that, on the basis of the contractual guarantee of preference in all subsequent colonization contracts for that area, Bennett and Meany signed with the government of Guatemala on April 8, 1835, a subsidiary contract for carrying out the promised colonization of the Lake Izabal region. This maneuver apparently was intended to separate the obligation to colonize from the privileges of exploitation granted in compensation, but the concessionaires made no great-

38. Draft letters to Meany and Bennett, May 4 and May 6, 1837, AMG, Expedientes, 1837, n.f.

39. The file of documents on this subject is in ANG, leg. 2401, exp. 50016.

er effort to comply with the new commitment than with the old. They continued, however, to cut wood at their pleasure anywhere within the limits of their grant until Bennett's death in 1838 and for several years thereafter Thomas Phillips, executor of Bennett's estate in Belize, maintained the operations in the interest of the partnership.[40] The government of Guatemala several times ordered an investigation of the Bennett and Meany woodcutting activities,[41] but no restrictions appear to have been imposed on them.

In 1843 Meany and William Hall, the attorney representing Bennett's estate in Guatemala, informed the government of Mariano Rivera Paz that the disrupted partnership was unable to fulfill its agreement to colonize and requested that it be relieved of that obligation. After some study of the matter, the government acceded to the petition on July 11, 1843, and ordered that the authorities proceed to measure the 1,500 *caballerías* of land that the partners had contracted to buy and for which they had delivered the stipulated 1,000 rifles. To accept a specific, measured tract of land, however, would probably restrict the woodcutting operations of the contractors to that single area. This curtailment of their activity they managed to avoid, and indiscriminate woodcutting continued as before.

The anomalous situation was recalled to the attention of the government late in 1844 or early in January 1845, when Phillips tendered to the customs house in Izabal the sum of 865 pesos in payment for mahogany trees cut on his order. Ironically, this gesture of good faith caused the government of Guatemala, now presided over by Rafael Carrera, immediately to scent fraud. It instructed the customs house to accept the proffered payment without prejudice to such rights of the contractors as Congress might subsequently recognize, ordered investigation of all woodcutting operations by Bennett and Meany in the region of Lake Izabal, and asked Congress to determine whether the proceeds from mahogany cut under the contract belonged to the partners or to the government.[42] In an attempt to head off the impending mischief, Meany petitioned the Congress in May to validate the earlier recision of the partners' obligation to

40. The events presented in this and the following paragraph are reported in the historical statements contained in the unsigned *informe* to the Secretaries of the Constituent Congress, July 8, 1845, and the *dictamen* of the Committee on Finance approved by the Congress on Sept. 18, 1845, ANG, leg. 1395, exp. 32384.

41. See, for example, Gerónimo Paiz to Minister of Finance, Oct. 14, 1842, ANG, leg. 3224, exp. 66790, n.f.

42. The instructions and reports are in ANG, leg. 1399, exp. 32738, leg. 3619, exp. 84764, and leg. 228, exp. 5125.

colonize and to proceed to measure the purchased 1,500 *caballerías* of land for which the contractors had authorized agents in Europe to recruit colonists in Germany. The Congress was not moved by this evidence of new-found virtue and proceeded beyond determination of the rightful claimant to the proceeds from mahogany cutting to examine the partners' original contract and their record of performance on it.

To the Congress the question was entirely clear. The contract was before all else an agreement to colonize; all rights and privileges granted to the concessionaires were contingent upon performance of that paramount obligation. The legislative body had authorized the government only to enter into agreements that embodied this principle, and any substantive modification of such contracts required analogous legislative concurrence. Failure of the government to consult the legislature when in 1843 it released the contractors from their obligation to colonize therefore invalidated that action and left the original agreement binding in all of its parts. The confessed inability of the concessionaires to discharge their basic obligation nullified their entire contract, including their right to purchase the tract of 1,500 *caballerías* for what was manifestly only a token payment. The failure of the contract to stipulate procedures in the event of cancellation left the adjustment of claims between the parties as the only step necessary to terminate the transaction. Such a settlement would require the contractors to pay to the government the difference between the value of the mahogany they had cut and that of the rifles they had delivered. The recent proposals of the former partners to colonize could not be considered under the old contract and would have to be made the subject of entirely new negotiations with the government.

Consistent with the principles thus laid down the Congress proceeded to close out the Bennett and Meany contract. This end it proposed to achieve by three actions: abrogation of the governmental *acuerdo* of July 11, 1843, and return of the contract to its original status; authorization to the government to act as it thought fit on Meany's request for cancellation of the contract; and conclusion of the whole transaction in a fashion neither onerous to the state nor prejudicial to the interests of Meany and Bennett's heirs. The steps taken by the government in accord with the legislative authorization were to be reported to Congress for its approval. The executive signed the measure on September 23, 1845,[43] but the record does

43. Informe, July 8, 1845; Dictamen of the Committee on Finance approved by Congress, Sept. 18, 1845.

not make clear what action the government took to carry out the intent of Congress. It appears, however, that the Izabal agreement was rescinded at this time but that, for reasons akin to those that impeded the settlement of the Chiquimula contract, the government was not able to determine and to collect the amount due to it.

No quantitative calculation of the resources sacrificed by Guatemala as a direct result of the colonization contracts is possible from the materials available for this study. The evidence at hand, however, suggests that neither Galindo nor the Eastern Coast Company was able to cut any appreciable quantity of mahogany from the uncontested portions of their grants. The immediate loss of large areas of both cessions that Gálvez had hoped by that device to save put those resources permanently in hands of residents of Belize. The territory granted to Bennett and Meany remained within the territorial limits of the state, but the choicest mahogany stands were despoiled and the logs exported through Belize. The resources pledged by Guatemala as the price of internal development and of territorial security against the encroachments of mahogany cutters from the British Settlement were thus exploited for the profit of the very individuals whose activity they had been hazarded to restrain.

VI

FOREIGNERS

OR NATIVE SONS?

Experience convinced Gálvez early in his administration that un-aided Guatemalans were incapable of accomplishing the swift develop-ment of their native state. This derogation of his compatriots was due, not to any belief that they lacked innate capacity, but to the conviction that the Spanish colonial system had deprived them of opportunity to develop those personal attributes and material capa-bilities necessary for the reconstruction of their society. His admira-tion of the rapid advances achieved by other western European states while Spain and her dominions in America remained largely specta-tors made it only natural that he should turn to those countries as the most obvious source of the elements required to produce a similar transformation of Central America.

Gálvez conceived of the colonization contracts as a means of achiev-ing in Guatemala a development analogous to that of the most advanced countries of the world. He hoped to have the miracle wrought directly on the land and covertly on the population. He envisioned the settlement of European immigrants on the empty northern wastes; the application of European capital, technical knowl-edge, and labor to the resources of the state; and the emulation by nationals of the skills, the work habits, and the desirable qualities of civic life practiced by the immigrants. Gálvez purported to con-ceive of this tutelage function as a means of raising the level of culture, civic responsibility, and productivity among the local popula-tion of Guatemala, but he may also have entertained another motive. In common with other leaders of European descent, Chatfield ob-served, he sought the co-operation of foreigners because of "the necessity of repressing the ambitious and restless designs of the mulatto class [which he defined later as 'this mixed race'] in the country, who are continually plotting and with uncertain success to sieze upon the Chief Government of the Republick."[1]

1. Frederick Chatfield to Lord Palmerston, No. 22, Nov. 12, 1834, FO 15/14, fol. 298.

It was entirely probable, Gálvez believed, that Europeans could be persuaded to forego the advantages offered by their own countries and brave the hazards of the Guatemalan wilderness only if unusual inducements were offered them. The contracts therefore provided for both entrepreneurs and settlers a variety of special privileges, concessions, and immunities that set foreign colonizers apart as a distinctive group favored over native sons. Among the most important of these inducements were economic and fiscal advantages, exemption from certain obligations demanded of citizens that might prove unproductive or onerous to new arrivals, and privileges granted in accommodation of dissimilar cultural and political traditions.

The government might be thoroughly convinced that such concessions were necessary and expedient, but popular opinion could well be less charitable. The imponderable question was whether a society reared in traditional suspicion of outsiders could sustain the shock of sudden, intimate association with foreigners on a large scale. Specifically, would the inhabitants find it tolerable that aliens enjoyed advantages not shared by native sons? Could the equality made dear by the orators of independence be reconciled with privilege? Could the conformity of a prescriptive culture accommodate diversity? Could an aggressive religious orthodoxy tolerate dissent? It was perhaps inevitable that these and other related questions should be made domestic issues both by individuals who believed their personal interests to be adversely affected and by politically ambitious persons who were alert for areas of controversy that could be agitated to partisan advantage.

Whether or not the citizens of Guatemala were in accord with Gálvez on the desirability of the ends he sought, not all of them concurred in the means by which he thought to achieve them. When news of the Bennett and Meany concession in Chiquimula reached Gualán, the Municipality of that Motagua River town met on September 28 to draw up a protest which it requested the *jefe político* of the department to forward with his own recommendations to the government of the state. The municipal corporation asked for nothing less than suspension of the agreement. The objection was not that the contract disposed of the land but that the new proprietors were foreigners. Reduced to its simplest dimension, the protest was stated in one sentence: "If the . . . land is national property, we are members of this nation, and with better right it belongs to us; therefore we oppose its being sold to foreigners."[2]

2. *De la Municipalidad de Gualán al C. Gefe político del departamento,* Sept.

The more sophisticated arguments of the Municipality, however, comprised a challenge to the two major assumptions of the colonization contracts. It asserted that foreign ownership of the lands in question could result only in national disaster, and it insisted that the government was entirely mistaken in believing that the agreement could yield the expected economic benefits. If revenue was the justification for the transaction, it believed that the government would have been better advised to meet its fiscal needs by levying and collecting a tax on the citizens of the state.

To the Municipality, as to Gálvez, the colonization agreement bore directly on the Belize boundary question, but with contrary expectation. If English proprietors were allowed to take possession of the northern coast, it predicted a repetition of the history of the British Settlement. There a site "loaned" by the King of Spain to British subjects for woodcutting had been fortified and supplied with all the trappings and machinery of government, and the restricted area originally designated had been expanded without authorization until the current generation of woodcutters was working within a league of the mouth of the Río Dulce. The contract, it was true, required the foreign settlers to subject themselves to the laws of the state, but who, the petitioners inquired, would guarantee the execution of that provision? The best cabinets of Europe, they remarked, had found no way to bind another government to observe even the most solemn treaty obligation. In their view the contract imperiled the territorial integrity, and perhaps the existence, of the state. Assuming a political motive for the contract, they counseled that a wiser government policy would be to fortify the principal points on the northern coast so that they would not be, as they then were, at the mercy of anyone who chose to take them.

The expectation of economic benefits from the contract the Municipality considered to be entirely without foundation. The argument that foreign colonizers "would transmit to us their industry and capital" it rejected as contrary to experience. The coasts of Belize, it pointed out, were colonized by Englishmen who had paralyzed Central American commerce and had drawn off millions in cash and products taken in exchange for the flimsy "figured stuff" in which the textile merchants dealt. Should Englishmen gain possession of the Caribbean coast and of Lake Izabal, the maritime key to control of Guatemalan commerce, they would "precipitate us

28, 1834 [Guatemala, 1834], FO 15/14, fol. 312. The following three paragraphs summarize the principal arguments of the Municipality.

to total ruin." Owning the land, the English proprietors would also extract the precious woods and sarsaparilla to the prejudice of nationals who were beginning to exploit them. If the contract were consummated, the Municipality predicted, "this department can count itself the most unhappy and ruined of all those in the state."

The protest was made public in Gualán, and it was printed in the capital. There it must certainly have come to the notice of the government, although it was apparently not formally submitted as the Municipality requested. It also circulated in Belize where Cockburn was amused by the "Precious production" and, thinking that his colleague in Central America might be equally diverted by it, sent Chatfield a copy in case he had not yet seen it. The Consul considered it "intrinsically . . . beneath notice,"[3] but he was perhaps not gratified to observe that, in contrast with the officials of the Guatemalan government, the unsophisticated residents of Gualán had foreseen just such a possibility of alienating the grant as he had himself proposed to the British government only a few days earlier.

Although Gálvez did not take official cognizance of the Gualán petition, it was indirectly forced upon his attention by his political enemies. The Chief of State's term of office was approaching its close, and it was generally supposed that he would be easily re-elected. His Conservative opponents were desperately searching for some basis on which to discredit the popular Liberal leader before his reforms could take effect and so fortify the position of his party that to displace it would be impossible. Xenophobia appeared to them to be the most promising weapon with which to topple him from power. They therefore agitated the Belize question, and the recent colonization grants made to British contractors, to stir up popular feeling against foreigners and the government that dealt with them. In their effort to incite the simple folk to resistance they appealed to religious bigotry by characterizing the expected colonists as heretics. On October 31 the authorities detected a conspiracy the alleged objective of which was to overthrow the government and to destroy the lives and property of foreigners resident in Guatemala. The warnings that Chatfield and the acting French consul thought it necessary to give to the local authorities to "let the Publick distinctly comprehend that foreigners are not to be molested with impunity" did nothing to allay the irritation with outsiders.[4]

3. Lieutenant Colonel Francis Cockburn to Chatfield, Nov. 5, 1834, FO 252/8, n.f.; Chatfield to Palmerston, Nov. 12, 1834, fol. 297.

4. Chatfield to Palmerston, No. 20, Nov. 7, 1834, FO 15/14, fol. 276, and Nov. 12, 1834, fols. 297-298; Morning Herald (London), No. 16,384 (Feb. 17, 1835), p. [2].

The conspiracy was suffocated, and the Assembly granted the executive emergency powers to deal with all elements thought to bear responsibility for it. The portion of the decree that authorized the Chief of State to punish as traitors those who in a turmoil of agitation menaced or presented petitions to any state authority or those who by means of documents of any kind incited others to commit acts defined as treasonable[5] was interpreted in Chiquimula as denying to the residents the right of free expression. Voices could still be raised in praise of the government, however. The Municipality of the hacienda of San Jerónimo, in what may well have been an inspired address to the government, criticized the charges being made against the colonization agreements and defended Bennett and Meany against their detractors. It was warmly commended for its patriotic attitude.[6] The protest against the contracts was stilled, but it was a quiet of suppression, not of satisfaction.

If direct petition for cancellation of the Bennett and Meany contract was made suspect by law, the government could be made to face the same issues if confronted with an application for a woodcutting concession within the ceded area. José Mariano Dorantes presented such a request to the government, but on the basis of representations by Meany that the desired locality was already granted to the partnership, the authorities refused to consider the proposal. Hearing that instructions had already been issued to the departmental officials of Chiquimula to give Bennett and Meany possession of the land ceded to them, Dorantes petitioned the Assembly to suspend the order and, meanwhile, to define the relationships between nationals and the foreign contractors on four essential points left unclear by the agreement.

The burden of the questions Dorantes raised was, how do residents of Guatemala get access to the land granted to foreigners for colonization? Until the promised colonization was accomplished, he asked, were Bennett and Meany actually owners of the public lands in Chiquimula and of the thirty-six square leagues they proposed to buy for the price of one thousand rifles? If Bennett and Meany were owners of the land, under what terms should they sell or rent it to native sons as their vassals? Did the forests and valuable woods growing on the land belong to the government or to Bennett and Meany, and under what terms should the one or the other sell them? Paren-

5. Decreto legislativo, *Boletín Oficial* (Guatemala), No. 45 (Nov. 2, 1834), p. 541.

6. Ciud[adan]o Ministro G[ene]ral del S[upremo] G[obierno] del E[stado] de Guatemala, Dec. 7, 1834, and draft letter Al gefe dep[artamenta]l de Verapaz, Dec. 18, 1834, ANG, leg. 3355, exp. 73910.

thetically Dorantes pointed out that if the real purpose of the contract was to colonize the land, allowing nationals to fell the trees would clear sites for easier occupation by settlers, and the government would enjoy the benefit of income derived by nationals from the exploitation. His fourth question was, in case Bennett and Meany were owners of the land, under what terms could nationals who wished to settle on the coast be admitted as colonists, what price should they pay to buy or to rent the land on which they settled, and might they freely select anywhere, except within the purchased areas, an advantageous spot to live?

These embarrassing but fundamental questions the Assembly referred to the Committee on Petitions. That body declared that the issues were important to the state and recommended in consequence that the petition be referred to the Committee on Public Prosperity. The Assembly approved this disposition of the problem on March 10, 1835, but thereafter it appears to have allowed a deep silence to settle over the entire question.[7]

Bennett and Meany, however, could not afford to ignore the outcry. Apparently hoping to forestall any general revision of their contract that might eliminate the more advantageous provisions, Meany proposed to the government on March 21, 1835, a number of explanations to clarify the rights of nationals under the agreement. He suggested that the contractors be authorized, until they were able to bring colonists from Europe, to sell unoccupied lands within their grant to residents of the state who wished to settle and cultivate them. The land ceded for the exclusive use of the contractors would be excluded from this arrangement, but it would be opened to residents of Chiquimula for fishing, for cutting sarsaparilla, and for planting corn or other grains. Should they wish to colonize within those confines, plant other crops, or cut wood they would be required to negotiate with the government which would set terms in agreement with the proprietors. From all of these concessions, however, the partners reserved the territory between Punta Lechuga and the Guapinol River, including the San Marcos and San Francisco Rivers, which comprised the eastern and southeastern margins of Lake Izabal, because they had chosen that area as part of the thirty-six square leagues they were allowed to purchase.[8]

This petition, also, the government referred to the Assembly for

7. Petition of José Mariano Dorantes to the Asamblea Legislativa, n.d., ANG, Congreso, 1834, No. 151, fols. 10-11, unclassified.

8. Petition of Carlos Antonio Meany, March 21, 1835, ANG, Congreso, 1834, No. 151, fols. 12-14, unclassified.

its consideration. The legislative body, however, seems to have been unable to determine a policy by which it was willing to be bound. The questions thus raised in several different ways received no public answer, but they were still posed in private.

Gálvez himself inadvertently re-opened the public controversy. He was re-elected in February 1835 and after three times rejecting the proffer of the Assembly finally accepted the office.[9] As a gesture of conciliation toward the citizens of Gualán he wrote to assure them that his best endeavor during his second term would be bent toward developing the prosperity and well-being of the Department of Chiquimula. He would not rest, he promised, until he had successfully concluded the proposed construction of roads, navigation of rivers, and cultivation of wastelands. When the letter was read in Gualán on April 19, some forty-five citizens of the town seized the opportunity it afforded them to restate their objections to the Bennett and Meany contract. The Chief of State's offer of such extensive benefits, they observed, under normal circumstances could have had no effect but to electrify the inhabitants and to cause general rejoicing. But enthusiasm was smothered on this occasion by knowledge that for Gálvez to make good his promises the greater part of the Bennett and Meany contract would have to be changed. The manifest reluctance of the government to hear complaints on the subject, however, made such a development improbable. Therefore, claiming their "sacred right of petition, expression, and censure" and denying any intent to foment rebellion or attack on the government, they addressed the municipal corporation to state their grievances.[10]

The burden of the protest again was that the rights of nationals had been infringed by the grant of the lands to foreigners. The argument, however, was developed along different lines from before. Major emphasis was given to the legality of the transaction with minor attention to the realism of the expectation that material benefit would be derived from it.

It had long been easy, the argument ran, to deceive an ignorant people with the appearance of good by assuring them that, as owners of the land and the natural products that came from it, they were the actual beneficiaries of the government's solicitude. But the people also owned the public wealth, and they constituted a power that

9. Lorenzo Montúfar, *Reseña histórica de Centro-América* (Guatemala, 1878), II, 175-80.

10. Petition of the citizens of Gualán, April 24, 1835, ANG, Congreso, 1834, No. 151, fols. 15-21. The following ten paragraphs summarize the principal arguments advanced in the petition.

knew no superior other than the laws they imposed upon themselves by means of legislators chosen for that purpose. Sovereignty resided in the people, and government merely executed laws. Any executive, therefore, was the servant of the people from whom he drew his authority.

By means of the contract in question, a grant of incredible size and value was made without the approval of the people. The executive had no authority to cede exclusive privilege to land that belonged to the nation, and the Assembly, even though its ratification was required for the simplest treaty, had played no visible role in the transaction. Even had the legislative body approved the measure, it had no authority to act contrary to the desires of the people. Usurped power exercised in this and every other case was a nullity because it was not ratified by the people. Any measure taken in the interest of some against the good of others was a mockery of the people and an enormous crime that ought to be condemned and forever forgotten.

The residents of the country had no quarrel with the objective of colonizing the uninhabited lands of the state. In the present instance, however, equality of opportunity between foreigners and native sons to undertake the project should have been assured by opening the contract to bids. And if the welfare of the immigrants who were expected to settle the ceded areas was of any concern to the government, the lands should have been granted to them in emphyteusis, but with no exclusive privileges, as was the practice in the United States and in the Río de la Plata. Moreover, the action of the government had been contrary to enlightened public policy in that it threatened to fragment the state. Even despotic governments tried to increase the area of their countries, but that of Guatemala offered to break up what it already possessed into a number of pieces, with great prejudice to the interests of the inhabitants.

The petitioners rejected the possibility that the cession could have been made deliberately to bring about their ruin. They could therefore conclude only that it was done in ignorance of the enormous size of the cession and of the miseries suffered by the inhabitants because of past wars and of the commitment of their persons and their property to bring to power the same government that now forgot them. Gualán, for example, possessed only a square league of land that supplied resources for not more than one-tenth of its needs. No other area fulfilled its requirements so well as that ceded to Bennett and Meany, for from that territory the residents made their livings by cutting sarsaparilla and wood, making boats, and navigating the rivers. Allowed the same privilege of exploiting the surrounding public lands as were the residents of Yucatán, the inhabitants of Chiquimula could, by enriching themselves, contribute to the public welfare and develop the ports of the north by colonizing them properly, without the fetters and obstacles inherent in the Bennett and Meany agreement.

The contractors, on the other hand, were incapable of fulfilling their obligations because they were without the necessary capital. Bennett's lack of funds was demonstrated by the "miserable way he now carries on his woodcutting operations at Santa Cruz to the north of Izabal." Meany was no more than a broker for European merchants who carried about with him samples of the goods and commodities his patrons wanted to sell. He was in debt five hundred pesos, had confessed his inability to pay, and had ventured to hope that collection would not be attempted by legal proceedings. To raise funds he could not himself supply he carried "map and compass" about the capital in an attempt to sell shares in the enterprise. Bennett was also alleged to have sold in London one thousand shares at two hundred pesos each to raise money for the company's operations. "These men," the petitioners asked derisively, "drained of ability and credit, will colonize our land and make us happy?"

The funds raised by the sale of shares in the enterprise would not result in colonization of the ceded lands. Indeed, the agreement contained no performance guarantee to assure such an outcome. Rather, the money would be used to bring in gangs of laborers who for twenty years could be used to plunder the concession, after which the contractors would be free to select their thirty-six square leagues of purchased land wherever they chose. Even if the territory were subsequently opened to exploitation by residents of the country, they would find the land swept clean of its resources and themselves deprived of advantages that were rightfully theirs.

Perhaps the basic difficulty was that the government was responsive to the interests of the capital but not to those of Chiquimula. It was a common saying, the petitioners recalled, that a government did much good simply by doing no evil. "Why do we not observe this maxim?," they inquired. "Is it not the duty of a government to maintain the whole state in quiet and peace, and to promote the welfare of all?"

If the contract remained in force, the petitioners prophesied that Gualán would be left "completely orphaned and in misery." Ignorant people already gave credence to a rumor that the government had ordered the inhabitants bound and handed over to the Englishman to whom they had been sold. Proof of the report they saw in the delivery to Bennett of eighteen men and six women expelled from the town of Zacualpa who were compelled to work for him without pay of any kind except for sustenance. It was to escape a similar fate that residents of the district, such as those of the valley of Sinsin, were emigrating to Honduras. They were also menaced by the possibility that the one thousand rifles Bennett and Meany offered in payment for the thirty-six square leagues of land would be used, if they were actually delivered, "to make war on us if necessary" to enforce the contract.

The Municipality of Gualán forwarded the petition of the citizens to the Assembly with its strong endorsement. The memorial truthfully described the situation of the department, it asserted, and the views expressed were shared by all the residents. The Municipality stated its own fear that the contract placed the state in danger of imminent invasion. Its argument, however, was tenuous. England and Spain were friends, and Spain, France and Portugal were governed virtually by orders from Austria and Russia. In this situation, "should we, without forces or assistance to resist, blindly hand ourselves over to foreigners?" "Think on these things," the Municipality cautioned the Assembly, lest the people be given reason to believe that although the evil was pointed out in time, their counsel went unheeded. The views expressed were those of a provincial Municipality, but the mighty should not overlook the advice of the lowly. Indeed, it observed, no one shows himself greater than when, recognizing his errors, he corrects them. This the members trusted the patriotism of the deputies would accomplish.

The protest from Gualán set off a wave of similar addresses to the government. In rapid succession the Municipalities of Esquipulas, Quezaltepeque, Chiquimula, San Nicolás, Zacapa, Santa Elena, Estanzuela, and Santa Lucía also petitioned the Assembly.[11] These actions were obviously inspired. The timing, the similarity in content and statement, and the references to information supplied by citizens of Gualán suggest that the later documents were composed as variations on the Gualán theme. There is no reason, however, to reject them

11. Petitions of the Municipalities of Esquipulas, May 12; Quezaltepeque, May 13; Chiquimula, May 16; San Nicolás, May 26; Zacapa, May 31; Santa Elena [page carrying date missing from the microfilm copy]; Estanzuela, June 6; Santa Lucía, June 7, 1835; all in ANG, Congreso, 1834, No. 151, fols. 22-23, 34-53, unclassified. The Zacapa and Santa Lucía memorials were identical except for orthography.

as invalid on that ground. Whether spontaneous or induced, they expressed attitudes that were deeply rooted and passionately held. They presented no new basic arguments, but they elaborated the fabric of justification for the request that the agreement be nullified.

The Municipalities expressed no opposition to the purposes of the colonization agreements and no objection to foreigners as colonists under what they defined as proper conditions. Most of the petitions did not even raise the issue, but in some there was overt agreement that Guatemala was underpopulated; that the inhabitants, as a result of Spanish rule, were ignorant of agriculture, the arts, and the means of fostering them; and that encouragement of colonization by foreign immigrants was an effective means of setting about the learning process. The principal question raised, however, was the expediency of such a step under existing conditions. Several of the memorials pointed out that the political systems of the republic and of the individual states were not yet fully established and that dissidents within the country and political exiles without would gladly join with foreigners who might be similarly disposed to alter the political order. In their view, current internal conditions were not propitious for such a step.

These considerations were intimately related to one of the basic issues raised in the memorials. Every Municipality feared for the territorial integrity of the state and for independence itself. The record of Belize they cited as an overpowering argument against the settlement of British colonists on the northern coasts. The attitude was based on the conviction that Bennett was an agent of British governmental policy, as the woodcutters of the Settlement were assumed to have been before him. Under what the petitioners viewed as identical circumstances, the residents of that establishment had converted a simple privilege to cut wood into a title claim to the site of the original concession, as well as to the additional areas over which without authorization they had extended their operations.

What had happened in Belize could occur with even greater ease in Guatemala because of the more extensive privileges conferred by the colonization agreement. The contractors were authorized to settle on their lands an unlimited number of colonists. Assuming that because the entrepreneurs were English the settlers would also be of that nationality, the Municipalities feared that the cession would fall under the control of a homogeneous population reared under different customs and governed under different laws. Once in possession of the land, no one could guarantee their performance in good faith of the obligations imposed upon them by the colonization agreement. Might not the imported population come ultimately to dominate native sons and force them to live under an alien culture and alien law? Might not Bennett, an active agent of expansion in Belize, wish to make a second gift of territory to the British crown? In that case the record of British policy toward Central America left no basis for doubt of the result. The Municipality of Chiquimula professed to "see close at hand the chains prepared for us by the British government that has never entertained favorable intentions toward Central America" and expressed its own preference of "a perilous liberty to tranquil slavery."

The threat to the political integrity of the state was enhanced by the economic advantages enjoyed by the foreign colonizers. They owned the ports of the north and were authorized to import through them duty-free goods in any quantity. Under these conditions their merchandise could undersell all possible local competition. These advantages over native sons, the Municipality of Quezaltepeque predicted, they would use to "make silent war on us" until, rich with the proceeds of their exploitation, they became the economic masters of the country.

Resentment against the special privileges granted to foreign colonists transcended fear of the consequences that might result from the economic advantages conferred upon them. "This abundance of benefits that no native son has been able to obtain depresses and stuns us," the corporate body of Estanzuela confessed. Inferior status to foreign newcomers was a poor reward to the native-born who paid the taxes assessed by the authorities, performed the public services required of them, risked their lives and their property during the recent civil war to bring to power the very officials who now forgot them, and bore in silence the poverty and misery that resulted from participation in that struggle. The Municipalities could find no basis in justice or expediency for creating a group of specially privileged citizens. If concessions were to be offered for colonization, let them be opened equally to foreigners and to native sons.

The most bitterly resented feature of the contracts was the cession of public lands to foreigners. The Municipalities criticized the extent and value of the grant, the disregard for legal procedures in its execution, the restrictive effect of foreign ownership on the ability of local residents to make a living, and its probable depressing influence on the prospects for national development. Their conclusion was that the government had acted without knowledge, without judgment, and without legal authority.

The enormous size of the cession filled the Municipalities with consternation. Bennett had been granted more land in Guatemala, they alleged, than many potentates governed in Europe. Furthermore, he obtained it far more easily. The great monarchs were accustomed to add territory to their dominions by intrigue, by force of arms, and by the sacrifice of thousands of victims. Bennett obtained his empire at the cost of a thousand rifles and the promise of a fourth-part of the proceeds of his operations, but the payment of that obligation was made dubious by the omission from the contract of any stated basis on which to calculate the government's share. Moreover, the authorities had assured the new proprietor the leisurely enjoyment of exclusive privilege in his imperial-sized domain by binding themselves to enter into no other similar agreement.

Not only did the cession to Bennett and Meany transcend the bounds of reason, it exceeded the limits set by law. The federal enactment of 1824 specified colonization grants of one million square varas for each family and a like amount for the contractor who established them. The state law of 1825 governing the breakup of public lands in Guatemala reserved one-third of the total public domain for purposes of colonization. The authorities ignored the standards set by both of these laws when they made the grant to Bennett and Meany. They ceded all the public lands within specified boundaries without relationship to the number of colonists specifically called for by the contract.

The lands granted to Bennett and Meany were alleged to be the most fertile and the richest in resources to be found anywhere within the republic. The authorities were ignorant of the value of the cession and were deceived in the transaction. The foreign proprietors had no intention of accomplishing the development expected by the government. They intended only to extract the riches from the land, perhaps by luring their propertyless compatriots to their service by promise of a fragment of the prodigal gift they had received from the government of Guatemala. "We will never acceed," the Municipality of Chiquimula declared, "to colonization achieved by giving away and selling the best and most fertile lands to the ambitious and evil-intentioned foreigners—to giving all the public lands of the department to Englishmen."

The grant to the contractors, the Municipalities alleged, left citizens of the state without the means to carry on their accustomed occupations and thus to provide for their necessities. Except under terms of vassalage to the foreign proprietors, native sons were now barred from the lands from which they had previously obtained the products they could sell abroad. The result of the government's action had therefore been to rob the inhabitants of the department of their patrimony and to confer it upon foreigners.

The method of executing the contract they also attacked as irregular. The denounced lands were not opened to public bidding, and hence, the government lost the opportunity to obtain the better price many citizens of the state would gladly have paid for the concession. After the contract was let, the authorities did not follow the usual procedures for validating a governmental action. Although the laws, decrees, and other measures of the government were required to be printed in the *Boletin Oficial*, the contract had never been published in the official newspaper. This secrecy displeased the residents of the state, for in it they thought they discerned the intent to paralyze their right of petition. They hinted that the excesses of which they complained might be the result of a venal arrangement between the contractors and government officials.

The Municipalities were unanimous in the opinion that the contracts conferred not the slightest advantage on the state. "Sad experience has taught us," the officers of San Nicolás observed, "that no good is to be expected from foreigners, for they act always in their own interest." Esquipulas was more specific: "The machines they introduce, and the great populations they establish will bring us no advantage, for they will take care to bring operators of the machines and will teach us nothing, for we well know their selfishness; their works will be for their own advantage and nothing for us; they will, like leeches, suck the blood of native sons." Zacapa perhaps stated the general view most cogently. "In vain," that body wrote, "can they try by studied arguments to make us believe that the contract offers great advantage to the state. We are of a contrary opinion, for we touch with our hands the evils, the misfortunes, and the dangers to which it exposes the whole nation."

Although the principal function of the memorials was criticism, they offered some constructive proposals for the guidance of governmental policy. Some of the suggestions dealt with the general problems of colonization, others with specific details and arrangements. As was predictable, the primary concern of the Municipalities was for the land and the resources to which they hoped to regain access.

The municipal bodies presented a variety of proposals for the more rational disposition of the ceded area. The general principle on which all agreed was that foreigners should be admitted to exploitation of Guatemalan resources only under limitations that would avert prejudice to the rights of nationals. Because of the scarcity of available land in the interior of the Department of Chiquimula, cessions should be restricted to the coastal areas where they would not affect the interests of nearby towns. Grants should be limited in extent to the parcels stipulated by law, the remainder to be reserved for other proponents or, it may be assumed, for exploitation by nationals. An even more desirable alternative would be to allow native sons to acquire the land and to sell the standing trees to foreign cutters. This procedure would make the income available internally to supply the needs of the inhabitants and those of the government. Preferable to the wholesale cession without cost to Bennett and Meany would be acceptance of the offers made by individual cutters from Belize to buy standing timber. From the proceeds of these sales the government could set up a fund to promote settlements and employ commissioners to enlist colonists abroad. The ceded lands contained resources in sufficient quantity to produce a superabundant revenue for this purpose and perhaps even a surplus from which, they suggested with heavy irony, the authorities might choose to relieve the distress of some of the established native towns.

Colonization by Europeans might be invited when the internal situation was settled enough to make it expedient. Special concessions, however, should not be offered. Foreign settlers should pay the same taxes as the native-born, be subject to the same obligations for public service, and live under the same departmental government so that residents would have some local recourse should their relations with the immigrant colonists result in friction that could be resolved only by authority. Promotion of colonization by commissioners abroad offered special advantages worthy of consideration. Such representatives of the government could choose the best, the most virtuous, and the most accomplished applicants from all countries for admission to the state. Furthermore, a diversity of nationality, language, and cultural heritage among the colonists would establish an equilibrium within the settlements and thus avert the danger to the unity and integrity of the state that might result from a concentrated homogeneous foreign population.

All the Municipalities asked that the government nullify the Bennett and Meany contract or modify it to bring it into accord with the principles stated. They claimed right to the attentions of the government by virtue of past sacrifices, services, and loyalty to the existing regime and argued the obligation of a popular government to heed the protests of its constituents. Should their petitions not be heard, they hinted that they might be forced as a last resort to avail themselves of the right of revolution. The regime that made the cession, the Municipality of Chiquimula declared, by "contravening the principles the republic and the state have proclaimed, has ceased to be a government and has degenerated into a tyrant." All of Central America, it averred, was disturbed by the contract. Hence, prudence dictated that "we try to avert the evils that may ensue, and not expose ourselves to a disastrous war."

The government was not without defenders, although the voices lifted in its support sound strangely akin to those that had proposed the measures under attack. A pamphlet entitled *Pequeño catecismo político sobre colonizaciones,* signed "Dr. Castrillo," and dated Zacapa, May 30, had all the earmarks of a government defense of its own actions.[12] It was a question and answer review and rebuttal of the objections raised by the dissenting Municipalities. The protest of Chiquimula, in particular, drew the fire of the pamphleteer.

The oracle that supplied the answers to the questions was inclined to view the memorials presented by the Municipalities less as protests than as a form of rebellion. The action of the state authorities was based on both federal and state law; hence, the opposition of the Municipalities was equivalent to defiance of law. Moreover, their remarks on the conduct of state officials ranged from lack of proper respect to outright libel.

The Municipalities professed to recognize the need for colonization and to agree on the benefits it could confer, but in reality they despised the idea. Basically they placed a higher value on a wilderness from which forest products could be extracted than they did on settled, prosperous, civilized communities. They therefore retarded rather than assisted the efforts of the government to bring enlightenment to the country, and they obstructed rather than facilitated the development of free institutions.

The opposition to selling or giving away land to promote colonization the pamphlet characterized as entirely incomprehensible. If an end was desirable, so also were the means by which it was achieved. Furthermore, such disposition of public lands had been authorized by federal law for eleven years and by state law for ten years, and there had been no protest. The state law set aside one-third of the

12. [Guatemala, 1835].

available public lands for purposes of colonization, but the remaining two-thirds could be disposed of to private individuals for any use whatever. The very best lands should be made available for colonization, for the immigrant settlers were the bearers and teachers of civilization, the greatest possible good. If they were willing to endure the rigors of a burning climate to transform the wilderness into a garden, the government, with decency, could offer them for their efforts no less than the best available land, without cost and with full title.

The area of the land granted, far from being excessive, was less than the amount authorized by law. The federal law allowed a plot measuring one thousand varas in length and in width to each family and an equal amount to the contractor who established it. For the one thousand families promised under the contract this allotment would call for plots one million varas in linear extent for the families and an equal amount for the contractor. This extension was equivalent to four hundred leagues and, being promised in the square, the total authorized cession would exceed by far the area actually granted.

The argument that the cession dismembered the state was equally without foundation. The lands became the property, not of a foreign monarch, but of private individuals who were specifically made subject to the laws of Guatemala. If chains were being prepared for any one, it was for the colonists, for they were required to swear fidelity to the constitution of the republic and to that of the state and to live subject to local law. To cite Belize as an analogous case was a fallacy, for the King of Spain did not require the British subjects who occupied that concession to live under Spanish law.

On the issue of legality the Municipalities were far more vulnerable than was the government. Their declared opposition to the execution of the laws of the republic and of the state placed them dangerously close to insurrection. Moreover, the procedure of the Municipality of Zacapa in calling a meeting of residents to consult on the question was not in accord with law and must have been intended either to give greater authority to its protest or to allow it to escape responsibility for it. These "shameful, illegal, and impolitic" measures "would not be able to justify before the government the conduct of Municipalities that try, with the backing of simple people, to upset the wise dispositions of the government and of the whole republic."

What, then, was the proper attitude for the Municipalities to adopt? "They should co-operate with the government to spread enlightenment; aid it actively and consistently to establish colonies, [which offered] the only hope of obtaining roads and industries, and the only means of impeding the usurpation of the territory of the republic by foreigners; carry on a war to the death against political and religious fanaticism, that rob [us] of a thousand benefits and produce a thousand evils; undeceive those misled by the fallacies and sophistries of the mahogany cutters; and above all, meditate seriously on their actions."

During the summer of 1835, both the federal Congress sitting in San Salvador and the Guatemala Assembly faced the problems raised by the cession to Bennett and Meany. The Congress was not directly concerned, but the dissent of the towns in Chiquimula practically ended any lingering possibility that it would take action on the pending ratification of the contract. The Assembly was confronted with virtual insurrection against certain features of the agreement. The protests from nine Municipalities in Chiquimula stated the objections of the opposition, and the proposals made by Meany on March 21 suggested modifications, acceptable to the contractors, that might remedy some of them. With the Assembly lay the choice between attempting to eliminate the features of the contract to which native sons objected or accepting the possibility that protest might ripen into revolt.

In its deliberations on the memorials from Chiquimula, the Assembly demonstrated no comprehensive grasp of the issues raised. Whether deliberately or inadvertently the committee to which the petitions were referred largely misconceived the nature and import of the criticisms. It interpreted the issue to be the terms of the federal law of 1824 and the faithfulness with which they had been executed by Guatemalan authorities who approved the contract. It therefore failed to come to grips with many of the fundamental questions raised by the memorials.

The committee assumed that the federal law and the contract were, for practical purposes, identical. The objectives were the same and, if the contract were signed in accord with the prescribed terms to achieve the purposes of the law, there could be no legitimate objection to the means of which the state government had availed itself. To make its point clear, the committee restated the principles on which the colonization law rested. Population, it asserted, was the fountain of prosperity, for wealth was produced by the labor of man; hence, the government that best understood its own needs encouraged the increase of its population in proportion to the capacity of its resources to provide a livelihood. Every foreigner who settled in Central America, assuming that he was not a mendicant, was useful because he brought capital to spend or to invest in some productive enterprise or because he intended to carry on some useful occupation. Active and virtuous artisans emigrated from one country to another only because of necessity, and the state that acquired such residents obtained something of far greater value than extensive territorial possessions; hence, governments that did not welcome such useful additions to their populations were only half-civilized. On the basis of these principles the first federal Congress had passed an astute law that authorized the states to exchange land which they possessed in superfluous quantity for population which they sorely lacked.

For ten years no state had taken advantage of this beneficent legislation. Now that Guatemala had done so a chorus of protests had arisen against the contract. The criticisms, however, were not directed against the law that authorized the transaction but against the terms by which the intent of the law was carried into effect. Nonetheless, the provisions of the contract were in accord with the provisions of the federal law; the Assembly had ratified the agreement, and it had been sent to the federal Congress for similar approval. The contract, the committee alleged, was entirely legal. In indignation it rejected the imputation that the Chief of State and the Assembly had betrayed the interests of the state for money.

The fear that the contract would allow a combination of European powers to threaten the territorial integrity of the state the committee found equally ridiculous. That apprehension, it believed, arose because the memorialists confused a legally regulated grant to an individual with a cession of dominion to another state. The grant of land, it insisted, was not excessive in extent nor were the other concessions over-generous in view of the absence of other offers to colonize and the urgency of the project in view of those "who hope to work not alone for posterity."

The misconceptions held by the Municipalities, the committee believed, could not have arisen from a simple reading of the contract. They must have been inspired, it conjectured, by mahogany cutters whose personal interests were tied to maintenance of the *status quo*. It therefore conceived the opposition to be the ephemeral manifestation of dissatisfaction among local mahogany interests. If freed from the unwelcome association with woodcutting, the colonization project could go forward "in all its majesty." The committee was uncertain, however, whether or not the privilege to cut wood was included in the concession. Its first thought was to assert flatly in its recommendation to the Assembly that no such right had been granted, but caution produced a substitute statement. It presented instead the equivocal declaration that the legislative body trusted the government would act "in the manner most suitable to the interests and reputation of the state, trying thus to calm the animosities that have arisen, separating the work of colonization from the business of wood-cutting." This recommendation the Assembly adopted on August 30,[13] but the government apparently gave no serious attention to the problem until it faced a crisis on the issue.

During the fall of 1835 the Chiquimula contract became the focal point of a rebellion forming under the banner of Nicolás Espinosa, Chief of State of El Salvador. The movement was alleged to have as its objective the overthrow of the federal government headed by Francisco Morazán and the regime of Gálvez in Guatemala. Whether Espinosa was in fact the author of the scheme or was trapped by a plot engineered by his enemies as Lorenzo Montúfar implies, emissaries operating in his name tried to capitalize on disaffection in Guatemala to neutralize that state while operations were carried on in El Salvador against Morazán. Gálvez believed that his position was threatened, and agents from El Salvador justified his fears by inciting the residents of Chiquimula to revolt.[14]

The Bennett and Meany contract was the chief issue used by the agitators to win support in both El Salvador and Guatemala. They obtained a copy of the agreement and printed twenty-one of the most offensive articles for distribution in support of their charges. Morazán and Gálvez, they told the people, had betrayed the country and its independence to the English. For a huge sum of money they had sold the north coast of Guatemala to Englishmen, and four ports on that coast were already in enemy hands. There the foreign proprietors were fortifying positions so that they could not be expelled from the country and were preparing from those bases to launch a war on Central America. These preparations would have availed them nothing, however, had they not been aided from Central America by the traitors Morazán and Gálvez and even by some of the inhabitants who artlessly served the tyrants without realizing that they trod the road of death.

The only hope remaining to the population was to overthrow Morazán and Gálvez while there was yet time. If the traitors were

13. Opinion of the committee, July 27, 1835, ANG, Congreso, 1834, No. 151, fols. 54-57.

14. Montúfar, *Reseña histórica*, II, 192-93.

allowed to escape to the English colony, they planned to use British forces to subdue Central America. Their purpose, and that of their English masters, was to put the inhabitants to the sword.

The English expected to take possession of the lands Central Americans had inherited from their forefathers. No surviving native resident would be able to earn even as much as half a real among them, for if one lone colonist, Bennett, had been able to sweep away their commerce, what opportunity would be offered in a country entirely dominated by them?[15]

This propaganda aroused many of the simpler folk of El Salvador to a frenzy of excitement, and it won adherents among even the more sophisticated levels of society. Uprisings occurred in several Indian villages and in a few of the larger towns. Chiquimula also appeared to be responsive, and the clandestine movement of agents between that department and El Salvador alarmed the authorities on both sides of the frontier. In response to an urgent appeal for help from the federal government Gálvez sent aid in troops and in cash. Ironically, the money was raised by means of a forced loan levied on the towns of the department that had protested the contract.[16]

Gálvez also took measures to insure the maintenance of quiet in Chiquimula. He ordered Mariano Trabanino, the *jefe político* of the department, to inquire into the conspiracy, to arrest and send to the capital the leaders of the disaffection, to make certain that no arms fell into the possession of the rebels, and to use the garrison as necessary to prevent violence against the authorities. The troops dispatched to El Salvador were routed via Chiquimula and were instructed to remain there as an added deterrent to insurrection until they were called for by the federal authorities.[17]

The crisis was short-lived. Espinosa relinquished his official position in mid-November, and late in the month he began his journey into exile. The centers of disaffection were quickly suffocated, and the menace of open revolt was dissipated.[18] Fear of the consequences

15. Miguel Alvarez, federal Minister of Foreign and Domestic Relations, to Gálvez, Nov. 8, 1835, ANG, leg. 16263, exp. 53129, n.f., and Dec. 7, 1835, ANG, leg. 164, exp. 3428, fols. 5-6; *Informe que el Secretario de Relaciones hace . . . sobre la conducta . . . del licenciado Nicolas Espinosa . . .* ([San Salvador?], 1836), pp. XVII, XX, XXIII; Chatfield to Palmerston, No. 6, Feb. 26, 1836, FO 15/18, fols. 61-62.

16. Colonel Mariano Trabanino, *jefe político* of Chiquimula, to Gálvez, Dec. 1, 1835, ANG, leg. 16263, exp. 53129.

17. Gálvez to Trabanino, Nov. 7, Nov. 12, and Dec. 8, 1835, ANG, leg. 16262, exp. 50968, n.f.; and Nov. 27, 1835, ANG, leg. 16263, exp. 53129, n.f.

18. Montúfar, *Reseña histórica*, II, 193.

to be expected from the Chiquimula contract had been widely disseminated, however, and unrest was not stilled by the collapse of armed resistance. For some time Gálvez and the federal authorities maintained a lively exchange of information on suspects, and a thin trickle of prisoners moved from El Salvador and Chiquimula to Guatemala City. Although the government of Guatemala undertook at the beginning of the crisis to ease the cause of resentment, the issues that had given strength to the insurrection were fundamentally unresolved.

Perhaps moved by the necessity of taking action to stifle the disaffection in Chiquimula, Gálvez attempted to moderate the opposition by revising the offensive contract. At almost the identical moment that he ordered the use of force if necessary against the citizens of the department, he reached an agreement that he hoped would remove the cause for discord. A series of six explanations to the contract, accepted by Meany for the partnership on November 5, 1835, stated certain principles intended to protect the rights of native sons. Unoccupied lands adjacent to towns and those that intervened between *ejidos* were specifically excluded from the terms of the grant and the settlement of colonists on them prohibited without the concurrence of the municipal authorities of the nearest town. Similarly, the prior cessions of public lands made by the Assembly to the members of the armed forces who had participated in the siege of Omoa were specifically validated and excluded from the terms of the grant. Residents of the state were guaranteed free and unrestricted use of the waterways within the cession and the right, on the basis of written concessions and the promise to pay a contribution in an amount to be fixed later, to cut from its sarsaparilla, wood, or any other forest product for export. Any resident of Chiquimula, the state, or the republic who wished to do so could settle as a colonist in any of the new towns and enjoy there all the privileges granted to foreign immigrants. They could also acquire shares in the enterprise with the same responsibilities and benefits as other holders. The contractors were expressly forbidden to sell or cede to any foreign government any of the lands granted to them. Finally, the conditional nature of the cession was reiterated and the stipulation added that should the required number of colonists not be settled within the specified time the contract was voided.[19]

A surviving fragment of a kindred document suggests that another

19. Articles of agreement signed by Meany for himself and Bennett, AMG, Comunicaciones, 1835.

agreement was reached between Meany and the government two days later. A final page, signed by Meany and dated November 7, carried the last few words of Article 8 and Articles 9 and 10 of what appears to have been either a more comprehensive arrangement or an extensive supplement to the earlier explanations. The eighth article related to the increase in price, by arrangement with the government, of something, possibly land, at Santo Tomás. Article 9 expressly revoked the additional articles to the original contract proclaimed on the last day of the preceding January. These explanations had redefined the boundaries of the tract set aside for the exclusive use of the contractors; had allowed the contractors, within the six *caballerías* reserved to the government at Santo Tomás, to use the area needed for building dwellings and warehouses in the town; and had required that the colonists swear fealty to the constitution of the republic, as well as to that of the state. The tenth article allowed the contractors to count toward the total number of colonists they were required by the agreement to establish within their grant any settler they brought into the country regardless of the place he might choose to reside.[20] Gálvez may have been thinking of dispersing foreign colonists among native residents of the country; Meany was undoubtedly thinking of developing San Jerónimo.

The first series of six explanations was given the force of the law when it was issued as a governmental decree on December 21, 1835.[21] Whether the second was repudiated, otherwise rendered inoperative, or kept a secret because of the further concessions it made to the contractors, the sources do not make clear. It seems never to have been made public, and its contents were apparently unknown to the critics of the contract. The later vigorous attempts of the partners to enlist laborers for San Jerónimo, however, suggest an agreement with the government on the substance of Article 10, at least.

However far Gálvez may have thought he had gone in meeting the objections of the residents of Chiquimula, his measures fell short of their insistent demands. In January 1836 the Municipalities of both Chiquimula and Esquipulas again petitioned the Chief of State to suspend the contract at least until the federal Congress could act upon it.[22] The Chiquimula address was referred to the Assembly in routine fashion, but Gálvez incorporated the product of second

20. *Ibid.*

21. Alejandro Marure and Andrés Fuentes Franco (comps.), *Catálogo razonado de las leyes de Guatemala* (Guatemala, 1856), p. 28.

22. Petition of Chiquimula, Jan. 4, 1836, ANG, leg. 1395, exp. 32348; Petition of Esquipulas, Jan. 13, 1836, ANG, Congreso, 1836, No. 62, fols. 1-3, unclassified.

thoughts in the recommendation with which he transmitted the Esquipulas protest.

Whether as a result of his own meditation or influenced by the arguments from Chiquimula, Gálvez had come to recognize that certain features of the contracts might indeed hazard the security of the state. In his message to the opening session of the Assembly in February he remarked, "Foreigners who wish to become members of the Republic and subjects of our laws can settle among us and enjoy the advantages that our soil offers; those that may come to dispute with us a single part of it, those that want to be in Central America the advance agents of European dominion, are our enemies." In response to Chatfield's suggestion in early March that compared with the Bennett and Meany contract Guatemala might reap greater advantage from opening its mahogany stands to Belize cutters, he opposed the fatal objection, previously rejected as invalid when argued by the dissidents of Chiquimula, in a single scornful question: "How can we give authority to cut to those who dispute with us ownership [of our territory] with no better original title than another woodcutting concession?"[23]

In submitting the Esquipulas memorial, Gálvez admitted that although the government had executed the agreements in good faith to promote the public welfare it might have erred in certain provisions and details of the contracts. The fear that an entirely English colony might ultimately join forces with Belize to separate from Guatemala might have some basis in reality. The declaration of the inhabitants of the Mexican state of Texas suggested that such action could indeed be taken by colonists possessing national affinity with an adjacent established community. He therefore suggested that the Assembly might, without breaking faith with the concessionaires, pass a general law requiring that colonies already contracted for and those that might be agreed upon in the future be constituted, after the population reached one hundred individuals, of not more than one-third of any single nationality.

The Committee on Government apparently overlooked the changed attitude of the Chief of State, and its report to the Assembly followed the pattern established by earlier legislative bodies on the same issue. It argued that the Esquipulas petition was based on "fear born of ignorance, which the Municipality itself recognizes." It would be

23. Gálvez to Chatfield, March 18, 1836, FO 252/12, n.f.; "Mensaje del Jefe del Estado de Guatemala, Dr. Mariano Gálvez, al abrirse las sesiones ordinarias de la Asamblea Legislativa, en 1836," *Anales* de la Sociedad de geografía e historia de Guatemala, II, No. 3 (March, 1926), 312.

ridiculous and shameful on such grounds to suspend the contract and thus to injure the concessionaires and prejudice the reputation of the government. The example of Texas gave cause for some concern, but the relatively small number of families called for by the agreement presented no hazard to the security of the state even if the colonists were all of the same nationality. It recommended approval of the law proposed by Gálvez for future colonies, but it saw no reason to include those already contracted for. This report the Assembly remanded to the Committee on March 8.[24]

Before a new opinion could be given, a long petition from the Municipality of Zacapa came to the Assembly. It rehearsed many of the arguments previously presented, but it elaborated one in a fashion that finally compelled attention. The Committee on Petitions ruled that the memorial deserved consideration, so it, too, was referred to the Committee on Government. The case made in the Zacapa document changed the opinion of the Committee and resulted in an entirely different recommendation to the Assembly.

Careful examination of its previous arguments, the Municipality pointed out, would reveal that it had opposed not colonization but the means by which the government had been led to believe settlement could be accomplished. It agreed that, properly conducted, colonization was the source of riches, industry, and prosperity; the fount from which sprang the improvement of agriculture and the arts; in short, the means by which free nations could aggrandize themselves with the greatest rapidity. But colonization demanded the offer of inducements appropriate to attracting useful foreigners, not adventurers who abandoned their own country because another offered them superior opportunities for their speculations. The Bennett and Meany contract failed to make this distinction. The Municipality attacked the agreement because it impeded colonization rather than promoted it.

The Chiquimula contract was a design for adventurers, the memorialists alleged. It ceded to the concessionaires the only wealth the state possessed under terms that allowed them to exploit for their own profit resources that should be reserved as a means of attracting colonists. Bennett and Meany had established their numerous woodcutting operations on the richest and most appropriate land for colonization and had left for habitation the inaccessible and deadly wilds that could be settled only at such obvious loss that even a fool

24. Opinion of the Committee on Government, March 2, 1836, ANG, Congreso, 1836, No. 62, fol. 4, unclassified.

would not be attracted to them. These locations could be colonized, if at all, only after fifty years of effort and at a cost of thousands of families. If, indeed, the contractors ever brought colonists, the immigrants would see that the proprietors had already appropriated the best of everything for themselves and had reserved the worst for settlers. Would not colonists, under those circumstances, either return to Europe or consider themselves defrauded?

The greatest weakness of the agreement, however, was that it required the contractors to give no guarantee that they would comply with the obligations they assumed. Indeed, the great hurry with which they selected and cut the best mahogany would immediately convince any observer that they promised to colonize only as a pretext to obtain authorization to cut wood. When their real motive was discovered they would already have made themselves rich by their deception and have prejudiced Central Americans by depriving them through fraud of what belonged to them.

The time period stipulated for completion of the first stage of colonization, the Municipality pointed out, had expired without compliance by the contractors. It therefore suggested that sufficient legal grounds already existed for cancellation of the agreement. Even were this not so, the overwhelming evidence to support suspicion of deception should compel such action without delay. In view of these considerations, the Municipality entreated the Assembly to nullify the contract immediately.[25]

This testimony from Zacapa stated an issue in terms that seized the imagination of the Committee on Government. To get to the major point in its recommendation, it brushed aside many of the objections raised by the Municipalities as born of misinterpretation of the articles in question or of ignorance of law and politics. The point it thought worthy of the consideration of the Assembly was the possible conflict of interest between the contractors and the government.

The contract, it pointed out, nowhere contained either a performance guarantee or a clear statement on the use of resources prior to colonization. The concessionaires were neither specifically authorized to exploit the resources of their grants nor expressly enjoined from doing so. These omissions should be remedied. The Committee therefore proposed to the Assembly a statement instructing the government so to define the Bennett and Meany agreement that the contrac-

25. Petition of Zacapa, April 8, 1836, ANG, Congreso, 1836, No. 62, fols. 5-10, unclassified.

tors would be required either to refrain from cutting wood until they had fulfilled their obligations to colonize or to give satisfactory guarantees that they would pay for the trees they had already extracted and those they might cut in the future as assurance against the possibility that they would not fulfill the requirements upon which that privilege was conditioned.[26] This recommendation the Assembly approved on April 29, 1836, and the government proclaimed the order on May 21.[27]

Almost exactly a year later the government recognized that the circumstances hypothesized by the Municipality of Zacapa were a reality. It therefore annulled the contract for non-performance of obligations and thus, belatedly and with little credit to itself, ended the controversy.

The author of the *Pequeño catecismo* ended his appeal to the Municipalities in 1835 with an exhortation to responsible thinking. "It will not be many years," he warned, "until the minutes and expositions signed by the municipalities will be read either with admiration or with derision . . . and there will be a gradual, but very just, judgment of the barbarity that existed in Chiquimula in 1835, during the very century of liberty and enlightenment." He proved to be a prophet of sorts, but a less discerning one that his pretentious words seemed to imply. The protests of the Municipalities were undoubtedly re-read in 1837, but probably with more admiration than derision. In "barbarous" Chiquimula at least the judgment must have been that, more than the ordinary people of Guatemala, the officials of the government required tutelage in the ways of Europeans.

26. Opinion of the Committee on Government, April 23, 1836, ANG, Congreso, 1836, No. 62, fols. 11-13, unclassified.
27. Orden legislativo No. 38, May 21, 1836, ANG, leg. 408, exp. 6679, n.f.

VII

WILDERNESS SETTLEMENTS:
NEW LIVERPOOL AND SANTA CRUZ

The agreements they signed with the Guatemalan government required all the contractors to become colonizers. To the state this obligation was the pre-eminent function of the concessionaires, the *raison d'être* for the contracts, the major hypothesis from which all else in the colonization agreements depended. Successful establishment of immigrant settlers was the prior condition by which the *empresarios* were required to validate the concessions made by their contracts.

However explicitly the state may have intended to impose its hierarchy of values, the contracts it accepted bound the concessionaires to no such system of priorities. Indeed, the agreements stated the obligations of the contractors in imprecise and widely varied terms. No minimum number of colonists was stipulated either for Galindo's grant or for the Bennett and Meany cessions north of Lake Izabal, and settlement had to be demonstrated only after five and twenty years respectively. The Verapaz, Chiquimula, and Totonicapán agreements were more exacting. They required the concessionaires progressively to settle families to the number of one hundred, two hundred, and one thousand over stated time periods. The Eastern Coast Company agreed to meet these conditions at intervals of two, four, and ten years; Bennett and Meany at three, five, and ten years. The contracts thus required all the entrepreneurs to show performance of their obligation to colonize, but only after they had been left in possession of their grants for extended intervals of time during which they were free to make use of them as self-interest might propose.

All available evidence suggests that Bennett and Meany intended to exploit to the maximum the privileges conferred by their contracts without regard for the obligation to colonize. If such was indeed their purpose, they performed precisely to plan. Bennett had no interest in recruiting colonists for the concessions where he expected only to exploit the forest resources; his efforts would be better rewarded if he enlisted laborers for the hacienda of San Jerónimo, which he planned to develop as an agricultural enterprise. The Guatemalan government appears to have become an unwitting collaborator in his designs if indeed it agreed in November 1835 to count as settlers established under the partners' colonization contracts immigrants who took up residence under their sponsorship anywhere in the state. Under this liberal interpretation of his obligation, Bennett attempted on several occasions to seduce into his service at San Jerónimo colonists brought to Guatemala by the Eastern Coast Company, but when he became convinced that Englishmen could not endure the rigors of the climate he imported Portuguese laborers in the hope that they would perform more satisfactorily.[1] In discharge of the obligation to colonize their concessions, however, Bennett and Meany appear to have enlisted not a single foreign colonist and, until the last of their grants was threatened with cancellation for non-performance of obligations in 1845, there is no evidence that they made any effort to recruit settlers abroad. By that time the government of Guatemala was convinced that the partnership was guilty of bad faith, and it nullified the contract.

Galindo's efforts to secure settlers for his grant progressed through several stages, each of which appears to have been an opportunistic expedient made necessary by the failure of the preceding scheme rather than a part of any developing, comprehensive plan. His first proposal was to sell the land in plots of 160 acres to residents of Belize. He obviously expected this maneuver to force mahogany cutters to become legal property holders, if not colonists in the sense desired by Central America. He alleged, however, that colonization of his grant was his major objective and one aspect of his proposed regime seems to have been intended seriously to encourage settlement. His argument that purchase of plots within his concession would contribute to agricultural development and to the "perfect security and stability of your Settlements & improvements thereon"[2] suggests intent to invite the British inhabitants to establish ranches

---

1. James Wood, *The Adventures, Sufferings, and Observations of James Wood* (Ipswich, 1840), p. 32. Plácido Flores, *jefe político* of the Verapaz, certified on Feb. 26, 1837, that more than 100 Portuguese laborers had been imported by Bennett and Meany earlier that month and settled at San Jerónimo (FO 252/9, n.f.).

2. Juan Galindo, "To the Inhabitants of the Spanish Side," Aug. 2, 1834, and a printed version of the same bearing a postscript dated "Guatemala, October 11," both in CO 123/46, n.f.

and plantations in adjacent Central American territories where the prohibitions of the Anglo-Spanish treaties against acquisition of land titles and cultivation and processing of agricultural staples within British Honduras were inoperative. This scheme the officials of Belize thwarted by supporting the woodcutters of the Settlement in their claims of title to the area as far west as Garbutt's Falls.

Meanwhile, inhabitants of the Petén began to take up residence along the Belize River in the vicinity of McAulay's Falls where the rumor became current that Galindo would soon appear to drive out the British. Galindo denied any knowledge of this development, but Chatfield believed that these settlers were in fact located by Galindo to spy on British cutters who might attempt without payment to him to cut wood on his land west of Garbutt's Falls.[3] Being nationals of Guatemala rather than foreigners, however, they could not qualify as colonists under the terms of Galindo's concession.

Balked in his efforts from Central America to obtain settlers to prove up on his grant, Galindo made use of his diplomatic mission to the United States and England to try to recruit colonists abroad. In New York he arranged to have his lands offered for sale through the office of Henry Dammers, at 7 Broad Street. The small advertisement, however, did not escape the watchful eyes of British agents who called it to the attention of the government. The British consul in New York was duly instructed to publish a warning to all prospective purchasers that Great Britain denied the legitimacy of Galindo's title and, hence, that the authorities in British Honduras would prevent anyone who purchased land from Galindo from taking possession of their alleged property.[4]

About a month after the Central American envoy arrived in England, John Waldron Wright reported to Guatemala that Galindo had completed an arrangement with a Dutch company which would send out settlers the following year to occupy his grant. Chatfield heard the report in Guatemala and repeated it to the Foreign Office, and early in 1836 Palmerston warned the Dutch government against allowing its citizens to involve themselves with the disputed territory. The Dutch Foreign Minister denied knowledge of any company in his country that intended to colonize in Central America and de-

3. Lieutenant Colonel Francis Cockburn to Frederick Chatfield, Nov. 22, 1834, FO 252/8, n.f.; Chatfield to Cockburn, Dec. 18, 1834, ABH, Letters Inwards, 1826-1848, Records 10, fol. 38.

4. James Hyde, Agent of British Honduras in London, to Lord Palmerston, Oct. 26, 1835, FO 15/17, fol. 240; Cockburn to Lord Glenelg, Aug. 17, 1835, and Colonial Office note to Foreign Office, Nov. 13, 1835, both in CO 123/46, n.f.

clined, should there be one, to intervene in a private matter in which the government had no interest.[5]

Whether or not the report of the Dutch arrangement was fact or fiction, no settlers appeared from that source to colonize Galindo's grant. If such plans had been made, the British warning may have overawed the individuals concerned and induced them to abandon the project. It seems likely, however, that no such agreement was actually reached. Before the British Cabinet had considered Chatfield's report, Galindo informed Gálvez that delays to his colonization efforts made it necessary for him to request an extension of the time allowed for meeting his obligations.[6] It seems hardly probable that Galindo's soaring optimism would have allowed him to think of failure had a pending agreement offered even remote expectation that he might be able to colonize his grant.

From early 1836 forward Galindo apparently abandoned hope of immediate success in recruiting settlers for his concession. He plunged into a variety of other projects and only occasionally did his attention return to the Petén. Then his chief concern was not to find colonists to occupy his grant but to prevent its incorporation into that of the Eastern Coast Company.

The London company, meanwhile, gave evidence that it intended promptly to validate the title to its Guatemalan concession. Whether its efforts were directed, as its critics alleged, toward only token performance of obligations in order to secure its right to land and privileges on which it intended later to speculate or whether it proposed seriously to colonize in anticipation of profits which might result from substantial development, it is difficult to determine. It appears that elements of both speculation and serious purpose were combined in the Company's operations. Only a dichotomy of interest, it seems, could have induced the directors to sustain a controversy with the British government in defense of their right to exploit mahogany stands south of the Sibún while attempting simultaneously to establish a colony on the Polochic as a first requirement toward validating their Guatemala grant. Such duality of purpose produced hesitations and delays that gave a subsequent board reason to charge that "an unaccountable supineness . . . accompanied by a want of

5. Chatfield to Palmerston, No. 30, Dec. 19, 1835, FO 15/16, fol. 282; Palmerston to Sir Edward Desbrowe, British Minister to The Hague, No. 12, April 22, 1836, FO 37/198, n.f.; Desbrowe to Baron Verstolk de Soelen, Dutch Foreign Minister, April 26, 1836, and Verstolk de Soelen to Desbrowe, May 25, 1836, FO 37/200, n.f.
6. Galindo to [Mariano Gálvez], Dec. 31, 1835, AMG, Comunicaciones 1835, n.f.

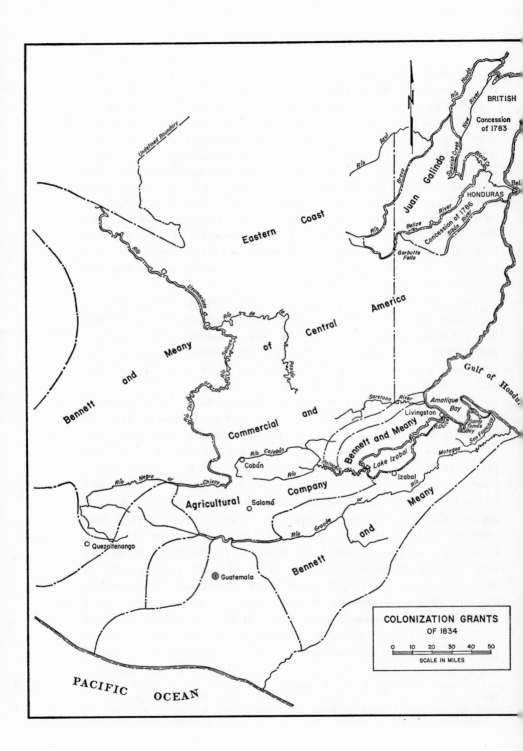

COLONIZATION GRANTS
OF 1834

0   10   20   30   40   50
SCALE IN MILES

unanimity in their councils . . . palsied the hopes of the Proprietary. . . ."[7]

This characterization by their successors, however, seems not to have identified the principal shortcoming of the directors. They were probably men whose small experience, few resources, and slight knowledge rendered them incapable of planning and conducting an enterprise of the magnitude they attempted. Chatfield recognized those limitations and urged Gould as he left Guatemala to "press on the attention of those who undertake the executive duties of the Company, that their plans must be well digested, and proper measures taken to prevent disappointment at the outset, or it is needless to anticipate any thing but a recurrence of those disastrous scenes, which in too many instances terminated such schemes of foreign enterprise."[8] This excellent advice the directors either chose to ignore or did not know how to apply. The principal failure was not that they deliberated too long but that they vacillated until a crisis was upon them and then acted hastily on the basis of slight knowledge and with inadequate preparation.

The Company's first significant step toward fulfilling the terms of its charter was to employ a superintendent for the projected colony in the Verapaz. For this position the directors selected Thomas Fletcher, a former resident of several of the West India islands and a man of recognized "talents, energy, and excellent reputation." Fletcher left London on June 1, 1835, sailed by way of Trinidad to pick up his family, and then proceeded to Guatemala.[9] His immediate task on arrival was to survey the lands within the Company's concession and to select and prepare a site for the reception of the first settlers. Subsequently he would superintend the colony and oversee the operations carried on directly in the interest of the Company.

From the fall of 1835 through the summer of the following year, the directors initiated a variety of other projects. They acquired a steamboat for service in Central American waters and obtained from the Guatemalan government a monopoly of steam navigation on the waterways within their grant; they published promotional literature to attract prospective investors and emigrants to their enterprise; they

7. *Brief Statement, Supported by Original Documents, of the Important Grants Conceded to the Eastern Coast of Central America Commercial and Agricultural Company by the State of Guatemala* (London, 1839), p. 2.

8. Chatfield to Thomas Gould, Sept. 30, 1834, FO 252/9, n.f.

9. Draft letter Carlos Salazar, Minister General, to John Waldron Wright, Aug. 22, 1835, ANG, leg. 1395, exp. 32333; Thomas Fletcher to Chatfield, Aug. 26, 1835, and William Campbell Gillan to Chatfield, May 8, 1839, both in FO 252/6, n.f.

recruited colonists and arranged for their transport to Verapaz; and they defended the validity of their concession before the British Cabinet against the claims asserted by the residents of Belize. Their show of activity must have generated a certain low-voltage confidence in the prospects of the Company, for its shares rose from 7 and 8 in July to 12½ by mid-December 1835. By early February 1836, however, the quotation had fallen again to the level of the previous July.

Simultaneously with the employment of a superintendent for the Verapaz colony, the Company began to take steps to qualify for some of the collateral privileges offered by its charter. The letter to Gálvez in which John Waldron Wright announced the appointment of Fletcher reported also that the directors had purchased a shallow-draft steamer which was expected to sail for Central America in October. The ship was delivered in mid-September and from that time forward she apparently became a familiar sight in London Dock. She was appropriately christened "Vera Paz" and registered at London Customs House with Jeremiah Barrett and William Crozier as owners and Crozier as master.[10]

Early in October the Company secretary informed Gálvez directly that the steamer had been purchased and announced the intent of the Company to exercise the option granted by its contract to bid for the monopoly of steam navigation within the limits of its grant. About a month later his successor in office proposed conditions under which he requested that the Guatemalan legislature confer upon the Company the monopoly of steam navigation of Lake Izabal and the Polochic River for a period of eighteen years. To earn this privilege the Company committed itself "to keep on those waters the Steam Boats necessary for all commercial purposes," to devote its best efforts to removing obstacles to navigation from the waters of its grant, to carry without charge the mail of the national government over the regular itineraries of the steamers, and to aid the national government to suppress smuggling on all the waterways of its concession.[11]

These propositions the executive branch passed on to the Assembly, which in turn referred them for study to the combined Committees on Legislation and Commerce. These bodies fretted over the ambiguities of language in the proposal and the absence in Guatemala of any accredited agent of the Company with whom acceptable

10. Copy of Certificate of British Registry [of "Vera Paz"], No. 415, CO 123/56, n.f.

11. J. Hammond to Gálvez, Oct. 9, 1835, ANG, leg. 3619, exp. 84739; Rest Fenner to Salazar, Nov. 5, 1835, ANG, leg. 7555, no exp. number, and a virtual duplicate dated Nov. 11, 1835, ANG, leg. 3616, exp. 84466.

clarifications could be reached. They were particularly concerned that the terminology of the proposal afforded no basis for precise understanding of the Company obligation and established no standard of performance capable of enforcement. The conditions of the monopoly had to be given definite statement, the Committees believed, before the concession could be approved or rejected. They therefore proposed that the Assembly add as "explanations" to the concession such conditions as were necessary to accomplish the objectives of the state without compromising the interests of the Company. On this basis, accepting the principle that exclusive privileges were "one of the most efficacious means that reason dictates" for promoting the prosperity of the state, they recommended granting the concession requested by the Company.

The Assembly acted favorably on the recommendation of the Committee. On April 9 it approved the concession of the monopoly for eighteen years, the time to be counted from January 1837. The Company was to lose the privilege, however, if by August 1837 it did not have at least one steamboat in operation on the assigned waters and if by the end of 1838 it did not have the required complement of vessels in service. The government was authorized to define, either by number of vessels or by total tonnage, the standards of service the Company was obligated to maintain and to fix penalties, ranging from cash fines to loss of the monopoly, to be assessed should it fail to comply.

As a general standard, the Assembly suggested that the Company be required to provide steam tonnage equal to three-fourths of the total capacity of the sailing vessels then operating. Its special privilege would be protected by a regulation that any steamboat judged by a competent court to be guilty of infringing the monopoly was to be confiscated, both the vessel and a fine of 5,000 pesos assessed against the owner to go to the aggrieved party. These conditions were to be communicated to the directors and, if accepted, the provisions when published by the government were to have the force of law in Guatemala. On April 23, 1836, the government informed the petitioner of the Assembly's action,[12] and presumably the conditions were accepted, for the Company was subsequently recognized to hold a monopoly of steam navigation in its area.

Three days after the Guatemalan Assembly granted the monopoly

12. The expediente detailing the government's action is in ANG, Congreso, 1836, No. 23, fols. 1-8, unclassified. Orden legislativo No. 24, of April 9, 1836, and the government's draft letter of notification of April 23 are in ANG, leg. 408, exp. 6668.

of steam navigation requested by the London directors, the Minister General sent to the legislative body a second communication dealing with Company affairs. It was an excerpt from Galindo's letter of the previous December 31 reporting that the old directors, who were "without money, knowledge, or influence," had been replaced by men of wealth and prestige who could give the Company a more capable administration. He warned, however, that even these distinguished officers would be unable to accomplish much if the British government continued to deny to the concessionaires possession of those parts of the grants disputed by Belize. For this reason he had promised to the new directors a one-year extension of time for fulfilling their contract if they joined him in representations that secured British recognition of the boundary claimed by Central America.

Although the Assembly denied that Galindo possessed authority to act for the state in the matter, it approved the conditional one-year time extension he proposed. The Representative Council, however, in mid-May 1836 refused its sanction to the measure. Its objections were taken on two grounds. It feared that the condition attached to the extension might be interpreted as tacit recognition of the usurpation by residents of Belize of the territory over which "the State since Independence acquired an unquestionable right." Moreover, it overlooked the reported change of directors and argued that the state would gain no advantage by granting an extension of time to a company "without money, influence, or knowledge." It was already on the verge of default on its obligations and an additional year would probably not increase its chances of success. The terms of the contract, nevertheless, would bind the government during the additional period to accept no other proposals of a similar nature, however advantageous they might be.[13]

The action of the Representative Council nullified the time extension, but Gálvez did not share its pessimistic view of the Company's prospects. He was informed on Fletcher's activity in the Verapaz, and the directors' application for a monopoly of steam navigation he regarded as no idle gesture. He daily expected news that the first immigrant settlers had entered the country and that the steamer had arrived at Izabal.

Imminent as the sailing of the "Vera Paz" had appeared to be when the steam monopoly privilege was applied for, the vessel remained at her moorings in London Dock. The reasons for delay of

13. The expediente on this transaction is in ANG, Congreso, 1836, No. 72, fols. 1-8, unclassified.

her departure are not entirely clear, but a part of the explanation probably lies in the controversy over possession of the territory disputed between Belize and Guatemala. The Company originally planned for the vessel to carry the mails and to engage in the coasting trade at some half-dozen points between Lake Izabal and the port of Belize.[14] This design could not be executed, however, because half of the ports at which the steamer expected to call were situated within the disputed area to which the authorities at Belize were instructed to resist approach by Company agents. Until the question of sovereignty was settled, therefore, the utility, and perhaps even the safety, of the steamer in Central American waters were questionable.

The vessel, however, was not entirely useless in London. Colonists embarking for the Verapaz observed the steamer with "her colours flying as if ready to start as soon as she had completed her cargo" and were cheered to think that she would soon appear in Central American waters. Prospective investors and emigrants may have found in the names "Vera Paz" and "London" inscribed at top and bottom of the circular brass plate set in her wheel reassurance that the remote Guatemalan province was thus intimately linked with the imperial capital on the Thames.[15] Her solid bulk in London Dock may have been the Company's best recruiting device.

Recruiting colonists was in fact the directors' principal concern as the date approached by which they were obligated to establish the first contingent of settlers. They therefore began a publicity campaign intended to attract to their Central American colony a share of the tens of thousands of immigrants who annually abandoned the British Isles to find homes overseas.[16] During the latter part of 1835, or early in 1836, they published *Hints on Colonization,* which argued that "emigration and emigration alone" could cure the economic ills of all classes in England. After examining some of the less agreeable characteristics of the United States, Canada, Van Dieman's Land,

14. *Hints on Colonization, particularly with reference to the Valuable Grant made by the Supreme Government of Central America, to the "Eastern Coast of Central America Commercial and Agricultural Company"* (London, [1835?]), p. 14.

15. Wood, *Adventures,* p. 8; John Lloyd Stephens, *Incidents of Travel in Central America, Chiapas, and Yucatan* (London, 1842), I, 23-24.

16. W. S. Shepperson states that an average of more than 65,000 persons left the British Isles each year during the decade of the 1830's to settle in British America, the United States, or the South Pacific. Of the 75,417 individuals who departed during 1836, only 293 sailed for destinations other than the United States, British North America, and Australia and New Zealand (*British Emigration to North America: Projects and Opinions in the Early Victorian Period* [Oxford, 1957], pp. 19, 258). The Company's concession obviously lay outside the areas of the world most favored by potential settlers.

Australia, and Texas, the pamphlet reached the predictable conclusion that Verapaz was the preferred spot for English colonists to settle.

During 1836 two additional publications appeared, both intended to acquaint investors and emigrants with opportunities in the Verapaz. *Information for Emigrants* offered extracts from the works of such official observers of Guatemala as George Alexander Thompson and J. Haefkens as sources of impartial information on "the climate, the natural products, the nature of the government, and other interesting particulars of the State" in which the Company's colony was situated. The pamphlet was offered for sale at threepence, a price calculated to put it "within the reach of the humblest members of the community, whom it particularly behooves to render themselves acquainted with the new and wonderful field which the colony of Verapaz opens to British industry and enterprise." A brief flier addressed *To Respectable Emigrants of Small or Large Capital* was prepared for prospective colonists. It reproduced the advertisement for colonists currently appearing in provincial newspapers, described the advantages of climate and production offered by the colony in the Verapaz, summarized six of the most favorable concessions made by the Company's charter to immigrants, described the site chosen for the first settlement, and finally, outlined the terms on which land was sold to settlers and the rates of passage to the colony. *Hints on Colonization* and *To Respectable Emigrants* were printed by Robert Sears & Co.; *Information for Immigrants* was issued under the imprint of another publisher.[17]

The nature of the colony the promoters intended to establish in the Verapaz emerges in at least hazy outline from these publications. The enterprise was to be an exploitation colony divided between the Company and private investors, large and small. Forest resources offered opportunities for immediate exploitation by those who had the interest and the capital to go into the business. Mahogany, logwood, Western pine, and other woods were described as abounding in the Company's holdings, but of these the Company reserved all mahogany for itself. The opportunities for developing plantation agriculture on the West Indian style it asserted to be virtually unlimited, for sugar, cotton, coffee, cocoa, cochineal, indigo, tobacco, rice, and tea were said to grow as in their natural habitat. A supply

17. *Hints on Colonization*, 16 pp.; *To Respectable Emigrants of Small or Large Capital* (London, [1836?]), 2 pp.; *Information for Emigrants; or A Description of Guatemala* (London, 1836), 15 pp.

of cheap labor, either Indians from Cajabón and other native towns or free Negroes of good character and industrious habits who would be encouraged to emigrate from Jamaica, was promised to investors possessed of sufficient capital to consider large-scale operations.

Cleared land in the vicinity of the settlement was offered for sale in tracts of forty acres at a graduated price based on priority of application. The first one hundred settlers would pay ten shillings per acre; the second one hundred, fifteen shillings; and subsequent purchasers, a higher price. Uncleared land was offered in any quantity at the rate of five shillings per acre to the first one hundred purchasers, seven shillings sixpence to the second one hundred, and higher prices to all subsequent buyers. Land was to be paid for in three equal installments, the first in cash at the time of purchase, the second not later than the end of the second year after location on the land, and the third not later than the end of the fourth year. Immigrants lacking capital to purchase land were promised opportunity to become proprietors by assurance that they would be employed on Company projects at wages of six shillings per day.

So remote had the origins of their company become in the memories of the directors that they proposed to make their Verapaz settlement the means of accomplishing the moral regeneration of the inhabitants. "Missionaries of every sect will receive full protection," their literature intoned, "and many privileges will be granted them, the benefits which they will confer, by spreading the principles of that religion which creates 'peace on earth and good will to men,' being fully appreciated. . . . The education of the young will be sedulously promoted, and every possible encouragement will be given to societies of a religious and ennobling tendency; the benefit of the whole colony being considered to lie in the improvement and moral elevation of each individual composing it." To encourage the establishment of individuals who "are calculated to add stability and importance" to the colony the Company offered free grants of land to a few select first settlers.[18]

These opportunities for a new life in the Verapaz the Company publicized principally by its formal publications, but it proclaimed the same message by newspaper advertisements to a wider audience from among which it might hope to attract a larger number of actual emigrants. Beginning in November 1835 the London papers announced the imminent departure of the "Vera Paz" and the schooner "Mary Ann and Arabella" with immigrant settlers for the Company's

18. *Hints on Colonization*, pp. 8-10, 14-15; *To Respectable Emigrants*, p. 2.

colony. Virtually identical announcements appeared the following spring in some provincial newspapers. Interested individuals were invited to obtain further details from Mr. George Bishop, 28 Jewry Street, Aldgate, or at St. John's Coffee House, Cornhill, London, or from Mr. Samuel Noller, Debenham, Suffolk.[19]

By this combination of appeals the Company enlisted and dispatched between the middle of May and the first week of August of 1836 three shiploads of emigrants. The schooner "Mary Ann and Arabella," Captain Spence, sailed from London on May 14; the schooner "Lord Charles Spencer," Captain Milward, on June 16; and the brig "Britannia," Captain Whattam, on August 6. All three vessels were property of William Crozier. At each of these sailings, the "Vera Paz" was described as virtually ready to cast off, and the "Lord Charles Spencer" carried the news to Central America that the steamer had actually put to sea with the directors aboard but had been forced to turn back.[20] Although expected momentarily at the colony, its departure from London was postponed from week to week.

The colonists enlisted were a motley crew. Driven either by desperate need to settle a stipulated number of families on Guatemalan soil within an all too short time period or content to deliver a sufficient number of human beings to validate a land title, the Company appears to have accepted anyone who presented himself as a prospective settler.[21] Selection of emigrants for their promise as successful colonists either was abandoned as impracticable or was never seriously intended. In one respect alone did the Company observe its announced policy in enrolling colonists. If moral regeneration

19. "To Respectable Emigrants of Capital," adv., *Morning Herald* (London), No. 16,623 (Nov. 28, 1835), p. [1]; "To Be Dispatched in the First Week in May," adv., *Suffolk Chronicle* (Ipswich), No. 1357 (April 30, 1836), p. [1]; "To Respectable Emigrants of Small or Large Capital," adv., *Suffolk Chronicle* (Ipswich), No. 1359 (May 14, 1836), p. [1].

20. Wood, *Adventures*, pp. 8-9, 19; "Shipping Intelligence," *Morning Herald*, No. 16,765 (May 16, 1836), p. [4], No. 16,793 (June 17, 1836), p. [4], No. 16,837 (Aug. 8, 1836), p. [4]. I am indebted to Mr. John L. Lochhead, Librarian, The Mariners Museum, Newport News, Virginia, for information on the class and ownership of the vessels which he supplied from Lloyds *Register of Shipping* for 1836.

21. James Wood's experience demonstrates the casual attention given by the Company to enlisting emigrants and assisting them to prepare for their transfer to Guatemala. He had originally intended to emigrate to Canada, but at the last moment changed his mind and decided to join seven other young men from Ipswich who were going to Verapaz. At the end of April 1836, he applied for passage, obtained it easily, and sailed in mid-May with the first group of settlers. He implies that the only information on the colony supplied by the Company was a paper—evidently the publication addressed *To Respectable Emigrants of Small or Large Capital*—handed to him in London (*Adventures*, pp. 7-8).

was one of the objectives of the establishment, the undiscriminating acceptance of applicants gave the directors opportunity for spectacular achievement.

In all the Company sent out some 225 colonists aboard the three vessels. By some strange circumstance the lists of settlers regularly promised to the government by the Guatemalan port authorities, if ever compiled, seem not to have survived. Two passengers, however, James Wood from the "Mary Ann and Arabella" and Frederick Crowe from the "Britannia," left some record of the groups of which they were members. These accounts, and occasional mention of names in public documents, permit identification of some of the colonists, but most of them of necessity remain anonymous.

The "Mary Ann and Arabella" carried sixty-odd emigrants, the majority of whom came from the eastern part of County Suffolk. They varied in age from one and one-half years to forty. Most of them were a "respectable sort of people, following different trades, and carrying out with them a little property." Among the group were eight "lads from Ipswich," including Wood, James Canham, Joseph Chiverton, and Stephen Watts; John Dyer, his wife, and eight small children; Mr. Gough, a bricklayer, his wife, and two children; Mrs. Poppleton, a widow, and her two sons; and Dr. W. King. They left England in good spirits, sanguine of the prospects for success of their venture. After a troubled voyage of some seven weeks the ship anchored off the bar of the Río Dulce on July 3, 1836.[22] It was the misfortune of the emigrants from temperate Europe to arrive on the Guatemalan coast in tropical midsummer, at the height of the rainy season.

The "Lord Charles Spencer" arrived at the bar on August 10 almost eight weeks out of London. She brought sixty-six passengers bound for the colony.[23]

The "Britannia" transported some ninety-odd prospective residents for the new settlement. Except for Crowe, the only members of the group who can be identified are those heads of families, perhaps with some admixture of passengers from earlier vessels, whose names appeared on an 1838 list of colonists treated by a physician in Belize.

22. Wood, *Adventures,* pp. 9-10, 21, 29, 33, 54; "Emigration," *Suffolk Chronicle* (Ipswich), No. 1359 (May 14, 1836), pp. [2-3]. Wood gave the number of passengers as 68, but if his count was no more accurate than were the dates and the days of the week he assigns to events, the figure cannot be accepted as precise. The Alcalde of Izabal reported 63 colonists (Valentín Ampudia to Minister General, July 9, 1836, *Semanario de Guatemala,* No. 11 [July 16, 1836], p. 44).

23. Ampudia to Minister General, Aug. 16, 1836, *Semanario de Guatemala,* No. 18 (Sept. 1, 1836), pp. 75-76.

The families so recorded (with the number of individuals reported in each) were: Bulger (3), Carrol (1), Connor (3), Cooker (1), Fitzgerald (3), Joiner (5), Lynch (1), Lynch (4), Lyons (3), McManus [or MacMinnis] (5), Sweeney (3), and Sweeney (4). Two unnamed Dutch families were also noted on the list.[24]

If Crowe's estimate of their character is to be accepted, his companions were capable of contributing little to the colony beyond an increase in the population. Even allowing for puritanical standards he may have applied in consequence of a subsequent religious experience, the passengers he describes were essentially misfits. Among the lot he found "probably not one who was really adapted for the enterprise, and small indeed was the aggregate amount of respectability which the entire band conferred upon it. There was, however as rich a variety of race, language, and occupation as could well be collected within the same limits. Above a score were Israelites, and with the exception of an equal number of Metropolitan tailors, this was by far the largest number which could be classed together by any tie less common than that of humanity. Among the rest there were some Irish labourers and their wives, a German organ grinder with a musical family, including some girls who were dexterous players on the tambourine, and several inexperienced youths, who preferred adventures afar off to honest industry at home." From "these excrescences of a dense and corrupt population (the very elements which society already constituted naturally threw off)," Crowe remarked, the Company proposed "to constitute a new society, and to lay the foundations of a prosperous state." In addition to this human cargo, the "Britannia" was reputed to carry stores sufficient to provision the settlement for several months.[25]

The voyage of the "Britannia" was a nightmare. Sanitary precautions had been neglected, and the passengers, who were "huddled together in the narrow hold and steerage" of the ship, suffered the consequences. Smallpox broke out immediately and for want of proper care spread rapidly. At one time there were seventeen cases aboard, but by some miracle only three deaths resulted. Water be-

24. Manuel Arias to Ampudia, Oct. 23, 1836, reported 93 passengers, but Ampudia to Minister General, Oct. 24, 1836, put the figure at 91 (both in ANG, leg. 1102, exp. 24429). Frederick Crowe (*The Gospel in Central America* [London, 1850], p. 517), says only that nearly one hundred colonists embarked, but the passengers' petition at Belize rounds the number off at 90 (Memorial of "Britannia" passengers, Nov. 8, 1836, CO 123/48, n.f.). The family names are given in Dr. Tuthill's list of the sick he attended (Minutes of a Public Meeting Held at Belize, March 5, 1838, CO 123/52, n.f.).

25. Crowe, *Gospel*, pp. 517, 519.

came scarce before the vessel cleared the English channel, and what remained soon putrefied in the uncared-for casks. Nevertheless, the captain refused to yield to the passengers' demand, when Madeira was in sight, that he put in to the island to take on fresh water. Filth and vermin increased as the vessel moved into warmer latitudes, until even the "hardiest mariners declined to sleep below." The captain was drunk during much of the voyage, and management of the vessel fell to the mate, who did very well under heavy disadvantages but was unable to compensate for his superior's incapacity. Discipline collapsed, and there were brawls and fights, and "open immorality practised in the cabin." One wretched young girl thought to commit suicide but changed her mind just before she dropped overboard. The only pleasant incident of the voyage appears to have been the celebration by the Jewish passengers of the Feast of the Trumpets in the captain's cabin. After ten miserable weeks at sea the "Britannia" made the mouth of the Río Dulce on October 21.[26]

When the first immigrant ship arrived off Livingston, Fletcher had barely completed minimum preparations to receive the colonists. By virtue of several postponements of the intended departure date of the vessel he had been allowed some ten months in Guatemala, during which he was expected to create a suitable habitation for Europeans in the virgin wilderness of the Verapaz. Had the directors possessed the slightest knowledge of the environment in which they proposed to establish a colony, they might have realized the proportions of the miracle they demanded.

Fletcher landed in Belize August 18, 1835. During the last week of that month he took advantage of Bennett's offer to forward a letter to Chatfield accompanied by an introduction provided by Thomas Gould. He announced his purpose, because of the brief time allowed for performance of his duties, to forego a visit to the capital and an opportunity to see Chatfield in person in order to proceed immediately to the Verapaz. He bespoke the Consul's protection, however, should it prove necessary and his good offices with the Guatemalan authorities to assist him in carrying out the assignment entrusted to him.[27]

26. *Ibid.,* pp. 517-18.
27. Fletcher to Chatfield, Aug. 26, 1835, n.f. Cockburn had previously informed Chatfield of Fletcher's arrival. On August 19 he wrote (FO 252/8, n.f.): "A Brig arrived yesterday from Barbados in which a Mr. Fletcher came a passenger. Report says he is the superintendent for the New Central American Land Company—So far I had written when in came Mr. Bennett and the identical Mr. Fletcher. He seems a gentleman-like, intelligent, and moderate person. He left England about the first of June—from whence he proceeded to Trinidad as I understand him,

Fletcher's instructions required him to find a suitable location for a first settlement on the Polochic River as far upstream as the Company steamer could safely navigate. The probability that the impressions of the first settlers communicated to friends and relatives at home would vitally affect the success of the colony required that the site be hospitable to its new inhabitants as well as productive under their tutelage. This consideration ruled out any possibility of establishing the settlement in a freshly made forest clearing. Felling the trees would be an impossible task during the rainy season, even if time and labor were available to achieve it, and if successfully accomplished the constricting forest surrounding such a location and the clutter of decaying vegetation swarming with insects would be conducive neither to good health nor to good spirits. Fletcher was therefore directed to seek a natural clearing at a sufficient elevation to ensure dryness, a pleasant temperature, and relative freedom from mosquitoes and other troublesome insects. When he found these conditions associated with a good water supply and land suitable for growing provisions and for cultivating plantation crops, he was to begin constructing there the temporary habitations for the new arrivals.

Fletcher's reconnaissance along the lower Polochic convinced him that the directors described conditions that could not be found in the region. His search confirmed Chatfield's observation after an

---

there to settle some private affairs. From Trinidad he made his way to Barbados and from the latter place has come on to Belize. It seems the appointment of superintendent was *offered* to him thro one of the Directors. I should think him well qualified for the office. He is a Native of the East Indies and has been in the Service of some [of] the South American Republics. He proceeds from hence under the guidance, advice, and direction of Bennett, to whom he seems consigned by the Company, to Verapaz and intends making his immediate preparations on the Polychike River for the reception of about 50 families which he expects out in a few weeks. He brings a Letter for you, I suppose from Gould, from whom he brings me one, soliciting my kind offices and *implying* that the Government at home are aware of the views and intentions of the Company and that Lord Glenelg has entered into the subject of the Boundary question with Captain Gould. Of course my observations to Mr. Fletcher were that as far as he was concerned I should be happy to show him any kindness or attention in my power but that I must be distinctly understood as knowing nothing officially about the Company. I shewed him the Boundary which we claim to the Sarstoon and to the Westward and further informed him that I considered myself as instructed by my Government to prevent any encroachment thereon. I stated this in the hearing of my *Secretary* (Dickinson) and *Mr. Bennett* to prevent the possibility of future mistake. I do not envy him his next six Months employment. If he succeeds it will be a miracle—but I wish he may for I anticipate benefit rather than evil to this Settlement from a successful result to the views of the Company. They are getting out a Steam Boat."

earlier expedition that good sites for a settlement were exceedingly rare, "the mountainous and rugged character of the interior not offering a great choice of spots, especially to those who must endeavor to combine proximity of a Town with a communication to the coast by water navigation, and a salubrious climate." Fletcher found only one location, a plot on which the forest had been recently felled, that approximated the conditions laid down by the directors. Unfortunately for the Company's project, however, the property was already in the possession of an influential cleric, C. J. Chacón, on the basis of a grant made to him by the local authorities pursuant to his request of August 18, 1834. To resolve this difficulty Fletcher first went to Salamá to consult with Plácido Flores, the *jefe político* of the department, and then, although reluctant to raise a delicate issue in his first official communication, he appealed to the government of Guatemala. On October 4 he wrote from Bennett's hacienda, San Jerónimo, to the Minister of Foreign Affairs to request that Gálvez confirm the title to the Company. He was relieved to have the prompt response that the archives of the government recorded no grant of the land in question and that certainly it could not have been legally alienated subsequent to the colonization agreement. The authorities gave him possession of the site, subject to his reimbursement of Chacón for the cost of the clearing.[28]

By the same mail that brought him the reply from the government, Fletcher received two letters from Chatfield. One was an earlier communication redirected to him from Izabal, and the other was written with knowledge of the request the agent had just made of the Guatemalan government. Both were disturbing, for the Consul disapproved of the area in which Fletcher proposed to situate the colonists, and he hinted that trouble might result from a clash between the Company's interests and those of a powerful individual. Fletcher's reply was appreciative but determined. "I feel extremely obliged to you," he wrote, "for the Interest you evince in the success of our Settlem^t. also for the good advice contained in your last Letter, of which, under other circumstances I might have availed myself, but in the present moment from various causes too tedious to trouble you with in this letter, I am sorry it is out of my power to do so." Mindful of the work he had to accomplish in limited time, Fletcher elected to disregard Chatfield's advice that he turn south to Guate-

28. Fletcher to Foreign Minister of Guatemala, Oct. 4, 1835, ANG, leg. 3616, exp. 84468; Fletcher to Chatfield, Oct. 11, 1835, FO 252/6, n.f.; *To Respectable Emigrants*, p. 2.

mala City to consult with informed individuals on the best sites for the settlement of Europeans in the Verapaz and chose instead to return north to the Polochic.[29]

The site on which Fletcher now established his family and began his preparations consisted of some 14,000 acres of land situated near the foot of a mountain ridge on the left bank of the Cajabón River a short distance above its confluence with the Polochic. The town, planned as the hub of an extensive agricultural settlement, was to be located in the clearing some two miles from the river on the brow of one of the low hills that fell away from the range behind. Fletcher estimated it to be some forty-five miles southeast of the large Indian town of Cajabón situated farther upstream and ten miles northeast of the river port of Telemán on the Polochic. By some vagary of imagination, perhaps because he believed the steamer could reach the river landing, he called the isolated, landlocked spot New Liverpool.[30]

Fletcher and Chatfield disagreed fundamentally on the merits of the site. They differed in their views on the probability that the steamer could cross the bar at the mouth of the Polochic to ascend the river, but the agent admitted that the Consul correctly equated location of the settlement on a pine ridge with acceptance of poor soil. He argued, however, that there was an abundance of excellent land for cultivation in the immediate vicinity. Basically, the two men disagreed on the appropriateness of the locality as an environment for European constitutions and for the achievement of the Company's objectives. Chatfield argued that European agriculturalists would be unable to endure the climate and that the situation was too exposed to the effects of internal turmoil. He suggested as a far more suitable spot in both respects the locality of San Luis far to the north in the Petén and close to the southernmost outposts of Belize. Fletcher could retort only that the instructions under which he labored allowed him no such geographical latitude of choice.[31]

The disagreement over the selection of a site for the settlement

29. Chatfield to Fletcher, Sept. 21, 1835, and Oct. 8, 1835, FO 252/9, n.f.; Fletcher to Chatfield, Oct. 11, 1835, n.f.

30. *Brief Statement*, p. 21; *Brief Statement, Supported by Original Documents, of the Important Grants Conceded to the Eastern Coast of Central America Commercial & Agricultural Company by the State of Guatemala* (2nd ed.; London, 1840), p. 133; Colonel Remy de Puydt, head of Belgian Exploratory Commission, to Comte de Hompesch, president of the Belgian Colonization Company, Feb. 5, 1842, AMAE, 2027, fol. 2.

31. Chatfield to Fletcher, Sept. 21, 1835, n.f. and Oct. 8, 1835, n.f.; Fletcher to Chatfield, Oct. 11, 1835, n.f.; Chatfield to Gálvez, July 22, 1836, FO 252/13, n.f.

revealed with sudden clarity the discrepancy between the views held by Chatfield and by the directors on the proper nature of the incipient colony. The Consul had not abandoned his conception of an establishment essentially tributary to Belize and contributing to the growth of the existing center of British influence; the directors thought in terms of a competitor to the British Settlement, which they hoped would quickly supplant its older rival.

Disregarding Chatfield's objections, Fletcher began within the hilltop clearing to prepare a habitation for the expected colonists. By arrangement with Plácido Flores in Salamá, he obtained Indian laborers from the neighboring towns to form his work force. Under his direction the Indians planted a field of corn, began to construct temporary dwellings for the settlers, and perhaps enlarged the clearing.[32] He was still engaged in these tasks when the first immigrants arrived. However distressing to the colonists his absence might be, he could not interrupt his work at New Liverpool to go down to the coast. He did not meet the ship when it anchored at the mouth of the Río Dulce.

Some premonition of the conditions under which they would live during the ensuing months may have come to the immigrants on the "Mary Ann and Arabella" as they stood off Livingston. They had expected Fletcher to meet them, but when he did not appear the captain left the colonists aboard the vessel and went in search of him. During the interim the passengers subsisted on pineapples, plantains, and bananas, for which they bartered with Carib canoemen who visited the ship.[33] Perhaps the novelty of the primitive environment and the exotic fruits obscured the portent of the experience, but there was more and worse to come.

Within a week or so the captain returned with a small coasting schooner, the "Albion" owned by Marshal Bennett, obtained through the good offices of Valentín Ampudia, a merchant and the alcalde of Izabal. The shallow-draft vessel crossed the bar to take off the colonists, but because it could not accommodate the total number of passengers only the younger people and their baggage were disembarked. They proceeded first to Izabal where the captain arranged for pirogues to take them aboard at the mouth of the Polochic for the journey upstream. Then the captain returned to his vessel to prepare the remaining passengers for disembarkation, and the schooner sailed for the rendezvous with the canoemen at the bar of the

32. Wood, *Adventures*, pp. 13, 23; Fletcher to Chatfield, Oct. 11, 1835, n.f.
33. Wood, *Adventures*, p. 10.

Polochic. After spending the night on the schooner the colonists transferred to the dugouts and began the tedious journey against the current of the river. Insects annoyed the passengers night and day, and the swamps and marshy banks of the stream made it impossible for them to leave their cramped quarters in the boats even to sleep. After four or five miserable days of travel, they reached the landing of the settlement, and a few days later the second contingent joined them.[34]

If, as the directors had supposed, the success of the colony depended upon the first impression of the settlers, the enterprise was doomed. A single look convinced the new arrivals they had been deceived and swindled. At the river landing they found only a native-style shed, built to protect their baggage until it could be carried to the settlement, and the Indian architects of the work standing along the bank of the stream "almost naked, wearing only a piece of coarse cotton cloth round their middle." By following the two-mile track through the forest they reached a clearing some half a mile long by half as broad in which the town was situated. There they found Fletcher.[35]

For all of the agent's care to secure an open spot for the settlement, New Liverpool appeared to the immigrants to be situated in "a wild forest, inhabited by all sorts of wild beasts, and surrounded by rocky mountains higher than the clouds." The clearing was a confusion of standing stumps and felled trees from which the "brushwood was slightly burnt off." A few huts had been constructed, but stumps still encumbered the earth floors of the structures so that the first task of the tenants was to clear the obstructions from their dwellings. Some corn growing on the site gave hope of a limited future harvest but no promise of a sustained supply of provisions. If any of the colonists had purchased land at the Company's offices in London, they must have been dismayed to calculate how few certificates entitling the bearer to forty acres of cleared land could be honored from that tiny rectangle enclosed by forest.

The preparations for the settlers were probably as thorough as could have been expected of Fletcher, granted the time and resources at his command. To arrivals fresh from London, however, the encompassing wilderness was terrifying, and the facilities prepared for them appeared primitive beyond belief. The site bore no resemblance

34. *Ibid.*, pp. 10-13; Ampudia to Minister General, July 9, 1836, *Semanario de Guatemala*, No. 11 (July 16, 1836), p. 44.
35. This and the following ten paragraphs are based on Wood, *Adventures*, pp. 12-26.

to the earthly paradise described in the Company's promotional propaganda, and there was nothing in the environment that their imaginations could conjure into a new Liverpool and certainly nothing to suggest an improvement on County Suffolk. The total lack of any contact with the outside world after the canoemen returned to Izabal left them marooned in a vast, unbroken solitude. In these circumstances the prompt arrival of the steamer became as much a psychological imperative as it was a material necessity.

Hard on the heels of disillusionment came suffering. Swarms of insect pests made day and night alternating tortures. The bites of a tiny fly opened into "great holes in our legs, and causing them to swell." Another fly deposited an egg beneath the skin that developed into a worm the size of the end of a little finger. *Niguas* embedded themselves in feet, and the resulting sores virtually crippled the victims. Scorpions lurked in clothing, and cockroaches found their way into trunks to destroy stored garments. Ants covered the ground, invaded houses, and sometimes swarmed on beds. Because it was the rainy season snakes left their normal habitat and took refuge in the thatch of the houses. From these hiding places coral snakes, barber poles, and a black snake, the bite of which was reputed to bring instant death, sometimes fell at night upon the beds beneath and terrified the occupants into frantic torchlight searches for the lethal intruders. Endemic fevers, of which malaria appears to have been the most common, struck the Europeans and reduced them to shaking debility. The women and children suffered most, but after a short time only a handful of able-bodied men could be mustered to do the necessary work.

In the hope of escaping from their misery the colonists entreated Fletcher to move the settlement to another site. Early in August he yielded to the point of leading an expedition in search of a more favorable location. A party consisting of the interpreter, five Indians, and half of the ten colonists who began the climb reached the summit of the neighboring mountains, but nowhere along the ridge could they find a suitable location for the settlement. With only the memory of restful sleep in the deliciously cool, insect-free mountain air, they were forced to return dispirited to New Liverpool. Nevertheless, they continued to importune Fletcher to establish them in a better place, but he insisted that he could do nothing more until the steamer arrived. He was able, however, with a work force of thirty Cajabón Indians who responded to his request for laborers, to clear some land at the foot of the mountain.

Hope in the colony now centered on the appearance of the "Vera Paz." The original stock of provisions brought from Europe was nearly exhausted, and until the steamer arrived with new supplies the colony had to go on short rations. When the vessel still did not appear, and a mission to Telemán to obtain a cow for slaughtering was unsuccessful, food became so scarce that the settlers had to subsist on such game as the physically fit could kill. The supply was never large, for the hunters were few and the rainy season impeded their efforts, but they sometimes brought in a wild turkey, partridge, wild pig, or monkey. On one occasion at least they killed a lap, an animal spotted like a leopard but only about half its size, and pronounced its meat superior to fowl. When the Indians of Cajabón brought corn and made tortillas for them, the settlers believed that they had been saved from starvation. Thereafter they lived on game and Indian corn.

During this crisis in morale at the settlement, Marshal Bennett appeared in the craftily devised role of savior. He proposed that the colonists accept employment at his hacienda of San Jerónimo, which he described as situated in fine, cool country near Salamá where provisions of all kinds were plentiful and cheap. He offered transport to the hacienda, wages of a quarter of a dollar a day, land, and a cow to all agriculturalists or artisans who would join him. Two or three families yielded to his inducements to escape from the "horrid place," but the majority, feeling "already deceived" and "in a certain manner sold to Marshal Bennet," determined to reject the offer and to wait to "see if the steamer would come out."

In mid-September two sailors for the "Lord Charles Spencer" arrived at New Liverpool in search of the Company agent bearing news that the second group of colonists had long been standing off the mouth of the Río Dulce. Fletcher returned with them to conduct the new arrivals to the settlement, but Wood persuaded the sailors to carry a warning letter to the passengers describing conditions at the colony. The deterrent effect of this information the sailors may well have enhanced by their own account of a huge snake that, from an overhanging branch, obstructed their passage along the track between the settlement and landing until a shotgun blast stretched its twenty-foot length harmlessly on the ground. Circumstantial evidence suggests also that Marshal Bennett or his agents may have tampered with the immigrants. At any rate, when Fletcher appeared at the ship, they refused to accompany him to New Liverpool and demanded instead to be established at Santa Cruz on the northern shore of Lake Izabal. Whether or not Fletcher and the colonists were aware of the significance of the choice, the settlers disembarked at Santa Cruz became residents of the territory ceded to Bennett and Meany. Thus, both theoretically and actually they were virtually lost to the Company.

Fletcher regarded Santa Cruz, nevertheless, as the Company's "lower settlement" and did his best to provide for its needs. The same lack of communications that prevented the settlers from abandoning New Liverpool, however, isolated the two settlements from each other and made mutual assistance virtually impossible. Bennett was not similarly handicapped. Santa Cruz lay within the area of his normal operations, and the settlers there were in consequence exposed to his blandishments. He apparently took some pains to foster a patronal relationship which he dramatized by supplying the settlers with corn when they had no other food. The purpose of his solicitude became evident a short while later when he attempted to recruit the residents, as he had earlier those of New Liverpool, as laborers for his hacienda of San Jerónimo. Again, a few individuals were enticed away, but the majority decided that "they would rather die where they were, than to go up the country to be made slaves." After this rebuff, Bennett discontinued his benefactions, and the settlers began to suffer for lack of food. Many were stricken with fever, and the members of the group were reported to be "dying off very rapidly."

Fletcher, meanwhile, returned to New Liverpool with two recruits from among the last arrivals. He brought welcome news that deprivation would shortly end, for the steamer would arrive within a few days. But again the expectation was disappointed, and again the agent sent to Telemán, this time with success, to buy animals for slaughter. Fletcher's troubles were compounded by the arrival of a resident of Santa Cruz bearing the news that the lower settlement was in desperate condition. The agent therefore arranged an emergency trip to Izabal to secure provisions for the colonists, but he could obtain only some Indian corn. Gough decided to seize the opportunity afforded by the arrival of the dugout to escape. He contracted with the canoeman to deliver him and his family to the coast, and they quit the colony.

In October Fletcher determined to unite the two settlements by a temporary road. Using a work force of fifty Indians he obtained from Cajabón and Chamiquín and augmented by the interpreter and five able-bodied men of the colony, he began clearing a track in the direction of Santa Cruz. The work was interrupted after four or five days when the party returned to the settlement to harvest the corn planted before the colonists arrived. Thereafter, until the supply was exhausted, this corn, supplemented by game, provided the sustenance of the colony. The work crew then returned to cutting the road. After the trace had been cut over a mountain, across a swampy area, and over another mountain, provisions ran out. The party then returned to the settlement, and the Indians scattered to their homes. Shortly thereafter, the captain of the "Britannia" appeared in search of Fletcher.

When the third immigrant ship arrived at the bar of the Río Dulce on October 21, the passengers found neither the representative of the Company nor a vessel of shallow draft to take them off. The captain therefore left the colonists aboard while he went first to Izabal and then to New Liverpool to find Fletcher. Somewhere along the route, he must have met the Gough family bound for the coast. Had each known the role the other was soon to play in his own life, the encounter could scarcely have been a casual one. During the journey one of the Gough children died, and the surviving members of the family arrived at the bar half-starved, half-clad, their bodies emaciated and covered with insect bites and sores. These apparitions were taken aboard the "Britannia" where they related to a highly excited audience their catalog of misery and suffering. This dramatic exposé corroborated to the indignation of the immigrants the reports of misery at New Liverpool brought by Marshal Bennett, who had earlier come aboard to make his oft-rehearsed offer of inducements to desert the Company and to enter his own employ. It particularly aroused the wrath of a violent and voluble Irishwoman, identified as Mrs. MacMinnis, who had achieved a position of some influence among the passengers by her commanding presence and by effective use during shipboard commotions of a nimble and profane tongue. Briefly she bewailed her folly in leaving Europe, but having learned of the proximity of Belize from the pilot of a mahogany vessel who offered to direct the immigrants there, she resumed her more familiar role of leadership to perpetrate a mutiny.[36]

The Irish virago persuaded the settlers to refuse disembarkation on territory belonging to the Company and to demand that they be landed instead at the British Settlement. After seizing the firearms in the cabin, the conspirators awaited the return of the captain and

36. Wood, *Adventures,* p. 26; Crowe, *Gospel,* pp. 518-19; Major John Anderson to Colonial Office, No. 22, Nov. 15, 1836, CO 123/48, n.f.

the Company agent to carry out their plan. When these unsuspecting individuals finally appeared, they were allowed to come aboard and to go down to the cabin where they were confined as prisoners of the aroused passengers. The captain insisted that the colonists disembark because they had already consumed all the provisions the vessel carried. Fletcher suggested that they go ashore to await the arrival of the steamer. The passengers demanded that the unhappy officials give orders to weigh anchor and to set sail for Belize. The captain refused on grounds that the provisions were exhausted; Fletcher, on the basis that he had no authority on shipboard.

A violent altercation ensued between captors and prisoners during which the redoubtable Mrs. MacMinnis apparently demonstrated complete mastery of a vocabulary proverbially ascribed only to sailors. When the determined passengers declared their intent to navigate the vessel themselves, Fletcher counseled the captain to feign acquiescence to their demand while he went ashore to arrange with the Guatemalan officials at Livingston to overhaul the departing ship and remove the colonists by force. In execution of this strategem, Fletcher went on deck to ask that he be allowed to disembark if the vessel were got under way for Belize. The rebels agreed to this arrangement, and the captain gave the order to weigh anchor and make sail. When Fletcher asked to be put over the side, however, the passengers, suspecting him of some treacherous design, reversed themselves and forced him to accompany them to Belize. So the colonists had their way, and triumphantly, but perhaps without cognizance of their wry musical pun, they played "Rule Britannia" as the prow of the vessel held steadily for the Settlement.[37]

On the evening of November 8 the ship made Belize. Acting Superintendent Major John Anderson had been forewarned by both Bennett and the former French consul, who was en route from Guatemala to Europe, that the "Britannia" lay off the Río Dulce and that the aroused passengers intended to force the captain to take them to Belize. Anderson had therefore consulted the Magistrates on the course to follow should the immigrants succeed in their design. That body expressed hope that admission could be denied the colonists in order to avert exposing the Settlement to persons of bad character and to unfortunates who were likely to become public charges. The Superintendent shared these misgivings, but he found no justifiable grounds on which to deny British subjects the right to land in a British settlement. He therefore gave orders that any arriving ship

37. Crowe, *Gospel*, p. 519; Wood, *Adventures*, pp. 26-27.

carrying a large number of passengers be required to anchor in the quarantine ground and that the captain alone be permitted to land.[38]

When these orders were executed on the arrival of the "Britannia," some of the passengers apparently misinterpreted the proceedings to mean that they were being placed under arrest as mutineers.[39] That night they prepared a memorial stating their grievances and praying that they be taken under the Superintendent's protection. Fletcher also addressed Anderson to request that he be restored to his rightful liberty. He complained that he had been compelled by force to suffer the "villainous insults of a set of low and desperate adventurers" and the "noxious vermin" and "execrably bad" water aboard the vessel, and he requested that he be "allowed to lay before your Excellency my complaint for the acts of daring outrage committed on me and the vessel."

On the morning of November 9 Anderson convened the Magistrates to consider with him the petitions he had received and to hear the testimony of the principals in the controversy. He ordered Fletcher released immediately from all restraint and asked him, the captain of the "Britannia," and a deputation of three of the passengers (which seems to have included Mr. Gough) to appear before the assembled officials. Fletcher frankly confessed that he was without resources to honor the commitments made to the immigrants by Company officials in London. There was no cleared or cultivated land to be delivered to them, no housing beyond some thirty rude huts, no food other than Indian corn and an occasional bullock for slaughtering, and a complete lack of such amenities as salt meat, flour, coffee, and sugar. There were no tools for cultivation other than hatchets and machetes and no possibility of paying wages higher than two reales (about a shilling a day instead of the promised six) from which the cost of food would be deducted and the balance applied against any outstanding obligations to the Company. Moreover, he had found the previous immigrants unsuited to sustained labor in the climate in which the colony was situated. The present group added to that inherent deficiency a temper and disposition that would put his already miserable life in actual danger. Anderson counselled that the disputants seek some reasonable accommodation of their differences. He reproved the passengers for the violence of their actions against Fletcher and informed them that they were unlikely to be allowed

---

38. Except as otherwise noted this and the following five paragraphs are based on Anderson to Colonial Office, Nov. 15, 1836, and enclosures.

39. Wood, *Adventures*, pp. 27-28.

to disembark at Belize. Neither government nor Settlement funds would be disbursed to help them, and the inhabitants were opposed to their remaining. Under these circumstances, he suggested that the parties try during the day to reach an amicable agreement under which they could proceed with the project for which they had been sent out.

The Superintendent was surprised when he encountered Fletcher during a morning ride the following day to discover that the agent had made no effort, and intended to make none, to reach an accommodation acceptable to the immigrants between the promises of the Company and his available resources. Rather, he insisted that the conduct of the settlers had been equivalent to piracy and that the Superintendent should conduct them by force to their intended destination. Anderson pointed out that the piracy charge would have to be formally brought and heard in a competent court in Jamaica and would require the presence of Fletcher himself, the accused passengers, and the ship. The idea of the use of force he rejected out of hand on grounds that the enterprise was a private commercial venture and that the use of British troops on foreign territory might easily be interpreted as aggression. Should the colonists be allowed to land in Belize, Anderson pointed out, and should Fletcher have any basis for an action against them that lay within the competence of any court within the Settlement, he might bring formal charges against them. Under such circumstances, however, he should consider that the costs might be great and that the penury of the immigrants would inevitably throw the financial burden on him. At this disquisition on the intricacies of British legal procedure, Fletcher exhibited such unseemly irritation that the Superintendent rode away from him. Apparently convinced that he could never find justice within Anderson's jurisdiction, Fletcher left the Settlement the following day.

After the agent's departure, Anderson allowed the colonists to disembark. His decision was apparently reached in part because Fletcher had disdainfully refused even to talk with the immigrants who had so ill-used him. More important, however, was his impression that Fletcher had some arrangement with Bennett to strand the unfortunate colonists somewhere in the region of Lake Izabal where the mahogany cutter could enlist them on his own terms to settle on the Santa Cruz site within his concession.

If the immigrants believed that their change of destination had enabled them to escape completely the perils and hardships they feared at New Liverpool, the illusion could only briefly have been maintained. They found themselves, it is true, in a long-established community that afforded some amenities not to be found in a raw clearing, but Belize itself was scarcely more than a tropical outpost squeezed between the forest and the sea. Tropical diseases were endemic to the Settlement, and only a few months before the "Britannia" appeared the town and its dependent mahogany works had been swept by cholera. Anderson insisted that the epidemic was over before the immigrants arrived, but it is probable that some cases remained. Moreover, the colonists themselves may have brought ashore the contagion of smallpox from the epidemic aboard the vessel. At Belize, in short, they suffered much of the physical discomfort and many of the hazards to life that might have been expected in the wilderness settlement they had disdained.

Fletcher, meanwhile, made his way back to New Liverpool. He was a long time in transit, perhaps because he paused en route to make the "protests and affidavits on the subject [of the 'Britannia' affair], possibly for the purpose of making matters appear in a false and erroneous light," against which Anderson thought it expedient to warn his superiors. From Fletcher's reports, or from another source, the government of Guatemala was able in mid-November to inform the federal government of the unfortunate affair that had deprived the state of nearly one hundred immigrant colonists.[40]

It was mid-December when the agent again appeared on the Cajabón. He found the colonists desperate. Illness was widespread at both settlements, and the residents at Santa Cruz were dying in numbers, although by some miracle those at New Liverpool escaped. Fletcher resumed work on the road to the lower settlement, but after cutting only a few miles the work gang returned to New Liverpool. Food was scarce, the steamer did not come, and no more that $2,000 remained in the agent's fund for local purchases. Even that small sum appeared to be useless, for when he tried to buy provisions at Belize, he was balked by the embargo placed by the government of Guatemala on imports from the Settlement as a quarantine measure against the spread of cholera. The New Liverpool settlers were again saved from starvation by slaughtering a young bullock obtained from Telemán. In their desperation the residents tried "all methods we could devise to get out of the place," but when Fletcher promised that if the steamer did not arrive within a month he would try to find

40. Anderson to Colonial Office, Nov. 15, 1836, n.f.; Alvarez to Gálvez, Nov. 25, 1836, ANG, leg. 165, exp. 3439, fol. 12.

some way to get them out, they agreed to spend Christmas there. It must have been a cheerless holiday.

Shortly after the beginning of the new year the Indian laborers from Cajabón reappeared. Fletcher intended to resume work on the road to Santa Cruz, but it was by then a completely futile undertaking. Only three of the Europeans were able to work, and the colonists of both settlements thought only of escape. Gradually, as means could be devised, they abandoned the disintegrating communities. By the summer of 1837 the settlements were deserted.[41]

Many of the difficulties of the settlement had their origin in the misconceptions held by both the London sponsors and the individual colonists about the territory they were to occupy. Forced in some measure to remedy their absolute ignorance of the area they had been granted, the directors selected and published from the accounts of recent European observers in Guatemala passages that described the country in most attractive terms. It is not unlikely that in the process they came to believe that these selections stated the whole truth. Otherwise it seems improbable that any of the directors would have considered hazarding his life to make even a voyage of inspection to the Company's holdings.

Nevertheless, the directors had access to more accurate information than they either divulged or acted upon. Gould had at least passed through the area in which the settlements were subsequently located, and Galindo's arrival in London at a crucial stage in the Company's preparations put them in direct contact with the ranking authority on their region. Moreover, Chatfield had specifically recommended to Gould, in the interest of realistic planning, that the Company make use of Galindo, "for he has travelled much in the part of the Country named in your Contract, and possesses a greater local knowledge of it, than any other Person in the Republick whose information can be deemed of any value."[42] Whether because of negligence in discovering what they might easily have learned or because they deliberately misrepresented to colonists the nature of the country within their grant, the directors were to some degree guilty of enlisting emigrant hostages for delivery to Guatemala in return for validation of their title to the land.

Whatever the reason for their misinformation, the colonists had an entirely erroneous conception of the country to which they were

41. Wood, *Adventures*, pp. 28-29, 33; William Hall to Chatfield, Aug. 4, 1837, FO 252/18, n.f.; *Brief Statement*, 1840, p. 60.
42. Chatfield to Gould, Sept. 30, 1834, n.f.

going. Wood relates a simple incident that makes this fact abundant-
ly clear. While the immigrants on the "Mary Ann and Arabella"
waited for the captain to return with Fletcher, some of them went
ashore at Livingston and after walking "a mile or two into the
Forest" came upon a patch of sugar cane. Recalling the assertion in
the Company literature that the plant grew wild in Guatemala, they
helped themselves, only to discover that they had appropriated private
property. When the owner of the field understood the situation, however, he gave them some canes and a sample of white rum. The same
imprecise knowledge of the environment is manifest in Wood's indiscriminate use of the term "Spaniard" to identify any native resident of Guatemala other than an Indian and his wondering comment
that the site of New Liverpool "was very subject to storms; indeed
the thunder and lightning were most dreadful, so that the ground
would sometimes shake beneath our feet; and there was nine months'
rain during the year." The revulsion that settlers accustomed to the
precisely manicured countryside in England felt for the forest and
its inhabitants suggests also that the colonists were not properly informed of the wild state of the country they were expected to tame
and cultivate. One of the purposes for which Wood wrote his *Adventures* was to inform prospective immigrants of the conditions of
life they could expect to encounter in several possible areas of settlement in the New World.[43]

In the dispersion of the settlers both Fletcher and Bennett played
significant but somewhat enigmatic roles. Some circumstantial evidence existed for Major Anderson's suspicion that Fletcher had an
understanding with Bennett. The mahogany cutter had been the
agent's mentor in Belize, had forwarded his mail, had provided him
with living quarters at San Jerónimo when he went to Salamá, had
been appointed an honorary director of the Company in October
1835,[44] and had relayed to the Guatemalan government Company
communications relating to arrival of settlers. The puzzling procedure
of settling Company immigrants on Bennett's land at Santa Cruz and
Bennett's attempts to lure away each successive group of Company
colonists also suggest some strange relationship.

Fletcher approved the transfer of colonists from the Company
project to Bennett's employ, and on some occasions even fostered such
moves. He reported to his superiors, however, that the arrangement
allowed him to recall the settlers at any time that the status of the

43. *Adventures,* "Introduction," pp. 10-11, 13.
44. Rest Fenner to Carlos Salazar, Nov. 11, 1835, ANG, leg. 3616, exp. 84467.

settlement invited or required their return. The explanation of his conduct may lie in his conclusion that European immigrants were incapable of sustained labor in the environment to which they were confined at New Liverpool.[45] Powerless for the moment to ameliorate the unfavorable conditions, he wrote to the directors asking that no more colonists be sent out for a time, and he perhaps agreed to "lend" some of those in residence to Bennett on hire until improved surroundings could be provided at New Liverpool. Bennett on the other hand, appears to have seized the opportunity to shop for European colonists at the bargain counter inadvertently set up by the Company at his very doorstep. His active recruiting among the settlers was perhaps the best justification for the charge made in Guatemala that the "seductive influence" of Belize[46] had intervened to ruin the settlements and to destroy a potential rival.

Further circumstantial evidence of the "seductive influence" of the British Settlement could be gleaned from the pattern of dispersion followed by the colonists fleeing their wilderness homes. A few went farther up the Polochic and then inland to San Jerónimo or Guatemala City. Most of them, however, tried to work their way to Izabal or to Livingston where they hoped they might encounter a vessel bound for Belize. Some found at least a temporary residence in the Bay Islands, but most eventually made their way to the British Settlement. There they found employment and, as Crowe remarked, "had they been industrious, they might have done well." Some, such as Mr. Gough, apparently did find a satisfactory situation and stayed on to become respected members of the community.[47]

Most of the immigrants who arrived in Belize ultimately confirmed the fears of the Magistrates that they would become public charges. It cannot be assumed, however, that this situation developed solely because the colonists were indisposed to work. Sickness was an important contributing cause. Many of the refugees had contracted diseases before they reached the Settlement, and others succumbed after they arrived. The Public Medical Officer testified in early November 1837 that more than 140 of the immigrants had been admitted to the public hospital, the majority of them suffering from serious illnesses that required extended care. Others less critically ill he attended in

45. *Brief Statement*, 1840, p. 132; Anderson to Colonial Office, Nov. 15, 1836, n.f.
46. *Memoria de la Secretaría Jeneral de Estado del supremo gobierno de Guatemala . . . presentada a la Legislatura de 1837* (Guatemala, [1837]), p. 19.
47. Wood, *Adventures*, 32-35; Crowe, *Gospel*, pp. 519-20; *Brief Statement*, 1840, p. 60. Gough was apparently a partner in the Belize firm of Welsh & Gough in 1842, and was appointed acting treasurer of the government there in 1844.

his office or at various residences in the town. A private physician claimed in the spring of 1838 that he had attended some thirteen or fourteen additional families of colonists totalling some forty-eight or more persons. Some of the sick died, and most of the survivors were ready to quit the tropics. Those who had sufficient resources or who could otherwise obtain passage eventually returned to Europe or emigrated to the United States. As late as the spring of 1840, however, the Superintendent asserted that the Settlement was spending £16 per month on surviving immigrants.[48]

The settlers who went inland had similar histories. A few died of accidents and many more of disease, including the wife and seven children of one of the men who succumbed to Bennett's offer of employment at San Jerónimo. The colonists at the hacienda complained of lack of food and mistreatment, and some of them at least experienced the terror of domestic anarchy when the partisans of Rafael Carrera sacked the property in March and May of 1838. Two or three poor English families, survivors of the Verapaz colony, were reported to be living in Guatemala City in the summer of 1838, one of whom must surely have been John Dyer. After his former master left him at New Liverpool, Dyer accepted employment at San Jerónimo, but after the Carrera attack he went to Guatemala City. There Carlos Rodolfo Klée engaged him to superintend his carpenter shop, but after a year and eight months in that position the volume of business so declined that he was again forced to search for employment. Knowing no Spanish, he found no work. Destitute and desperate he appealed to Chatfield in 1839 for aid to get his family to Belize where he hoped to be able to raise enough money to return to England.[49]

The total colonization effort thus produced a net gain of scarcely a person to the population of Guatemala. Of some 225 immigrants embarked by the Company in London, ninety-odd never touched Guatemalan soil. The dispersion of the two settlements that were

48. Minutes of a Public Meeting Held at Belize, Nov. 6, 1837, CO 123/50, n.f.; Minutes of a Public Meeting Held at Belize, March 5, 1838, n.f.; Colonel Alexander Macdonald, Superintendent of Belize, to Lord Russell, April 11, 1840, CO 123/57, n.f.

49. Wood, *Adventures*, pp. 29-30, 32; Chatfield to Palmerston, No. 40, June 23, 1838, FO 15/20, fol. 264; Petition of British subjects at San Jerónimo to Chatfield, March 30, 1838, and Petition of John Dyer to Chatfield, Sept. 16, 1839, both in FO 252/6, n.f. The British subjects who signed the petition from San Jerónimo were Domingo Knoth, Samuel Mason, Richard Charles Murray, William Knoth, Joseph Carter, J. Wibleshauser, Henry Giles, Samuel Langford, Edward Braffet, and George Overton. William Knoth was subsequently the Company superintendent in the Verapaz.

established left some individuals in Guatemala, but most, if not all, of these seem later to have emigrated. Perhaps the only ones who remained in the country were those whose graves marked the site of Santa Cruz or the routes by which the disillusioned Europeans sought escape from the inhospitable wilderness in which they had been interned.

Gálvez was a partner in the chagrin over the collapse of the colonization effort, for he had done everything in his power to insure the success of the enterprise. He issued advance instructions to departmental and local officers, particularly those at ports, to give every assistance to Fletcher and the colonists, and his orders appear to have been faithfully executed. He wrote letters of greeting to the new arrivals, watched developments at the settlements with avid interest, and concerned himself, for want of more active participation, "that they be given liberal rules for their political and judicial administration, according to the agreements." He awaited the arrival of the "Vera Paz" as expectantly as did the colonists and suppressed his impatience by exchanging with Chatfield the latest reports on its anticipated appearance and discussing the probability that it would be able to cross the bar of the Río Dulce.[50] His disappointment at the successive delays was as real, if not as poignant, as that of the settlers. Only inadvertently, by establishing the quarantine on communication with Belize calculated to prevent the spread of cholera, did the government impede the actual work of colonization in any way.

The Company had no cause for complaint against the Guatemalan government, but it was distressed by two of its actions. There was some dissatisfaction in London because of woodcutting grants allegedly made in contravention of the Company's agreement, and the cession of Santo Tomás to Pulleiro, Balcarzel, and associates in January 1837 disappointed the hope of the directors that they might obtain at least that part of the grant Bennett and Meany had forfeited. Fletcher's visit to the bay in March 1837 at the invitation of Balcarzel may have encouraged hope that the Company might yet acquire the concession, for the associates were encountering difficulty in fulfilling their commitments. The Guatemalan quarantine on commerce with Belize that frustrated Fletcher's attempt to supply the colony from that source also impeded the associates in the movement of laborers, tools, sup-

50. Circular to *jefes departamentales* of Chiquimula and Verapaz, 1835, ANG, leg. 3605, exp. 83553; Gálvez to Chatfield, March 16, July 15, July 27, 1836, FO 252/12, n.f.; Chatfield to Gálvez, July 22, 1836, FO 252/13, n.f.; *Brief Statement*, 1840, p. 142.

plies, and provisions. Balcarzel complained to Carlos Salazar, the Minister General, that he had been kept for twelve days "in this vale of delight with arms folded for want of something in which to employ them" because local officials capriciously halted all traffic "on the excuse of executing orders dictated at a distance of 60 or more leagues from here." He denied the existence of a cholera epidemic in the British Settlement and demanded that the Minister General "see to it that [the quarantine] is lifted, and that they do not hinder us."[51]

The associates cleared the site for the town but, in the process, their refusal to admit the threat of cholera may have helped to bring the disease to Guatemala. Before 1837 had run its course, they were forced to recognize that cholera was sweeping the north coast, and on the basis of that "fortuitous circumstance" they applied to the government and received an extension of six months in the time allowed for the completion of their contract. When the lumber and other construction materials they ordered from the United States were delivered in May, whether because of the epidemic or for want of funds, they were unable to proceed with the construction. The lumber was therefore stored under a shelter on the site and placed in the care of a watchman, and thus it remained a year later when George W. Montgomery visited the bay. By the summer of 1837, therefore, the projects of both the associates and the Company were moribund.[52]

The government of Guatemala was disposed to explain away the Company's failures and to accept its obvious exertions as evidence of good faith. Gálvez gave proof of this attitude when, after the Company had delivered but a single shipload of immigrants within the time period allowed for establishment of one hundred families, he did not terminate the agreement. Rather he recognized the dispatch of the other two vessels as demonstrating that the Company intended to honor its commitments and, on November 5, 1836, granted it a one-year extension of the time allowed for the performance of its obligations. His confidence in the Company was undoubtedly reinforced by its effort to secure from the British government recognition of the Central American claims to the territory disputed by Belize.[53]

51. Juan José Balcarzel to Salazar, March 11, 1837, ANG, leg. 3220, exp. 66296.

52. Extension of contract, 1837, ANG, leg. 1395, exp. 32724, fol. 4; George W. Montgomery, *Narrative of a Journey to Guatemala, in Central America, in 1838* (New York, 1839), pp. 41-42.

53. *Memoria que el Secretario general . . . presenta a la novena Legislatura del estado, leida el 12 de febrero de 1836* (Guatemala, [1836]), p. 4; "Mensaje del Jefe del Estado de Guatemala, Dr. Mariano Gálvez, al abrirse las sesiones ordinarias de la Asamblea Legislativa, en 1836," *Anales* de la Sociedad de geografía e historia de Guatemala, II, No. 3 (March, 1926), 312.

When, after more than a year of effort, the Company's hopes were dashed by the statement in November 1836 of the formal British claim to the disputed area, the secretary forwarded copies of the correspondence to Gálvez as evidence that the directors were entitled to such consideration as might be accorded for an earnest if unsuccessful defense of his country's territorial integrity. The Chief of State had prepared a gracious acknowledgment of the Company's service and was on the point of dispatching it when the British partner in the firm of Klée, Skinner & Company brought to him a report that caused him to withhold the letter.

George Skinner had just returned from London with the latest news from the British capital. He volunteered to Gálvez the allegedly authoritative information that the Company existed only to defraud the public in England, that its operations in Guatemala were only a strategem designed to beguile unwary investors with the illusion of achievement, and that it actually intended to accomplish nothing. This thesis accepted, the rumors that the Company commanded no capital and the evidence of its failures in Guatemala acquired a sinister significance. Gálvez became convinced that the allegations against the Company were true, and he prepared to annul its contract. Two potential beneficiaries of that action, it may be assumed, did nothing to weaken his resolve. Skinner's German partner, Carlos Rudolfo Klée, hoped to obtain the colonization contract, if it fell vacant, and Galindo was facing the necessity of obtaining a new contract, if he were to save his own grant from the Company's control. Chatfield observed with self-righteous complacency the failure he had prophesied. He asked to be provided with copies of the decree as soon as it appeared, but he did not involve himself in the issue. Not so Carlos Meany, Bennett's partner. He tried locally to undo the damage caused by Skinner's "mischievous and malicious tongue" and, when he could press the issue no further, he requested Fletcher to come to the capital to take up the defense of the Company's interests.[54]

In an atmosphere frigid with distrust Fletcher began discussions with Gálvez. The conversations elicited from the Chief of State his reasons for giving credence to the allegations against the Company, but they made no progress toward restoring his faith in its integrity. Gálvez actually did not cancel the contract, but communication be-

54. Copy of Carlos Antonio Meany to Leonard S. Coxe, Sept., 1837, in Hall to Chatfield, Sept. 8, 1837, and Chatfield to Hall, "Private," Sept. 1, 1837, all in FO 252/18, n.f.

tween Fletcher and the Chief of State was suspended and so for all useful purposes was the agreement. Under these circumstances, Meany wrote to Leonard Coxe during the first week of September urgently recommending that the provisional committee in charge of the Company's affairs send out a commissioner with full powers to resolve the impasse.

Almost simultaneously, a reconstituted board of the reorganized Company in London had decided on the same step. In consequence, Young Anderson, the Company's special commissioner, arrived in Izabal in November 1837. And ironically for Fletcher, to whom it was consigned, the "Vera Paz" dropped anchor at the same port shortly thereafter. Remembering the recent months of fruitless toil and unrequited suffering, the agent must have found, for himself and for the vanished settlers, some pungent statement of the concept "too little and too late."

VIII

DISASTER SURMOUNTED

The more dynamic posture assumed by the Eastern Coast Company in Guatemala late in 1837 was the result of a major re-orientation of its affairs in London. The change was intended to result in more vigorous prosecution of the colonization effort and more aggressive action to convert into profit some of the privileges granted by its contract. To reach these objectives, however, the Company would have first to regain the confidence of the Guatemalan government and persuade it to revalidate the colonization agreement. The new administration was pledged to achieve both the immediate and the remote goals. It could not have known, however, when it set the course that developments at home and in Central America would delay for two years any opportunity for actual operation.

Rival factions had apparently been striving for control of the Company for some time previous to the re-organization. The issues are nowhere made clear, but the nature of the controversy can perhaps be surmised. It appears that the conflict developed between the original speculators concerned primarily with raising the market price of Poyaisian securities and the investors who wished to capitalize on the opportunities afforded by the Guatemalan concession and between those to whom the affairs of the Company were of paramount importance and those to whom they were a minor consideration. The reform group seems to have taken the view that the Verapaz concession was more valuable in its own right than as an adjunct to speculation in Poyaisian securities and that the affairs of the Company merited greater attention than the prestigious directors selected by Galindo were willing to give them. Perhaps because their major concerns lay elsewhere, these men, with the exception of Peter Harris Abbott, appear to have made little if any contribution to the advancement of Company interests during their tenure. The reform group therefore wished to install an administration that would act with vigor and responsibility to develop the latent agricultural and commercial empire in Guatemala that had been placed within their grasp.

By early October 1836 the proponents of change succeeded in having Abbott, Charles H. Bourjot, and W. Gordon Thomson named as a provisional committee to supplant the directors in the management of Company affairs. They obtained from the Cabinet a statement of British territorial claims that allowed them to define the portion of their grant in which they could operate without contest, but lack of capital and of a declared policy prevented them from giving any effective assistance to the struggling settlements in the Verapaz. They were, however, eager to learn the true state of Company affairs in Guatemala. They appear to have been the "esteemed friends" in whose interest H. Roper of Lloyds, on the basis of a letter of introduction furnished by an official of the Foreign Office, inquired of Chatfield in March 1837 about the progress of the colony and the Company's prospects for future accomplishment.

Roper was particularly concerned, now that the boundary question with the British government was resolved, to know whether or not the Company's grant had been finally ratified by the federal government "to render it complete and perfect." Absence of such assurance, he pointed out, "completely paralyses their operation" and should the Company proceed "without it I fear our success must be exceedingly doubtful." Chatfield could honestly plead lack of official information to parry the direct questions raised, but his comment that the settlers were reported to "have all left the place selected for their residence, a circumstance that need not create surprise the vicinity of the Cajabón being generally considered very little suited to be the location of Europeans," could not have been reassuring to the questioner.[1]

Despite the prognosis of paralysis and the absence of the recognized antidote for it, the committee refused to believe that the Company could not be revitalized by proper treatment. In this confidence, a general shareholders' meeting on April 10 appointed a committee to draft a plan for more efficient management of the Company's interests, and another held on May 30 received the report. The shareholders considered the proposals at a series of three adjourned sessions, and on July 12, they unanimously adopted the plan for reorganization. It recognized that the Verapaz grant would require a heavy capital investment to become productive, but it proposed to raise the funds to undertake the task. To this end, it provided for a modification of the financial structure and for a new board of

1. H. D. Scott to Frederick Chatfield, March 3, 1837, and H. Roper to Chatfield, March 6, 1837, FO 252/6, n.f.; Chatfield to Roper, July 1, 1837, FO 252/9, n.f.

directors, the members of which promised energetic and efficient administration of Company business.[2]

The new board appears to have been constituted to put the management of Company affairs in the hands of a small number of men capable of carrying on the multi-faceted operation in Guatemala. Two of the directors, Peter Harris Abbott, who was retained as chairman and it may be assumed financial expert of the board, and Charles H. Bourjot, an established London merchant, were carried over from the provisional committee. The third member was Adam Murray, a surveyor and land agent. In addition to the useful experience they brought to their positions, the members must have given some modest prestige to the enterprise, for all three were listed among the peers of England.[3]

The new financial arrangements set the capital of the Company at £200,000, represented by 10,000 debentures at £20, only half of which were issued. These securities were to pay an annual return of 4 per cent, although some of the directors protested that interest should be paid only out of profits, in the expectation that the promised income would attract new capital. Proprietors were notified to deposit their shares at the Company office and on each to pay an assessment of thirty shillings to entitle them to a receipt which they could subsequently exchange for a debenture. If this measure failed by September 8 to produce the expected return of £5,875 10s the directors were authorized to cover the deficit by selling reserved debentures on such terms as to them seemed advisable. Shares upon which the assessment was not paid were declared forfeited to the Company.[4]

2. This data comes from classified announcements published in the *Morning Herald*, No. 17,079 (May 27, 1837); No. 17,084 (June 3, 1837); No. 17,100 (June 22, 1837); No. 17,135 (Aug. 3, 1837); Young Anderson to Chatfield, Oct. 28, 1838, FO 252/6, n.f.

3. Abbott was chairman of the board as early as Sept. 15, 1837 (Abbott to the President of Guatemala, Sept. 15, 1837, ANG, leg. 7550, no exp. number. The names of the three directors appear in the Santo Tomás cession, dated Oct. 15, 1838, *Brief Statement, Supported by Original Documents, of the Important Grants Conceded to the Eastern Coast of Central America Commercial & Agricultural Company by the State of Guatemala* (2nd ed.; London, 1840), p. 37. Murray's office is listed in *Robson's London Directory for 1836* (London, 1835), p. 593, at 47 Parliament Street, to which he had just moved from 61 St. Martin's Lane, Charing Cross. The three names appear in *Robson's Court Guide with Analysis of Peerage for 1837* (London, 1837), respectively pp. 77, 90, and 159.

4. The figures on capitalization and debentures issued and the comment on interest come from the *Brief Statement, Supported by Original Documents, of the Important Grants Conceded to the Eastern Coast of Central America Commercial and Agricultural Company by the State of Guatemala* (London, 1839), unnumbered leaf following title page. The remaining data was given in classified announcements in the *Morning Herald*, No. 17,135 (Aug. 3, 1837); No. 17,139 (Aug. 8,

Before the change in the financial structure of the Company had been completed, another speculation in Poyaisian securities akin to the one that had been its own beginning gave unanticipated urgency to the plans of the new management. A group outside the Company who had invested heavily in MacGregor's bonds and land certificates determined to gain control of the securities by the device of having the Poyaisian land grant conferred on them. To this end they dispatched Thomas Hedgecock, an experienced trader on the Mosquito Shore, who in May 1837 obtained from Robert Charles Frederick, the current Mosquito "King," a concession of the same territory granted by his father to MacGregor. Hedgecock also induced "His Mosquito Majesty" to request his ancient ally, the monarch of Great Britain, to allow mahogany cut on the Mosquito Coast to be shipped direct to British ports under the same favorable duty accorded to wood cut in the Bay of Honduras and cleared through Belize. The speculators thus emulated those woodcutters of the Settlement who sought to circumvent Marshal Bennett's virtual monopoly by resurrecting as an independent source of mahogany concessions the half-forgotten tradition of a sovereign Mosquito kingship.[5]

Hedgecock returned to England in July, and in October the speculators sprang their trap. They announced that the new concession superseded the MacGregor grant and that all securities based on the former title were worthless, but could be incorporated under certain conditions into their venture. They demanded that all holders of valid Poyaisian documents issued prior to 1834 present their certificates and pay an assessment of one per cent of their value as a condition of having them recognized by the new regime. As an inducement to co-operate, they offered a plan to cut and export mahogany and other natural products from the concession as a means of paying interest on the recognized securities.[6]

1837); No. 17,145 (Aug. 16, 1837); and No. 17,151 (Aug. 23, 1837). Assuming that the expected return was calculated as the product of the assessment paid on all shares, the outstanding shares would number 3,917.

5. These events are covered in general outline in Robert A. Naylor, "The British Role in Central America Prior to the Clayton-Bulwer Treaty of 1850," *Hispanic American Historical Review*, XL, No. 3 (Aug., 1960), 376, and can be found in detail in the documents in FO 15/19, FO 53/44-45, and CO 123/57-58. The associates sold a part of the grant to another group of speculators who formed the British Central American Land Company. The part they retained formed the basis for the York and Lancashire Central American Land and Emigration Company. The two groups co-operated under the commonly accepted name Black River Company.

6. These arrangements were described in classified announcements appearing

The announcement appears to have caught the Eastern Coast Company completely unawares. At first it was inclined to deny the pretensions of the new proprietary group, and the Poyaisian Office, which it seems to have controlled, counselled all security holders to read a promised exposé of the new scheme before they yielded to the demands of the pretenders. The new promoters, however, convincingly defended the validity of their concession, and in consequence, a hurried assembly of the threatened holders in mid-November reached the decision to send J. M. Belisario as their own agent to the Mosquito Coast to try to salvage their interests.[7] The Company seems to have been a principal participant in this action.

The proprietors of the Eastern Coast Company meeting late in November, however, recognized that they had been outmaneuvered. The Company was unable to pay the assessment on the securities it had accepted in payment on its own shares, and it therefore determined to return the documents to the original owners in order to give them opportunity to take such measures individually as they thought fit to protect their investments. Because the Company securities could not be distributed in time to permit the owners to present them within the specified deadline, the new proprietors magnanimously extended the period to accommodate them.[8]

The defection of the Company resulted in the abandonment early the following year of the scheme to send Belisario to the Mosquito Coast. Nevertheless, the Company alleged to the Colonial Office that Hedgecock's grant was invalid because the chieftain who made it had previously docked the entail in return for an annual payment and other considerations and because the mahogany cutting rights had been given by Honduras to Morazán for twenty years. These representations, however, the Company must have made more to curry favor with the General, to whom it sent a copy of the letter, than from any hope of preserving the value of the securities it had returned.[9]

As a result of these developments, the Company was forced to surrender certificates representing some 1,600,000 acres of land in Poyais, the entire first issue of three per cent Poyaisian stocks listed at

on the first page of the *Morning Herald*, No. 17,189 (Oct. 6, 1837); No. 17,199 (Oct. 18, 1837), and No. 17,211 (Nov. 1, 1837).

7. *Morning Herald*, No. 17,205 (Oct. 25, 1837); No. 17,206 (Oct. 26, 1837); No. 17,233 (Nov. 27, 1837); and No. 17,267 (Jan. 5, 1838).

8. *Morning Herald*, No. 17,227 (Nov. 20, 1837); No. 17,241 (Dec. 6, 1837); and No. 17,247 (Dec. 13, 1837).

9. *Morning Herald*, No. 17,343 (April 5, 1838); Leonard S. Coxe to Francisco Morazán, Dec. 15, 1837, enclosing a copy of Coxe to Lord Glenelg, Nov. 27, 1837, MSS., Morazán Papers, Latin American Library, Tulane University.

£800,000 face value, and some £82,000 face value in five per cent stock certificates.[10] The Company's nominal assets were thus reduced to the value of its holdings in Guatemala, its original purpose was nullified, and its only remaining business was the project into which it had been inadvertently directed as a result of the grant Gould had obtained in Guatemala.

It was fortunate, under these circumstances, that the Company's new administration was committed to more vigorous prosecution of the colonization enterprise. Before they were aware of the calamity that had befallen their assets, the directors had begun to take steps to retrieve the near disaster in Guatemala. They hired Young Anderson, a half-pay officer and a resident of the West Indies for many years, as superintendent of the Company's operations in Central America and dispatched him in mid-September 1837 to Guatemala. They instructed him to restore good relations with the government of that country and then to obtain revalidation of the Company grant in Verapaz, recognition of its right to cut mahogany, acknowledgment that the first one hundred families had been sent out in accordance with the terms of the original agreement, and postponement of the date by which the Company's remaining obligations were to be discharged. He was also to secure confirmation of the monopoly of steam navigation and to enhance the value of that privilege by acquiring Santo Tomás, if inspection of the bay and its environs showed the site to be salubrious and to offer feasible routes of communication with the interior. Finally, he was to survey the country within the Company's grant and select for settlement locations that afforded suitable climate and soil, security from internal disorder, and facility of access from the sea.[11]

The Company also prepared to send out the "Vera Paz" as soon as possible. In October title to the vessel was passed from Jeremiah Barrett and William Crozier to Peter Harris Abbott and Charles Bourjot. Francis Riley Cobb was employed as her captain under a three-year contract that placed him under the orders of the directors or their agent when he arrived in Central America. On October 27

10. These are the figures given by the Company (Coxe to Morazán, Dec. 15, 1837). The new proprietors calculated the Company-held securities at 1,200,000 acres in land certificates, and £640,000 in bonds (*Morning Herald*, No. 17,241 [Dec. 6, 1837]). The discrepancies may be accounted for by the method of discounting Poyaisian securities announced by the new proprietors (*Morning Herald*, No. 17,211 [Nov. 1, 1837]), and by their refusal to recognize land certificates issued in payment of interest on securities.

11. Robert Glasgow Dunlop, *Travels in Central America* (London, 1847), p. 278; *Brief Statement*, 1840, pp. 57, 59-60, 163; Anderson to Chatfield, Oct. 28, 1838, n.f.

the vessel cleared from the port of London and in company with the sloop "Turbot," Captain Pearson, began her long-delayed voyage to the Bay of Honduras.[12]

Anderson arrived at Izabal on November 20, 1837. He had urgent business to transact for the Company, but he found Guatemala so gripped by internal convulsion that for more than six months he was unable to travel any great distance into the interior. Three times during that period he attempted the journey to the capital and as often was driven back by guerrilla activity.[13] Before he could reach the seat of government the regime of Gálvez had been overthrown.

The rebel forces that terrorized Guatemala were partisans of Rafael Carrera, the nominal chief of the insurrection of the *montaña*. The rebellion had begun as a local uprising in the eastern part of the state in the summer of 1837, but it developed rapidly into a general revolt against the government of Gálvez. As the movement gained momentum guerrilla bands disrupted commerce, impeded communication, virtually halted travel, and reduced local officials to tenuous and transitory authority. Anderson and Fletcher themselves experienced the effects of the turbulence when a force from Chiquimula under a certain Dorantes invaded Izabal and carried off against their protests twenty-three stands of arms that had apparently been imported as a part of the cargo of the "Vera Paz."[14] The internal disorder was compounded by the appearance of cholera. The ravages of the disease, the attempts of the government to establish an effective quarantine, and the appearance in the villages of doctors sent to treat the victims added to the excitement and the terror of the inhabitants.

The Company's interests were affected by the rebellion, not alone because of the loss of property and Anderson's detention on the coast but because the colonization contracts were one of the issues agitated to produce the unrest. The approaching elections in Guatemala gave all political opponents of Gálvez, including dissidents in his own party, unusual reason and opportunity to attack his regime. It was scarcely avoidable, in these circumstances, that the xenophobia so effectively cultivated during the recent Espinosa revolt should reappear in trappings appropriate to the current situation.

Opponents of the regime resuscitated the objections to the cession of public lands to foreigners and alleged that, in consequence, native

12. Certificate of British Registry [of the "Vera Paz"], No. 415, CO 123/56, n.f.; Minutes of a Meeting of Magistrates in Belize, Feb. 5, 1838, CO 123/55, n.f.; "Shipping Intelligence," *Morning Herald*, No. 17,208 (Oct. 28, 1837), p. [4].

13. Anderson to Chatfield, Oct. 28, 1838, n.f.

14. Anderson to Chatfield, Oct. 28, 1838, n.f.

sons and their families had been left without means of livelihood. They taunted the Chief of State with his "great projects" and charged him with venality. They recalled the slowness with which he had responded to warnings that Bennett and Meany were engaged in fraudulent operations and alleged that, had he collected the amounts due the state under the contract, the treasury would be overflowing rather than bankrupt. These grievances were taken up by Carrera and their reform made a part of his program. Three of the sixteen demands, on the basis of which he recruited his *división de reforma,* related to the colonization agreements. He insisted that foreigners be given neither employment nor lands to the prejudice of nationals, that the grants to foreigners of lands belonging to the people be revoked, and that Gálvez be required to give an accounting for the funds that should have been paid to the state under the Bennett and Meany contract.

Class interests and religious intolerance were also drawn upon to inflame popular sentiment against the colonization enterprises and their domestic patrons. Artisans, or propagandists who put words in their mouths, alleged that foreigners harbored in the country by the artifices of the Gálvez government had brought about their economic ruin and had deprived their families of bread. It was darkly hinted that the Catholic religion was marked for extinction as a part of the conspiracy between the government and foreigners and that the temples of Catholic worship might be profaned by heretics and even converted into stables for accommodation of their animals. These charges were cited as proof that Gálvez entertained evil intentions toward the mixed-bloods of Guatemala and that the purpose of his regime was to remake the state under alien institutions and with an imported population.

The cholera epidemic provided the climactic link in the chain of circumstantial evidence. The appalling toll of deaths gave plausibility to the charge that the government was deliberately poisoning the simple folk as a step toward wholesale extermination of the native inhabitants preparatory to repopulating the country with foreign heretics. Indeed, the vanguard of the new proprietors was already established in the Verapaz.[15]

15. Addresses to various government officials, ANG, leg. 16267, exps. 53157, 53170; "Editorial," *La Oposición* (Guatemala), No. 11 (Nov. 25, 1837), p. 51, and "Comunicado," *La Oposición* (Guatemala), No. 13 (Dec. 10, 1837), p. 59; *Conciudadanos,* hoja suelta signed "Un Artezano" (Antigua, Guatemala, 1837); *Noticia al Congreso federal de la revolución de Guatemala* [Guatemala, 1838], pp. vi-vii; *Profesión de fe política,* hoja suelta (Guatemala, 1837), p. [3]; Lorenzo Montúfar,

This agitation helped at once to sustain the revolt and to reduce the ability of the government to combat it. Late in January 1838 Carrera threatened Guatemala City. With the capital under attack Gálvez resigned, and on February 2 Pedro J. Valenzuela, the Vice Chief, assumed the executive power. That same day the departments of western Guatemala seceded and under the name of Los Altos set up the sixth state in the Federation. In the remaining portion of Guatemala Valenzuela proved unable either to control the insurrection or to command popular support. On July 23 he gave way to Mariano Rivera Paz, the presiding officer of the Representative Council, who assumed the government under the title of Councilor Chief of State. Two days later in response to the popular demand the government decreed the convocation of a Constituent Assembly.[16]

While insurrection altered the authorities with whom he would treat when he reached the capital, Anderson employed his enforced residence on the coast to perform some of his assigned duties. In order to gather data on which the directors would base their plans, he tested the climate of the area, and he made a thorough reconnaissance of the region that included Santo Tomás, the lower Motagua, and the river and lake waterways from the Río Dulce to Telemán. He chose a site for a settlement on the Boca Nueva River near its junction with the Polochic, and he formed a favorable opinion of Santo Tomás and its possibilities. These observations made somewhat at leisure would considerably advance his mission, if and when he reached the capital. Until then he could only wait.

A part of the time that might have been relatively unproductive Anderson needed to arrange for the operation of the "Vera Paz" in Central American waters. The steamer arrived at Izabal, apparently late in 1837, and immediately encountered difficulties that required all the skill and authority both Anderson and Fletcher could command. An immediate misunderstanding developed with officials at Izabal over payment of duties and fees on the vessel and her cargo in Guatemalan ports. The captain became embroiled in altercations that ultimately involved Fletcher and Anderson, and an impasse developed over final control of the vessel that was broken only by laying the case before the Magistrates of Belize. Once that issue was resolved a new dispute arose with the authorities in the Settlement over the

Reseña histórica de Centro-America (Guatemala, 1878), II, 84-85, 360-61, and "Documentos," pp. 370-72; Chatfield to Palmerston, No. 17, June 26, 1837, FO 15/19, fols. 101-2, 104.

16. Alejandro Marure, Efemérides de los hechos notables acaecidos en la república de Centro-américa (Guatemala, 1895), pp. 101-2; 105-6, 115.

status of the steamer and the duties and fees that could properly be assessed against her.[17] When they had made the best arrangements possible in Belize for the "Vera Paz," Fletcher and Anderson parted. Fletcher sailed for England to make his final report and to leave the Company's employ. Anderson returned to Izabal hoping that the internal situation of Guatemala had calmed sufficiently to permit him to transact his business.

By late June or early July 1838 travel had become secure enough that he began his journey to Guatemala. On July 25, in what must have been one of the first official acts of the new Councilor Chief of State, he presented his credentials to Mariano Rivera Paz. The following day his position was recognized and he entered formally on his negotiations.[18] He immediately encountered an obstruction, however, for he found that the time extension he was instructed to arrange had already been negotiated with the Valenzuela government a few days earlier by Juan Galindo.

The arrangement to which Anderson found his employers committed was not one over which either he or they could rejoice. Galindo purported to negotiate for the Company as honorary director but, beyond the three-year extension of time he obtained for it, the benefits of the agreement were entirely for himself. He secured the assent of the Guatemalan government to the perpetual separation of his own grant from that made to the London directors, an extension of its boundaries toward the south at the expense of territory originally included in the cession to the Company, and a postponement of four years in the date by which he was required to fulfill his contract. For all these concessions, he obligated himself and the Company within four years to construct, under the conditions stipulated in the Verapaz contract, the road between Salamá and the port of Refugio on the western end of Lake Izabal.

Anderson was outraged when he discovered the perfidy of the honorary director. He wrote Galindo a blistering letter of reprimand denouncing the total absence in his nature of the virtue suggested by the first word of his title, stripping him of any formal connection with the Company, repudiating the agreement he made, and warning him that even as a private individual he intended to have nothing to do with him. A copy of the letter he sent to Rivera Paz with the

17. Anderson to Chatfield, Oct. 28, 1838, n.f. On difficulties of the "Vera Paz," see Chapter XI, pp. 255-59.

18. Anderson to Chief of State, July 25, 1838, ANG, leg. 7555, no exp. number, n.f., enclosing letter of introduction from P. H. Abbott, Sept. 15, 1837.

request that the contract he cancelled as illegally executed and with the explanation that the former directors of the Company had appointed Galindo an honorary member of their body in the belief that he "was an honest man." As soon as the directors learned of the transaction they wrote to Morazán in similar anger to repudiate the contract and the individual who made it.[19]

Having neutralized the effect of Galindo's interference, Anderson was free to open his own negotiations. In one respect the unauthorized compact should have reassured him, for it showed that current official opinion was no less favorable to colonization proposals than Gálvez had been. Although the insurrection that brought him to power was anti-colonization, anti-foreign, and particularly anti-British, Valenzuela showed a most friendly and forgiving attitude.[20] The executive *acuerdo* by which he approved Galindo's proposals absolved the contractors of responsibility for failure to meet their obligations and attributed the delays in their performances to such untoward circumstances as political vicissitudes and the current civil war. He even found in the insurrection itself justification for greater attention to colonization projects. Beyond the considerations on which Gálvez had promoted foreign settlements as a vehicle of development, Valenzuela saw an even greater need for accomplished and industrious colonists because of "the tendencies shown by the uncouth masses of the population to overturn all the principles on which civilization and prosperity of the people are founded."[21] If Anderson's proposals were given an equally sympathetic reception by Rivera Paz, the Company representative might have reason to be grateful that his negotiations had been delayed.

Anderson hoped to transact his principal business with the government by means of two contracts. The questions of pending obligation and privilege could be resolved by an understanding on the status of the original agreement. The cession of Santo Tomás would require an entirely new arrangement. It appears that Anderson opened negotiations on both fronts at the end of July by making proposals for validating the Verapaz agreement and submitting bases for the cession to the Company of the port and district of Santo

19. Anderson to Chatfield, Oct. 28, 1838, n.f., and enclosures; Coxe to Morazán, Jan. 15, 1839, MSS., Morazán Papers, Latin American Library, Tulane University.
20. Chatfield reported that the ordinary people believed all foreigners to be Englishmen (Chatfield to Palmerston, No. 17, June 26, 1837, FO 15/19, fol. 104), and several other contemporary observers remarked on the same curious misconception.
21. Copy of acuerdo ejecutivo, July 17, 1838, FO 252/6, n.f.

Tomás.[22] The necessity of disentangling the confusion created by Galindo's unauthorized action delayed the first negotiation, but the second proceeded without reference to the outcome of the first.

The negotiation was not an effortless process, however; Anderson chafed at the continuing insurrection that distracted the government from the conduct of normal public affairs and at the deliberateness with which the new officials went about their business.[23] Unanticipated developments that had perverted or frustrated the intent of the original grants revealed contingencies against which negotiators of new agreements might demand safeguards, and the bitter and prolonged criticism of the first contracts had suggested several modifications that would probably be demanded by public opinion.

The transaction was also complicated by the existence of rights acquired by nationals in the region of Santo Tomás subsequent to the default of Bennett and Meany. During the previous May, the government had commissioned Galindo in partnership with Miguel Moscoso to open a road from Santo Tomás to the Motagua and to build a warehouse at the river terminus of the road and another at Los Encuentros where the Izabal trail crossed the stream. As compensation for this service it granted the contractors the exclusive right for twenty years to cut mahogany from a large tract of public lands in the vicinity of Lake Izabal and the Motagua River, a part of which lay within the district Anderson hoped to obtain.[24] Even more important, the contract under which Pulleiro, Balcarzel, and associates had undertaken to open the port had not been cancelled. Finally, a large woodcutting grant to Angel Floripes in the area was pending before the government.

Acting for the Pulleiro associates, Balcarzel attempted to forestall a concession to Anderson that would supersede their own. In a petition dated August 1 he reminded the government that his firm had cleared the site for the town at Santo Tomás and had imported lumber for the buildings but had been prevented from completing the work by the failure of the government to reimburse them as agreed for their outlay in clearing the town site. He claimed expenditures of more than 11,000 pesos on construction materials and some 750

22. I have not found the original proposals. The published version of the confirmation of the Verapaz Charter (*Brief Statement*, 1840, p. 32), refers to proposals of June 30, but this must surely be an error for July 30, unless Anderson opened negotiation by mail from the north coast before he presented his credentials.

23. Anderson to Chatfield, Oct. 28, 1838, n.f.

24. The terms of the contract are summarized in the opinion of the special committee which examined Anderson's proposals, Aug. 16, 1838, ANG, leg. 3220, exp. 66300, fols. 1-5. I have not found the original.

pesos for the salary of the watchman who guarded them, plus some 4,000 pesos spent in clearing the site. Moreover, the associates at the behest of the government had constructed several improved routes of communication for the extraction of mahogany, subject to negotiation of a satisfactory basis for making their use public. In this category he claimed that, under the direction of the English engineer Henry Gardiner, they had opened a canal between Graciosa Bay and the San Francisco River at a cost of 3,000 pesos and had drawn plans for a similar waterway between the San Francisco and the Motagua. The completed work would give direct outlet from the lower Motagua to the Bay of Honduras. He asserted also that they had completed the road between Santo Tomás and El Mico left unfinished by Velís in 1836 and had constructed a road between Santo Tomás and the Motagua three months or more before Galindo and Moscoso had offered to build it. Before the government entered into any new arrangements for opening the port, he invited it to consider the accomplishments of the Guatemalan company and the unfulfilled obligations of the government toward it.[25]

Balcarzel's petition and Anderson's proposal for the cession of Santo Tomás the government submitted to a special commission composed of Felipe Molina, Juan Antonio Martínez, and Pedro Aycinena, who was substituted at the last minute for Manuel Francisco Pavón. This group found three categories of impediments to the cession proposed by the Company agent. Their most significant objection was to the grant of political power to be exercised in Guatemala by residents of a foreign state and subjects of an alien government. They pointed out also that the government was already bound by conflicting contracts with the Pulleiro associates, and with Galindo and Moscoso, and by several woodcutting concessions in the area that it had no alternative but to honor. Several technical difficulties likewise stood in the way of the arrangement. The federal colonization law prohibited contracts with foreign companies composed of more than three individuals, and the same act specified land grants of one million square varas per family, one each for the colonist and for the contractor. Several of the conditions suggested by Anderson would require new legislation, and hence, the government could promise no more than to request the enactment of the appropriate laws. Finally, the commission found Anderson's credentials inadequate to the negotiations he had undertaken because he lacked power of attorney from the directors. Rather than delay the proceedings unnecessarily, how-

25. Petition of Balcarzel, Aug. 1, 1838, ANG, leg. 1399, exp. 32724, fols. 4-5.

ever, the commission proposed that any arrangement reached with the
agent be made conditional upon receipt within six months of formal
ratification by the directors.[26]

The commission believed that its objections could not be accommodated by revision of the articles proposed by Anderson. After discussions with the Commissioner, therefore, it drew up and submitted
to the government a contract that it believed would reconcile the
interests of the state with those of the concessionaires. It proposed,
if the obstacles imposed by the federal law could be removed, to
grant a block cession similar to those included in the earlier agreements. It protected the rights that nationals had already acquired by
exempting from the terms of the contract all lands that were the
property of individuals or of established towns. It did not, however,
provide for any subsequent disposition of those properties that had
been granted to individuals for a specified term of years or of those
that were given under qualifying conditions.

The principal care of the commission was to safeguard the political
authority of the state within the cession. To this end it vested the
government with powers of appointment and review that would give
it substantial control over the municipal officials and the military
forces of the colony. Specifically, it required approval by the Chief
of State of the individuals appointed by the municipal government
to the offices of judge and fiscal and approval and appointment by the
Chief of State of a person nominated by the municipality as commander of the local militia. The other officers of the militia were to
be nominated by the commander and appointed by the Chief of
State. The regulations governing the offices of judge and fiscal were
to be decreed by the Chief of State in accord with the municipal
government. For twenty years all measures adopted by the municipal
government to levy taxes and to make public expenditures were made
subject to approval first by the representative of the Company and
then by the Chief of State. Measures disapproved by the representative could be passed over his veto by a two-thirds majority of the
municipality, but in these cases the Chief of State could give final
approval only after prior consultation with the Assembly and the
Representative Council.[27] These arrangements would obviously leave
the representative of the Company in a relatively weak position between the municipal authorities and the Chief of State.

26. The draft of the appointment letters is in ANG, leg. 1398, exp. 32654; the
opinion of the committee is in ANG, leg. 3220, exp. 66300, fols. 1-5.
27. Draft contract, submitted Aug. 23, 1838, ANG, leg. 1399, exp. 32725, fols. 1-5.

Anderson's objections to the commission's action came promptly. On September 18 he wrote to Rivera Paz in barely restrained anger to complain of the discouraging tone of the report and of the harsh terms in which the draft contract was framed. The commission's attitude, he observed with scarcely veiled condescension, seemed hardly appropriate to a country whose present state put it in obvious need of industrious immigrant settlers, not alone because of the increase in wealth they could be expected to produce by development of agriculture and commerce but "as a means of assuring the liberty and well-being of the cultured portion of the population [now] menaced by a savage faction." The same conditions, he pointed out, made it necessary to adopt something more than ordinary measures to induce capitalists to hazard investment in an enterprise that required large immediate expenditures and offered only remote and uncertain profits. The commission proposed a contract that admittedly offered "obvious and incalculable" advantages to the government but rewarded the Company only with privileges the value of which was made uncertain by circumstances. There was no mistaking the threat implied by his observation that the time allotted by the directors for his stay in Guatemala had already expired and that he was prepared, with a contract or without it, to return to England.

The commission's technical objections Anderson brushed aside as ill-considered or based on misconceptions. He saw no point to the challenge on the structure of the Company after the government had recognized it and had long been bound to a contract with it. To question his own powers was "improper and inopportune" after they had been recognized by the Chief of State. Only ignorance of the procedures followed by companies could have led the commission to consider inadequate documents issued in accord with the practise of all boards of directors and attested to by no less a personage than the Lord Mayor of London. Those same documents had been recognized as valid by a court of law even in the hostile environment of Belize.

Twenty-one of the twenty-eight articles of the proposed contract Anderson was willing to accept as the commission drafted them or with only slight changes, but those that embodied the objectionable conditions he insisted would have to be substantially altered. The modifications he suggested would remove all competitors from the fields of Company endeavor, make it proprietor of virtually everything of value in the district of Santo Tomás, and give it substantive control over the officials and policies that affected its operations.

To eliminate all competing activity and to bring all property under Company ownership Anderson asked that where possible existing grants be extinguished immediately and that the Company be made the beneficiary of the remaining conditional concessions when they expired. To this end he requested that the project to open a road from Santo Tomás to Los Encuentros or El Mico on the Izabal trail be abandoned; that the road being constructed by Galindo and Moscoso become the property of the Company when finished or, if it was not completed, that the fine established as a penalty by the contract be paid to the Company; and that the woodcutting privilege granted to Pulleiro and associates in recompense for constructing buildings at Santo Tomás be cancelled at once for non-fulfillment of the conditions imposed. The contractors, however, should be given an additional twelve months in which to erect the buildings and to establish the promised twenty Canary Island families at Santo Tomás. Should they fail to do so, their privilege should pass to the Company. In any case, the government should reimburse the associates for their expenditures in clearing the land and opening roads and include these works without cost to the Company in the Santo Tomás grant. Finally, the pending woodcutting grant to Colonel Angel Floripes should be limited to fifty *caballerías* and the concession should be disposed of at public auction as provided for by law. The residue of the requested cession should then be included in the grant made to the Company.

He also suggested provisions that would assist the Company in its steam navigation projects. To protect the Company's monopoly he proposed that administrators of customs houses at all ports of the state be required to refuse loading and unloading privileges to steam vessels not belonging to the Company. He also requested that one-half of the warehousing fee collected at Santo Tomás be allocated to removal of obstacles to navigation in the Motagua River.

Perhaps the most controversial of Anderson's demands related to the authority of the Company representative in relation to the Chief of State. He argued with some reason that the arrangements proposed by the commission would be cumbersome in operation and would almost inevitably lead to disputes and that the Company could not risk placing in the hands of any individual not in its employ the power of decision over the heavy investment it would have to make. He could plead also that the successful execution of the project rested on the principle of mutual aid, responsibility, and confidence. He placed himself, however, in the awkward position of insisting that the government repose a degree of confidence in the Company that he was obviously unwilling to reciprocate. In defense of his position he argued lamely that the Company would feel secure could the powers suggested by the commission be exercised always by a man of the stature of the current Chief of State but that a subsequent incumbent of less enlightened views might use the prerogatives of his office to destroy the colony.

Anderson suggested specific changes that would shift important areas of authority from the Chief of State to Company employees. He proposed that the resident agent of the Company be ex-officio commander of the militia and as such be responsible to the Chief of State, that the municipal authorities appoint the judge and fiscal without the requirement of government approval, and that local ordinances levying taxes and disbursing municipal funds be subject to approval by the Company representative alone. In a similar vein, he requested that the contract contain specific declarations that under no circumstance was the commerce of the port to be interfered with "by the intemperance of military men" and that the military arm of the state be permitted within the district only when called for by a magistrate to assist the civil authorities or to help repel an invasion. To give the Company control over residents of the colony he proposed that the contract require all new arrivals to appear before the provost marshal to give assurance of their good conduct under penalty of expulsion. Should anyone fail to leave on order of the municipal authorities, he could legally be treated as a vagabond.[28]

The difference of views between Anderson and the commission appeared irreconcilable. Hopeful that another negotiator might be able to reach an agreement, however, Rivera Paz on September 25 appointed José Antonio Azmitia, Minister of Government, Justice, and War, to continue the discussions. On October 1 Anderson presented a draft contract that incorporated his demands and in two weeks of conferences obtained agreement to his major requirements. The points he yielded involved no substantive concession. On October 15 the negotiators signed an agreement, subject to ratification by the Assembly, and on November 1 Azmitia transmitted it to the Chief of State who ordered it submitted to the legislative body at its next session.[29]

The contract ceded to the directors of the Company the port of

28. Exposition of Anderson, Sept. 18, 1838, *ibid.*, fols. 15-18.
29. The acuerdo ejecutivo on the appointment of Azmitia is in ANG, leg. 3220, exp. 66300, fols. 5-6; the letter transmitting the contract, leg. 1413, exp. 33007.

Santo Tomás and a narrow strip of territory, denominated the District of Santo Tomás, stretching into the interior behind it. The lateral limits of the District were defined as the Polochic-Lake Izabal-Río Dulce waterway on the north and west and the Motagua River on the south and east. Upstream, the boundary was set at an imaginary line drawn from the confluence of the Cajabón with the Polochic to the point on the Motagua nearest the town of San Pablo, above Gualán; in the opposite direction it was formed by the line of the seacoast between the mouths of the Río Dulce and the Motagua. The territory and waters of the entire District, including all islands lying within three leagues of the coast and excepting lands owned by individuals and those reserved for existing towns or owned by them under special title, the government assigned to the Company with absolute right of possession and free use. Although the pending transaction with Floripes was not specifically mentioned, the government also reserved lands in the process of transfer to other concessionaires, but it pledged itself to grant no more than fifty *caballerías* from the cession. It was calculated, deducting the excepted areas, that the District contained 8,000 *caballerías* of good land. This area the government ceded to the Company as absolute property, with power to sell in whole or in part the land itself or its rights thereon to individuals or to other companies. The contract specifically asserted the sovereignty of the state over the cession and declared that no provision of the agreement could be interpreted to infringe that power.

The Company was to have possession of the entire District for a period of ten years during which it was to select where it saw fit the 8,000 *caballerías* assigned to it. At the expiration of that interval the selected portions were to be measured and the boundaries marked in order to determine whether the total extent exceeded or fell short of the designated area. If more than 8,000 *caballerías,* the Company could buy the excess land at a price set by two appraisers appointed one each by the government and the Company. If less than the agreed upon area, the government was to make up the deficit from public lands, if any should remain at that time, anywhere in the state at the election of the Company.

In return for the cession the Company obligated itself to execute a variety of projects that were expected to contribute to the development of the state and the nation. It agreed to build a number of needed roads, to establish steam navigation on the principal waterways, to build a commercial town on the Bay of Santo Tomás, and to colonize the town and the District principally with foreign immigrant settlers. In case of default on any of the substantive obligations it assumed, it agreed to pay to the state a fine of 5,000 pesos, and the government gave a reciprocal guarantee of performance on its commitments to the Company. The Company was released from liability, however, should the state fail to honor its obligations, and the government agreed to notify the Company of any shortcoming and to allow it a year's time in which to remedy the deficiency before the fine was assessed.

The Company obligated itself to construct within three years a cart road from Santo Tomás to the Motagua and, if practicable, a cart or pack road between the port and the outlet of Lake Izabal. Should Galindo and Moscoso complete the road they had undertaken to build between Santo Tomás and the Motagua, the finished work would be put at the disposition of the Company under terms to be agreed upon at that time. The government declared that it was bound by no existing contract for opening a road from Santo Tomás to connect with the Izabal trail, and it promised within the next six years to sign such an agreement only with the Company. If at the expiration of that period the road had not been built, the government could thereafter receive offers from other proponents and, should the Company elect not to make a better proffer, could conclude an agreement with another contractor and assign to him from the Company's grant the land necessary to carry out the project.

The Company also contracted within three years to have three steamboats in operation on the waterways within its grant. It committed itself to place river steamers on the Polochic and the Motagua and to keep the "Vera Paz" in service between Izabal and Belize. If any of the vessels should cease to operate, the Company agreed to replace it within three years.

The government granted the Company monopoly control over the improved facilities for transport thus established. The roads it constructed were recognized as its absolute property, and it was authorized to assess and collect for their use a stipulated tariff of tolls that could be lowered, but not raised, without the consent of the government. It was also guaranteed an absolute monopoly of steam navigation on each of the major waterways within and bordering on its grant, contingent upon establishment of service within the specified time. Subsequent failure to keep any vessel in operation for as long as three years would result in loss of the monopoly over the route to which it was assigned. To safeguard the Company's privilege the government agreed that any vessel judged by a competent court to be guilty of infringing the monopoly would be declared forfeit to the Company and that a fine of 5,000 pesos would be assessed against the owner for the benefit of the Company. It also pledged to request that the federal government instruct the administrators of all customs houses to deny the privilege of loading or discharging cargo to steam vessels not the property of the Company and that it exempt the Company's steamers and all other vessels owned or operated by it from tonnage duties in all the ports of the republic. Should this latter privilege be refused, the Company could at its option, but under penalty of loss of its monopoly, retire its vessels from service in Central America.

The Company agreed to present to the government within one year a plan for a commercial town at Santo Tomás. The port city was to occupy an area no smaller than a mile square, within which sites were to be reserved for a *comandancia,* a customs house, a municipal building, churches, and parks. The streets were to be of adequate width, straight and intersecting at right angles. The Company was to begin constructing houses and other buildings as soon as possible in order to accommodate the population at the earliest feasible date.

To assist the Company to build and to improve the town, the government made several special concessions. It authorized the builders to fell timber needed for the construction of houses on any convenient land, even that granted for woodcutting to another concessionaire. It allowed the Company to make use of the area cleared by Pulleiro and associates subject to compensating the government in an amount equal to the authenticated costs of clearing a comparable extent of land. It also agreed to request the federal government to approve special fiscal arrangements intended to stimulate development of the port. It was to ask that the tonnage duty collected at Santo Tomás be allocated to improvement of the port, the town, the fortifications, and other means of defense and that the warehousing fees assessed there be assigned in equal portions to improvement and enlargement of the public warehouses at the port and to removal of obstructions to navigation in the Motagua. If the permission were granted, the funds for both purposes were to be administered by a commission of three members, one the representative of the Company and the other two appointed by the government and the municipal authorities of Santo Tomás.

The Company pledged itself to establish one thousand foreign families as residents of the town and the District over a period of twenty years. The first one hundred families were to be settled within three years, the second one hundred within eight years, and a total of five hundred by the end of ten years. Within the next decade it obligated itself to settle another five hundred families, but it was not limited to that number. Immigrant settlers of any nationality could be brought as colonists, but at least one-fourth of the total number were to be Spaniards or Portuguese from Europe or from the islands, Germans, or Maltese. Emancipated slaves, however, could not be counted as satisfying the conditions of the contract. Central Americans could also settle in the colony under the same rules and regulations established by the Company and the municipal government for other residents. All foreign colonists were to swear fidelity to the republic and to the state and to obey their laws. The Company was authorized to appoint an agent who would reside in the town.

The settlers were allowed to set up a municipal government that was to be largely autonomous in local affairs. A municipal council of six members was to be elected by a majority of votes of the residents of the District who had an annual income of two hundred pesos or more. Membership on the council was restricted to residents who had an annual income of five hundred pesos or more, but individuals otherwise eligible were disqualified if they were illiterate, had a criminal charge pending against them, or had been convicted of a crime against the state or the well-being of the community.

The council was to be the legislative body of the colony, but for twenty years its ordinances were subject to review by the Assembly of the state. Each of the six members in rotation was to serve a term of one month as a police judge, to hear civil cases involving not more than fifty pesos, and as chief of police. The size of the police force was to be fixed by the Chief of State in accord with the Company representative and that body was to remain exclusively under civilian control. Residents of the District were required to pay such taxes as were levied by the council to meet the expenses of local government and the administration of justice, to maintain a competent police force, and to sustain religion and public education.

The council was authorized to appoint a muncipal executive officer (*alguacil mayor, magistrador ejecutor,* or provost marshal) who was to carry out local ordinances and use the police power to maintain order, give security to peaceful inhabitants, and apprehend lawbreakers. All new arrivals were required to appear before him to give satisfactory assurance of their good conduct. Persons who did not comply were to be expelled from the colony, and if they refused to leave when notified, they were to be treated as vagrants.

The council was also given power to appoint a judge and a fiscal, whose identities were to be communicated to the Chief of State, and to establish regulations governing those offices. The judge, the fiscal, and the Company agent were to be ex-officio members of the council. The judge was also to hear civil cases involving more than fifty pesos and to preside over jury trials in criminal cases that fell outside police jurisdiction. Capital sentences were subject to review by the Supreme Court of Justice of the state. After twenty years the Livingston Codes were to be observed in the colony if the inhabitants so desired.

The local military force was to consist of a militia made up of all male residents between the ages of sixteen and fifty-four. It was to be governed by such regulations as might be agreed upon by the Chief of State and the municipal council in accord with the Guatemalan constitution, subject to several specific limitations. The Company representative was to be commander and, as such, responsible to the Chief of State to whom he was to propose for appointment candidates for the other offices. The militia could be used only within the District, and the regular military was excluded from that area, except in case of invasion, unless called by the local authorities.

The Company, its employees, the colonists, and their descendants were guaranteed the protection of the government and security of their persons and property, within the ability of the state authorities to assure them, on the same basis as other residents of the state. They enjoyed equal rights with the native-born to bequeath their real and intangible property, and the relatives of persons dying intestate could inherit under the laws of the state regardless of their place of residence. Settlers were assured freedom of conscience and the right without interference of any kind to the public exercise of any religion.

The contract granted certain fiscal privileges as a stimulus to development of the new settlements. Colonists were exempted for twenty years from all legal monopolies and from all contributions and taxes except import and export duties from which they were not specifically released. They were allowed duty-free export of their own products, those of any Central American state, or those of foreign origin that had been naturalized by legal importation. They were permitted free import of all national products; foreign goods that had paid duty elsewhere in the republic; foreign tools, implements, and machinery useful to agriculture or the development of the arts; materials for building houses; books and other articles for moral instruction; uniforms, arms, and ammunition for the police and the militia; and food imported by the Company for its employees or colonists, or by the settlers for their own consumption.

Certain special economic opportunities were offered to the Company. Both the Company itself and the colonists it brought in were free to engage in any occupation of their choice, including mining. All mineral deposits discovered within the cession were to be the property of the Company, and it was authorized to exploit them as it saw fit on condition of paying to the government one-tenth of the net profit on the enterprises. It was also given the exclusive privilege, as against all foreigners, of hunting and fishing in the territory and waters included within its grant, and it was guaranteed an absolute monopoly of woodcutting of all kinds, and of exploitation of all natural products within its cession, on its coasts, and along the margins of its rivers and lakes. The same exclusive privileges were to be extended to such temporary concessions as had been excluded from the grant as they expired, were cancelled, or otherwise fell vacant. These resources it could exploit directly, or it could dispose of its rights in whole or in part to anyone.

Both the Company and the colonists were permitted to arrange voluntary apprenticeship contracts with anyone wishing to settle at Santo Tomás. These agreements would be recognized as valid whether executed within the republic or in a foreign country. No such engagement could be executed, however, for a period longer than five years, and none could be made with emancipated slaves. Slavery was prohibited in the colony, as it was elsewhere in the republic.

Because the regular Assembly had adjourned and the Constituent Assembly would not convene until Anderson had returned to England, the contract granted the Company a period of eight months within which to send a commissioner to Guatemala with full powers to ratify the contract. During that period the government committed itself to sign no agreement that might even indirectly affect the privileges assigned to the Company.[30]

As soon as the cession of Santo Tomás had been arranged, Anderson turned to the task of revalidating the Verapaz contract. On October 29 the government notified him that it had conceded the three-year time extension requested on condition that the Company, as a penalty, erect an iron bridge at the Motagua River crossing of the road between the capital and the Verapaz. The following day,

30. Contract for the cession of Santo Tomás, Oct. 1, 1838, ANG, leg. 1399, exp. 32724, fols. 19-27.

Anderson acknowledged the offer and proposed additional articles for a decree that would formalize the transaction. Some of his suggestions were intended to clarify the status of certain obligations assumed by the parties to the original agreement; others were new conditions that on the basis of earlier discussions with Rivera Paz he hoped to have included. The Chief of State accepted the proposals, and on November 8 decreed the new arrangement, subject to ratification by the Assembly.[31]

To clarify the status of responsibilities assumed under the original agreement, the government declared that the obligation to settle the first one hundred families had been entirely fulfilled and that it granted a time extension of three years on each of the other intervals at which accomplishments were subject to review. Thus, the second group of one hundred settlers should be established by August 14, 1842, and the remaining eight hundred by the same date in 1848. The termination of the twenty-year period was postponed until 1858. The government also agreed to protect the Company in its right to cut wood within its concession and to annul all concessions since made for that and other purposes contrary to the tenor of the original agreement. The contract with Galindo approved the previous July it specifically revoked.

In return for the time extension, the Company agreed within three years to construct an iron chain suspension bridge across the Motagua. The government allowed it, however, to utilize the masonry, abutments, timber, and other materials it had already prepared for that purpose and promised to assist in transporting the bridge parts between Telemán and the construction site. Moreover, the government granted to the Company ownership of the completed structure for a period of twenty years during which it was authorized to collect a schedule of stipulated tolls for its use. At the expiration of twenty years the bridge was to become the property of the state.

The agreement also confirmed to the Company the monopoly of steam navigation conferred by the Santo Tomás charter and extended its provisions to include the territory comprised within the original Verapaz grant. The waterways leading to the Bay of Honduras were already covered by the Santo Tomás concession, but the new agreement added the Chixoy, Pasión, and Usumacinta Rivers to the

31. Anderson's letter of Oct. 30, 1838, proposing conditions, is in ANG, leg. 7555, no exp. number, n.f. The Rivera Paz decree incorporating the terms of the cession is printed in translation in *Brief Statement*, 1840, pp. 32-36. I have not found the original. The following digest of provisions is based on the published version.

monopoly. The Company agreed to put a steamer on those waters within three years of the date on which the government notified it that official statistics showed the volume of traffic to be sufficient to make the operation profitable.

With his negotiations in Guatemala successfully completed, Anderson was prepared to return to Europe. He fell victim, however, to a "painful indisposition" that prevented him for a month or more from leaving the capital. During his illness several developments occurred that boded no good for the arrangements he had just concluded. Galindo, unchastened by the repudiation of the contract he had negotiated in the name of the directors and by the low opinion of his ethics expressed by Anderson, again busied himself with projects that bore directly on the Company's operations. And a correspondence that Anderson established with Chatfield in December gave the Consul the opportunity he had "taken measures" to invite in order to express his "unbiased" opinions on an undertaking he characterized as "a waste of British Capital & Lives."[32]

Galindo projected himself into Company affairs by means of two documents prepared on December 17. One was a letter to the directors inviting them to another involvement in a disputed title to Poyaisian land. The other was a road construction project submitted to the government of Guatemala. The letter to the directors alleged that the government of Honduras had ceded to Galindo the unoccupied lands on the Mosquito Shore of that state east of those granted to Morazán. As the new proprietor he offered to validate the Company's title to the lands in Poyais to which it held certificates dated prior to 1833 in the hope that the step would "lead to the profitable employment of British capital within my property."[33] The earlier decision of the directors to surrender their Poyaisian securities, their disastrous experience with titles granted by Central American authorities but disputed by British subjects, and their poor opinion of Galindo's integrity were probably sufficient to insure that the invitation to vassalage was ignored.

The proposal Galindo submitted to the government of Guatemala, however, was not disregarded. He offered to construct within four years the road between the port of Refugio and Salamá that the Company had declined to build, and in consequence, he claimed from the land ceded to the Company in Verapaz the block of territory four

32. Anderson to Chatfield, Dec. 1, 1838, and Carlos A. Meany to Chatfield, Dec. 15, 1838, both in FO 252/6, n.f.; Chatfield to Palmerston, No. 13, March 5, 1839, FO 15/22, fols. 99-100.
33. Copy Galindo to Directors, Dec. 17, 1839 [for 1838], FO 252/18, n.f.

leagues square reserved for the port and the strip of land a league in width on either side of the entire route. On the same day that it was submitted, Rivera Paz accepted the offer. His decree of approbation declared the new contract to be a clarification of the November 8 agreement with Anderson.[34] It is doubtful that the agent was more disposed on this occasion than he had been previously to claim for the Company the privilege of building the road, but he undoubtedly resented the loss of the land and the ability of Galindo again to intrude in what he must have regarded as exclusively a Company affair.

The correspondence with Chatfield Anderson established after an earlier letter had gone astray. On October 28 he had written to the Consul to report the Santo Tomás concession and to request his advice on the best places to establish settlers. Somewhere between Guatemala and San Salvador, however, the letter apparently fell into the hands of Carrera's partisans, and it was never delivered. On December 1, while he was ill in Guatemala, Anderson again had occasion to address the Consul and to enclose a copy of the earlier letter. Chatfield's reply of December 19 reached Anderson after he left the capital, but he continued the debate from Izabal on January 18, and the Consul had the last word in the exchange on February 5.[35]

Chatfield used the correspondence to renew with Anderson the argument begun with Fletcher on the appropriate place and type of activity for the Company's operations. The discussion ranged over a wide variety of topics, but the basic concern in the Consul's mind was the possibility that a successful establishment at Santo Tomás might undermine the commercial position of Belize. His pessimistic analysis of prospects in that area was intended to dissuade the Company from attempting a settlement there.

Chatfield argued that the underdeveloped state of Guatemala made the country uninviting as a field for investment. The absence of internal security, of industry, of domestic capital for economic expansion, and of population that could provide an extensive potential market, all made it doubtful that sufficient economic opportunity existed to justify an attempt to establish a port of deposit in competition with Belize. Moreover, there was no visible field for profitable investment of foreign capital in the port area. Indigo and cochineal

34. Galindo's proposal of Dec. 17, 1838, and acuerdo ejecutivo of acceptance, ANG, leg. 3618, exp. 84638, n.f.

35. Chatfield enclosed copies of the entire exchange with his dispatch No. 13 to Palmerston, March 5, 1839, fols. 103-39. The following digest of arguments is based on that source.

were the only important commercial products of the state, and neither was cultivated in the vicinity of Santo Tomás. Tobacco and sugar might be developed as export staples, but not by the labor of European colonists and certainly not at a competitive price with established centers of production. Moreover, agricultural development was handicapped by absence of extensive areas of level land suitable for large-scale cultivation.

On specific details of Anderson's plan, Chatfield pointed out what he believed were grave miscalculations. Santo Tomás, he observed, could be assumed by its own history, as well as by analogy, to be no more healthful to Europeans than such notoriously pestiferous towns as the ports of Omoa, Izabal, and Gualán on the Motagua, where the Company would probably find it necessary to keep an agent. The disease rate in these places showed that unhealthfulness was not a local condition but one characteristic of a substantial portion of the territory the Company proposed to colonize. Moreover, the area lying behind Santo Tomás was unsuited to cultivation, and communication by land with Gualán was made impossible by lack of pasturage for mules and by swampy terrain that made roadbuilding infeasible. Even assuming the existence of a road, distance and other problems would make freight rates from the port excessively high.

The whole plan for steam navigation he believed to be unrealistically conceived. The Motagua was obstructed by sandbars, rapids, and fallen tree trunks that could be removed to allow the passage of a steamer only at exorbitant cost, even assuming the improbable condition that the necessary laborers could be obtained to do the work. The Polochic carried insufficient water over its bar to permit the entry of even a shallow-draft steamer, and such a vessel, even if put into operation, could not safely navigate the open water between the mouth of the Río Dulce and Santo Tomás. Even assuming that steam traffic were established on the Polochic, the effect on commerce would be negligible until an all-weather road was constructed between Telemán and Salamá.

Chatfield, in short, could find no merit in any aspect of Anderson's plan. His best advice was to abandon as impractical all idea of occupying Santo Tomás. If additional reason were needed for reaching such a decision, he suggested that, although the nationality of settlers brought to the port might be of no concern to Guatemala, the British government might disapprove a colony of foreigners located so close to Belize. As an alternative to colonization at Santo Tomás he repeated the suggestion he had earlier made to Fletcher that the Company establish its settlements in the Petén and seek their access to the sea through Belize and by way of the Usumacinta River.

Anderson challenged most of Chatfield's facts, and he rejected all of his conclusions. He pointed out with some asperity that he "did not solicit an opinion as to the proposed introduction of settlers into this Country—that being a matter already decided upon, but merely requested to be favoured with the result of your experience as to the best locations for their establishment." He denied that Santo Tomás was insalubrious, but he pointed out that his plan allowed for such a contingency. The site would first be cleared to expose it to the drying effect of sun and air, then agricultural laborers would be brought in from the Spanish or Portuguese islands, Malta, the Bahamas, or southern Europe. Merchants and other residents whose occupations required no great physical exertion or exposure to the sun and rain would probably find the climate acceptable. If after trial, however, the locality proved uncongenial to Europeans, they could be removed to more temperate zones in the interior.

Chatfield's other arguments Anderson rejected as irrelevant or based on misconceptions. The scanty population, he pointed out, was the best justification for the colonization project, not an argument against it. Settlements of Europeans would increase the security of the country and extend civilization to the other inhabitants. The limited number of commercial productions likewise was no handicap, for the natural products of the country were much esteemed in the markets of the world and required only "industry, capital, and peace" to make them exportable. As they stood, they offered "inducements for colonization such as no other country possesses."

That Santo Tomás might come to rival Belize remained to be proved. The British flag, he conceded, gave the Settlement advantages that for some time would be unmatched by any commercial depot in Central America. But on any other ground, he asserted, it would be "an act of humanity" to abandon the pestiferous place. He predicted that before many years the town would be deserted, for, when the residents became acquainted with the superior advantages afforded by Santo Tomás, they would elect to establish themselves at the Guatemalan port. The implied threat that the British government might restrict the freedom of its subjects to make such a choice or prevent the establishment of nationals from other European states at the port he threatened to contest in the Parliament if necessary.

Anderson could chide the Consul for his tardy expression of opposition to the Company's enterprise after he had earlier given the appearance of "a favourable disposition," but he could scarcely fail to observe that many of the points were well taken. Moreover, the Company could assume, in making its plans, that the opinions of the Consul would be communicated to the British government and that they might be adopted also by the Cabinet.

When Anderson was again ready to travel early in January 1839, some two and one half months had elapsed since the Santo Tomás contract was signed. To relieve the Company of the handicap imposed by this initial delay, he obtained the agreement of Rivera Paz that the time period allowed for fulfillment of the Company's obligations would be counted from January 1, 1839, rather than from the preceding October 15.[36] Secure in the belief that he had placed the Company's interests in an unassailable position, he departed from the capital for Belize. He had scarcely left the country when a chain of domestic events began rapidly to undermine the arrangements he had just completed.

During the first few months of 1839 Guatemala experienced a significant political re-orientation. Encouraged by a military victory over Carrera at Villa Nueva followed by a treaty of peace with the guerrilla leader and emboldened by the presence of Morazán in Guatemala, the Liberals believed themselves secure enough to ignore the call for a Constituent Assembly issued under pressure of popular discontent the previous July. They therefore convoked the regular Assembly which, acting under the aegis of Morazán, restored Mariano Rivera Paz to his position as President of the Council and in his stead named Carlos Salazar, the Liberal hero of Villa Nueva, as provisional head of the government. Thus provoked, Carrera renewed the civil war. In mid-April he entered Guatemala City and re-installed Rivera Paz as chief executive.[37]

From this time forward Conservatives dominated the government and dictated its policies. On April 17 Rivera Paz declared the bonds with the Federation dissolved and formally assumed for Guatemala status as an independent nation. The Constituent Assembly, convened late in May, ratified this decree and later conferred upon the chief executive the title of president. It legislated a political redivision of the country that created Izabal and the Petén, both significantly related to the Company's projects, as districts presided over by commandants who were made directly dependent on the government and

36. Acuerdo ejecutivo, Jan. 3, 1839, ANG, leg. 1395, exp. 32352, n.f.
37. Marure, *Efemérides*, pp. 107-8, 111, 113.

independent of the corregidores who were made the chief administrators of the newly-delimited departments. On August 17 the Assembly reconstituted the Consulado de Comercio, suppressed by the Liberals in 1829, and clothed it with its original attributes.[38] As a national state Guatemala assumed the authority, previously vested in the Federation, over the ports within its borders, and it restored to the recreated merchant guild of colonial origin its quasi-public responsibility for public works.

In expectation that the state would exercise its new power, Juan José Balcarzel petitioned the government on August 19 to open the port of Santo Tomás. He urged either that it continue directly the work begun by the Pulleiro associates or that it reimburse the contractors for their expenditures in clearing the site so that they could proceed to erect the buildings for which they had imported the materials.[39]

The Assembly also took up the question. On November 5 it asked the government to provide, with its comments, copies of all contracts ceding lands to foreign companies and of all woodcutting concessions currently in force. In preparation of the *expediente* requested by the Assembly, the executive asked the Consulado to give its opinion on the contract signed with Anderson the year before and invited that body to extend its remarks "to anything related to land or water transport it may think appropriate for the good of the state, and to whatever, at least cost, would contribute to its prosperity." He also obtained from Juan Piñol, the commandant at Izabal, reports on the operations of Pulleiro and associates that showed extensive use at a variety of locations on the north coast of the woodcutting privilege granted to the partners in compensation for the work done at Santo Tomás.[40]

Before the documents requested by the Assembly were gathered, the legislative body adjourned. During the last days of the session, however, without waiting for the report of the government, it authorized the Consulado to undertake an extensive program of road con-

38. *Ibid.*, pp. 114-16; *Colección de los decretos de observancia general, expedidos por la Asamblea Constituyente del Estado de Guatemala, en los años de 1839 y 1840* (Guatemala, 1840), Decretos No. 16, June 15, 1839, pp. 8-9; No. 65, Dec. 3, 1839, pp. 99-104; No. 43, Sept. 12, 1839, pp. 40-42; No. 50, Oct. 2, 1839, pp. 54-65; and No. 36, Aug. 17, 1839, pp. 33-34.

39. Petition of Balcarzel, Nov. 19, 1839, ANG, leg. 1399, exp. 32724, fols. 6-7.

40. The legislative and executive requests are in ANG, leg. 1413, exp. 33007, fols. 2-3; Piñol's report is in leg. 1399, exp. 32724, fols. 11-13.

struction and port improvement, some parts of which had already been assigned by the contract to the English company.[41]

Anderson, meanwhile, was occupied with Company business in Belize and in the Verapaz. In early March he warned residents of the Settlement who were reported to be cutting mahogany from Company territory "to quit the said lands forthwith, under all the prejudices which will accrue to them in case of default," and he cautioned merchants against buying such timber from any but Company agents. He also requested residents to present for adjustment and settlement all claims against the steamer "Vera Paz" and the defunct settlement at New Liverpool. This activity led Superintendent Alexander Macdonald to remark that although the Company's project had been "a perfect failure" it still "lays claim to a jurisdiction quite independent." From Belize Anderson returned to the Verapaz. There he made further explorations in the vicinity of Panzós and began to prepare the site he had selected on the Boca Nueva for occupancy by settlers. When the work was well started, he left John MacKenney in charge as resident agent and began his return voyage to Europe.[42]

Anderson reached England on September 9, 1839, after an absence of almost exactly two years.[43] Whether or not he carried a report of recent adverse trends in Guatemala, he brought the directors good news. Despite the insurrection that had overthrown Gálvez he had secured the restoration of the Company to its privileged position, and to offset the loss of its Poyaisian assets he had obtained revalidation of its Verapaz grant and had negotiated a new cession of the District of Santo Tomás. With fifteen million acres of Guatemalan real estate at its disposal to develop and exploit, the Company might be on the eve of its first substantial achievement.

41. *Colección de los decretos . . . de 1839 y 1840*, Decreto No. 64, Nov. 29, 1839, pp. 96-99.

42. *The Belize Advertiser*, I, No. 21 (March 2, 1839), 108; Macdonald to Glenelg, No. 11, May 6, 1839, CO 123/55, n.f.; *Brief Statement*, 1840, pp. 69, 129, 147.

43. *Brief Statement*, 1840, pp. 17, 57.

IX

COMMERCIAL TOWNS:
ABBOTTSVILLE AND SANTO TOMÁS

Young Anderson returned to London in the fall of 1839 bearing official documents and firsthand information that enabled the Company finally to formulate plans for its Central American operation. The agent's frequent reports from Guatemala had kept the directors informed of the progress of his negotiations, but details of the arrangements he concluded were often lacking. The principal outlines of the Santo Tomás cession, for example, they learned from the summary sent by Anderson, but his acceptance of Meany's advice not to trust a copy of the document to the mails, "lest it fall into other hands,"[1] left them without full knowledge of the agreement until his arrival. For similar reasons they were only generally acquainted with the plans for developing the Company's concessions he formulated as a result of personal observation. On the basis of the information they received, however, the directors had been able to forecast the nature and intent of the operations they would be required to undertake and to make preliminary preparations to discharge the responsibilities to which the new agreements committed them.

During Anderson's absence the Company virtually completed the reorganization intended to give it more effective management. The directors added four new board members: Parker Duckworth Bingham, a commander in the Royal Navy; John Dawson, a merchant and ship broker of Billiter Square; William Hood, of Upper Bedford Place; and John Spurgin, M.D., a member of the Royal College of Physicians. Philip Dottin Souper left his position as secretary of the South-Western Railway Company, of which Abbott was a director, to accept the corresponding post with the Company in substitution for Leonard S. Coxe, who remained as cashier and accountant with

1. Young Anderson to the Directors, n.d., *Brief Statement, Supported by Original Documents, of the Important Grants Conceded to the Eastern Coast of Central America Commercial and Agricultural Company by the State of Guatemala* (London, 1839), p. 58.

responsibility for accepting at the central office applications from prospective land purchasers and immigrants. Some twelve additional agents were appointed to perform this function in other cities of England, and in Ireland, Scotland, and Wales. By the beginning of February 1839 the Company offices had been moved from the Lombard Street Chambers at 33 Clements Lane to 60 Moorgate Street, near the Bank. During 1840 the directors made two new appointments. They named David Pollock, Q.C., of 3 Pump Court, Temple, who had been standing counsel for the South-Western Railway, an eighth member of the board, and James A. Winsor replaced Souper as secretary.[2]

The financial measures taken during the interim of preparation lifted the Company, by the fall of 1839, from threatened bankruptcy to fiscal solvency. By early November the directors could report income of £18,011 10 s received from assessments paid on converting shares to debentures, sale of shares not converted, and proceeds from a call that was met on all but eighty-five of the outstanding five thousand debentures. They had spent £6,797 2s to achieve "the almost miraculous change in the position of the Company," £7,317 8s 7d to pay off old debts inherited from the previous administration, and £3,780 9s 6d in interest on debentures. Entirely free of debt, the Company had a small balance on deposit with its bankers, Glyn, Hallifax, Mills & Co.[3]

Revitalized at home and restored to privileged status in Guatemala the Company renewed its public appeal to investors and to emigrant settlers. During the spring or early summer of 1839 it issued a *Brief Statement, Supported by Original Documents, of the Important Grants Made by the Government of Guatemala to the Eastern Coast of Central America Commercial and Agricultural Company*, the most pretentious of its publications to date.[4] The booklet incorporated two of the pamphlets previously published, but it contained much new material. It presented to the judgment of public opinion the

2. Except as otherwise noted this information comes from *Brief Statement*, 1839, unnumbered leaf following title page, and p. 118. Pollock's name first appears among the board members in an advertisement "Emigration to Central America," *The Colonial Gazette* (London), No. 68 (March 11, 1840), p. 183.

3. Eastern Coast of Central America Commercial and Agricultural Company, *At a General Meeting of Proprietors Held at the Jamaica Coffeehouse on Monday* [May] *the 25th inst., the Directors presented the following Report* (London, [1840]), pp. 4-5. The reprint in *Brief Statement, Supported by Original Documents, of the Important Grants Conceded to the Eastern Coast of Central America Commercial & Agricultural Company by the State of Guatemala* (2nd ed.; London, 1840), pp. 166-67, gives the interest payments as £7,780 9s 6d.

4. 137 pp.

controversy between the Company and the British government over the territory lying between the Sibún and Sarstoon Rivers, reproduced the Verapaz contract in Spanish and in English translation, and gave a digest of the principal features of the Santo Tomás cession. Its avowed purpose was to extol to the "friends of emigration the unparalleled advantages" afforded by the Company's two concessions for the investment of "capital in money or labour."

The Company announced its purpose to divide and sell the lands within its holdings as urban sites and as large and small agricultural plots. It also offered employment on its own projects to agricultural workers and skilled artisans without capital. To speculators it held out the prospect of natural productions of enormous value awaiting only a means of transport to make their owners rich and of fertile soil situated in a benign climate requiring only cultivation by immigrant settlers or cheap Indian labor to burst forth in fecund production of an amazing variety of agricultural staples. To merchants it proffered access to a rich existing commerce and the possibility of vastly expanded operations as local cultivation was extended and improved transport facilities were provided, particularly over the trans-isthmian route to the Pacific. To philanthropists it pictured a rich but empty territory capable of furnishing homes and sustenance for the poor and needy of Europe. To emigrant land purchasers and contract laborers it offered opportunity to acquire land and ultimately to achieve independence by hard work. By these varied appeals the Company hoped to attract both capital and settlers for its projected towns and agricultural settlements.

Anderson's return to London initiated the final phase of the Company's preparations. In anticipation of a meeting of the proprietors the agent submitted to the directors a series of reports on his negotiations and his observations in Guatemala. He described the opportunities opened to the Company by the two contracts, discussed and rebutted Chatfield's objections to his proposals, and recommended a course of action that he believed would put the concessions to their most profitable use.[5]

Anderson's plan must have staggered even the most inventive proprietor of a company hitherto distinguished for reckless imagination. He sketched a design for a vast commercial and agricultural empire built upon the concessions granted by Guatemala and unified by a

5. These reports were printed under the title *Mr. Anderson's Report* (London, [1839]), 138 pp., and were substantially reproduced in *Brief Statement*, 1840, pp. 57-102. Except as otherwise noted the outline of Anderson's plan that follows is digested from the *Brief Statement* reprinting.

system of land and water transport monopolized by the Company. To attain the goal he described, however, the Company would have to put steamers in operation on the Bay of Honduras, the Motagua River, and the Río Dulce-Lake Izabal-Polochic waterway; establish commercial towns on the Bay of Santo Tomás and on the Polochic near the head of steam nagivation; construct roads connecting those waterways and linking them with the markets and centers of production in the interior; and establish agricultural settlements in the temperate highlands of the Verapaz lying farther inland.

Santo Tomás was to be the deepwater port and the hub of the commercial empire. It would be served at first by the steamer "Vera Paz" from Belize or Havana, but subsequently it might shake off dependence upon any intermediate station and be supplied by direct commerce with European ports. Through Santo Tomás merchandise and colonists would enter the country and local products would be exported. The port would be connected with the Motagua and with the Río Dulce by roads terminating in wharves at which steamers operating on those waterways could lade and discharge cargo without having to cross the treacherous bars that obstructed the river mouths.

The town at the head of steam navigation on the Polochic likewise was to be a commercial center. To enable it to fulfill this function it was to be linked by river steamer with the wharf at the Río Dulce end of the thoroughfare leading from Santo Tomás and connected by new and direct routes with Guatemala City and with the Petén. The road toward the capital was projected to bypass Salamá and to join the existing track south and west of that town at a spot called Llano Grande, near the site at which the Company was required to erect the penalty bridge over the Montagua. The Petén road would follow the Boca Nueva River until it flanked the mountains and then continue north to a projected town near Poptún which would command the headwaters of the Usumacinta River. As the focal point from which this system of land and water transport radiated, the river town was expected to engross the commerce of the Verapaz, the densely populated highlands of Guatemala from the capital to Quezaltenango, and the adjacent provinces of Mexico.

The establishment on the Polochic was expected also to serve as the *point d'appui* for several larger projected agricultural colonies. These settlements were to be established away from the river at more temperate and healthful elevations in the interior of the Verapaz along the new roads leading to Guatemala City and to the Petén. Toward the capital Anderson recommended an agricultural establishment at,

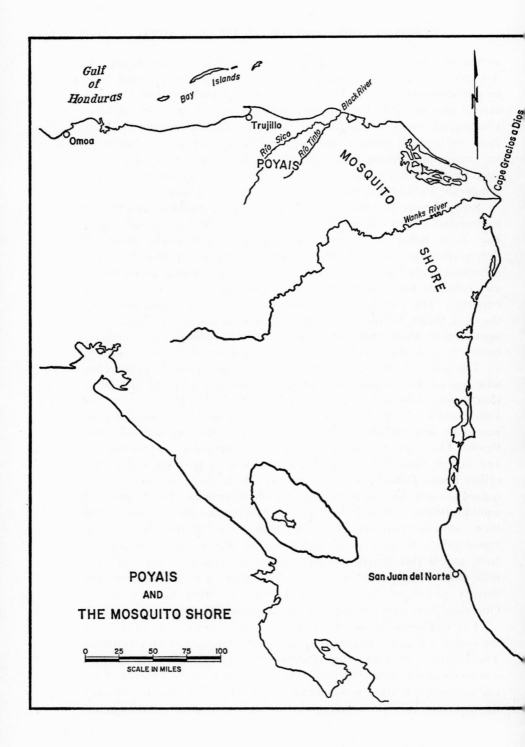

Gulf
of
Honduras

Bay Islands

Black River

Omoa

Trujillo

Río Sico

Río Tinto

Cape Gracios a Dios

POYAIS

MOSQUITO

Wanks River

SHORE

San Juan del Norte

POYAIS
AND
THE MOSQUITO SHORE

0   25   50   75   100
SCALE IN MILES

or near, Chamiquín and a second at Pampá, a day's journey farther inland. Along the Petén road he proposed that similar centers be established on the small plain at the foot of the mountain range and on the tableland above called Trece Aguas. The river town would be the reception center for colonists and supplies bound for the settlements and the commercial depot at which their products would be gathered for shipment to Santo Tomás.

The Motagua River route was expected in similar fashion to monopolize the commerce of the Department of Chiquimula as well as that of the states of Honduras and El Salvador. Ultimately it might be made the water link in a system of trans-isthmian transport that would displace the arduous and costly voyage around the Horn. By thus "extending the view" to the Pacific, the promoters could conjure up a vision of Santo Tomás grown into "an entrepot of British goods, whither the traders from all ports, even the extreme ends of the western shores of America, might resort, to select what each requires for his peculiar market. From Vancouver's Island to Chiloe, comprising ninety degrees of coast, every spot would be benefitted" by such a development.[6] The Company was obviously dreaming of creating at Santo Tomás nothing less than a nineteenth-century English counterpart of Spanish Portobello in the heyday of the fabled isthmian trade fair.

Anderson recommended that the Company move toward its ultimate goal by planning and undertaking an orderly succession of projects, each based on a realistic assessment of local conditions. By this means it could meet its obligations within the time periods set by its contracts and avoid the precipitous haste and concomitant lack of preparation that had resulted in failure of its earlier effort. Beyond their planning, however, the proprietors would have to supply both capital in sufficient amounts to accomplish the desired ends and proper administration. Good management would require the Company to provide "efficient local superintendence," establish a surveying and exploring department that should include native mahogany hunters, and set up a local office supplied with staff and funds adequate to its responsibilities.

As the first in the sequence of projects, Anderson proposed that the Company make the essential preparations to receive colonists in the Verapaz. The major requirements for this step would be to provide necessary means of transport by water and by land and to build a reception center for immigrants near the head of navigation on the

6. *Brief Statement*, 1839, pp. 10-13; *Brief Statement*, 1840, pp. 58-60, 67-68.

Polochic. This order of priorities would validate the Company's monopoly of steam navigation, give it control of the commerce of the Central American isthmus, and facilitate its colonization efforts by providing a means of transport for settlers and, later, for their products and imports. The measures would also afford the Company an immediate source of revenue. Income could be anticipated from sale of town lots and agricultural lands, sale of mahogany and other timber, production and sale of tobacco free of the government monopoly, rental of houses in the commercial town and reception center, commissions and fees for storage paid on merchandise in transit on the Polochic, tolls collected for use of the roads it constructed, and freights and fares paid by patrons of its steamers.[7]

During his stay in Guatemala Anderson had anticipated the establishment of such a town. He had examined all eligible spots within reasonable distance of the head of steam navigation on the Polochic from which easy access might be had to the river port of Panzós and to the road that ran through Telemán to the capital. On the left bank of the Boca Nueva River about a mile and a half from its confluence with the Polochic he discovered a site on the brow of a ridge, at the end of a spur thrust out to the brink of the stream from the mountain range beyond. Immediately behind the house and clearing owned by Antonino Sotela and at the crest of an escarpment that rose some forty yards above the level of the river, he found two gently ascending slopes, one behind and stepped above the other. This site overlooking the Boca Nueva and the Polochic he chose as the site of the town, which he named Abbottsville in honor of the chairman of the board.[8]

The locality Anderson described as offering advantages unmatched at any point along the margins of the Polochic. The lower course of the Boca Nueva, he believed, could at slight cost be cleared for navigation by a small steamer but, should he have underestimated the difficulty of the project, the Company could with almost equal convenience maintain its wharf and a store at Panzós on the Polochic. In the immediate vicinity of the site there was abundant soil adapted to the production of European fruits and vegetables, plentiful good water for drinking and domestic use, and a supply of native laborers willing to work for low wages. He believed that the elevation of the

7. *Anderson's Report,* pp. 89-90; *Brief Statement,* 1840, pp. 71-72.
8. Some details of the description were filled in by Colonel Remy de Puydt, head of the Belgian Exploratory Commission, to Comte de Hompesch, president of the Belgian Colonization Company, Nos. 1 and 2, both dated Feb. 5, 1842, AMAE, 2027, n.f.

plateau was sufficient to insure a salubrious climate for Europeans not engaged in heavy labor, although he admitted that they might not find it entirely comfortable. Average temperatures were higher than at any of the sites proposed for agricultural settlements, and plague had been known to strike there. Mosquitoes were troublesome, although less so than they had been at New Liverpool, but he believed that they could be eliminated altogether by felling the forest and exposing the soil to the drying action of the sun. Sotela's clearing in front gave an initial advantage in this respect.

Just before he left Guatemala Anderson had begun to prepare at Abbottsville a reception center for colonists. He had the vegetation cleared from the site, several houses erected, and others under construction. On his departure he left John MacKenney in charge with instructions and funds to proceed with the clearing above and below the town site, to plant corn and other food crops, and to start a large garden.

Anderson recommended that the Company complete the preparations he had begun. He proposed that it send out a shallow-draft steamer for service on the Polochic; materials to construct twenty frame houses at Abbottsville and minimum furnishings to equip them for occupancy; eighteen artisans skilled in building trades, two smiths, four gardeners, and twelve laborers, all with the implements and tools required by their trades; seeds for provisions and for commercial crops; a small supply of American lumber; and medicines for all the personnel. This step successfully accomplished, the immigrant settlers later sent out would find on their arrival an established village with houses available for rent and locally-grown provisions available at moderate cost; sites for agricultural settlements chosen and cleared where those who had purchased land could be settled; company plantations laid out for the production of coffee, tobacco, and cotton on which those who came out as laborers would find employment; and communications open toward the interior by means of the roads constructed by the Company and toward the sea by means of the Polochic steamer.

The proprietors assembled in a general meeting on November 25, 1839, to consider Anderson's report and to determine the Company's future course.[9] The directors submitted a plan of action to carry into effect Anderson's recommended immediate program, together with a statement of capital requirements and of the current financial status of the Company. They proposed to send out at once two steam vessels,

9. The following account is based on *Brief Statement*, 1840, pp. 168-69, 171-72.

one for the outward voyage and the other constructed for navigation of the Polochic and Lake Izabal; to discharge the penalty assessed for extension of the Verapaz contract by construction of a simplified chain suspension bridge invented and perfected by Dr. Spurgin; and to send Anderson in charge of a group of artisans and laborers to complete preparations at Abbottsville for reception of settlers. These investments they expected to be self-liquidating from revenue collected as a consequence of increased movement of persons and goods resulting from the availability of improved facilities for travel and transport. Should all other sources of income fail, however, the directors calculated that the total cost of the Company's future operations at home and abroad could be met, with a balance for division among the proprietors, by sale of no more than a tenth-part of the land in the District of Santo Tomás to which it had just obtained title. Pending ratification of the cession by the Guatemalan Assembly, however, no immediate plans were made either for its disposition or for its development.

In the prevailing mood of optimism the proprietors approved the recommendations of the directors. To provide the capital needed for immediate outlays they authorized the issuance of the remaining 5,000 debentures. The directors were instructed to offer the securities at such time and on such terms as would be most advantageous to the Company, but they were permitted to accept a discount rate no greater than five per cent.

During the next few months the directors prepared the Verapaz expedition. They acquired a shallow-draft steamer, which they christened the "Polochiquito," for service between Lake Izabal and Abbottsville, but they apparently abandoned the idea of providing the larger ocean-going vessel. They also recruited artisans and agricultural laborers for imminent departure to the Verapaz. Their brochure, *Emigation to Central America*,[10] offered two-year work contracts

10. (London, 1840), pp. 10-12. This statement of conditions was accompanied by an application form dated London, January 1, 1840. It appears, therefore, that these were the approximate terms on which the Company recruited the artisans sent out in late February. A somewhat different set of conditions, apparently drafted more to forestall a repetition of the "Britannia" affair than to achieve the constructive purpose of 1840, was stated in the laborers' contract published in the *Brief Statement*, 1839, pp. 129-31. These earlier contracts were to cover three years, bound the laborer to accept such work for such period of time (or no work at all) as the Company agent might assign, and to accept remuneration at the current level of wages in the country, plus use and occupancy of forty acres of land (under pledge to clear at least three acres each year) which would be deeded in full title at the end of his contract if the conditions had been satisfactorily fulfilled.

in the Verapaz to a limited number of able-bodied, married craftsmen of certified character between the ages of eighteen and forty-five. They particularly sought artisans skilled in the trades related to building, but they also hoped to enlist gardeners, smiths, and tree-fellers. They offered to furnish tools, pay good wages, and provide without cost steerage passage and rations during the voyage and living quarters and a food allotment at Abbottsville to the artisan, his wife, and children younger than twelve years of age. Children older than twelve could be taken out as apprentices, but in such cases the youths were required to work for the Company at fair wages to repay the cost of transport and maintenance. Working days were to be from six to six, with three hours off for meals. One month's pay was offered in advance upon signature of the contract, and wages were to start on the day of arrival in the colony. Employees were to forfeit two days' pay for neglect, drunkenness, or refusal to work, and twice the local value of any tool misused or lost. Wages would be suspended during periods of sickness, but food, medicines, and care were to be provided. Applicants were required to present a marriage certificate and references attesting to their honesty, sobriety, industriousness, and good character. Should the contract not be renewed by mutual agreement at the end of the two year period, the artisan would be a free agent, and for good conduct during his period of service the Company promised to grant him ten or fifteen acres of land.

By early 1840 arrangements for the expedition were complete, and it was dispatched from London on February 21 aboard the bark "St. Lawrence," Captain Huggup. The principal function of the group was to prepare the town site and the agricultural locations for the reception of settlers who were to follow. It appears, however, that the artisans were to be assigned plots of land which they were expected to cultivate and on which they would erect houses and become permanent settlers. With this justification the Company was able immediately after the vessel sailed to announce the establishment of the colony as an accomplished fact.[11]

To claim status of a colony for the work force was perhaps an exaggeration, but the lading of the "St. Lawrence" marked the enterprise as a serious attempt in that direction. On deck she carried the "Polochiquito" and two large boats for loading and unloading cargo. In her hold were a twelve-months' supply of provisions for the party; pre-fabricated houses to be erected at Abbottsville and furnishings to

11. Printed Company notice of sailing of the "St. Lawrence," with dates filled in by hand, Yale University Library.

198 EMPIRES IN THE WILDERNESS

equip them; fifteen iron water tanks; a variety of instruments, tools, utensils, and implements; twenty-nine shotguns with ammunition; and nearly one hundred tons of coal for use by the steamers. Also included in the cargo was a model of the iron chain suspension bridge sent for the approval of the President.[12]

The personnel of the expedition consisted of sixty-eight individuals. The principal figures were Anderson, who returned with his family to the Verapaz as Company superintendent; Count Maurice d'Adhemar, a French gentleman who had agreed to act as the Company surveyor; and the Reverend E. Rudolph W. Krause, a German Lutheran clergyman engaged to serve as schoolmaster and to minister to the religious needs of the settlers, who emigrated with his family. The remaining passengers included three purchasers of forty acres of land who accompanied the party as colonists and twenty-eight English and German artisans and laborers, some married and accompanied by their families, who went out in the employ of the Company. A disenchanted later-arrival at the settlement described the group as composed of English artisans, German laborers, French roués, Irish soldiery, and Portuguese peasants, most of whom were "very little, if anything, superior, in a moral point of view, to those who had mutinied on board the Britannia." For reasons analogous to those that prevent identification of the earlier Company settlers, most of the members of the work party cannot be distinguished as individuals. The few who managed by good or evil fortune to escape anonymity were a Mr. and Mrs. Bailey, Henrick Gunther, August Feldmann, Georg Hoffman, Peter Keller, a Mr. Mylord, and John Withers. Most of the immigrants were said to be Catholics.[13]

About two o'clock in the morning of Easter Sunday, April 19, the "St. Lawrence" anchored off the mouth of the Río Dulce. As day broke, the passengers were cheered to discern the "Vera Paz" lying in the river on the other side of the bar, and they were even more

12. Eastern Coast of Central America Commercial and Agricultural Company, *Report of the Directors, to a General Meeting of Proprietors, 18th August, 1840* (London, [1840]), p. 5; *El Tiempo* (Guatemala), No. 94 (May 7, 1840), p. 375. The arrival at Izabal in late February of some 17,000 feet of lumber and nine barrels of beer consigned to "George" Anderson may imply that the "American lumber" requested by Anderson was waiting for him at his arrival (ANG, leg. 2391, exp. 49928). Prefabricated "Immigrant houses" offered for sale in London (*Times*, No. 14,114 [Oct. 14, 1842], p. 1), may reveal the source of the cottages sent out for erection.

13. *Report of the Directors*, Aug. 18, 1840, pp. 4-5; *Brief Statement*, 1840, p. 68 n.; Frederick Crowe, *The Gospel in Central America* (London, 1850), p. 527; Manuel J. Piñol, Corregidor of Verapaz, to Minister of Government, June 10, 1840, *El Tiempo*, No. 106 (June 20, 1840), p. 424.

heartened, when a short time later the steamer's boat pulled out to them, to observe the robust health of the crew. Anderson offered immediate return passage to any individual who wished to abandon the enterprise, and when no one accepted the proffer the transfer of passengers and cargo to the "Vera Paz" began. Meanwhile, the Count d'Adhemar departed for Abbottsville to inform MacKenney of the arrival of the party.[14]

On April 30 MacKenney reached Izabal to meet the new arrivals, and on the following day the "Vera Paz" steamed into the harbor. While the passengers remained aboard the larger vessel, the "Polochiquito" was put through a trial run that gave great satisfaction to her handlers and compelled the admiration of the spectators. This augury of commercial development on the Polochic Juan J. Piñol, the commandant at Izabal, pridefully reported to the President of the country who considered the event to be of such importance that he ordered the letter published.[15] The collector of customs expressed in more practical form the satisfaction of the government with the Company's performance by sparing the passengers the ordeal of baggage inspection. When the expedition was ready to move, Anderson engaged five of the pirogues used in the lake and river traffic to assist in conveying the baggage and some of the colonists to Abbottsville.

The little flotilla left Izabal on May 4 to rendezvous at the mouth of the Polochic. The "Vera Paz" carried most of the colonists, but some were assigned, along with the baggage, to three of the pirogues and the remainder to the "Polochiquito," which also towed the remaining boats. The exceptionally shallow water over the bar of the river, the result of a protracted drought, caused apprehension that even the "Polochiquito" might not be able to cross. Anxiety was dispelled, however, when she navigated it triumphantly and, safely on the other side, took aboard the women and children. Anderson put Mr. Rush, the engineer of the "Vera Paz," and a native sailor in charge of the little vessel, and she steamed her way upstream, followed by the men and the baggage in the flotilla of dugouts. At Panzós the passengers transferred from the "Polochiquito" to small boats for the short trip up the Boca Nueva to Abbottsville. The party reached

14. Except as otherwise noted, the account of the arrival of the party and its journey to Abbottsville comes from Anderson's report to the secretary of the Company, May 12, 1840, published in *Report of the Directors*, Aug. 18, 1840, pp. 1-2 (Notes).

15. Juan J. Piñol to Minister of Government, May 1, 1840, ANG, leg. 3616, exp. 84472, fol. 1. The arrival and departure of ships, boats, and passengers at Izabal during this episode is recorded in ANG, leg. 2391, exp. 49928, and leg. 3221, exp. 66365.

its destination on May 9,[16] exactly three weeks after the "St. Lawrence" anchored off the Río Dulce.

The immigrants found the promised living quarters in the town only partly completed. Some of the large native-style houses begun on the site were ready for occupancy, but others afforded only thatched roofs without walls. The available housing was assigned to the new arrivals, and as construction proceeded at an increased tempo with the assistance of the European artisans, the entire party was settled in houses within a short time. When Manuel J. Piñol, corregidor of the Verapaz, came from Salamá to visit Abbottsville at the end of the month, he, Anderson, and the Count d'Adhemar planned the arrangement of the settlement and marked sites for a Catholic chapel and a municipal building. An emigrant from Belize who later joined the colony remarked that the town was far from wisely planned but that it was "many degrees better than New Liverpool."[17]

First priority in construction at Abbottsville was given to dwellings that would enable the settlement to serve as a reception center for colonists. For the time being, therefore, the lumber for the Company storehouse was allowed to remain at Izabal while the "neat boarded cottage[s] constructed in London" were assembled on the locations chosen for them, and some individuals began to erect private dwellings. The houses, whether imported or of local construction, were ranged along either side of the rugged path, or street, that ascended the slope from the lip of the escarpment. The elevation afforded the householders a wild and romantic vista. The last cottage at the end of the street was "perched upon the edge of a precipice overhanging a considerable plain," and its "latticed verandah commanded a view of the Boca Nueva . . . and of gigantic forest trees extending along a wide valley, and spreading their continuous mantle of rank verdure over the very summits of the bold and lofty ranges of mountains which bounded the scene to the north and to the south, at once setting limits to the sweep of the mighty Polochic, and seeming to the eye to terminate only where the broad ocean was known to commence."[18]

It was intended that the Company houses should serve only as temporary residences, first for the work force and then for successive

16. Letter of Henrich Gunther, Georg Hoffman, and August Feldmann, printed in *Report of the Directors*, Aug. 18, 1840, p. 4 (Notes).

17. M. J. Piñol to Minister of Government, June 10, 1840, p. 424; Crowe, *Gospel*, p. 526.

18. Anderson to Secretary, May 12, 1840, p. 2 (Notes); Crowe, *Gospel*, pp. 526, 529, 530.

parties of immigrants. The members of each new group were expected to build private dwellings within six months and to vacate Company facilities to allow accommodation of the next party. In early June Anderson calculated that he would be prepared by November to accommodate one hundred immigrant families should they be sent out, but he later postponed the date until Christmas.[19]

As buildings rose on the townsite at Abbottsville, the environs began to show the results of labor applied to the soil. In early June Anderson reported a Company clearing nearly a mile long and about half as wide partly planted to corn. Land was apparently assigned to artisans as well as to colonists, and private individuals began gardens and bought livestock both for their own use and in the expectation of later sale. By mid-August fields of corn, pastures, and farms stocked with cows, pigs, and poultry stretched away from the town in several directions. While crops were maturing, the workers were supplied with provisions by Indians from the surrounding country who came to sell their produce under the shelter that had been erected to serve the town as a market. A company store provided the settlers with such reminders of home as soap, sugar, cheese, and beer.[20]

The work regime under which these improvements were accomplished differed slightly from that announced by the Company's literature in England. Anderson fixed the stipulated nine-hour working day between five in the morning and seven in the evening with a five-hour interval at the middle of the day. During the two or three hours of most oppressive heat no one was allowed to labor either at his own or on Company projects. Although the Superintendent reported that all of the artisans fell to their tasks with "hand and heart," he had special praise for some members of the group. Several of the English workers had proved invaluable, but all the German members of the work force distinguished themselves by their industriousness and their fine spirit.[21]

Health conditions in the town were reported to be remarkably good. Medical care was provided by re-employing Dr. Henry pro tem, apparently until Dr. W. King could resume service as regular doctor.

19. Eastern Coast of Central America Commercial and Agricultural Company, *Emigration to Central America* [London, 1840], pp. 6-10; Anderson to the Directors, No. 1, June 4, 1840, *Report of the Directors,* Aug. 18, 1840, p. 3 (Notes).

20. Anderson to Directors, June 4, 1840, p. 3 (Notes); Eastern Coast of Central America Commercial and Agricultural Company, *Emigration to Vera Paz, Latest Intelligence from the Colony* [London, 1840?], p. [1]; M. J. Piñol to Minister of Government, June 10, 1840, p. 424.

21. Anderson to Secretary, May 12, 1840, p. 2 (Notes); Anderson to Directors, June 4, 1840, p. 3 (Notes).

The workers arrived during the season of greatest heat and rain when plague was rampant in the surrounding country and along the river. Chamiquín and Tucurú suffered serious losses of population as a result of the epidemic, but there was little or none of the disease at Abbottsville. Soon after their arrival a few of the laborers contracted colds and slight fevers, but Anderson observed that by their conduct they had done "all they could to bring it on." About a dozen suffered from a tropical malady that the Superintendent attributed to gorging on ripe bananas, plantains, and pineapples. The testimony of Reverend Krause, however, suggests that these gastronomical excesses may not have been entirely voluntary. "Our principal food is plantains," he wrote to his brother and sister, "a most delicious fruit, which we can have the whole year." His determinedly cheerful explanation that "we cook them, roast and fry them, in different ways" may have been interpreted by his relatives as an enthusiastic endorsement of tropical cookery, but the evidence of attempt of varied preparation to relieve dietary monotony would probably have been understood by another group of English colonists who settled at Plymouth under another London company some two centuries earlier. Despite early evidence of health, some of the residents of Abbottsville fell victim to disease or to overindulgence, for Crowe describes a graveyard at the two-year old settlement in which "a few of England's exiles—convicts of penury and vice—lay mouldering beneath the soil."[22]

During the first months of its existence Abbottsville gave promise of achieving the status planned for it. In spite of some defections the population increased slightly, and by the end of 1840 it numbered some eighty persons. The growth, it appears, was due primarily to the accession of a few immigrants from Belize and of some Ladino families in addition to that of Antonino Sotela who were attracted by the free expenditure of Company funds. Indians who came on other missions often stayed for a time to work at such tasks as cultivating crops, clearing land, or opening roads and in this fashion temporarily added one hundred or more natives to the population of the town. The new market for foodstuffs and labor at Abbottsville caused an even more significant demographic shift in the Verapaz. Indians established two new villages near the settlement, one at Chactilá, two leagues from Abbottsville, formed by residents from San Pedro Carchá and San Juan Chamelco and the other called

22. Anderson to Directors, June 4, 1840, pp. 2-3 (Notes); Rev. Krause to relatives, June 4, 1840, in *Report of the Directors*, Aug. 18, 1840, p. 3 (Notes); M. J. Piñol to Minister of Government, June 10, 1840, p. 424; Crowe, *Gospel*, p. 533.

Polochic. More than one hundred native families from established towns were reported to be disposed to settle in each.[23]

The promising development of the colony, however, was abruptly arrested during the fall of 1840. The change was due in part to declining support from the directors in London and in part to a reversal of policy by the Guatemalan government. For more than a year the climate of opinion in the capital had grown steadily cooler toward foreign companies as agents for accomplishing national development and correspondingly warmer toward national enterprise. This attitude was clearly ascendant in the Constituent Assembly when it reconvened on July 1, 1840, and resumed its consideration of the Santo Tomás question.

On August 6, Deputy Manuel Francisco Pavón, the current Prior of the Consulado and long recognized as a Conservative leader in Guatemala, proposed to the Assembly that it authorize the government to take directly the steps necessary to open the port of Santo Tomás. The Committee on Commerce, to which the measure was referred, asked before giving a report on the subject to know the views of the executive branch. The Assembly therefore sent the Pavón proposal to Luis Batres, the Minister of Finance, for an opinion and repeated the request made during its previous session that the President's office supply relevant background material on Santo Tomás. Each of these officials independently asked the Consulado to express its views on the issue before the Assembly. On September 5 the merchant guild endorsed the Pavón proposal in a brief letter to the Minister of Finance, and on October 8 it submitted to the executive a report intended to demolish the grounds on which the Anderson contract had been justified.[24]

The specific interests the Consulado sought to advance may have differed from those that motivated the critics of the earlier Bennett and Meany agreement, but the arguments it presented against the Santo Tomás contract were essentially the same. It pointed out that circumstances at the time offered the government no alternative to the agreement if it wished to accomplish its beneficent objectives. Civil war racked the country, the government treasury was empty, and there was a notable absence of the spirit of enterprise that else-

23. Crowe, *Gospel*, pp. 525, 527; M. J. Piñol to Minister of Government, June 10, 1840, p. 424. The comment on the disposition of the Indians to emigrate to the new towns does not appear in the published report, but the manuscript copy in ABVP contains the sentence.

24. This entire transaction is documented in ANG, leg. 1399, exp. 32724, fols. 1-3, 36-41.

where made it possible to accomplish great projects. The reestablishment of peace, however, had since so improved domestic prospects that the peculiar advantages originally conferred by the contract had largely disappeared.

Benefits as great as those originally anticipated would unquestionably accrue from opening the port, the Consulado averred, but the contract signed with Anderson paid an excessive price for them in concessions and privileges. The territory ceded was enormous in extent and contained resources of great value. Moreover, the situation of the grant on the northern coast and the inclusion within it of the best port in the country made the concession not merely injudicious but dangerous to the security of the nation. The exclusive privileges granted to the colonizers accorded them status superior to that of the native-born inhabitants, and this discrepancy could be expected to generate hatreds that would produce only unhappy consequences. Other provisions of the contract compounded this evil, for the ceded lands and privileges were destined to benefit, not the colonists, but a foreign company which was permitted to speculate on its concessions while maintaining the colonists in a situation of dependency and isolation that would make it difficult to establish mutually advantageous relations with the remainder of the state.

The assumption that foreign settlement was inevitably advantageous, the Consulado alleged, had been proved fallacious by the experience of other nations. It was unquestionably beneficial to a nation to receive industrious immigrants who mingled with the local citizenry, but foreign colonists settled in separate communities and allowed to maintain customs and laws distinct from those existing in the remainder of the country presented an entirely different prospect. Settlements of such character might well come to assert pretensions that could not be reconciled with the common good and that might endanger the very independence of the state. Mexico, for example, had achieved the colonization of Texas by means of land concessions that were virtually identical with those made by the contract to the Company, and the example of successful revolution by those colonists might encourage foreign settlers in Central America to carry the parallel one step further. The British conversion of trading factories into political sovereignty in India and the facile expansion of the population and power of the United States against Indian and European-derived neighbors alike both pointed up the hazard of permitting a foreign lodgement within the national territory.

Without regard to other considerations, the Consulado believed it impolitic for a government freshly installed in power by general revolt to risk giving cause for new public unrest. This tenet was especially relevant to the current authorities because the recent popular agitation had in part been produced by emphatic disapproval of just such concessions as those granted in the Santo Tomás contract. To ratify the agreement would be to give enemies of the new regime a basis for reviving popular discontent.

In the opinion of the Consulado the best interests of the state required that the government itself open the port and establish the town of Santo Tomás. Were the contract to be approved, the government would be prevented from undertaking the task and the state would be denied the advantages that would accrue should its own efforts accomplish the project. It recommended, therefore, that the Santo Tomás agreement be denied ratification.

In this climate of adverse opinion the government submitted the Anderson contract on Santo Tomás to the consideration of the Assembly. On October 15 it transmitted to the legislative body the file on the negotiation of the agreement, the dossier relating to the project undertaken by the Pulleiro associates, and the opinions on the subject given by the Consulado. It made no recommendations but confined its remarks to an explanation of the circumstances under which each document was produced.

On October 22 the Committee on Commerce, consciously accepting and virtually repeating the arguments of the Consulado, recommended that the Assembly refuse ratification to the Santo Tomás contract. It professed complete accord with the objectives the government had sought to attain in the negotiations with Anderson, but it found the resulting agreement disadvantageous under current circumstances. The deficiency lay, not in the essence of the contract, but in those conditions which violated the principal of reciprocal benefit. The Santo Tomás contract thus disposed of, the Committee recommended adoption of the Pavón proposal.

The decree drafted by the Committee on Commerce was unanimously adopted by the Assembly on October 27, approved by Rivera Paz, and promulgated on October 30. The measure denied ratification to the Santo Tomás contract, annulled it in all its parts, and authorized the government in consultation with the Consulado to establish and colonize the port of Santo Tomás. A hint of vindictive intent can be discerned in the instruction given to the executive that he arrange, by appointment of a special agent if necessary, to have the decree published in London.[25]

25. Decreto No. 107, *Colección de los decretos de observancia general, expedidos*

The favorable terms won for the directors by Anderson's insistence during the negotiations two years earlier proved to be the fundamental obstacle to the ratification of the contract. In contrast to their suspicion of the Company, however, neither the Committee nor the Assembly appears to have thought it remarkable that the Consulado had been given double opportunity to advance its own monopolistic interests by advising against those granted to a potential rival. There is no evidence to suggest that Anderson or any other agent of the Company attempted to avert the disapprobation of the contract or for that matter that they were aware it was under consideration. Whether inevitable under the circumstances or due to the negligence of its agents in Guatemala, this major reverse suffered by the Company signalized an abrupt decline in its fortunes.

When Anderson learned the fate of his Santo Tomás agreement, he must have realized that the key to the Company's projected operation had been removed. The land in the District that the directors had chosen to regard as capital had been repossessed, as had the deepwater port that was to have served as the entrepôt of a projected commercial empire. Henceforward, any development it might accomplish in Guatemala would have to be achieved on its own resources and entirely within the Verapaz. In that area Anderson might yet salvage for the Company a portion of his plan by establishing the proposed interior agricultural colonies and by opening a system of land routes emanating from the head of navigation on the Polochic. To these two tasks he now devoted his particular attention.

To enable him to make a definitive selection of sites for agricultural settlements, Anderson began a series of explorations that seem to have been intensified after the legislative disapproval of the Santo Tomás contract.[26] In August 1840 he sent Mr. Mylord to reconnoiter the region of Trece Aguas to the west and north of Abbottsville. The party reached the area without difficulty, examined the valley, and pressed on to an even larger one beyond. They reported enthusiastically on the relative accessibility of the country to the northwest and on the fertility, agreeable temperature, and beauty of

---

por la Asamblea Constituyente del Estado de Guatemala, en los años de 1839 y 1840 (Guatemala, 1840), pp. 173-75.

26. This and the following two paragraphs are based on reports of developments in the Verapaz furnished by the Eastern Coast Company to the Belgian Colonization Company in Brussels and digested by the Belgians for the information of their own government in a document headed: Des Dépêches reçues de Verapaz, en dâte du 10 mar 1841, donnant à la Compagnie Commercial et Agricole de Côtes Orientales de l'Amerique Centrale les renseignements suivantes, sur ses establissements dans ce département, n.d., AMAE, 2027.

the sites for colonization afforded by that region. Anderson himself later confirmed the evaluation of the earlier party and planned to prepare sites in that direction for the location of the expected colonists. He surveyed a ridge route to the area over which he proposed subsequently to open a mule trail and in the course of his examination discovered a hill-top site that he believed admirably suited for a settlement. He probed the interior until he reached Senahú and marked the inviting valleys on either side of the town as appropriate locations for agricultural communities. He also explored west and south of Abbottsville as far as Purulhá, where he was impressed by the fine grassy plain which he believed capable of providing pasture for herds of domestic animals.

In expectation that colonists would soon arrive to occupy the sites he selected west and north of Abbottsville, Anderson began to open trails to link them with the settlement and with the Polochic. By the spring of 1841 these roads were reported to be almost completed. Anderson now informed the directors that he lacked only hard-working agriculturalists to reinforce the pioneers in the Verapaz in order to develop the resources of the country thus made accessible. These reports made good propaganda for the Company in Europe, but they produced no colonists in Guatemala. The only agricultural settlers actually established were a transferred group of workers who came out in 1840. In response to the request of the German laborers that they be moved to an environment cooler than Abbottsville, Anderson constructed a road to a locality some eight miles distant identified as Benny perte (perhaps an attempt to render in French Benichaj, a place in the *municipio* of Senahú), and apparently settled them there.

Anderson's road-building program also included a new trace from the Polochic in the direction of the capital. Reports from the colony early in 1841 announced that work crews would soon finish a new and shorter road to the river that was expected to facilitate the movement of goods by eliminating the necessity of transporting them to Abbottsville. This deliberate by-pass of the Company settlement implied that Anderson had abandoned the plan to establish a commercial entrepôt at the head of steam navigation on the Polochic. Shortage of funds and loss of Santo Tomás were undoubtedly causes contributing to the decision, but the determining consideration must have been that the "Polochiquito" seems to have disappeared soon after its initial voyage. Without the little steamer, commerce on the Polochic would be carried as before in pirogues which could navigate the shallower water above Panzós. Telemán would probably continue, therefore, as the principal river port, and Panzós would be used chiefly by contraband traders who found it expedient to disembark their cargoes at some distance from the watchful eyes of the authorities upstream. Deprived of the key element in his plan to establish control over the commerce of the Polochic, there was little reason for Anderson to give high priority to the now largely meaningless adjunct services that had been projected for Panzós or Abbottsville. The new road was perhaps intended to enhance the position of Panzós and to allow the Company to collect tolls that would compensate in part for the revenue the steamer had been expected to earn.

The Company also undertook to keep river commerce at Panzós under surveillance. Responsibility for this function rested primarily with MacKenney, but Pedro Pérez, resident agent who served gratuitously at the port, performed the actual inspections. The effectiveness of the control suffered, however, because Pérez commanded no force with which he could compel pirogue owners to submit to his jurisdiction and because his unremunerated position gave him little basis on which to claim status as a public official.[27]

These operations along the river probably produced no significant fraction of the revenue the directors had anticipated from that source, but they were sufficient to involve the Company in a protracted misunderstanding with the Guatemalan government over measures adopted to suppress illicit commerce. It appears that contraband trade by way of the lightly-policed Polochic had long been a common occupation of the inhabitants of the region. Among the contemporary practitioners of the business, Antonino Sotela, the original settler on the site at Abbottsville, was one of the principal operators, but his close relations with Pedro Oliva, a resident of Telemán of like character and the power in local affairs, had afforded him immunity from official interference. Shortly before the Company work force arrived at Abbottsville, however, the government took measures intended to control illicit commerce on the river. On the basis of reports that an extensive contraband traffic in *aguardiente,* tobacco, arms, and powder was being conducted through Company territory at Panzós, the corregidor of the Verapaz prohibited the disembarkation of cargo of any kind at that port. After Abbottsville was occupied, Company agents at Panzós joined with Guatemalan officials at Telemán and Chamiquín to make the embargo effective.

27. Juan MacKenney to the President of Guatemala, Feb. 26, 1841, ANG, leg. 3661, exp. 74283, n.f.

In early November 1840 it was reported that Sotela was conducting a contraband shipment of powder up the river. The suspect had already passed beyond Telemán when the news reached officials at that place, but MacKenney dispatched an express messenger to Andrés Santa María, the law enforcement officer at Chamiquín, informing him that Sotela was reported to be in his jurisdiction. On the basis of this information Santa María organized a pursuit party that overtook Sotela at Tucurú. The contrabandist and his companions tried to buy their way out of difficulty, but Santa María spurned their offer, seized the fourteen or sixteen *arrobas* of powder they carried, and took it in person to Salamá where he turned it over to José Dolores Gutiérrez, the corregidor. That official, however, was annoyed rather than pleased by the coup. He required Santa María to replace from his own funds the money he had taken from the local treasury to pay the expenses of the expedition and allowed him no compensation for his horse, stolen while he was in Salamá.[28]

Perhaps because of this episode the contraband traders, writing as pirogue owners of Izabal, petitioned in February 1841 for relaxation of controls on the river trade. They represented the regulations in force along the Polochic to be arbitrary dispositions adopted by Company officials at Panzós in connivance with the authorities at Chamiquín for the purpose of diverting to Abbottsville the provisions that the pirogue owners had traditionally purchased at Panzós to supply the population and the garrison at Izabal. They were prohibited, they alleged, from buying foodstuffs at the river port, and in consequence, the residents of Izabal were bordering on starvation. They requested, therefore, that the central government give orders to the officials of the river towns requiring them to withdraw the regulations that impeded the provisions trade. Gerónimo Paiz, the new commandant at Izabal, forwarded the petition to Guatemala with his full approval. Without investigating the charges, the central government issued orders as requested and directed the corregidor to see that they were observed. Ignacio Córdova, the new incumbent, complied with the instructions, but he protested to the government that the real objective of the petitioners was to destroy the controls over contraband for which the trade in provisions was only a cloak.[29]

28. M. J. Piñol to Minister of Finance, Feb. 14, 1840, and José Nicolás Aparicio, Consulado agent at Telemán, to Minister of Finance, Nov. 3, 1840, ANG, leg. 3360, exps. 74273 and 74279, n.f.

29. Petition of pirogue owners to Corregidor and Commandant of Izabal, Feb. 18, 1841; draft letter to Superintendent at Abbottsville, Feb. 27, 1841; draft letter to Corregidor of Verapaz, Feb. 27, 1841; all in ANG, leg. 3222, exp. 66526, n.f.;

On almost the very day that the corregidor pointed out to the central authorities the mistaken assumption on which they had acted, those officials instructed him to increase his vigilance to thwart contraband. The government had received positive evidence that a clandestine shipment of powder destined for Los Altos was entering the country by way of Panzós. The corregidor, therefore, was to give orders to the guard along the river and to the officials at Abbottsville to hunt down the cargo. With some exasperation the corregidor pointed out that measures to halt the practice which the government now found it necessary to combat had been in effect until they were revoked on superior orders as a result of representations made by individuals who sought to free their illicit operations of all impediment.[30]

Perhaps because inspection was tightened along the river as a result of the latest government orders, Paiz again protested to the central government in September 1841 that in disregard of specific instructions MacKenney still obstructed the provisions trade. He alleged that in execution of an embargo imposed by MacKenney Pérez had seized at Panzós several demijohns of liquor cleared through the customs house at the lake port "for no reason but that they were imported by a resident of Izabal." In response to this appeal, the government repeated its instructions to Company and Guatemalan officials at the river ports and ordered them not alone to refrain from obstructing, but actively to assist, the trade in provisions.[31]

Whatever the justification of the participants, the controversy trapped Company agents and the Guatemalan authorities who acted in concert with them between hostile officials at Izabal and in Guatemala City. The aggressive action taken by Paiz could be explained either by a personal involvement in the contraband trade or by an overriding concern with adequate provisioning of the port under his command. The evidence of the market for local produce at Abbottsville gives some reason to believe that the existence of the colony may have deranged the accustomed pattern in distribution of foodstuffs, but the central government appears to have disregarded the relevance of contraband to the dispute. It therefore supported its own citizens

Corregidor of Verapaz to Minister of Government, March 5, 1841, ANG, leg. 3361, exp. 74283, n.f.

30. Draft letter to Corregidor of Verapaz, March 8, 1841, and Corregidor of Verapaz to Minister of Government, March 11, 1841, ANG, leg. 3361, exp. 74283, n.f.

31. Gerónimo Paiz to Minister General, Sept. 24, 1841; draft letter to Corregidor and Commandant of Izabal, Oct. 2, 1841; both in ANG, leg. 3222, exp. 66640, n.f.

in what it conceived to be a simple conflict of requirements between an established national port and an incipient foreign settlement. The disfavor into which the Company had lately fallen undoubtedly made it easier for the authorities to make their choice, and the recurring harassment of which each thought the other guilty must have further eroded confidence on both sides.

The deterioration at Abbottsville soon began to undermine the morale of the colony. Toward the end of 1840 Reverend Krause abandoned his post and the settlement and took his family to Guatemala City.[32] Dr. King also was tempted to leave the Company's employ. In July 1841 Paiz proposed to the central government that the Company physician be employed to attend the population and the garrison at Izabal at a monthly salary of 40 pesos to be paid in part by popular subscription and in part from receipts at the local customs house. The government refused to consider the proposition, but the evidence of a shipment of construction materials consigned to King at Izabal during the fall of 1841 suggests that the doctor may have decided to risk the appointment on the basis of local resources alone. The issue of employing an official physician in Izabal, however, was still pending in 1843.[33]

To assume the duties abandoned by Krause, Anderson employed Frederick Crowe, who originally came to Central America under Company auspices as a colonist aboard the notorious "Britannia." Landed with the other passengers at Belize he had settled there, had married a French widow of some means, and had come under the influence of Mr. Alexander Henderson, the local representative of the Baptist Missionary Society, and become a convert. The position at Abbottsville interested him as a stepping stone to the work of evangelization he wished to carry on in adjoining communities of Spanish speech. He therefore accepted Anderson's offer to conduct the school in the Company settlement with the understanding that he might on his own responsibility undertake religious work among the colonists and the natives.

Crowe pursued his religious purpose in all of his activities. He took advantage of the grant of religious liberty in the colony to import Bibles which he distributed as widely as possible. He used

32. Crowe, *Gospel,* p. 525.
33. Paiz to Minister General, July 30, 1841, and Aug. 13, 1841, and report on arrivals and departures of vessels at Izabal, Sept. 28, 1841, all in ANG, leg. 3222, exps. 66642, 66618, n.f.; *Al Sr. Secretario del despacho de gobernación del Supremo Gobierno* (*hoja suelta* signed Marcos Dardon and Manuel Santa Cruz dated Guatemala, May 8, 1843).

the New Testament as a text in his school, and he persuaded some of the national institutions to follow his example. He seized every opportunity to read passages to the natives in their homes, and later he did the same "publicly in the cabildo to the Spaniards." As his facility in the use of the language increased, he ventured some commentary on his texts. He gradually extended his activity to native towns as distant as Salamá, often with the aid of the local priest, but on occasion he aroused the antagonism of the Catholic clergy.

Crowe's heavy religious emphasis was not popular in Abbottsville. His school was not well attended, and his preachments were scorned by the inhabitants. His attempt to impose puritanical standards of conduct on a community grown lax in the criteria applied to personal behavior, among the members of which "the grossest immorality prevailed, and the most profane language was common," foredoomed his effort to failure. His religious services began with official approval, but "a very few addresses on their spiritual concerns sufficed to scatter the little congregation" and to range his original patrons "among the bitterest enemies of the truth." Indeed, some of his choicest shafts appear to have been directed at Company officials who "were themselves flagrantly outraging the laws of God." In consequence, he gave his attention principally to the native inhabitants and their children.[34]

Crowe's harsh judgment of his contemporaries may have been unjustifiably comprehensive, but evidence from a variety of sources confirms his observation that there was little enthusiasm among the colonists for the temperate and moral life he advocated. The Company had thought to forestall flagrant breaches of the peace and of ethics by outlawing liquor and games of chance in the colony, but the general absence of resources for wholesome amusement in the isolated settlement encouraged forms of social behavior that regulations alone were insufficient to control.

One basic difficulty Anderson noted in the first report he made to the directors from Abbottsville. The failure of the Company to recruit, as it had intended, a work force composed entirely of married men, he pointed out, exposed the colony to "the evils to be apprehended (already felt) from want of Female Emigrants."[35] The conduct of the settlers apparently confirmed the Superintendent's fears, but deviations from the moral code seem rarely to have been followed by disciplinary action. One such case, however, reached the Guate-

34. Crowe, *Gospel*, pp. 517, 522, 524-28.
35. Anderson to Directors, June 4, 1840, p. 2 (Notes).

malan courts. John Withers and Mrs. Helen Bailey, both members of the colony, were arrested at Abbottsville late in 1840 on the criminal charge of adultery. Mrs. Bailey was released to her husband who, after some consideration, decided not to prosecute the case. Withers, however, was retained in custody in Salamá for several weeks until, taking advantage of the special status he enjoyed as a member of the colony, he appealed to the central government. He was then ordered sent to Guatemala City, where in February 1841 the court stayed judgment on both individuals. Withers was allowed to emigrate from the country, but Mrs. Bailey remained to become the principal figure in the fire that virtually destroyed Izabal in 1842.[36]

Irresponsible behavior by residents at Abbottsville was encouraged by the absence in the colony of any regularly constituted governing authority. Perhaps because Company officials regarded the inhabitants as temporory employees rather than permanent colonists, they organized no municipal government among the settlers as authorized by the contract. Aside from Company officers, the only local authorities were those commissioned on an interim basis by agents of the Guatemalan government. During his visit to Abbottsville on May 30, 1840, Juan J. Piñol, the commandant at Izabal, took the first steps in this direction. He appointed John MacKenney police judge, named an *alcalde auxiliar* for the settlement, and left a body of police regulations that was solemnly proclaimed in the town. Some time later, during a tour of inspection by Manuel J. Piñol, the corregidor of the Verapaz, he and Anderson agreed upon a series of regulations that were intended to maintain order and to give the colonists security.[37]

Because the machinery of local government did not advance beyond this rudimentary state, the settlement remained in an anomalous position outside any system of regular administrative control. It was not counted among the municipalities of the Verapaz, and it had no clearly defined status within the framework of the Guatemalan government. It is perhaps best described as a Company work camp.

The special position accorded to the colony by the Verapaz charter was an administrative annoyance to local authorities that must have contributed to the deteriorating relationship between the Company

36. Juzgado de 1ᵃ Instancia de Verapaz y Peten, Estado que manifiesta el que tienen las causas criminales de los reos que existen . . ., Dec. 24, 1840, and Corregidor of Verapaz to Minister General, Jan. 1, 1841, both in ANG, leg. 3361, exp. 74283, n.f.; draft letter to Corregidor of Verapaz, Dec. 29, 1840, ANG, leg. 3360, exp. 74272, n.f.; *Gaceta Oficial* (Guatemala), No. 4 (March 29, 1841), p. 16; William Hall to Captain Carter, H. M. S. "Vestal," Jan. 18, 1841, FO 252/18, n.f.

37. M. J. Piñol to Minister of Government, June 10, 1840, p. 424; Des Dépêches reçues de Verapaz, en dâte du 10 mars 1841, n.f.

and the government of Guatemala. In November 1840, for example, José Dolores Gutiérrez, recently appointed corregidor of the Verapaz, innocently requested from Abbottsville the contribution assessed upon all municipalities of the department toward the cost of the new prisons then under construction. Anderson apparently made a gift of ten pesos to the fund, but he pointed out that the terms of the Company contract exempted the settlement from all such assessments and removed it from the jurisdiction of all Guatemalan officials save the President himself. The bewildered corregidor could only refer the Superintendent's reply to the central government and request that he be supplied a copy of the contract that defined the unique privileges enjoyed by the colony. The authorities in Guatemala City sustained the position taken by Anderson on the question of contributions, and they did not dispute his claim to immunity from control by all local officials.[38] In the heat of the controversy over the provisions traffic, resentful local officials represented the aloof separateness of the English agents as arrogance and contempt for nationals. Paiz, for example, informed the central government that when MacKenney imposed the embargo that Pérez subsequently enforced on the shipment of liquor at Panzós he had done so with insults to Pérez, to Paiz himself, and to the corregidor of the Verapaz. MacKenney was also alleged to have boasted that, because of his association with the Company, the corregidor had no authority over him.[39]

While the conduct of officials and settlers at Abbottsville thus fulfilled or frustrated the expectations of their employers in London and their sponsors in Guatemala, the Company directors made ready to proceed to the subsequent phases of their grand design. They proposed to construct the penalty bridge for the Motagua and to prepare to inaugurate steam navigation on the Usumacinta when called upon to do so by the government of Guatemala. Their most urgent requirement, however, was to recruit the settlers their contract required them to establish in the Verapaz. They hoped to enlist land purchasers in sufficient number to fulfill their obligation, but should they fail in that expectation, they recognized that they would have to send out at Company expense enough colonists to complete

38. Anderson to José Dolores Gutiérrez, Nov. 6, 1840; Gutiérrez to Minister General, Nov. 19, 1840; and draft letter to Gutiérrez, Nov. 24, 1840; all in ANG, leg. 3360, exp. 74272, n.f. In late 1841 the Corregidor of Verapaz was still requesting an official statement on the unique privileges granted to the colonists (J. E. Valdéz to Minister of Foreign Affairs, Nov. 13, 1841, ANG, leg. 3361, exp. 74283). The ten-peso contribution from Abbottsville appears in Documentos de gastos en reparac[ió]n de un edificio de carcel, Año 1840, in ABVP.

39. Paiz to Minister General, Sept. 24, 1841, n.f.

the quota.[40]   To this end in the spring of 1840, and with greater intensity during the fall and early winter, they gave wide publicity to the colony and to the opportunities afforded within their concessions.

The directors addressed prospective emigrants and investors chiefly through printed matter of various sorts. They began newspaper advertisements as early as March, and they issued four special publications before the end of the year, none dated precisely enough to permit accurate determination of sequence. One was a handbill flier, two were pamphlets, and the fourth was a second edition of the *Brief Statement.* The booklet, however, was so changed as to constitute a distinct publication, although it incorporated verbatim or in substance a number of the earlier brief tracts.[41]

By means of these publications the directors offered land for sale and passage to the Verapaz for emigrants who wished to establish residence within the Company's holdings. They offered forty-acre plots of agricultural land for £20, steerage passage for a man and his wife included. Investors with greater capital could acquire forty-acre plots in any number at the rate of five shillings per acre and, should they wish to emigrate, cabin passage at £25. Town lots one acre in extent sold for twenty shillings. The Company also offered employment at the colony to "a few Mechanics, and Agricultural Labourers, to make preparations for a large body, who are to follow" under terms identical with those stated in recruiting the original work force.[42]

The propaganda apparently provoked little response. The accounts of the fertile soil of the Verapaz and the varied resources it afforded brought no throngs of purchasers to the Company offices. Even abandonment of its former claim to all standing mahogany and the offer to confirm to the proprietor title to all the surface and subsoil resources of the land appears not to have quickened the interest of investors. Any favorable effect produced by publication of the

40. *Report of the Directors,* Aug. 18, 1840, pp. 6-7.
41. These publications have all been cited previously. For convenience they are relisted in the sequence in which they seem to have appeared. "Emigration to Central America," *The Colonial Gazette,* No. 68 (March 11, 1840), p. 183; *Emigration to Central America* [London, 1840], 14 pp.; *Emigration to Vera Paz* (London, [1840]), 8 pp.; *Brief Statement, Supported by Original Documents, of the Important Grants Conceded to the Eastern Coast of Central America Commercial & Agricultural Company by the State of Guatemala* (2nd ed.; London, 1840), 174 pp.; *Emigration to Vera Paz: Latest Intelligence from the Colony* [London, 1840], 2 pp.
42. The fullest single exposition is given in *Brief Statement,* 1840, pp. 118-20.

enthusiastic first reports solicited from officials and workers sent to Abbottsville was probably nullified by the simultaneous appearance of James Wood's graphic description of his *Adventures, Sufferings, and Observations*[43] at New Liverpool. In consequence, the sailing of the next immigrant ship which had been projected for September was first postponed until November, then until December, and finally quietly dropped.

Even had colonists been obtained, there was some doubt that the Company's financial resources were sufficient to see them securely established. The authorized sale of the remaining half of its debentures was apparently not accomplished, whether because the directors found no opportunity to offer them under the conditions stipulated by the proprietors or because capitalists were not attracted to the issue. Revenue from this source and from the sale of lands failing, the Company tried to raise the funds it required by calls on debentures. One call was made payable by June 1, but a large number of proprietors seems to have ignored it. The securities of those who did not cover the assessment when the period of grace was extended to November 28 were declared forfeit and were offered for sale at auction in early December. Another call of a guinea per share was made payable by February 16, 1841, after which date all debentures in default were again declared forfeit.[44]

The Company was unquestionably in financial difficulty, but it was not without hope, for it had a huge sale of land in prospect. The interest of the directors in a scheme for a European bank with Guatemalan connections had brought them into contact with a group of continental speculators whose purposes could be served by acquisition of a share in the Company's concessions. In this fashion the directors might yet secure the capital and the colonists they had been unable to enlist in Great Britain.

The idea of a banking venture in Central America originated in conversations between Thomas Fletcher, the Company's former superintendent in the Verapaz, and William Campbell Gillan, a partner in the firm of Bulmer and Gillan, Parliamentary Agents. Gillan interested the banking house of Ladbrokes, Kingscote & Company in the project, and together they secured the adherence of a group of "respectable Bankers, Merchants, and Gentlemen of the City of London," most of whom were known to be men "of property and mercantile

43. (Ipswich, 1840), 68 pp.
44. These actions were announced in advertisements in the *Morning Herald*, No. 18,143 (Oct. 31, 1840), p. [1], and No. 18,171 (Dec. 3, 1840), p. 8, and the *Times*, No. 15,589 (Feb. 9, 1841), p. 2.

reputation," to a memorial proposing the establishment of a British-sponsored bank in Guatemala. In May 1839 they dispatched Fletcher as their agent to Guatemala City, where in October he obtained from the government approval of a charter. The promoters of the bank specifically denied connection with the colonization venture, but the directors of the Company were sufficiently interested to report the project to a general meeting of shareholders in November 1839 and to discuss it with Gillan at a formal session in June 1840.[45]

Shortly after the English promoters obtained the charter from Guatemala, they were drawn into negotiations with Belgian capitalists who hoped to establish an Anglo-Belgian bank. The key figure in establishing this contract was Louis Henri-Charles Obert, a promoter of French birth engaged in trade and textile manufacturing in Brussels. His business affected by the industrial and banking recession that struck Belgium between 1838 and 1840, he sought a cure for the country's economic malaise in a union of Belgian and British capital to create opportunities that domestic merchants and existing banking institutions had failed to develop. These interests led him into negotiations with Gillan, representing the British proponents of the Guatemalan bank, through whom he established contact with the Eastern Coast Company. By mid-summer of 1840, Obert was acting as the Company's agent in Belgium.

To Obert, the two British projects afforded different avenues to the same Belgian objective. During the summer of 1840 he tried to convince the Belgian Minister of the Interior that in the interest of economic recovery the government should lend its support to an attempt to establish an Anglo-Belgian commercial bank dedicated to fostering commercial development and to assist local financiers to share in the opportunities offered by the Eastern Coast Company's concessions in the Verapaz and Santo Tomás. His expositions awakened official interest in neither project.

Balked in his purpose to establish an Anglo-Belgian bank, Obert gave his principal attention to the colonization scheme. Late in 1840 he published in Brussels in the Company's interest a *Mémoire sur le Guatemala*, essentially a translation of the revised *Brief Statement* brought up to date by inclusion of the first reports from Abbotts-

45. Information on the Guatemalan banking scheme is given in Gillan to Chatfield, May 8, 1839, and Fletcher to Chatfield, July 12, 1839, both in FO 252/6, n.f. The Guatemalan decree No. 52 chartering the bank is printed in *Colección de los decretos . . . de 1839 y 1840*, pp. 65-74. None of the memorialists named in the decree can be identified as associated with the Company. The Company reference to the bank project is in *Brief Statement*, 1840, p. 171.

ville. By this means he sought to arouse Belgian interest in the opportunity to achieve colonial establishments and commercial expansion in Central America by sharing the English company's privileges. Several times he renewed his overtures to the Minister of the Interior, but on each occasion his proposals were rejected. He did, however, interest a group of Belgian capitalists in the enterprise and was commissioned on behalf of his clients to attempt to purchase from the London directors a part of their concession. By late December 1840 the sale had been arranged, although some details remained for final determination.[46]

To the London directors the agreement could not have been more opportune. Should they wish to continue their Guatemalan project, the sale provided a miraculous windfall of capital for want of which their operations were languishing, and it brought into active collaboration a sub-contractor whose achievements would be credited against the performance standards they were required to meet to validate their grant. Should they choose to take a speculative profit, the transaction promised to yield in cash a sum exactly equal to the nominal subscribed capital of the Company in return for a fifteenth-part of concessions that had cost them practically nothing.

While the details of the sale contract were being arranged and the Belgian investors prepared to select their territory, the Company directors attempted to recoup their deteriorated position in Guatemala and to prepare as attractive a colonial exhibit as possible for examination by the expected Belgian commission. Late in 1840 they sent Captain P. D. Bingham, one of their number, and Adam Murray, Jr., the son of another director, on a special assignment to Central America. The mission signified that in the course of a year the board had lost confidence in Anderson. The grievances against him are nowhere made explicit, but it appears that he was held responsible for failure to avert the legislative disapproval of the Santo Tomás contract and that he was thought guilty of prodigal expenditure of Company funds and, perhaps, of malversation.[47]

The Company emissaries arrived in Izabal on February 6, 1841. Bingham was expected to secure from the Guatemalan government

46. Joseph Fabri, *Les belges au Guatemala (1840-1845)* (Brussels, 1955), pp. 24-31. The cover of Obert's publication bore the title *Mémoire sur le Guatemala et la colonisation du département de Vera Paz, Amérique du Centre;* the title page *Mémoire contenant un aperçu statistique de l'Etat de Guatemala . . .* (Brussels, 1840).

47. J. A. Winsor to Remy de Puydt, Dec. 15, 1841, and de Puydt to Comte de Hompesch, Jan. 15, 1842, both in AMAE, 2027, n.f.

restitution of the Santo Tomás grant and to bring Anderson under discipline and control. His officious and blundering behavior, however, alienated all with whom he came in contact. He temporarily displaced Anderson as Company superintendent and thereby weakened the position of both, for Anderson enjoyed the respect and admiration of the Guatemalan authorities. At Abbottsville he viewed everything with prejudiced eyes and took "such capricious measures that as a result of his actions the Colony . . . is practically reduced to nothing." He demanded that Anderson submit his accounts, but the Superintendent interpreted the request as a personal affront and refused to comply. In the capital Bingham failed to persuade the government to reinstate the Santo Tomás contract. His loose talk of the Company's sale to the Belgian capitalists, however, suggested to Guatemalan officials that the government had erred in believing subsidies necessary to obtain colonization agreements when in fact European contractors could be found willing to buy the privilege. His mission lowered the prestige of the Company and increased the hazards that threatened its project in the Verapaz.[48]

Had Bingham been a much wiser and more tactful man he might still have found it difficult to protect the Company in Guatemala against the consequences of its impecunious treasury. Toward the end of 1840 or early in 1841 it appears that support of the colony from London dwindled to nothing. Whether the circumstance was due to the inability of the directors to raise the necessary capital or to their anticipation of easy prosperity soon to result from the sale to the Belgians, the settlement suffered from the poverty of its sponsor. Salary payments fell behind, all but the most essential projects had to be suspended, and money for such out-of-hand expenditures as could not be avoided was advanced by local Company officials.

This situation was called to the attention of the Guatemalan government when some individuals had recourse to authority outside the Company in an attempt to secure satisfaction of their claims. The absence of any substantial institutional framework within the colony probably deprived the majority of the settlers of any mechanism through which they could claim their rights, but a few in more favorable circumstances found means to present their cases either to Guatemalan or to British officials. After Krause moved to Guatemala City, for example, he instituted action before the Tribunal of the

48. Memorial of David Pollock to Lord Stanley, Nov. 25, 1842, FO 15/14, fol. 259; de Puydt to Hompesch, Jan. 15, 1842, n.f.; report on arrivals and departures of vessels at Izabal, Feb. 1841, ANG, leg. 3222, exp. 66673.

Consulado to collect money he alleged to be due him from the Company and to recover from the customs house the furniture and baggage that Santa María had impounded at Telemán on Anderson's complaint that the minister had absconded with 160 Bibles belonging to the Company and 250 pesos of the Superintendent's money. In the spring of 1841 he had Anderson brought before the mercantile court where, in accord with practice, a swift and equitable agreement was sought. Anderson denied the competence of the Tribunal in the case and signed the records of its proceedings under protest. He insisted that Krause seek redress from Bingham, who was then in Guatemala. The bitter exchanges between the principals made no progress toward an agreement, but when Anderson recovered from Krause's baggage the property alleged to have been appropriated from the Company, his own claims were satisfied, and he prepared to leave the city. Krause, however, secured from the Tribunal an order restraining his departure until he had named a power of attorney competent to represent him to the conclusion of the hearings. Thus provoked, Anderson established his concept of the proper Guatemalan jurisdiction over Company affairs and, it appears, brought the case to an abrupt close by obtaining the consent of the President himself to represent him.[49]

Other members of the colony encountered even greater difficulty in finding competent authority before whom to lodge their complaints. John Withers prepared to emigrate from Guatemala claiming that the Company owed him back wages which the British vice-consul suggested he might collect through the courts at Belize.[50] In September 1841 John MacKenney presented to the President of the republic his claims for back salary and advances made in the interest of the Company to a total of not less than 2,000 pesos. Informed that the powers of the executive over the colony were to be delegated to the commandant at Izabal, he turned to Paiz for assistance, but when he learned that no such commission had been issued, he could only renew his importunities to the capital.[51]

The demoralization at Abbottsville was traceable at least in part to deteriorating authority of Company officials. The conduct of the settlers before Bingham arrived suggests that Anderson had main-

49. The action at Telemán is reported in Andrés Santa María to Minister of Foreign Affairs, March 3, 1841, ANG, leg. 2404, exp. 50194, n.f.; the hearings before the Consulado in ANG, leg. 3612, exp. 84385, n.f.

50. Hall to Captain Carter, Jan. 18, 1841, n.f.

51. MacKenney to Paiz, Jan. 3, 1842; MacKenney to Minister of Foreign Affairs, Jan. 8, 1842; both in ANG, leg. 3616, exps. 84477, 84478, n.f.

tained no strict discipline, but the ill-advised interference of the director must have weakened all control over the inhabitants, and certainly it embittered Anderson. Whether at Bingham's return to London or later, Anderson was permanently set aside and Murray appointed in his stead, apparently on grounds that the disgruntled agent had circulated rumors among the Guatemalans that Belgians would soon arrive to take possession of the country by force of arms. Anderson, however, remained in the colony, a dissident element whose prestige among the settlers and with Guatemalan officials must have prevented Murray from exercising the full powers of his position.[52]

During 1841 the already scant authority existing at Abbottsville completely broke down. Crowe remarked that the colony "was several times convulsed by intestine commotions, and was the theatre of more than one deed of blood." Sword and knife play were apparently commonplace, and on one occasion, when he attempted to pinion the arms of a man who threatened the alcalde with a knife, Crowe himself was stabbed. The corregidor of the department charged that MacKenney, as peace officer, did what the colonists wished, protected only the European residents, and denied the natives justice at the settlement. Andrés Santa María chided his good friend Mac-Kenney with the evidence that Pedro Pérez had several times been mistreated by a native in the town, once in MacKenney's own house, and that his attacker had never been punished. Santa María did not himself wish to intervene "because I see that everything depends on Mr. Sotela," but he suggested that MacKenney appeal to Paiz to establish order in the colony.[53]

The government had already considered such a step. The corregidor of the Verapaz in mid-November 1841 had urged upon the central authorities the necessity of establishing some effective governmental regime in the colony, and they had promised to supply regulations to accomplish that end. The President had taken advantage of the presence of Paiz in the capital in October to declare his intention of delegating to the commandant at Izabal his authority over the colony, but three months later the necessary orders had not been received. By that time even Company officials recognized the necessity of some authority in Abbottsville. On separate occasions both the Superin-

52. Winsor to de Puydt, Dec. 15, 1841, n.f.

53. Crowe, *Gospel*, pp. 528-30; Valdés to Minister of Foreign Affairs, Nov. 13, 1841, n.f., and Santa María to Macquine [MacKenney], Jan. 11, 1842, ANG, leg. 3361, exp. 74284, n.f.

tendent and MacKenney appealed to Paiz to assert authority that otherwise was non-existent.[54]

Its projected function largely vitiated, the anticipated reinforcement by other settlers apparently abandoned, and discipline among the resident population collapsed, Abbottsville rapidly disintegrated as a community. Early in 1842 the settlement was reported to consist of some thirty-five houses, most of them unoccupied. The better colonists had followed the example of Krause and had abandoned the settlement, some for more desirable locations elsewhere within the country, others for the United States. The population nevertheless had increased to some 120 or 125 as a result of settlement by Caribs or Negroes from the coast and of natives from elsewhere in the country. Colonists, however, accounted for only one-sixth of the total. Ladinos constituted a group equal in number to the colonists; Indians who established temporary residence while employed and Negro or Carib laborers and servants each comprised one-third of the residents.

The colony was far from the exemplary model of industry, skill, and sobriety imagined by the proponents of foreign immigration. The Indians were the backbone of the settlement. They were industrious, gentle, and possessed "all the traits that make up a hardworking man." The Negroes were also industrious but haughty and, because of their traditional associations on the coast, strongly partisan to the English. Some of the nationals worked a little and were well-behaved, peaceable, and sober, but some were undesirables and miscreants banished by the local authorities from communities elsewhere in the country. The colonists were "lazy, besotted, debauched, and buried in debts." They made no effort to extend the clearings, and they allowed those already in existence to grow up to weeds and brush. They planted no crops and tended neither the permanant plantings nor the livestock that roamed at will through the settlement and even into the dwellings. They lived in anticipation of receiving the wages the Company had allowed to fall in arrears, content while waiting to idle away the days lying in their hammocks and drinking. They subsisted on imported provisions and the fruits and vegetables brought to market by the Indians.[55]

Early in January 1842 crises of different sorts forced both Anderson and Murray to leave the miserable settlement to go temporarily

54. Valdéz to Minister of Foreign Affairs, Nov. 13, 1841, n.f.; Paiz to Minister of Foreign Affairs, Jan. 7, 1842, ANG, leg. 3616, exp. 84478.

55. De Puydt to Hompesch, Nos. 1 and 2, Feb. 5, 1842, n.f.; Report of August T'Kint, n.d., in AMAE, 2027, n.f.; Crowe, *Gospel,* p. 528.

to Belize. Anderson was suffering from a tumor on his leg that for the preceding six weeks had confined him to his bed. Murray was without funds from which to provide the urgent requirements of the colony. Together they set out for the British settlement, Anderson for medical treatment and Murray to try to raise money on the Company's credit. As passengers aboard the "Vera Paz," called from Izabal to a rendezvous at Santo Tomás, they served as an impromptu welcoming committee for the Belgian party just arrived to select and to take possession of a part of the Company's holdings.

X

BRITISH COLONY

OR BELGIAN?

The Belgian Exploratory Commission was sent to Guatemala to complete the transaction the Brussels capitalists had arranged with the directors of the Eastern Coast Company in Europe more than a year before. Persuaded of the benefits to be derived from participation in the Company's colonization project, the continental financiers had sent Obert to England in December 1840 to treat for a share in the enterprise. Accompanying him on the mission were Pierre-Emile van der Hecht, who represented the financial interest of Dirck baron van Lockhorst as well as his own, and Remy de Puydt, a colonel of engineers who had participated in the Dutch reconnaissance of a Central American isthmian canal route in 1830. This group approached the London directors with a proposal to buy a portion of their concessions in Guatemala. Within a few days they reached a tentative agreement to purchase one million acres from the Company's grants in the Verapaz and the District of Santo Tomás.[1]

Before the formal contract was drawn, however, the arrangement was vitiated. On January 25, 1841, London newspapers published the decree issued by the Guatemalan Assembly the previous October that nullified the Company's Santo Tomás contract.[2] Stunned by this development, of which the English directors professed complete innocence, the negotiators hastened to conclude their transaction. On January 30 they signed three documents that covered all foreseen contingencies. The first was a contract incorporating the terms of the original understanding, the second was a substitute agreement to become effective should the reports on the action of the Guatemalan Assembly prove to be correct, and the third was an order of transfer drawn by J. A. Winsor, the Company secretary, instructing the super-

1. Memorial of David Pollock to Lord Stanley, Nov. 25, 1842, FO 15/14, fol. 259; Joseph Fabri, *Les Belges au Guatemala (1840-1845)* (Brussels, 1955), pp. 30-32.
2. The *Times*, for example, carried the notice under the heading "Guatemala," No. 17,576 (Jan. 25, 1841), p. 4.

intendent in the Verapaz to allow the Belgians to select and to take possession of the first allotment of purchased land.

By these agreements the English company sold to the Belgians for a price of £100,000 sterling one million acres of "unoccupied, uncleared, and virgin land," together with a share in all the privileges and immunities granted by the government of Guatemala. The purchasers were to send agents to select their acreage, as much as one-fifteenth of the total in the District of Santo Tomás and the remainder in the Verapaz. If, however, the Santo Tomás concession had in fact been revoked and the English directors were unable to secure revalidation of the contract to permit execution of the original understanding, the Belgian purchasers agreed to accept the entire one million acres from the Verapaz concession. Within eight months they were to select 50,000 acres, 2,500 of which were to be claimed within the first half of the period, and to pay an installment of £10,000 on the purchase price toward which they made an immediate deposit of £500, refundable should the Company for any reason be unable to deliver the lands as stipulated.[3]

Having acquired the right to colonize in Guatemala, the Belgians made ready to exercise it as quickly as possible. They drew up statutes for a joint stock company and presented them for government approval; they prepared to send a commission to Guatemala to select the purchased acreage, and they began arrangements to sell land to prospective colonists and to organize the first party of immigrant settlers. Chiefly because King Leopold was interested in their plan and because a new Minister of the Interior, Baron Alphonse Nothomb, viewed their project with greater favor than had his predecessor, the government approved the statutes, and the Belgian Colonization Company (Compagnie belge de colonisation) began its formal existence. The contract signed by the original investors with the London directors assumed, it was ready for action.

The conditions of the official approval, however, forced the Compagnie to modify its plans for immediate operation. The government insisted that, until an exploratory commission had evaluated the prospects for successful colonization in Guatemala and had published its report in the *Moniteur Belge,* no land sales could be consummated, and no colonists could be sent to Central America. The Compagnie thus obtained the support of the Belgian government, but in the

3. All three contracts were published in French in the *Moniteur Belge* (Brussels), 11e Année, No. 282 (Oct. 9, 1841), pp. 4-11. The English originals of the substitute agreement and the transfer order are in AMRAHM, Oficier 1852, Carton 3, No. 2.

process its own organization was delayed, and the function of the projected exploratory commission was amplified from simple selection of purchased lands to include investigation of the feasibility of the project and inquiry into the appropriateness of the environment for the projected settlement of Europeans.

The change in status of the commission was not entirely agreeable to the directors, but it carried certain advantages. On the argument that the primary work of the mission was imposed by the official requirement, the Compagnie persuaded the government to lend a vessel, the "Louise-Marie," for the enterprise and to grant four officers leave with pay to serve as members of the commission. The delay imposed upon the Compagnie by the royal stipulation also enabled it to obtain a loan from the government and to secure postponement of the payment schedule agreed upon with the Eastern Coast Company.[4]

During the fall of 1841 the Belgian Exploratory Commission was constituted. It was composed both of representatives of the Compagnie and of official agents named by the government. The Compagnie contingent was made up of Colonel Remy de Puydt, head of the party; Captain Adrien Casimir Grosset Devercy, who served as secretary; Chevalier J. van den Berghe de Binckum, a specialist in commercial matters; Lieutenant of Engineers Honoré Joseph Carrette; and Lieutenant of Artillery Guillaume de Puydt. The government representatives were Auguste T'Kint de Roodenbeck, a young specialist in banking affairs and international law from the Ministry of the Interior; Lieutenant P. L. N. Petit, captain of the "Louise-Marie;" and Dechange, the ship's doctor. Bernard van Lockhorst was to accompany the commission as interpreter and draftsman.[5]

The preparations for dispatch of the exploratory commission brought the arrangements entered into with the English company under critical examination. The exchange of communications between Compagnie officials and various government officers developed the

4. The royal decree dated Oct. 7, 1841, approving and establishing, with conditions, the Compagnie belge de colonization was published in the *Moniteur Belge*, Oct. 9, 1841, pp. 1-4. The negotiations for participation by the government of Belgium in the Guatemala expedition can be followed in Remy de Puydt to Minister of Interior, July 25, Aug. 15, and Aug. 26, 1841; de Puydt to Minister of Foreign Affairs, Sept. 4, 1841; Compagnie to Minister of War, Sept. 18, 1841; incomplete, unsigned note, Ministry of Foreign Affairs to Ministry of Interior, Sept. 28, 1841; and Minister of War to Minister of Interior, Oct. 12, 1841, all in AMAE, 2027. The English company's version of its relationship with the Belgians is given in Memorial of Pollock, fol. 260.

5. Fabri, p. 40, and Notes 1, 2.

idea that the conditions of the contract were not altogether advantageous to the Belgians. Because the Eastern Coast Company held the grants on which the Belgian rights rested, the English directors stood between the subcontractor and the Guatemalan government in any negotiation, however vital it might be. The Belgians could alter this situation only by purchasing outright the concessions of the English company or by establishing direct relations with the government of Guatemala. Persuaded that direct negotiation of a commercial treaty would assist the Compagnie to achieve objectives beneficial to the nation, the Minister of Foreign Affairs appointed de Puydt a special commissioner and authorized him to begin conversations on that subject with the Guatemalan government.[6]

On mature deliberation the Compagnie also began to suspect that the purchase of land and rights from the English company might not have been necessary. Nullification by the Guatemalan Assembly of the contract signed with Young Anderson suggested the possibility that the government might be persuaded by a better offer to cede Santo Tomás, and perhaps it could be induced to grant the lands purchased in the Verapaz directly to the Belgian company in return for a payment no larger than that agreed upon with the English speculators. With these considerations in mind the Compagnie commissioned de Puydt to treat with any or all of the governments of the states of Central America for territorial concessions and, specifically, with the government of Guatemala for cession of the District of Santo Tomás or such other areas as might seem appropriate.[7]

Their internal maneuvers notwithstanding, the two colonization companies maintained superficially friendly relations for about a year after the sale was arranged. There were some changes in personnel among the English directors—Abbott appears to have died during 1841; Pollock replaced him as Chairman, and Adam Murray disappeared from the board—but the correspondence with the Brussels group was unbroken. Desiring to make the most of the Belgian collaboration, the London directors kept their continental associates informed of their actions and issued confident but studiously vague reports on the progress of their establishment in Guatemala. In early

6. De Puydt to Minister of Interior, July 17, 1841; Minister of Foreign Affairs to Directors of Compagnie, Oct. 12, 1841; both in AMAE, 2027. De Puydt's credentials to discuss commercial relations (Comte de Briez to Minister of Foreign Affairs of Guatemala, Oct. 18, 1841) are in ANG, leg. 1395, exp. 32354, n.f.

7. Affaire de la Vera Paz, intra-ministry memorandum, Director of the Division of Commerce to Minister of Interior, "Urgent," May 3, 1841, AMAE, 2027. A translation of de Puydt's commission from the Compagnie dated Oct. 29, 1841, is in ANG, leg. 1395, exp. 32354, n.f.

October Pollock, Bingham, and Winsor visited Brussels and were entertained at a banquet held to celebrate the establishment of the Belgian company. During their stay the English representatives observed disquieting evidence of activities and plans that suggested the Belgians might contemplate an independent operation. Their inquiry brought from the Compagnie the apparently candid assurance that the expedition to Guatemala had no purpose but to explore, although the Belgian government planned to take advantage of the opportunity to negotiate a treaty of commerce to aid the colonization effort. To avoid surprise by any developments, however, the English directors offered to name a special commissioner who would accompany and assist the exploratory commission. The Brussels company rejected their overture on grounds that the Belgian government would permit no one to accompany the commission who might influence the independent judgment of the members.[8]

Their offer refused, the directors of the English company determined to send a representative of their own to Central America. They believed it "incumbent upon them, in the performance of their duty, that this Company should be represented in Guatemala, during the sojourn of any commission from Belgium, by an Agent of both competent ability and undoubted integrity." For this mission they selected José María de Mora, the son of a distinguished Spanish gentleman, who for several years had been a resident of London. Mora was authorized to serve temporarily as the Company superintendent in the Verapaz to supervise the selection and delivery of land bought by the Belgian investors and to secure from the Guatemalan government restitution of the Santo Tomás concession and validation of the Verapaz contract.[9]

Two related and ostensibly co-operating missions thus departed from Europe for Guatemala almost simultaneously in November 1841. The "Louise-Marie" sailed from Ostend on November 9 and arrived at the Bay of Santo Tomás on January 6, 1842. Mora embarked from Liverpool on November 15 and, travelling via Belize, reached Abbottsville on January 25. While both commissioners were on the high seas the Company secretary addressed a letter to de Puydt blandly in-

8. Memorial of Pollock, fols. 259-61; *L'Indépendant* (Brussels), 11e Année, No. 281 (Oct. 8, 1841), p. [2]. The Brussels company submitted to the Belgian government an occasional summary of the information it received from the Eastern Coast Company.

9. Memorial of Pollock, fol. 261; J. A. Winsor to Remy de Puydt, Dec. 15, 1841, AMRAHM, O. 1852, Carton 3, No. 19; de Puydt to Comte de Hompesch, president of the Belgian Colonization Company, Jan. 15-Jan. 27, 1842, fol. 7, AMAE, 2027.

forming him that the directors had dispatched Mora to co-operate with the Belgian party during their mission to Guatemala and, by implication, to isolate them from what might prove to be embarrassing contact with Young Anderson, who continued to live at Abbottsville. Winsor alluded to misdeeds committed by the former superintendent against the Company as justification for the admonition that "a man who thus conducts himself in relation to those who have accorded him such absolute confidence certainly merits no consideration."[10] De Puydt did not need the warning. Before he could possibly have received Winsor's letter, he learned for himself the Company weaknesses it tacitly confessed and began immediately to complete the plan half-formed in Brussels to repudiate the engagement of his sponsors with the London directors.

From the Bay of Santo Tomás the Belgian commission announced its arrival to the captain of the "Vera Paz" and requested the promised transport to Izabal. On January 9 the steamer appeared. Aboard were Anderson, bound for Belize for medical treatment, and Superintendent Murray, forced by lack of support from the directors to seek in the British Settlement funds to sustain the Abbottsville colony. Murray requested and received from de Puydt permission to deliver the cargo of cochineal the vessel carried, but he promised that the steamer would return within a few days to transport the commissioners to Izabal. The following morning Petit and de Puydt went aboard the steamer to visit Anderson, whose malady confined him to his cabin. The conversation with the former superintendent supplied them with a significant amount of "interesting information about the country, and notably about the current state of the establishment of Abbottsville." Anderson was clearly disenchanted with the Company and spoke of leaving the country, but he "evinced a desire to return to Abbottsville to lend the members of the commission the assistance of his experience and his influence with the authorities."[11] Whatever the ensigns they had previously flown, the principals in the interview aboard the Company steamer could appropriately have hoisted forthwith pennants emblazoned with the emblem of the double-cross.

The "Vera Paz" sailed for Belize but was delayed there and did not return for two weeks. During the interim the Belgian commission had opportunity to reconnoiter the land and waterways in the

10. Fabri, p. 43; Memorial of Pollock, fol. 261; Windsor to de Puydt, Dec. 15, 1841.

11. De Puydt to Hompesch, No. 4, Feb. 11, 1842, fol. 1; Procès verbal, Livingston, Jan. 20, 1842, fol. 1; Rapport de Binckum, May 11, 1842, fols. 4-5; all in AMAE, 2027.

vicinity of Santo Tomás and the lower Motagua. The group, however, soon divided into Compagnie and government factions in dissent over the nature of their assignments and their relationship to each other. The government representatives interpreted their instructions to require them to conduct an independent investigation and to return a separate report on conditions in Guatemala and on the suitability of the area for European colonization. As a result of the breach, Petit moved the Compagnie delegation to Livingston on January 18, where two days later the three government delegates joined them and then, accompanied by Guillaume de Puydt and Devercy of the Compagnie contingent, continued to Izabal. On January 23 the "Vera Paz" overtook the small schooner in which the remainder of the Compagnie representatives had finally embarked and took them, too, to Izabal. There they found that, except for Devercy, the first party had proceeded to Abbottsville, and the Compagnie group followed. De Puydt, however, remained in Izabal for conversations with Cándido Pulleiro, interim corregidor of the District of Izabal as well as agent for the English company.[12]

Pulleiro confirmed and added details to Anderson's report on the miserable state of the Abbottsville colony and the English company's declining prospects in Guatemala. His remarks on the low esteem in which Englishmen were held in the country and his account of the rights he, Balcarzel, and others held at Santo Tomás crystallized the resolve that had been forming in de Puydt's mind since he arrived in the Bay of Honduras. On January 26 he signed a provisional contract, subject to government approval, to buy the rights of Pulleiro, Balcarzel, and associates at Santo Tomás. As a bonus he secured Pulleiro's promise of support for his plans in the capital.[13]

When de Puydt departed from Izabal for Abbottsville, he had elaborated a full design for the deception conceived in Brussels. He had made up his mind that the Compagnie should plant its colony at Santo Tomás, although "I do not wish to express my opinion in an official form until after a sojourn for a time in Abbottsville with the Commissioners of the Government, so that I will not be taxed with hastiness." He planned therefore to enter immediately into

12. Procès verbal, fol. 2; de Puydt to Obert, Jan. 16-Jan. 26, 1842, fols. 4-7, AMAE, 2027; Rapport de Binckum, fol. 6. The arrival at Izabal aboard the "Vera Paz" is recorded in ANG, leg. 3223, exp. 66689. By coincidence, Frederick Crowe was also a passenger on the steamer.

13. De Puydt to Hompesch, Jan. 15-Jan. 27, 1842, fol. 5; *ibid.*, No. 4, Feb. 11, 1842, fol. 2; unsigned, undated [Jan. 25, 1842?] fragment of letter on conversations with Pulleiro, AMRAHM, O. 1852, Carton 3, No. 155. The provisional contract is in ANG, leg. 1395, exp. 32368.

negotiations with the Guatemalan government for the cession of Santo
Tomás and to establish incontestable title by securing official ratification of the purchase contract he had signed with Pulleiro. Foreseeing
some difficulty because of the commitments made to the English company, he planned his operations "with a great deal of prudence."
Taking advantage of the disordered condition of Abbottsville and the
disrepute into which the Company had fallen and making use of
Anderson, whose disaffection with the Company and whose influence
with the government made him "an instrument that is momentarily
very useful," he hoped to influence the Guatemala authorities to
rescind the English company's contract in the Verapaz. The impecunious government of the country, he believed, might then be persuaded
to cede to the Compagnie for a small consideration the rights vacated
by cancellation of the English company's charter, but if not, he intended "to take measures here so that it will be possible to establish
that they have deceived us, so that if need be the 2,500 francs paid
in advance will not be lost." He proposed while in the Verapaz to
select the 2,500 acres the Belgians were obligated to accept immediately, but by requiring the London company's officials to guarantee that
the sale was approved by the Guatemalan government and that un-
exceptionable title could be delivered, he planned to establish evidence that the English company had defaulted on its commitment
as grounds for voiding the purchase contract.[14]

The administrative anarchy that prevailed in the Company's Verapaz establishment favored de Puydt in the execution of his designs.
Anderson continued to assert some claim to exercise of the powers
he had been granted as superintendent, and his friendship with
Carrera, Rivera Paz, and other individuals powerful in the government gave him great local influence. He refused to recognize the
authority of the new Company agent, and he took "malicious pleasure," during his absence in Belize, "in leaving Mr. Mora abandoned
to his own devices." The Company emissary, just arrived and
apparently not forewarned of the actual state of the wilderness colony,
awaited the arrival of the Belgians in Abbottsville, apprehensive that
the miserable condition of the place forebode ill for the commission
he had been sent to execute. Murray's extended sojourn in Belize
left authority in the settlement during the stay of the Belgians imprecisely divided between his delegate, Captain Barnett, and Mora.[15]

14. De Puydt to Hompesch, Jan. 15-Jan. 27, 1842, fols. 1-8; *ibid.*, No. 2, Feb.
5, 1842, fol. 9, AMAE, 2027; *ibid.*, No. 4, Feb. 11, 1842, fol. 2.
15. Young Anderson to de Puydt, May 21, 1842, AMRAHM, O. 1852, Carton 3,
No. 54; de Puydt to Hompesch, Jan. 15-Jan. 27, 1842, fols. 4, 7-8.

For about a week the Belgian commissioners remained in Abbottsville examining the settlement and its environs. Their peculiar interests did not dispose them to credit the English company with much
accomplishment, and the evidence they observed hardly required them
to form a judgment more favorable than they would wish of the
"miserable hamlet" and its indolent, drunken inhabitants. After this
brief period of joint observation the Belgians divided into work
parties to go about their assigned special duties. The government
representatives departed for Guatemala by separate routes, but Petit
and Dechange turned back at Gualán when the ship's doctor fell ill,
and only T'Kint appeared in the capital. Guillaume de Puydt and
Carrette began their scientific surveys and Remy de Puydt, after some
delay occasioned by the continued absence of Murray, went through
the formality of selecting the purchased lands with Captain Barnett.
He reserved the rights of the Compagnie, however, should the English agents be unable to convey clear title to the property, and he
advised the directors in Brussels to withhold further payments to the
London company until he could determine the validity of its title
to the lands that had been sold.[16] On February 14 he and Devercy
departed for Guatemala City.

During most of this time the Guatemalan government had received
no official notice that the Belgian commission had arrived in the
country. Private sources in the capital, however, soon circulated a
report originated by the Commandant at Izabal that an armed Belgian vessel had anchored at Santo Tomás expecting to take possession
of the bay. This news reached the ears of General Carrera who,
perhaps linking the event with the rumor attributed to Anderson
that armed Belgians would soon arrive in force to take over the
country or with the presence of blockading English vessels in Central
American waters, determined to investigate. He asked the government
to provide 200 veteran troops to enable him to reconnoiter the English warship—Carrera was reported to identify all foreigners as Englishmen—and to take such measures at Izabal and Santo Tomás as
were necessary for the security of the country. The government tried
to mollify him by explaining that Dutch colonists were expected to
settle in the Abbottsville colony and that, presumably, the ship in
which they arrived would be English.

In response to Carrera's repeated importunities the government

16. Rapport de Mr. A. T'Kint, May 23, 1842, fols. 1-2, AMAE, 2027; de Puydt
to Hompesch, No. 1, Feb. 5, 1842, fol. 1, AMAE, 2027; ibid., No. 2, Feb. 5, 1842,
fol. 7; ibid., No. 4, Feb. 11, 1842, fols. 2-3; Rapport de Dechange, May 11, 1842,
fol. 62, AMAE, 2027.

on January 29 finally asked Pulleiro to report on whether or not a Belgian ship had arrived at Santo Tomás bearing passengers who expected to solicit lands on which to settle. If so, the contract for the cession of Santo Tomás signed with Anderson in 1838 might give them reason to believe that they should negotiate with the agent of the English company. Should such be the case, the government instructed Pulleiro to state emphatically to the new arrivals that the Assembly had disallowed the contract with the English company, and hence, that any negotiations for the right to colonize in that area should be undertaken directly with the Guatemalan government. Pulleiro confirmed the arrival of a commission headed by de Puydt which purported to represent a Belgian company entirely independent of the London directors. He reported that he had shown de Puydt a copy of the Assembly's decree nullifying the contract signed with Anderson and that the Belgian commissioners were on their way to the capital hoping to negotiate an agreement for colonization of the north coast.[17] This information, which could only favor the hopes of the Belgian representatives, was passed on to Carrera on February 11. The evening of the following day T'Kint arrived in the Guatemalan capital.

T'Kint's brief mission in Guatemala yielded no conclusive information on the prospects of either the London or the Brussels companies. He hoped to discover whether or not the failure of the English company to fulfill its obligations would automatically annul its contract, should the Assembly not reconfirm its rights, and to explore the disposition of the authorities toward a Belgian colonization project. José Venancio López, who had been named two months before by the Council of Government as interim executive during the disability of Rivera Paz, would not attempt to provide answers. When T'Kint raised the points during a conference with López and Juan José Flores, the Minister of Finance and acting Minister General, and later put the question in writing, he was told that the power of decision rested exclusively with the Assembly which would reconvene within a few days. Before the legislative body could take action on either matter, however, T'Kint was forced to leave Guatemala to board the returning "Louise-Marie," but he carried away the impression that the attitude of the government was distinctly unfavorable.[18]

17. Rapport de T'Kint, fol. 31. Carrera's letters to Minister of Foreign Affairs, Jan. 25, and Feb. 16, 1842, and to Minister General, Jan. 26, 1842; the replies of Jan. 26, Jan. 29, and Feb. 11, 1842; and the inquiry to Pulleiro, Jan. 29, and his response on Feb. 5, 1842, are all in ANG, leg. 1395, exp. 32354, n.f.

18. Rapport de T'Kint, fols. 2, 6-7; T'Kint to Guatemalan Minister of Foreign

A few days before T'Kint terminated his investigations in Guatemala, Mora arrived in the capital, and on February 25 Remy de Puydt appeared and occupied the house placed at his disposal by Balcarzel.[19] During the next two months the English representative engaged the Belgian commissioner in combat, the stake of which was the life of the London company. It was an unequal struggle. Mora had the advantage of a few day's priority in arrival, but in every other respect he was at a competitive disadvantage.

Mora presented his credentials to the Guatemalan government on February 16. On February 21 he was authorized to submit in writing the representations of the English company, and two days later he presented his first memorial to the President.[20] He defended the Company's relative lack of accomplishment on grounds that "after having made great sacrifices and invested large sums for the colonization of the territory of Verapaz, it has seen the fruit of all of its efforts wasted because of malversation by some of its agents, and because of the enmity with which persons opposed to the prosperity of the country have constantly attacked it." The directors, nonetheless, had persisted in their efforts, and as a product of their exertions a Belgian commission had arrived in Guatemala to arrange for the settlement in Company territory of sober and industrious immigrant families professing the same religion as the native inhabitants.

Although the Company had been hampered by evil fortune, Mora asserted that it was on the verge of fulfilling its obligations. He reported that construction of the iron bridge for the Motagua River was almost completed when he left London and that it should at that moment be on its way to Izabal. The Company, he admitted, was responsible for erecting the bridge, but because transport of the structure from the seacoast to the construction site was to be arranged by the government, delays for which the Company was in no way at fault might greatly retard performance of the final obligation upon which its time extension had been conditioned. He requested, therefore, that the government declare the Company's responsibility discharged when the bridge was delivered at a Guatemalan port.

To contribute to the complete and efficient realization of the

Affairs, Feb. 19, 1842, and draft reply, Feb. 21, 1842, both in ANG, leg. 1395, exp. 32354. T'Kint left the capital on Feb. 22, and the Assembly began to transact business on Feb. 24.

19. Fabri, p. 57.

20. Acuerdo ejecutivo ordering translation of Mora's credentials, Feb. 16; translation returned Feb. 18; Mora authorized to make proposals, Feb. 21; and Mora's petition, Feb. 23, 1842; all in ANG, leg. 1395, exp. 32354, n.f.

objectives which the Company was assisting Guatemala to achieve, Mora asked that the government reconfirm it in possession of the ceded territory in the Verapaz. Thus assured of the stability of their interests, the directors could venture to increase the scope of their operations and thus hasten the day when previously unpopulated lands would be "covered by a numerous and industrious population submissive to the laws of the Republic." In order that the settlements thus established in the Verapaz might be able with advantage to dispose of the products of their industry, however, it was necessary that the government concede to the Company authority to establish warehouses at some point on the coast from which direct traffic with Europe could be conducted without interposition by the merchants of Belize. The most appropriate spot for such an establishment Mora, with feigned artlessness, left for the government to suggest, apparently in expectation that the promise of commercial independence from Belize would draw it unwittingly into renewed negotiation for cession of Santo Tomás.

On the very day that Mora's proposals were presented, however, the Guatemalan government recorded its disapproval. The executive ruled that the express rejection by the Assembly of the English company's contract for the cession of Santo Tomás closed that subject to discussion on any basis. Moreover, the Company had failed to comply with the stipulation of its Verapaz contract that required it within four years to settle two hundred families in addition to the one hundred promised during the first two years of the agreement. The government admitted that in 1838 it had conceded an additional three years for the introduction of the two hundred families, but it argued that, lacking ratification by the legislative body, the extension could not be considered valid. Even should the Assembly now approve the additional time, the Company would be obligated to fulfill the stipulations upon which the extension was conditioned, one of which was to manufacture and erect a bridge over the Motagua River. The government admitted its responsibility to assist in the transport and erection of the bridge, but it would recognize the Company's obligation as fulfilled only when the structure had been completed. It would certainly not accept simple delivery of the pieces to a Guatemalan port as satisfying the condition. The government, therefore, determined to bring the question of the English company's tenure immediately to the attention of the Assembly and to request it to decide whether to ratify or to disapprove the time extension granted in 1838. During the first days of March it communicated these observations to Mora and submitted the issue to the Assembly for resolution.[21]

Simultaneously with the executive action on Mora's petition de Puydt initiated negotiations on Santo Tomás. On March 2 he prepared a formal request for cession of the District as described in the disallowed contract with Anderson and under the same general conditions. He proposed, however, several modifications of the arrangement to make it more tempting. He offered to settle several hundred industrious European families of exemplary habits professing the Catholic faith and prepared to foreswear their previous allegiance and to accept Guatemalan citizenship. He offered to pay twenty pesos for each of the 8,000 *caballerías* assumed to be comprised within the grant, at the rate of 16,000 pesos per year for ten years. Finally, he promised general and specific aid to the government in locating, building, and arming fortifications on the north coast with a view to affording greater security to the country. The following day he sent the document to the President, together with a brief exposition on the merits of his proposals and on the unique advantages to be anticipated from Belgian sponsorship. On March 5 the executive forwarded this petition also to the legislature for consideration.[22]

The Assembly thus considered concurrently two possible contractors for the colonization of the Verapaz and of the District of Santo Tomás. The question of the Eastern Coast Company's contract was referred to the Committee on Government, and de Puydt's proposal was submitted to a special committee. The Committee on Government apparently did not know what action it was expected to take, and it therefore requested on March 11 that the government express its views on the question. The Assembly itself was also uncertain what course to pursue, if, indeed, it should act at all. It defeated a motion to declare resolution of the issue a matter of urgency, but Luis Batres referred to the President's statement that the arrangement compromised the peace and security of the state to justify his insistence that the importance of the question required the legislature to remain in session until it was decided. The Assembly,

21. Acuerdo ejecutivo disallowing Mora's petition, Feb. 23, 1842; acuerdo ejecutivo disposing of Mora's petition, March 1, 1842; draft reply to Mora, n.d.; draft letter submitting question of status of Company contract to Assembly, March 3, 1842, ANG, leg. 1395, exps. 32364, 32389, 32354, 32358, n.f.

22. Note relative au port de Santo Thomas, March 2, 1842, and Spanish translation, and de Puydt to the President, March 3, 1842, ANG, leg. 1395, exps. 32354 and 32387, n.f.; letter submitting proposal to Assembly, March 5, 1842, ANG, Congreso, 1842, No. 25, unclassified. A marginal note shows referral to a special committee.

however, was reluctant to act, and the executive made no haste to express the opinion requested by the Committee. For nearly a month the question was held in abeyance. Mora's professed ignorance of the Assembly's disapproval of the Santo Tomás contract, however, prompted the government to send him on March 15 a copy of the decree in question.[23]

De Puydt's similar proposal encountered no such delay. On March 11 the special committee recommended that the government be authorized to negotiate with the Belgians, and on the following day the Assembly approved the measure. This action was communicated to the government on March 15. The following day de Puydt submitted to the President the essential conditions of a contract, and during the remainder of March the Guatemalan government named a succession of commissioners until it found two willing to undertake the negotiation. On April 6 it informed de Puydt that Antonio Colón and Manuel Arrivillaga had been appointed as commissioners of the government, and the negotiations began.[24]

Sensing that the prize was about to slip beyond his reach, Mora apparently determined to gamble. Pretending to understand that the authorization to negotiate with the Belgian agent was a general commission to treat on the subject of Santo Tomás, he renewed his representations to the government. On March 17 he submitted an exposition in which he alleged the willingness of the Company to revise the offending articles of the disapproved Santo Tomás contract to meet such objections raised by the committee of the Assembly in October 1840 as could not be shown to rest on misconceptions. He attempted by reason and by citing the evidence of recent experience at Abbottsville to demonstrate that the Company had neither desire nor power to create conditions that would justify the fears of the committee for the sovereignty of the nation.

The following day Mora made nine specific proposals for modification of the rejected Santo Tomás contract in the spirit of his earlier memorandum. He offered to bind the Company to establish only Catholic colonists; to recruit at least one-half of the settlers in Spain, Italy, and the Spanish or Portuguese islands; and to require them

23. Committee on Government to Minister General, March 10, 1842, ANG, leg. 1395, exp. 32360, n.f.; motion of Batres, March 12, 1842, ANG, Congreso, 1842, No. 20, unclassified; acuerdo ejecutivo to send a copy of Decree No. 107 to Mora, March 15, 1842, ANG, leg. 1395, exp. 32357, n.f.

24. Dictamen of the special committee, March 11, 1842, ANG, Congreso, 1842, No. 25, unclassified; letter to Minister General reporting Assembly approval of the petition, March 15, 1842; de Puydt to President, March 16, 1842; and draft letter to de Puydt, April 6, 1842; all in ANG, leg. 1395, exp. 32354, n.f.

after arrival to submit themselves under all circumstances to the laws of the state. He matched de Puydt's offers to pay for the ceded land and to assist in the erection of fortifications on the north coast. He proposed that the government appoint all civil and military officials of the colony and that it garrison the city and the fortifications. Finally, he offered the services of the Company without charge as the agent of the Guatemalan government in Europe for discharging commissions, handling contracts, and performing other similar services. His claim that the past efforts of the Company entitled it to the preferential consideration of the government did not move the Guatemalan authorities. They appear to have persisted in their decision to treat the English contract for Santo Tomás as a closed subject.[25]

Some three weeks later, on April 8, the executive branch took cognizance of the request from the Committee on Government of the Assembly for a statement of views on the London company's Verapaz contract. The President resolved to advise against ratification of the time extension for three reasons: the remaining fraction of the extended period was too short to permit establishment of the required two hundred families and delivery of the penalty bridge; the Company was guilty of misconduct in selling a portion of the lands ceded to it before its title was confirmed by ratification of the time extension; and, finally, the contract was disadvantageous to the state because it disposed almost gratuitously of a tremendous extent of territory under conditions which threatened the security of the state. On April 12 these views were communicated to the Committee.[26] On this basis the Assembly denied ratification of the time extension granted to the English company and in effect nullified its concession in the Verapaz.

De Puydt waited for the action of the Guatemalan government neither on the London company's Verapaz grant nor on his own application for the cession of Santo Tomás before he moved to free the Belgian company from its obligation to the English directors. On March 11, the same day that the special committee of the Assembly recommended that the government be authorized to negotiate with him, de Puydt wrote to Murray demanding, in consideration of the pending forfeiture of the Company's concession in the Verapaz, that he guarantee unconditionally the Belgian company's title to the lands

25. Mora to Minister General, March 17, 1842, and Proposición relativa al puerto de Santo Tomás, March 18, 1842, ANG, leg. 1395, exp. 32354, n.f.

26. Acuerdo ejecutivo, April 8, 1842, and draft letter to Committee on Government, April 12, 1842, ANG, leg. 1395, exp. 32360, n.f.

it had agreed to purchase. Lamely, Murray complied, but the subsequent action of the Assembly made his assurance hollow. On April 23 the Belgian commissioner informed Murray that, in view of the forfeiture of the Company's charter, he had negotiated with the Guatemalan government a contract for the cession of Santo Tomás. The following day he communicated the same information to the directors of the Company in London.[27]

The contract for the cession of Santo Tomás that de Puydt thus reported was signed on April 16. The Guatemalan commissioners forwarded it to the executive on the same day, and López submitted it to the Assembly on April 20 with suggestions for only minor modifications. It was referred to the same special committee of the Assembly, which on April 22 recommended approval. Although admittedly identical in essence with the English charter previously disallowed by the Assembly, the committee alleged that modification of certain particulars in the Belgian contract had corrected the objectionable features of the earlier agreement. The sale of the land, for example, would for ten years provide an annual revenue of 16,000 pesos derived from resources that had lain unclaimed for centuries and that recent contracts had ceded gratis to other companies. Finally, it evoked the perennial dream of a flourishing port at Santo Tomás and steamers plying the Motagua to justify its appeal for approval of the contract.[28]

Action on the agreement was halted at this juncture when Pulleiro and Balcarzel presented a petition to the government asking that it ratify the contract Pulleiro had signed with de Puydt on January 26. De Puydt had previously signified his intent to acquire the rights of the Pulleiro associates to the site, but he had revealed neither to the government nor to the negotiators that a contract had already been signed. The petition, therefore, came as a complete surprise to the government. The argument that sale of their rights at Santo Tomás would relieve the government of its obligation to make the long overdue repayment to the associates aroused immediate apprehension that the Belgian company might intend to submit delinquent claims against the government, acquired from Pulleiro and Balcarzel, in satisfaction of the annual payments called for in its contract. López therefore referred the petition to the special committee of the As-

27. De Puydt to Murray, March 11, 1842, and April 23, 1842, and de Puydt to directors, April 24, 1842, all in AMRAHM, O. 1852, Carton 3, No. 51.

28. The contract is published in Manuel Pineda de Mont (comp.), *Recopilación de las leyes de Guatemala* (Guatemala, 1869), I, 824-31. The documents transmitting the agreement and the opinion of the special committee are in ANG, leg. 1395, exp. 32361, n.f., and leg. 3618, exp. 84653, n.f.

sembly which had considered the Belgian contract with the recommendation that it write into the agreement an express prohibition against any such procedure. The legislative body spent several days incorporating this and other minor refinements into the contract, and on May 4, after a short debate, it ratified the amended document.[29]

The applications for revalidation of the Verapaz contract and for the cession of Santo Tomás re-opened the issue of foreign colonization in all of its varied aspects. The negotiations produced a recrudescence of the traditional contrary opinions on the effectiveness of colonization as a means of achieving national development and on the prudence of entrusting such enterprises to foreigners. They also led inevitably to comparison and contrast of the Brussels company with the Eastern Coast Company and of the Belgian contract with the agreements signed with the London directors. The rejection by the Guatemalan government of the Eastern Coast Company's proposals was reasonably consistent with the trends recently manifested by public opinion, but its approval of the Belgian contract, which varied in no significant way from the terms offered by the London company, was a complete reversal of its position and a repudiation of the convictions it professed to hold when the Belgians arrived.

At the beginning of the negotiations, the Belgians found little Guatemalan enthusiasm for their proposed colony. Some important individuals, most of them merchants, favored cession of Santo Tomás to the Belgian company, however, and at T'Kint's arrival in the capital were gathering signatures on a petition to that effect. Their motives may in part be explained by Devercy's comment that the Belgian colony was "the hope of the whites," for Carrera, a representative of the numerically predominant "men of color," had just established himself by popular insurrection as the power behind the government. But the General had just acknowledged receipt of Pulleiro's report on the arrival of the Belgian commission by cautioning the Foreign Minister against acceding in any way to the propositions of the Compagnie, "be they what they may, for the results would be prejudicial to the State and even to the entire Republic, since the people, seeing a new foreign colony founded, will consider it the first link [in the chain] of their slavery."[30]

29. The Balcarzel petition is in ANG, leg. 1395, exp. 32368, n.f. The government inquiry, its recommended modifications, and the actions of the Assembly are recorded in ANG, leg. 1395, exps. 32357, 32361, 32362, n.f., and leg. 3619, exp. 84758, n.f. The manuscript decree approving the contract is in ANG, leg. 1395, exp. 32361, n.f.

30. Rapport de T'Kint, fol. 7; Captain Devercy to Obert, April 7, 1842, fol. 1,

T'Kint's investigations in the capital in mid-February revealed a general atmosphere as uncompromisingly hostile to foreign colonization agreements as was Carrera. The English company was in disrepute, and its Verapaz contract was expected to be annulled when the Assembly reconvened. President López and acting Minister General Juan José Flores opposed further colonization contracts and vowed that the government would not again grant to a company exclusive rights at Santo Tomás. A colonizer, however, willing to open a road or a river route between the port and the capital would be rewarded with important privileges but never again on a scale equal to those enjoyed by the English company. Because of the general fear that foreign colonists would ultimately wish to establish their independence on the pattern of Texas, the government insisted that all immigrant settlers in the future abjure the protection of their home governments and become Guatemalan subjects.[31]

When Mora arrived in Guatemala the decision had virtually been made against him. The "English party" in the capital may have given him some support, but it was more than counterbalanced by the anti-British sentiment in the country at large. The Company's record of incomplete performance on its contracts and divided councils among its personnel in Guatemala also weakened his position. Although he succeeded to Anderson's powers, he could assert no comparable influence, for the former superintendent retained the confidence and respect of Guatemalan officials, and disgruntled because of his treatment by the directors, he unwittingly or deliberately armed Mora's opponents for the offensive. His characterization of the Company as "a gang of swindlers" was quoted during the debate in the Assembly in support of the Belgian proposal.[32]

Even casual circumstance operated against Mora. On February 13

AMAE, 2027; Santos Carrera (for Rafael Carrera) to Minister of Foreign Affairs, Feb. 16, 1842, ANG, leg. 1395, exp. 32354, n.f.

31. Rapport de T'Kint, fols. 6-7.

32. Both Devercy and General William S. Murphy, Special Agent of the United States in Central America, speak of an "English party." Murphy, who was often misinformed, identified it as composed of English and other foreign merchants, who opposed the "native party" headed by Carrera, and credited it with great influence in the secret councils of state. Because Carrera was also present at these sessions, however, it attempted to accomplish its ends through the legislature (Murphy to Daniel Webster, Feb. 4, 1842, William Ray Manning (ed.), *Diplomatic Correspondence of the United States. Inter-American Affairs, 1831-1860*, III: *Central America, 1831-1850* [Washington, 1933], 173). Devercy (to Obert, April 7, 1842, fol. 1) remarks simply that it opposed de Puydt. The quotation from Anderson is in the *voto particular* of Juan José de Aycinena, May 4, 1842, ANG, leg. 1395, exp. 32354, n.f.

a fire broke out in one of the three buildings owned by the Company in Izabal and, fanned by the land breeze, destroyed twenty-eight houses in the town. The official reports on the disaster carefully avoided placing blame on the Company, and Pulleiro even commended the captain and crew of the "Vera Paz," which happened to be in port, for their heroic exertions to control the flames. The merchants and others who suffered loss as a result of the conflagration, however, must have noted that the blaze originated when a carelessly placed candle just before midnight ignited the combustible walls of the house occupied by "the English woman," Helen Bailey, one of the notorious central figures in the earlier judicial proceeding at Abbottsville. If, indeed, the merchants suffered injury from the destruction in Izabal, it was compounded when the government asked the Consulado to provide aid for the victims of the fire.[33] It seems hardly probable in the hostile environment of Guatemala that interest groups who sustained loss in the fire would absolve the Company of all responsibility for the disaster.

The circumstances under which the Guatemalan government rejected Mora's proposals suggest that its actions were determined by the prevailing hostility toward the Company rather than by any contemporary re-examination of evidence. On the same day that it authorized Mora to submit his propositions, the government inquired of José Francisco Barrundia whether or not it was correctly reported that the *expediente* on the Company's operations in the Verapaz had been in his possession and had been lost when his home was sacked during a recent uprising. If so, it asked whether he could recall the terms and conditions of the concession with sufficient exactness to be able, if presented a copy of the contract, to state whether or not it was accurate. Somewhat later the executive branch in effect confessed to the Assembly that some of the assertions it had made in justification of its refusal to consider Mora's proposals were unsubstantiated by the records in its possession. The extant documents proved, for example, that the Assembly had been informed of the executive *acuerdo* of November 1838 conceding a time extension to the Company for execution of its Verapaz contract, but they failed to reveal whether or not the legislative body had ratified it.[34] Finally, the President advised the Assembly against confirmation of the resubmitted *acuerdo* on grounds that the Company was guilty of mis-

33. This incident is recorded in ANG, leg. 3224, exp. 66835, n.f.

34. Draft letter to Barrundia, Feb. 21, 1842, and draft letter to secretaries of Assembly, March 3, 1842, ANG, leg. 1395, exps. 32357 and 32358, n.f.

conduct for acting, prior to ratification, on those articles of its agreement that allowed it to sell all or a part of its concession and of default for not acting, under the same circumstance, on those that stated its obligations.

The disenchantment of the government with colonization projects in general promised that de Puydt's proposals would be no more favorably received than were those of Mora. The day after the Assembly authorized the executive to negotiate with the Belgians, López told William S. Murphy, Special Agent of the United States in Central America, that he intended if at all possible to thwart the transaction. Asked to express his personal views on the cession, Murphy departed from his instructions to counsel against it "both, as it regarded the Present, & future interests not only of the State & People of Guatemala; but more especially in its bearing on friendly Powers" whose commerce might, in consequence, be excluded from the country. Both López and Flores concurred in these opinions and expressed their determination to present the matter for the action of the Council of Government. Murphy later understood that the Council had declared the decree of the Assembly unconstitutional and that, in consequence, the legislative body had been induced to repeal it.[35] The agent often misunderstood, or was misinformed, but if events transpired as he reported them, the conflict of opinion within the government may explain the difficulty encountered by the executive during the latter half of March in finding two commissioners willing to undertake the negotiation.

If Murphy's influence was any deterrent to action by the Guatemalan government, that impediment to de Puydt's success was removed when the envoy left the capital on March 30. The absence of Chatfield from the country also spared the Belgian opposition from any British representative, for "his substitute [William Hall] is almost a nonentity who dares to take nothing on himself." Had Chatfield been in residence, Devercy supposed, "he would have had sufficient credit to have all negotiations suspended until he asked for and obtained instructions from his government." In indirect fashion, however, British policy may have assisted de Puydt to obtain the cession he sought. Murphy appears to have been misinformed when he reported that Hall supported the Belgian petition as a means of securing to the Eastern Coast Company the benefits of the sale it had made to the Belgian promoters, but the presence of British warships off Central American ports to secure recognition of debts helped to

35. Murphy to Webster, June 16, 1842, Manning, III, 191-92.

produce a similar result. Some of the members of the Assembly thought it implausible that the naval units had been assigned to their announced mission and believed, rather, that they intended either to prevent ratification of the Belgian contract or to seize Santo Tomás before the cession could be consummated. To some degree, therefore, the actions of the Assembly on the English company's Verapaz contract and on the proposals made by de Puydt appear to have been taken to thwart what were assumed to be British designs.[36]

To overcome the intransigent opposition to his plans that remained in high places, de Puydt resorted to his ultimate means of persuasion. He decided "to negotiate as one negotiates here." Some five or six thousand pesos distributed as bribes so quieted the apprehension that had caused the Assembly earlier to disapprove similar contracts that the same arguments were unheeded when rehearsed by opponents of the Belgian concession. Under the same persuasion important functionaries of the state completely reversed their positions in the course of a few days. Carrera's adamant opposition expressed in mid-February so softened by April 15 that, provided by de Puydt with an advance copy of the agreement, he wrote to the special committee of the Assembly to commend the patriotism exhibited by the negotiators and to recommend approval of the contract. The Belgian historian Fabri records that when the Assembly was unable on April 25 and 26 to attain a quorum for the scheduled discussion of the matter, Carrera personally invited the absent members to attend the next session and on April 29 entertained de Puydt at a banquet, in the course of which he proposed a toast to the success of his negotiations. Apparently under the influence of Carrera, President López raised no official objection to the agreement. Fabri states that in the process of obtaining support for the Belgian, Balcarzel corrupted, among others, the President of the Assembly, Alejandro Marure; the Minister General, Flores; and Carrera's personal physician.[37] The conclusion is almost inescapable that Carrera, Flores, Marure, and perhaps the negotiators of the contract, the members of the special committee that recommended its approval, and some of the leaders of the Assembly were bought.

36. Devercy to Obert, April 7, 1842, fol. 1; Murphy to Webster, June 16, 1842, p. 189; Opinion of Ignacio Cordora and M. Santa Cruz to the Assembly, April 30, 1842, ANG, Congreso, 1842, No. 14, fol. 3, unclassified, and Manuel Pineda de Mont, Apuntes on deliberations of the combined Committees on Commerce and Public Credit relative to the British blockade, April 30, 1842, fol. 75, and his voto particular, May 4, 1842, fol. 86, British Museum, Add. MSS. 38510.

37. Devercy to Obert, April 6, 1842, fol. 1; Santos Carrera (for Rafael Carrera) to the special committee, April 15, 1842, ANG, leg. 1395, exp. 32354; Fabri, p. 61.

The proponents of the Belgian contract, whether convinced or corrupted, justified their position by restatement of the hopes and expectations that had traditionally motivated such projects. One of the principal advocates of the agreement was Juan José de Aycinena. He had refused appointment as a member of the negotiating commission on grounds that he had been accused of "desiring foreign domination," but this disability did not deter him from serving as a member of the special committee of the Assembly and writing its favorable report. Neither did it prevent him from publishing a *voto particular* in which he supported both the general concept of European immigrant colonies and the particular terms of the Belgian contract.

Aycinena sustained his approval of European immigration by a curious biblical argument. Assuming that Europe, by obeying the divine injunction to "Be fruitful, and multiply, and replenish the earth," had reached a state in which it could no longer provide sustenance for its people, the design of the Creator, fulfilled in the Old World, could be realized also in the New by assisting the surplus population to settle the vast and underpopulated continent of America. It followed that Guatemala could refuse European immigrants the opportunity to occupy and cultivate its empty, unused, and mortiferous lands only by committing an abomination in the eyes of God.

The Belgian contract, he argued, was an entirely satisfactory arrangement. There could be no legitimate objection to the settlement of colonists at Santo Tomás for the founders of the republic had proclaimed it a place of sacred asylum for all who chose to seek refuge in it and had in no way restricted the right of immigrants to acquire public lands in any part of the country, either on the coast or in the interior. Problems encountered under earlier colonization contracts had been resolved in the Belgian agreement by inserting new conditions binding on foreigners who established residence in the country. The Belgians agreed to recognize the sovereignty of the state and to establish settlers pledged to subject themselves to the laws and to the government of Guatemala. They proposed to purchase land and to acquire title on the same basis as local residents, without power to alienate the soil to any foreign nation or to break their political ties with the state. The often-expressed fear that the colonists would some day rebel was entirely without foundation. Just as the experience of Spain, England, and other colonizing powers showed that sons of European immigrants born in the New World were Americans rather than Europeans, so the sons of the settlers at

Santo Tomás would be Guatemalans, bound to the soil of their birth.

The Compagnie was of quite different quality from the "gang of swindlers" that composed the London company. It came to reach an agreement in good faith and with the intention of complying religiously with all of the conditions of its contract. Approval of the contract therefore offered the first real hope that the cherished dream of Guatemalan development would soon be realized.[38]

These views drew eloquent and withering rebuttal from some members of the Assembly who remained unconvinced either by argument or by money. True to the convictions they had manifested when the English Santo Tomás contract was under consideration, Manuel Francisco Pavón and Luis Batres opposed the agreement to the end and after it was ratified asked that their dissenting votes and their exposition be recorded in the proceedings of the Assembly. Their *voto particular* is a classic expression, in Socratic method, of the major objections to foreign colonization in general and to the Belgian contract in particular.

Batres and Pavón conceded that the Santo Tomás agreement incorporated certain safeguards absent in the Verapaz contract. Other aspects of the new arrangement, however, they believed made it even more dangerous than the earlier cession which the President had characterized as a threat to the security of the state. In justification of their fears they cited the strategic importance of the granted area and the implied right of the colonists to maintain their own fortifications and their own armament. To place in control of foreigners a portion of the country's territory "that contains the only two ports by means of which we can communicate with Europe, export our products, and provide for our necessities" was to risk economic strangulation. "If European populations are successfully established in the area that controls the only access to our country" and if, as was probable, the settlers became disaffected, Guatemalans could expect one day to "find ourselves walled in, tributary to our own colonists, with no communication and no commerce save that which they wish gratuitously to concede us."

Prudence, they argued, required more serious consideration of the probability that the settlers would revolt and establish their independence on the model of Texas. "What was Texas when it began," they asked, "and what is it today? Was it not a colony formed under the

38. Opinion of the special committee, April 22, 1842, ANG, leg. 1395, exp. 32361, n.f.; Aycinena to Minister General, March 21, 1842, ANG, leg. 1395, exp. 32354, n.f.; voto particular of Aycinena.

same illusions, with the same hopes, and with the same desire of accelerating time that has moved us in the approval of the contract with the Belgian company? And is it not today the cancer, the opprobrium, and the crowning evil that afflicts Mexico? Who assures us that our colony will not be for Guatemala what Texas has been for Mexico?"

To repose faith in the contractual reservation of sovereignty and in the pledged transfer of allegiance by colonists they believed was to ignore the history of British usurpation in Belize. One day the members of the Assembly might well be questioned by their constituents: " 'Did you not know that the King of Spain, upon making a simple, temporary concession to cut mahogany, not only reserved sovereignty and eminent domain, but expressly stipulated that those who came to make use of the privilege could not construct fortresses, nor even build houses, or plant crops? And did you not witness what resulted from that concession? Did not you, yourselves, hear the blows of the English axe devastating the whole coast only because a few fishermen were permitted to set foot on it? . . . With what prudence is it possible to trust in guarantees that consist only of a piece of paper? And from what source can the Assembly of Guatemala draw the power, belonging only to the Divinity, to make Guatemalans out of Belgians, Frenchmen, Swiss and other inhabitants of the continent of Europe?' "

They chided their colleagues for precipitate and stealthy action on an issue of great public concern without consulting, or even informing, the people. Well might the Assembly members, they averred, fear the day when an aroused public "may say to us: 'How in a matter of this sort, of this importance, could you decide to proceed so rapidly without hearing, or more accurately said, choosing not to hear, our wishes and our opinion? Can you call what you have done in two or three weeks a profound and mature examination of a matter that embraces so many and such important considerations? What urgency was there to conclude the matter without informing the public of it? Nothing, it appears, save that you feared to open the question to discussion.' "

Grave as were their objections to individual features of the contract and to the procedures by which it was approved, the result most to be feared, Batres and Pavón asserted, was successful achievement of the ends for which the agreement was signed.

Let us suppose that the project succeeds; that the beautiful city of Santo Tomás . . . rises as by magic; that . . . a canal or a railroad connects the bay with the Motagua; that . . . the river is furrowed by handsome steamers . . . ; that the colony . . . develops as a beautiful garden belonging to the state and subject to its . . . laws—let us for a moment enter a dream world . . . . [But suppose] the established population . . . becomes alarmed (as has already occurred in a similar case) . . . [and sees in] the contract . . . the first link of a chain forged to enslave them, what will we do? Is our government powerful enough to force compliance . . . [on them]? The Belgians . . . will make us comply willingly or by force . . . . But we will do nothing but tear ourselves to pieces internally, and in place of a beautiful city, of a magnificent port, of canals and rails, of steamboats and commerce, in place of a delicious garden formed in our imaginations, we will have wars—real wars, and cruel— slaughters, and devastations.

The contract being already ratified, it was too late to ward off the consequences of success should the Compagnie justify the confidence placed in it. In the interest of the country, however, Batres and Pavón hoped that their fears would prove vain and that the Belgian project would result in "nothing but a speculation as the Verapaz one has been."[39]

The colonization issue decided in Guatemala City, the foreign negotiators went their separate ways. Ignoring Mora, de Puydt began the journey by way of Gualán and Mico Mountain to rejoin the other members of his commission at Izabal where they expected to embark for Belize and Europe. Mora returned to Abbottsville from where on May 23 he made the empty gesture of informing de Puydt that he was assuming temporarily the office of superintendent and that all negotiations on matters of Company business should be conducted with him alone. Two days earlier Anderson had made the even more futile offer to deliver to the chief of the Belgian party, even though he was without specific orders to do so, the selected lands in the Verapaz as soon as the purchase price had been deposited with the Consulado. On May 28 he congratulated de Puydt on the complete success of his mission in Guatemala, accepted an invitation to meet him in Izabal, and offered his services to the Belgian company. He was searching, he admitted, for some means to return to Europe in the face of a personal financial crisis produced by the Company's

39. Voto particular of Pavón and Batres, May 6, 1842, ANG, leg. 1395, exp. 32345, n.f.

refusal to pay his salary and by its obstruction of his credit in Belize.[40]

The outlook for the Company in London was no less desperate than for its former superintendent in the Verapaz. The directors had apparently reposed their hopes almost entirely in the successful conclusion of the transaction with the Belgians and had done little during the intervening year to advance their projects in Guatemala. A brief newspaper notice records a desultory shareholders' meeting in December 1841, and in June of 1842 Winsor gambled a contribution of £5 to help "relieve the general distress" in response to a public statement by Sir Robert Peel. He enclosed a copy of *Emigration to Vera Paz* on the chance that the Prime Minister would read it and be persuaded to give official support to the proposition "that the labour of thousands of Emigrants, would be profitably directed" toward the Company's holdings in Guatemala. The directors also received the completed penalty bridge for the Motagua and early in 1842 shipped it to Izabal.[41]

In its expectation of assistance from the Belgians, the Company was progressively disappointed. The activities of the exploratory commission first caused the directors misgivings and then alarm. Informed of de Puydt's approach to the government of Guatemala for the cession of Santo Tomás, they immediately protested to the Belgian company which "repudiated all participation in, or knowledge of, the proposals so made." When expurgated versions of the commissioners' reports appeared in the *Moniteur Belge* during the early part of October 1842 and were summarized in the London *Times,* the directors again found reason to protest the bad faith shown by the commission. Had they known the content of the deleted sections, they would have realized the futility of their action. After some delay the Belgian officers replied in November that the actions to which the English directors objected had been taken by members of the government commission, not by those representing the Compagnie.[42]

40. Mora to de Puydt, May 23, 1842, and Anderson to de Puydt, May 21, 1842, and May 28, 1842, AMRAHM, O. 1852, Carton 3, Nos. 55, 54, 60.

41. *The Colonial Gazette* (London), No. 161 (Dec. 22, 1841), p. 808; Winsor to Sir Robert Peel, June 17, 1842, The Peel Papers, Vol. CCCXXX, fol. 272, British Museum, Add. MSS. 40510. The bridge reached Izabal in early June 1842.

42. Memorial of Pollock, fol. 262. The commissioners' reports appeared in the *Moniteur Belge,* 12e Année, Nos. 280-290 (Oct. 7-Oct. 17, 1842). The *Times* article dealing with the Company settlement at Abbottsville appeared in No. 18,110 (Oct. 10, 1842), p. 4. The Belgian minister in London, C. Drouet, reported the reaction of Company officials to the Minister of Foreign Affairs, No. 40 bis, Oct. 13, 1842, AMAE, 2027.

Realizing that they had been betrayed by the associates they had accepted as collaborators and frustrated in the expectation of acquiring means for survival, the directors of the Company appealed to the British government. A memorial on their behalf addressed by David Pollock to the Colonial Office on November 25, 1842, sketched at some length the duplicity of the Brussels company and emphasized the extensive part the Belgian government was reported to have taken in the affair. Should breach of contract be insufficient grounds for action by the British Cabinet, the directors pointed out the harmful effects on Belize that could be anticipated from a foreign establishment at Santo Tomás. They did not presume to ask, but they obviously hoped, for the support of the government in seeking satisfaction from the Belgian capitalists.

The Colonial Office was only mildly concerned. The spot the Belgians proposed to colonize might be "the key to the whole isthmus," but the officers of the Colonial Department saw no action the government could appropriately take to impede the project. They were relieved early in December to be able to honor Lord Canning's request that the memorial be forwarded to the Foreign Office and to inform the Company secretary of the transfer.[43]

For more than two months the Company heard nothing further from the memorial. Finally on February 21, 1843, Winsor requested James Stephen of the Colonial Office to grant an interview to a commission representing the board. The directors, he pointed out, had "already incurred great personal responsibility in their efforts to retain the very extensive and valuable Territory for the Benefit of British Emigrants," but they were no longer able alone to sustain the effort. Unless the government saw fit to take some action in their support they would "feel compelled by the next Honduras Mail to issue final notices to withdraw all Persons holding possession for this Company, and to terminate all further expenditure in the proposed Colony." They would take such action only with "the deepest regret that a District of many millions of acres, replete with the greatest advantages to the industrious Settler, and to the Colonial Trade of the British Dominions should be abandoned to Foreigners; and that at a time when the Directors still remain in indefeasible possession by a formal Grant or Charter confirmed to this Company by the government of Guatemala." On this petition Stephen jotted an ironical inquiry to George W. Hope: "Shall these gentlemen be told that

43. Memorial of Pollock, Nov. 25, 1842; and notes, and draft letter to Winsor, Dec. 10, 1842, CO 123/64, n.f.

you will be happy to receive them?" Hope denied any anticipation of pleasure in the assignment, but he granted an interview to Winsor at his convenience. The Company secretary, however, was forced to leave London on urgent personal business, and the directors requested permission for Dr. Spurgin to call on March 3 in his stead. If the conference took place, the record was not preserved in the Colonial Office.[44]

The Company's threat to terminate its settlement in the Verapaz scarcely required execution. Circumstances during the previous year had already virtually accomplished its destruction. Murray returned in late February 1842 from his sojourn in Belize with provisions for the colony, but there was little vitality left in the enterprise. The collapse of expectations raised by the mission of the Belgians and the forfeiture of the Company's charter in the Verapaz as a result of the maneuvering in the capital left the settlement without support, without purpose, and without hope.

Anderson returned from Belize late in April and attempted, by resuming contact with de Puydt, to re-establish his authority. When Mora arrived from his negotiations in the capital late in May, he dismissed Murray from the office of superintendent and himself assumed the post for a time. Circumstances, however, made the position meaningless. Anderson left the settlement at the end of May, and both Mora and Murray appear shortly to have abandoned the country. William Knoth then fell heir to the empty title.[45]

Gradually most of the remaining residents of the settlement drifted away. Crowe, however, remained. Supported by funds from the Baptist Missionary Society after the Company defaulted on his salary payments, he found Abbottsville a convenient point from which to carry on his missionary work. The virtual disappearance of foreign authority in the settlement, however, encouraged neighboring priests to claim religious jurisdiction over the area and to attempt to restrict his activity. Crowe therefore decided in September 1843 to leave his wife in the nearly deserted town and to take his stock of Bibles to sell at the great fair of Salamá, from whence he proceeded to the capital. When after an absence of some nine months he returned in the sum-

44. Winsor to Stephen, Feb. 21, 1843, and notations; Hope to Winsor, Feb. 27, 1843; and J. G. Butter to Hope, March 1, 1843; CO 123/66, n.f.

45. The movement of persons and cargoes at Izabal in 1842 is given in ANG, leg. 3224, exps. 66839, 66860, and 66884. Murray's dismissal was announced in Mora to de Puydt, May 23, 1842. Knoth was recognized as superintendent as early as July 1842 (Guillermo Knoth to Manuel Gatica, July 18, 1842, *Gaceta Oficial* [Guatemala], No. 54 [Aug. 3, 1842], p. 231).

mer of 1844 to take his wife to Guatemala City, the evidence of European occupation had all but disappeared. The central street of the town was overgrown with bushes taller than a man's head, and the houses were falling in on the livestock which had taken possession of most of them. Crowe's own kitchen fell with a heavy crash during the last night the couple spent in their house, "and the pretty English cottage in which we spent three years was soon as desolate as the rest."[46]

By mid-summer 1844 Abbottsville had ceased to exist as a European settlement. The colonists were scattered, and the principal figures had returned to Europe or were engaged in other enterprises in Guatemala. Young Anderson was proposing to the government, on his own behalf, projects of public benefit, and a year later he was operating his own mining company at Chiantla, near Huehuetenango.[47] John MacKenney was serving as interim corregidor of Izabal and confessing to the government that his short tenure in the position had hardly given him time to learn his duties.[48] Knoth was directing a work crew opening a new road to the iron bridge supplied by the Company, which had just been erected over the Motagua south of Salamá.[49] The Eastern Coast Company had withdrawn from Guatemala and left the field to its erstwhile Belgian protégé whose colony at Santo Tomás had begun its second year. By 1844 the Company offices had disappeared from the listings in the London directories. Like the host of the amate tree of the Guatemalan forest it had been strangled by the growth of its erstwhile guest.

46. Frederick Crowe, *The Gospel in Central America* (London, 1850), pp. 534, 535, 545-46.

47. Draft letter to Anderson, Aug. 16, 1844, ANG, leg. 1395, exp. 32376, n.f.; *La Aurora* (Guatemala), Trim. 3, No. 17 (Aug. 15, 1845), p. 67.

48. MacKenney to Minister of Foreign Affairs, Aug. 9, 1844, ANG, leg. 3633, exp. 85393, n.f.

49. *Gaceta Oficial*, No. 163 (July 19, 1844), p. 666.

XI

INFRASTRUCTURE

OR ANACHRONISM?

The Guatemalan government wrote into the colonization agreement its dream of attaining certain elements of an economic "infrastructure." In most instances this feature of the projects remained a dead letter, but the Eastern Coast Company made some serious effort to comply with its obligation to supply major improvements in communications within the country. Its various contracts required it to erect a permanent bridge over the Motagua River on the route between the capital and the Verapaz and authorized it to establish and monopolize steam navigation on the principal waterways of the state and to construct and hold as its own property a number of trunk roads intended to expedite travel and commerce. The directors were not able to build the roads they projected nor did they take full advantage of their opportunity to monopolize steam transport, but they inaugurated steam navigation in Central America, and they constructed and delivered the first iron bridge to be erected in the country.

These improvements were expected to be financially rewarding to the Company, as well as economically useful to the republic. They promised opportunity for earnings in fees and tolls and for monopoly control by the Company over the movement of commerce within the area embraced by its communications network. Neither the government nor the contractor, however, seems to have considered objectively whether the facilities were provided in response to need or in advance of demand or to have examined critically the assumption that the expected development was compatible with the necessity of earning an immediate return. As a long-term social investment the projects were probably sound, but as a profitable employment for private capital they were likely to prove anachronistic.

The first step taken by the directors of the Company to improve communications within their concession was purchase of the steamboat "Vera Paz" for coasting service in Central America. The vessel was square-sterned, caravel-built, had one deck and two masts, and was schooner-rigged. She was steam-powered, had one stack, and was designed to use coal as fuel, although circumstances in Central America forced her on occasion to become a woodburner. She was identified by sham quarter galleries, a standing bowsprit, and a female bust figurehead. Her wood plank hull was copper-sheathed, her hold afforded slightly more than eight feet of vertical clearance, and her capacity was rated at a fraction more than 87 tons. Aloft she measured slightly more than 93 feet from the fore part to the main stem to the after part of the stern post and nearly eighteen feet at her greatest width above the main wales. She was built by John Oliver and Son, of South Shields, County Durham, and was delivered to the Company in the fall of 1835.[1]

The directors planned for the "Vera Paz" to sail for Central America as a part of the Company's first colonization effort in 1836. Although she might have contributed materially to the success of the settlements, she was allowed to lie at anchor in London Dock for some two years while the directors debated the Belize boundary issue with the British government and corresponded with Gálvez to arrange the terms of the promised monopoly of steam navigation within their concession. Finally, the new directors, pledged to more energetic management of the Company affairs, dispatched the vessel, in company with the sailing sloop "Turbot," to Central America in the fall of 1837 consigned to Thomas Fletcher, their resident agent.

The arrival of the "Vera Paz" at Izabal was in every way inopportune. The Company settlements at New Liverpool and Santa Cruz were abandoned and beyond revival by any aid, material or psychological, the steamboat could provide. Guatemala was in the grip of the insurrection of the *montaña,* and the steamer's arrival found the country racked by civil strife, internal communications disrupted, Izabal isolated, and foreign commerce virtually halted. The vessel, therefore, was temporarily useless to the Company either in assisting to advance its own immediate projects or in earning revenue by carrying a share of the existing commerce of the region. Finally, whether because of the administrative disruption produced by the insurrection or because Gálvez had neglected to request the proper

1. Copy of Certificate of British Registry [of "Vera Paz"], No. 415, CO 123/56, n.f., and description of the vessel given by John Lloyd Stephens, *Incidents of Travel in Central America, Chiapas, and Yucatan* (London, 1842), I, 22, and George W. Montgomery, *Narrative of a Journey to Guatemala, in Central America, in 1838* (New York, 1839), pp. 41, 47.

action by federal authorities, the port officials at Izabal knew nothing of the privileged status expected for the steamer. Hence, instead of receiving the delirious welcome anticipated by the directors, the vessel was "subjected to vexations & expensive detentions."[2]

In the absence of specific instructions to the contrary the customs officials at Izabal considered the appearance of the "Vera Paz" as a routine arrival. They demanded payment of the usual tonnage fees and of duty on the provisions carried on board for the crew. These charges Fletcher refused to pay and threatened, if the port authorities persisted in their demands, to execute the instructions of the directors to lodge an official protest and return the steamer to England. After the "Vera Paz" had made three voyages between Izabal and Belize without payment of duty in the Central American port, the customs officials at the end of March 1838 consulted the federal Minister of Finance who referred the question to the authorities of the state of Guatemala. The government of Valenzuela, who had succeeded Gálvez in power, found nothing in the contract signed with the Company to justify its pretensions to immunity from port duties. The port authorities, therefore, exacted an "onerous tonnage duty" on the "Vera Paz." In July 1838 the federal government resolved the issue by exempting all steamers for two years from payment of tonnage duties in the ports of the republic, but the charges collected on the "Vera Paz" were not refunded. Two years later the government of independent Guatemala extended the concession for a like period.[3]

The discordant reception at Izabal was only the first of a succession of misadventures that befell the "Vera Paz." Scarcely had the vessel dropped anchor when Captain Cobb and his crew became embroiled in an altercation and another dispute erupted between the captain and a passenger. Fletcher attempted to escape involvement in the controversies, but he was not permitted to do so; as consignee of the vessel, all parties pressed their arguments on him. His attempts to reconcile the differences were fruitless, and in the end they drew upon him the accusation by Cobb that he had encouraged the crewmen in their "mutinous complaints." These circumstances perhaps

2. Young Anderson to Frederick Chatfield, Oct. 28, 1838, FO 252/6, n.f.

3. *Ibid.;* consulta of federal Minister of Finance with state government of Guatemala, April 20, 1838, ANG, leg. 2390, exp. 49924; "Discurso del Presidente del Congreso Federal, Diputado J. Basilio Porras, pronunciado al cerrar sus sesiones ordinarias aquel cuerpo el 20 de julio de 1838," *Boletín* del Archivo General del Gobierno (Guatemala), III, No. 3 (April, 1938), 450; Decreto No. 117, Nov. 9, 1840, *Colección de los decretos de observancia general, expedidos por la Asamblea Constituyente del Estado de Guatemala, en los años de 1839 y 1840* (Guatemala, 1840), p. 221.

recalled to the agent's mind the trauma of his experience with the "Britannia," for he determined to assert his authority over the vessel. His action on this decision produced open defiance from Cobb. The "Vera Paz" had no urgent business she could perform, but she was useless for any purpose until the impasse was broken. On the basis of a general agreement to accept the decision of the Magistrates of Belize on the controversy, Fletcher and Anderson took the steamer to the Settlement to lay the issues before the authorities there.

The Magistrates heard the case early in February 1838. On the basis of the documents presented to them they decided in favor of Fletcher's claim to jurisdiction over the vessel, but they also assessed the costs of the hearing against him. The agent then used the authority that had just been confirmed to him to discharge Cobb, who was given a termination settlement and returned with his wife to England.[4] The question of control of the "Vera Paz" was thus settled, but its difficulties were not ended. The Magistrates were preparing to repeat at Belize the reception given to the vessel at Izabal.

The appearance of the "Vera Paz" in the British port caused consternation among the local merchants. The aim of the Company, they correctly believed, was "to draw to itself the trade with the interior now carried on by the Inhabitants of the Settlement."[5] Company efforts in the past had resulted in complete failure, but the arrival of its steamboat to compete with local sailing vessels in the coasting trade suggested that it might yet accomplish some of its objectives.

The issue was opened when Fletcher requested Belize registry for the "Vera Paz." Superintendent Alexander Macdonald was inclined to grant the petition in the belief that steam navigation might prove a considerable advantage to the commerce of the Settlement. Knowing, however, that the "interests of a large class of the Inhabitants" were involved, he decided to submit the question to the Magistrates. That body voted unanimously to refuse local registry to the steamer. It asserted that several small local craft would be driven out of service by the larger, swifter, more dependable steamer, with consequent loss of employment to many inhabitants of the Settlement; that granting the request would establish a precedent upon which other British vessels trading with Central American ports could claim exemption

4. Minutes of a Meeting of Magistrates held at the Court House, Belize, on 3rd February, 1838, and *ibid.*, on 5th February, 1838, CO 123/55, n.f.

5. Alexander Macdonald, Superintendent of Belize, to Lord Glenelg, No. 11, May 6, 1839, CO 123/55, n.f. Except as otherwise noted the account of the controversy over charges assessed against the "Vera Paz" at Belize is based on this source.

from fees at Belize; and that, assuming the Company to possess a monopoly of steam navigation on Lake Izabal, any steam vessels from Belize operating to those ports would be required to pay the highest rates of duty. On the recommendation of the Magistrates, therefore, "the usual fees and duties to which British ships of her size and class are liable were assessed and collected."

The Company representatives insisted that the "Vera Paz" was entitled to equal status with the four local coasters engaged in the Izabal trade. They pointed out that, although the steamer was British-owned, it was "under the protection of the Government of Guatemala" by virtue of the Company's contract and that it would engage in the coasting trade in competition with ships which were not required to pay equivalent duties. Some of the competing vessels were larger, some smaller, than the "Vera Paz"; they were partly owned by British subjects, partly by foreigners; and they operated under Central American registry or with license from the Superintendent of Belize.[6] These arguments were in vain. Macdonald made it clear that no change in status would be considered unless a local resident could be induced to become a partner in ownership of the vessel.

The decision of the Settlement authorities put the "Vera Paz" at severe disadvantage in the Belize-Izabal trade. An obviously well-informed but probably subjective observer alleged in a Settlement newspaper some years later that the steamer was required on each entry at Belize to pay a tonnage duty of $32.62½ and fees of $18.25. By contrast other coasting vessels were charged no tonnage duty and fees of only $3.75 at a maximum.[7] Company officials calculated that the charges placed on the steamer would amount to some $2,000 during a year of operation. This sum, they pointed out, was "quite sufficient to annihilate any profits she was likely to make" and, hence, equivalent to driving her out of operation. They charged similar discrimination against the sailing sloop "Turbot." For this reason the steamer was withdrawn from service in June 1838, and her local agent posted explanatory notices of the action in Belize, but they were pulled down either by the intimidated agent himself or by a government official.[8]

6. Anderson to Chatfield, Oct. 28, 1838, n.f.

7. "Tonnage," *Honduras Observer* (Belize), I, No. 19 (March 31, 1841), p. [3], in CO 123/60, n.f. Macdonald alleged that the *Observer* was published by Andrew Kennedy, the Company's agent for management of the steamer, and his business partner Dr. John Young, for the purpose of attacking him (Macdonald to Lord John Russell, July 12, 1841, CO 123/60, n.f.).

8. Memorial of Peter Harris Abbott and Charles Bourjot, Sept. 6, 1839, CO

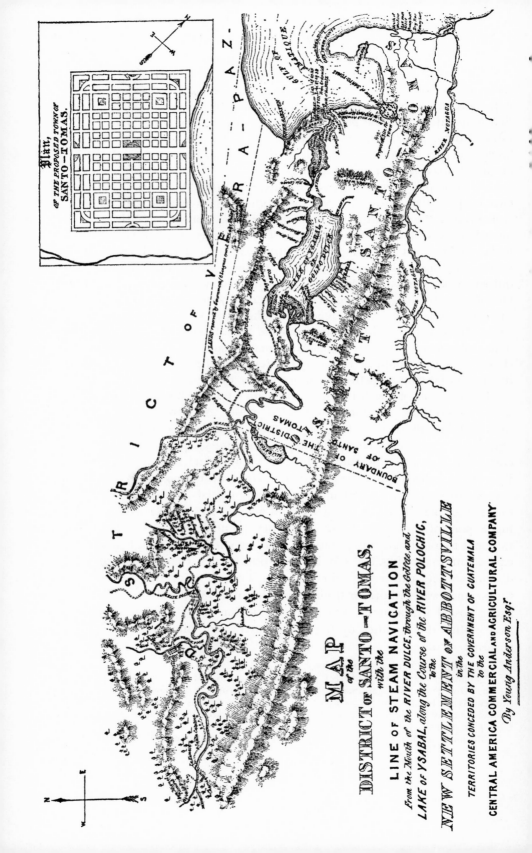

Plan,
OF THE PROPOSED TOWN OF
SANTO-TOMAS.

MAP
of the
DISTRICT OF SANTO-TOMAS,
with the
LINE OF STEAM NAVIGATION
From the Mouth of the RIVER DULCE, through the Gulfete, and
LAKE OF YSABAL, along the Course of the RIVER POLOCHIC,
to the
NEW SETTLEMENT OF ABBOTTSVILLE
in the
TERRITORIES CONCEDED BY THE GOVERNMENT OF GUATEMALA
to the
CENTRAL AMERICA COMMERCIAL AND AGRICULTURAL COMPANY
By Young Anderson Esqr.

The "Vera Paz" was finally put under colonial registry as the most advantageous arrangement open to her, and she resumed operation, apparently late in June 1838. The dispute over her status, however, continued for the remainder of the year. The new local agent for the vessel, Andrew Kennedy, kept the issue alive by addressing petitions to Macdonald, who on each occasion restated the condition under which a change of registry could be obtained. In exasperation Kennedy finally published the correspondence in a pamphlet designed to demonstrate the inequity of the treatment to which the steamer was subjected in protection of local vested interests.[9] The wrath of the authorities was the only tangible achievement of his attempt to obtain a favorable judgment from public opinion.

Finally, Marshal Bennett appeared before Macdonald in January 1839 to claim joint ownership of the "Vera Paz." The Superintendent promptly made good his promise and accorded the vessel coasting registry, although "neither its size nor the circumstances . . . perfectly warranted my doing so." Soon thereafter, Young Anderson, on his way back to England, removed Kennedy as local agent "for the plain reason that I hope his [Macdonald's] oppressive exactions will cease as soon as he knows your house has ceased to be our agents."[10]

The directors of the Company immediately began action at both the Colonial Office and the Board of Trade to recover the overcharges on the steamer which they alleged had been improperly levied and illegally exacted in Belize. The Colonial Office suspended judgment until it received from Macdonald the report it requested on February 8, but the Board of Trade promptly informed the Colonial Department that the Company was entitled to a refund if unusual or distinctive duties had been collected. When Macdonald's defense of his action arrived in London, the Colonial Office sent a copy to the Board of Trade, and some three weeks later, in response to an inquiry from the directors, it also furnished the Company a copy of the report. In early September the directors renewed their claims to recover £258 2s 6d in discriminatory charges and fees collected on the "Vera Paz" in fifteen voyages and on the "Turbot" in two voyages. On the basis of the accumulated evidence, the Board of Trade on September 12, 1839, ruled that the Company was entitled to a refund

123/56, n.f.; Tal W. Cox to Patrick Walker, Secretary of Belize, April 11, 1840, CO 123/57, n.f.

9. *Copy of Correspondence Relative to the Steam Boat "Vera Paz"* . . . (New York, 1838), in CO 123/57, n.f.

10. Anderson to Andrew Kennedy, March 3, 1839, CO 123/56, n.f.

of the overcharges and suggested that an instruction be issued to Macdonald to that effect.[11]

The Colonial Office, however, allowed the Superintendent additional opportunity to defend himself. Macdonald confessed that he could add little to his first report and could submit as new evidence only the plea that the Settlement had been put to "enormous expense in providing for the support of great numbers of the deluded victims of the Company who have sought refuge from their calamities in Belize." If the records are complete, the Colonial Office closed out the incident on July 3, 1840, by sending the directors a copy of the Superintendent's latest defense of his action. The critic of Macdonald's policies who wrote in the *Honduras Observer* in March 1841 alleged, however, that the instruction suggested by the Board of Trade had been sent and received but that the Superintendent had submitted it to the Magistrates who thwarted its execution by ruling that the extraordinary and differential duties were justified in view of the "many pauper immigrants, and much sickness" to which the Settlement had been exposed by the owners of the steamer.[12]

While the dispute over her registry was carried on in Belize and London, the "Vera Paz" began her operations. She offered passenger and cargo service of an unprecedented type between Izabal and Belize, but the troubled internal conditions in Guatemala probably restricted the traffic on which her profitable employment depended and prevented her at least temporarily from capitalizing on the advantage she might normally have anticipated.

The operation of the "Vera Paz" fell under the general responsibility of the Company superintendent in Guatemala, but only rarely was he able directly to exercise his authority. During his enforced residence on the north coast of Guatemala in late 1837 and early 1838, Anderson participated in the negotiations at Izabal and Belize that cleared the way for the operation of the steamer, and while he resided in Belize in the spring and summer of 1839 en route to Europe from his successful negotiations in Guatemala, he again took direct charge of arrangements relating to the vessel. On most other occasions, however, his residence elsewhere forced him to leave super-

11. The correspondence between the Colonial Office and Macdonald is found in CO 123/55, n.f. The Superintendent's defense of his actions is given in his dispatch to Glenelg, No. 11, of May 6, 1839. The communications between the Colonial Office and the Board of Trade, and the official correspondence with Abbott and Bourjot appear in CO 123/56, n.f.

12. Macdonald to Russell, No. 29, April 11, 1840, CO 123/57, n.f.; "Tonnage," p. [3].

vision of the steamer and of the freight and passenger traffic she carried to agents in Belize, Izabal, and Guatemala City. The management of the vessel itself, of course, was left to her master or captain. When the "Vera Paz" first appeared at Belize Leonard P. Cox was appointed her acting agent. In late June 1838, however, after a brush with the authorities over the publicity he gave to her withdrawal from service, Cox gave way to Andrew Kennedy, of the Belize firm of Young & Kennedy, who received the regular appointment. He served until Anderson withdrew the agency from him in March 1839 in the hope that relationships with the Superintendent would improve in consequence. The new agent for the steamer was Francisco Camoyano, a wealthy Spanish merchant resident in Belize, whose attempts a year earlier to dissuade George W. Montgomery from risking his life aboard one of "those new fangled inventions of the English" had convinced the United States agent that his recent acquaintance "evidently was no friend to steamboats, or to any thing English." At the same time the Company was represented in Izabal by Felipe Molló and in Guatemala City by the firm of Spanish merchants, Espada y Piloña, who had offered their services to the Company the previous December. By early 1841 Kennedy was again serving as Company agent in Belize, and in Izabal the agency had been changed to the firm of Ampudia y Pulleiro.[13]

The steamer was commanded by a succession of captains who varied greatly in competence and in tenure. Captain Cobb was appointed as her permanent master, but his dispute with Fletcher resulted in his dismissal before the vessel entered on active service. His immediate successor was apparently a Captain Neal, of whom an unflattering description was left by George W. Montgomery, who chanced to sail as a passenger on the steamer from Belize to Izabal in May 1838. Several incidents of the voyage made it evident that the captain "was very deficient in the knowledge of his profession, and still more so in energy and firmness of character." The sailors had

13. Information on the first two appointments comes from H. A. Grey to Young & Kennedy, Aug. 3, 1839, and Petition of Abbott and Bourjot to Glenelg, Feb. 4, 1839, both in CO 123/56, n.f.; and Anderson to Kennedy, March 3, 1839. Data on Camoyano comes from Loughman & Son to Rt. Hon. E. G. Stanley, March 27, 1843, CO 123/45, n.f.; Stephens, I, 13; and Montgomery, p. 39. Subsequent changes were reported in Anderson's "Avisos," published in *El Tiempo* (Guatemala), No. 7 (May 14, 1839), p. 28; and in "Aviso al público," *Honduras Observer,* I, No. 15 (March 3, 1841), [4], in CO 123/60, n.f. Espada y Piloña to Peter Harris Abbott, Dec. 8, 1838, *Brief Statement, Supported by Original Documents, of the Important Grants Conceded to the Eastern Coast of Central America Commercial & Agricultural Company by the State of Guatemala* (2nd ed.; London, 1840), p. 138.

no respect for his authority, debated his orders with him, and on occasion even threatened him. Command of the vessel shifted about among the captain, the pilot, and Anderson, who happened also to be aboard.

The anarchy aboard the "Vera Paz" was demonstrated with particular clarity when she reached the mouth of the Río Dulce. As the steamer approached the bar about noon the captain and the pilot engaged in prolonged debate over the proper course to steer until the helmsman, left to his own devices, ran her aground. An argument to affix blame for the mishap then ensued among all parties concerned, in the course of which no attempt was made to get the vessel off. Finally, a kedge anchor was rowed out and dropped, and the sailors by tremendous exertion worked her free and into deep water. She was barely underway when the helmsman again ran her aground. On the advice of the pilot the captain decided to make no effort to take her off but to wait until the high tide, subsequently discovered to be non-existent on that coast, floated her free When it became evident that the pilot was a charlatan and that a rising tide could not be expected to release the vessel, a square sail was hoisted and under the combined force of steam and evening breeze she edged across the bar with much thumping and scraping and late in the evening entered the Río Dulce.[14]

Mismanagement of this sort not unnaturally left the vessel in need of frequent conditioning. In June 1838 she underwent hasty repair, perhaps in part as a result of damage sustained on the voyage described by Montgomery. It appears that the officers and crewmen were accustomed to employ mechanics at Belize to tinker with the steamer, for in March 1839 Anderson announced that henceforward no work commissions should be accepted from the master or crew of the steamer. The owners would recognize and pay only such obligations as Anderson himself, or his duly appointed agent, contracted in writing. All persons currently holding claims against the vessel were advised to present them within fifteen days for examination and payment. This regularization of procedures was apparently preliminary to a general overhaul of the vessel, for Anderson advertised on May 1, 1839, that the "Vera Paz" was again in perfect running order and ready to resume her voyages between Belize and Izabal.[15]

14. *Copy of Correspondence,* p. 16; Montgomery, *Narrative of a Journey,* pp. 39, 40, 43-44.
15. "Public Notice," signed by Young Anderson, Supplement to *The Belize Advertiser,* I, No. 21 (March 2, 1839), 108, in CO 123/55, n.f.; "Avisos," p. 28; *Copy of Correspondence,* p. 16.

When the steamer returned to service she sailed under the command of Captain Juan López, whom Anderson described in his May 1 announcement as a "highly respected and experienced pilot." López served as master of the "Vera Paz" from May 1839 until January 1840.[16] He was the "small, weather-beaten, dried-up, old Spaniard, with courtesy enough for a Don of Old" who greeted John Lloyd Stephens "hat in hand" when the United States envoy came aboard the steamer at Belize late in October 1839. The engineer was an Englishman, William Rush, who, in physical contrast with his commander, stood "six feet three or four inches high and stout in proportion." The fireman, Philip, was a mulatto who had emigrated from Baltimore some eight years earlier in such haste that Stephens conjectured he might be wanted in Maryland as a fugitive slave. In addition to his employment aboard the steamer at a salary of $23.00 per month, Philip owned a house in Izabal where he maintained a common-law wife and was the principal architect-carpenter of the port. The remainder of the crew were "Spaniards, Mestitzoes and mulatoes, not particularly at home in the management of a steamboat."[17]

Thomas Griffiths, who succeeded López, held the position of captain from late January 1840 until mid-June 1841. His tenure of nearly eighteen months exceeded that of any other master of the vessel. Rush continued as engineer of the steamer, and after Griffiths gave up the command he served as her interim captain for about a month. During the fall of 1840 the vessel was withdrawn from service and repaired by John Uter of Belize, who made her timbers and all other visible portions from her copperline upwards as good as new.[18] About the middle of October she resumed her runs under the interim captaincy of John (or Joseph) Mulard, but Griffiths again took command late in November and served until he left the Company's employ in June 1841. He was succeeded by William Kelley who was responsible for the steamer until she was retired in mid-April 1842.

The "Vera Paz" operated in Central American waters over a total

16. The captains of the "Vera Paz" beginning with López, the sailings of the vessel, the cargoes and passengers she carried, etc., are recorded in the register of vessels entered and cleared at the port of Izabal: AGN, leg. 2391, exps. 44928-930; leg. 3220, exps. 66304, -5, -8, -11, -27; leg. 3221, exps. 66334, -38, -51, -63, -84, -90, -412, -13, -14, -50, -55, -79, -511, -12; leg. 3222, exps. 66542, -68, -74, -91, -617, -18, -20, -21, -27, -31, -34, -37, -47, -60, -66, -68, -73; leg. 3223, exps. 66689, -706, -52, -875. Except as otherwise noted the paragraphs dealing with these subjects are drawn from these documents.

17. Stephens, *Incidents of Travel*, I, 23-24, 37-38.

18. Deposition of John Uter, March 4, 1843, Proceedings of the Public Meeting held at . . . Belize . . . 6th March, and subsequent days, 1843, CO 123/65, n.f.

period of slightly more than four years. Her earliest voyages are not documented in detail, but by March of 1838 she was reported to have made three round trips between Izabal and Belize and by February 1 of the following year she was said to have made fifteen voyages. The record of the next eight months is blank, but between October 1839 and April 1842 she operated between the two ports at fairly regular intervals. Service was suspended for two and one-half months between the end of June and the middle of October 1840 while the steamer was undergoing repairs and again for two months beginning late in October 1841. During some twenty-four months of actual operation the "Vera Paz" made forty-six documented voyages in and out of Izabal. Two were exclusively on Company business, but the remaining forty-four were in the interest of general commerce.

The early sailings of the "Vera Paz" were determined largely by circumstance. Availability of cargo was the principal consideration, but other contingencies were also allowed to influence her movements. Montgomery, for example, records that his departure from Belize as a passenger on the steamer was delayed for a day, first because the crewmen did not appear on schedule and three or four hours were required to round them up and then because the sailors, brought aboard in a state of inebriation, refused to perform their duties and prevented the engineer from getting up steam.[19]

After the steamer was overhauled and placed under more competent management in the spring of 1839, Anderson committed her to a partial schedule. He announced that she would sail regularly from Izabal at a fixed hour on the third day of each month and as often between scheduled departures as cargo justified.[20] The steamer would thus be able to accommodate traffic in excess of a monthly minimum on the same informal basis as before, but passengers and shippers alike could plan with certainty on one fixed sailing date each month. However advantageous the announced schedule might have been to patrons, it could not be maintained. During the nine-months' period between October 1839 and June 1840 the "Vera Paz" made twenty round trips, but only once did she sail from Izabal on the third day of the month. On all other occasions she was from one to five days late.

Insufficient cargo was the principal reason for the irregular service, but the courtesies extended to John Lloyd Stephens suggest that it may also have resulted in part from the practice of accommodating

19. Montgomery, *Narrative of a Journey,* p. 39.
20. "Avisos," p. 28.

valued patrons to the disregard of the announced schedule. To serve Stephens' convenience the agent in Belize offered to delay the departure of the steamer for a few days, and he put her captain under orders to make such stops en route as his distinguished passenger might desire. On this basis the sailing of the "Vera Paz" was postponed for one day, and a stop at Punta Gorda, requested by Stephens, further delayed her arrival at her destination. Accustomed "to submitting to the despotic regulations of steamboat agents at home," this casual disregard of schedule was a flattering novelty to the fledgling diplomat,[21] but it was probably not so regarded by commercial interests.

In the spring of 1841 Andrew Kennedy put all sailings of the steamer on a formal schedule. He announced that she would leave Belize on alternate Thursdays beginning February 18 and sail from Izabal on Fridays of the following weeks.[22] For two voyages the "Vera Paz" adhered to her timetable, but then she fell behind and was never able to regain her schedule.

The "Vera Paz" offered advantages unmatched by other vessels engaged in the Belize-Izabal traffic. Her speed and relative independence of wind and weather allowed her under normal conditions to make the passage in either direction in from eighteen to twenty hours. Unusual circumstances, however, often greatly increased her sailing time. The voyage on which Montgomery was a passenger consumed more than forty-eight hours, but a detour to the Bay of Santo Tomás, stops there and at San Felipe to take aboard wood for fuel, and the delay incident to the groundings at the bar of the Río Dulce added greatly to the minimum necessary navigation time. Similarly, Stephens' trip appears to have required some thirty-two hours, several of which were added by putting in at Punta Gorda through unfamiliar waters and by the leisurely inspection Stephens made of the town. On the whole, however, the swiftness and dependability of the "Vera Paz" made her the favored conveyance for the mails and of travelers who wished to minimize their exposure to the pestilential climate of the north coast.

In addition to the advantage of dispatch, the "Vera Paz" afforded accommodations that Anderson alleged were superior to those offered by any competing vessel. Montgomery, however, did not find them beyond criticism. During the night he spent aboard the steamer in Belize harbor he recorded that "the small and rather crowded cabin

21. Stephens, *Incidents of Travel*, I, 13-14, 23-24, 28-32.
22. "Aviso al público," p. [4].

was intolerable from the heat and smell of bilge-water." His impression might be explained either by the lax regime permitted by Captain Neal or by the circumstance that a violent storm forced him to seek shelter in his quarters and to keep all openings tightly closed. John Lloyd Stephens' opinion tended to justify Anderson's boast. He considered the cabin "very comfortable," and he was delighted with the arrangement under an awning on deck of a seat from which he could watch the passing shore. Even the error of his unthinking assumption that meals would be furnished to passengers aboard resulted in no cause for complaint, for the ingenuity of his servant and the generosity of his only traveling companion, a priest whose friends in Belize had thoughtfully provided against this deficiency in the service, supplied him with food during the voyage. Although the clatter of the "panting monster" destroyed the romantic illusion of following the last track of Columbus in New World waters and the "unnatural bluster of our steam engine" shattered the pristine quiet of the Río Dulce, Stephens found the steamer voyage a delightful adventure.[23]

Her combination of desirable qualities made the "Vera Paz" the preferred means of travel over the Belize-Izabal route. Foreigners were amazed to find such a modern convenience in so remote an area of the world, and although they perhaps had less comparative basis for celebrating their privileged position, Central Americans were also happy to take advantage of the service. Merchants who went to Belize on business made considerable use of the steamer, and despite the ill favor into which the Company had fallen in Guatemala President Rivera Paz himself selected the vessel for the voyage he proposed in May 1841 to make with General Carrera to visit Omoa, Trujillo, and Belize. The trip was arranged to be a prestige performance with Captain Bingham, one of the directors then in Guatemala, taking command for the occasion, but the President was forced to cancel the plans before they could be executed.[24]

Granted the small volume of travel over the Izabal-Belize route, the "Vera Paz" was well patronized. On the forty-four commercial voyages she made between October 1839 and April 1842 she carried a total of some three hundred passengers. The patronage was not uniform, however, but tended to decline gradually and consistently. During the first eighteen voyages, when she carried slightly more than

23. Montgomery, *Narrative of a Journey*, p. 39; Stephens, *Incidents of Travel*, I, 24, 26-27, 34.
24. George U. Skinner to Macdonald, May 1, 1841, CO 123/60, n.f.

half of the total number of travelers, the steamer averaged a little more than four passengers per trip; during the next twenty-two she averaged slightly less than three; and during the last four, a fraction more than two. The decline in patronage may have resulted because the cost of the passage was prohibitive to all but the wealthiest patrons. Anderson advertised the fares in May 1839 as twenty pesos for cabin accommodation and ten pesos for steerage. However, a passenger accompanied by as many as eighty *zurrones* of domestic products or a like number of *bultos* of merchandise was allowed free passage.[25] This concession may well account for the popularity of the steamer with the merchants, and it may also explain the apparent increase in freight shipments while passenger traffic declined.

The record of the "Vera Paz" as a cargo carrier was the reverse of her experience as a passenger vessel. She appears to have begun rather poorly but to have increased her freight traffic as she became established in the business. She was virtually never without cargo on the Belize-Izabal run, but frequently she found nothing to lade at Izabal. Of the eighteen commercial voyages she made between October 1839 and June 1840 she sailed from Izabal in ballast on twelve occasions. Of the four trips she made between December 1841 and April 1842 she sailed twice with an empty hold. On the average she sailed in ballast from the Guatemalan port on more than forty per cent of her voyages. Quantitative estimates of the freight she carried are impossible to compute because of the practice of reporting cargo only by number of *bultos* or other equally indefinite designations. The commodities that comprised her cargoes were also stated in imprecise terms, but from the general descriptions given, it may be inferred that from Belize she carried principally European merchandise and from Izabal chiefly indigo and cochineal.

Available evidence provides little basis for determining whether or not operation of the "Vera Paz" was profitable to her owners. When her agent at Belize announced her withdrawal from service in June 1838 he alleged that everything she earned on her regular voyages was consumed by the duties exacted at the Settlement. He offered her, however, for charter trips between Belize and Izabal or Omoa, one way in either direction for the sum of $250 above tonnage duty.[26] Assuming, after the duty issue had been resolved, that when she sailed with cargo she carried a sufficient volume of freight to pay some return, her empty hold on so many of the Izabal-Belize runs must

25. "Avisos," p. 28.
26. *Copy of Correspondence*, p. 16.

have meant that her average profit was small, if not entirely non-existent.

Apparently in an attempt to increase the patronage of the "Vera Paz" the Company undertook to provide auxiliary services that might induce shippers to employ the vessel as a cargo carrier. In the spring of 1839 Anderson announced that the Company had purchased from Piñol and Croskey two houses in Izabal and was repairing them for use as warehouses. It therefore offered to handle transit shipments through the port city at a charge of four reales per *zurrón* or *bulto*. This service it apparently offered continuously until February 1842 when the carelessness of an employee resulted in a fire that totally destroyed the warehouses and a large part of Izabal as well.

The disaster at Izabal and the cancellation of the Company's Verapaz contract in the spring of 1842 ended the career of the steamer in Guatemalan waters. She was, therefore, laid up at Belize under the care of a custodian who lived aboard her. Archibald Montgomery, a resident of the Settlement, was appointed to act as her agent, but he apparently found no useful employment for her. For several months she rode idly at anchor, exposed to the sun and weather. To keep her seaworthy Montgomery employed John Uter in November 1842 to calk the seams that opened in the planking above her copper sheathing.

In early February 1843 the Magistrates of the Settlement offered temporary employment for the retired vessel. They decided to rebuild the power magazine in the harbor, and they sought a secure place to store the contents of the existing structure while its successor was under construction. The "Vera Paz" seemed to offer an ideal solution to their problem, for she could serve as a floating warehouse anchored at a safe distance from the town in case of an accidental explosion. The Magistrates rejected Montgomery's proposal to rent the vessel at $100 per month and his offer to sell her outright for $3,000, but they agreed on February 6 to rent her for $50.00 per month. The powder was stowed aboard and she was moored at an isolated anchorage in the bay. During the night of Friday, February 17, 1843, she disappeared. Investigation established the probability that careless workmen had laded her until she rode in the water well above her copper sheathing and that while lying at anchor she had shipped through seams that had re-opened in her dry planking enough water to sink her.

On behalf of the owners Montgomery immediately instituted a claim for $5,000, the alleged value of the vessel, plus the cost of collection. He first appealed to the Magistrates who refused to admit the claim, then to Superintendent Macdonald who declined to accept it as a public charge, and finally to the Public Meeting. That body deferred consideration of the petition in March, but on July 4 it appointed a committee of five to appraise the value of the steamer as of the day before she sank. The following day the Meeting approved the committee's recommendation that $1,250 be placed at the disposal of the Magistrates for the benefit of the owners of the "Vera Paz." On July 12 Colonel St. John Fancourt, the newly-arrived superintendent, refused to sanction this action on grounds that, far from settling the issue, the payment might be construed as admitting the justice of Montgomery's claim and, hence, lead to further litigation.[27] This negative decision by the Superintendent appears to have placed the claim as thoroughly beyond salvage as was the steamer herself.

In addition to the "Vera Paz" the Company sent out at least two other vessels for service in Central America. The "Turbot" accompanied the "Vera Paz" on her outward voyage, and the "Polochiquito" came out aboard the "St Lawrence" with the work force sent to Abbottsville in the spring of 1840. Compared with the "Vera Paz" each of these vessels had a short and relatively uneventful history in the New World.

The "Turbot" was a sailing sloop of 112 tons commanded by Captain Pearson on her outward voyage. She was apparently not intended, as was the "Vera Paz," to play an integral role in development of the Company's concessions in Guatemala, and if she was, the disappearance of the Company's settlements and the deteriorated state of Central American commerce caused her to be diverted immediately to other service. The known facts about her career in Central American waters are few indeed. She was said to have made two voyages into Belize in March and April 1838, after which she was reported lost off the Wanks River on the Mosquito Shore. This scanty evidence affords basis for nothing more than a conjecture that she was employed in the rapidly developing mahogany business on the Mosquito Shore. If this surmise is correct, she may have been used to transport mahogany for other cutters, or perhaps logs bought by the Company from other operators, or conceivably timber cut by the Company on lands to which it claimed title by virtue of its purchase from Gregor MacGregor. Whatever the nature of the operation, it was abruptly terminated by the almost immediate loss of the vessel.

27. Proceedings of the Public Meeting held at . . . Belize . . . 6th March, and subsequent days, 1843; *ibid.*, 3rd and subsequent days of July, 1843; Fancourt to W. J. Coffin, Chairman, July 12, 1843; all in CO 123/65, n.f.

Short as was the career of the "Turbot" it was not without controversy, for she was involved with the "Vera Paz" in the dispute over duties and charges levied at Belize. The Company claimed that discriminatory charges were levied against both vessels, but the authorities at Belize maintained that, because the "Turbot" was the same size as the other coasting vessels operating out of the Settlement, she "was admitted at once to their privileges." Because of her infrequent entries, however, the "Turbot" played only a minor role in the controversy.[28]

The "Polochiquito" was a small, shallow-draft steamer intended for freight and passenger service on the Lake Izabal-Polochic River route. No description of her has been discovered, beyond Crowe's reference to "the light and graceful *Polochiquito*," but it may be assumed that she approximated Anderson's specifications. If so, she was an iron steamer constructed to draw no more than eighteen inches of water and capable of towing a barge laden with some eight tons of cargo. She was designed to burn coal, but experimentation after she arrived in Guatemala waters allowed Anderson to report that she "answers admirably with fire-wood" that could easily be obtained for her at New Liverpool and on the north shore of Lake Izabal.

The "Polochiquito" appears never to have passed beyond the stage of trials in New World waters. As soon as she arrived she was disembarked and put through an entirely successful test on Lake Izabal. Immediately thereafter she made a triumphant maiden voyage across the lake and up the Polochic carrying the newly-arrived colonists and their baggage to Panzós. A short time later Anderson took her out of sheltered inland waters for an ocean trial, perhaps with the idea that if she were able to navigate the open roadstead to Livingston or to Santo Tomás she could spare the "Vera Paz" the hazardous crossing of the bar at the mouth of the Río Dulce. The little steamer performed well, the Superintendent reported, when "tried at sea with a stiff breeze right ahead and through a surf, such as the ship's boats in harbour could not head."[29]

Anderson's passion for testing the "Polochiquito" may account for the circumstance that the record of the little steamer falls suddenly mute. She must certainly have been lost, although no mention is made of such a tragedy. The self-conscious avoidance of all mention

28. Macdonald to Glenelg, May 6, 1839, n.f.; Memorial of Abbott and Bourjot, Sept. 6, 1839, n.f.

29. *Brief Statement*, 1840, p. 68; *Emigration to Vera Paz: Latest Intelligence from the Colony* [London, 1840?], p. 2; Frederick Crowe, *The Gospel in Central America* (London, 1850), p. 526.

of the vessel, however, suggests a calamity caused by negligence or irresponsibility of a Company official. It may not be beyond reason to conjecture that she was swamped by an unusually large wave during a sea trial, or that she was wrecked by a boiler explosion produced when an inexperienced fireman fed quickly combustible wood too rapidly into her fire box, or that she sank as a result of hull damage sustained while testing the navigability of the Boca Nueva or some other river within the Company's grant. Whatever her fate, the "Polochiquito" disappeared before she made a single commercial voyage. She was entered out of Izabal on her maiden trip, but never again did she appear on the register.

The loss of the "Polochiquito" was a heavy blow to the Company's dream of empire in Central America. Again, as in his report of September 1839, Anderson might have warned the directors "that your whole scheme of colonization will fail, unless such a steamer be provided before another immigrant be sent to the country."[30] The vessel was no less essential to the directors' commercial ambitions, for if it was not promptly replaced the Company lost its monopoly of steamer service on the waterways of the Verapaz, and without the river traffic the "Polochiquito" was expected to develop its exclusive privilege of steam navigation over the Izabal-Belize route was scarcely worth maintaining. When the "Vera Paz" was withdrawn from service on that run, the Company's last claim to monopoly was lost.

Ironically, the "Vera Paz" was retired only a short time before the bridge for the Motagua, the Company's second major contribution to improved communications in Guatemala, required transport over the route it had abandoned. When the shipment reached Belize, it had to be transported to Izabal aboard one of the sailing vessels which had formerly been a competitor of the steamer in the coasting trade.[31]

The Company constructed the bridge to discharge the penalty imposed by the government of Guatemala in November 1838 as a condition of extending for three years the period allowed for fulfilling the obligations assumed under the Verapaz agreement. The directors adopted for this purpose the plan of an iron chain suspension bridge invented by Dr. John Spurgin, one of their number, and a model of the proposed work was shipped for approval to the President of Guatemala when the work force was sent to Abbottsville in the spring of 1840. The design was apparently accepted, for in the summer of the

---

30. *Brief Statement*, 1840, p. 69.
31. Arrival and departure of vessels at Izabal, ANG, leg. 3224, exp. 66882.

same year the directors decided to proceed with manufacture of the structure and estimated that its cost would not exceed £1,200. The actual cost, as reported in Guatemala, however, was £2,500. Before the work was finished the Company's position in Guatemala had deteriorated almost beyond salvage, but the emphasis Mora gave to the imminent arrival of the structure in his representations to the government in the spring of 1842 suggests that the directors had chosen to gamble that completion of a major project might restore their prestige. The bridge was therefore shipped to Central America, and an engineer was sent out to superintend its construction.[32]

The bridge arrived at Izabal on June 3, 1842, the unassembled parts grouped to form a total of 289 loads weighing some one hundred pounds each. Andrew Kennedy & Company, the commercial agent of the directors in Belize, paid the transport charges on the shipment to the Guatemalan port where it was delivered to the Company representatives, Ampudia y Pulleiro. Disembarked at Izabal, the bridge was stored in the warehouse of the consignees to await shipment up the Polochic and overland to the Motagua.[33]

The means that had to be employed to convey the heavy cargo from the lake port to the construction site on the upper Motagua manifested with dramatic clarity the primitive state of internal transport in Guatemala which the Company's operations had been expected to improve. With equal forcefulness the expedients adopted to defray the costs of carriage revealed the puny resources from which both the government of Guatemala and the Company attempted to finance the major projects of development to which they committed themselves.

The terms of the penalty required the Company, with the assistance of the government, to deliver the bridge to the Motagua and to erect it at the chosen site. William Knoth, the superintendent at Abbottsville, tried dutifully to fulfill this obligation. He contracted with Basilio Chaverría to transport the shipment by pirogue from Izabal to Telemán and sent to Belize to obtain from the Kennedy firm the money necessary to pay the freight. By mid-July the Com-

32. Eastern Coast of Central America Commercial and Agricultural Company, *Report of the Directors, to a General Meeting of Proprietors, 18th August, 1840* (London, [1840]), p. 6; "Puente del Río grande," *Gaceta Oficial* (Guatemala), No. 114 (Aug. 4, 1843), p. 464; Guillermo Knoth, Superintendent at Abbottsville, to Manuel Gatica, Corregidor of Verapaz, July 18, 1842, *Gaceta Oficial*, No. 54 (Aug. 3, 1842), p. 231.

33. Arrival and departure of vessels at Izabal, ANG, leg. 3224, exp. 66882; Francisco Infiesta, Consular deputy at Salamá, to Gatica, Dec. 17, 1842, ANG, leg. 3361, exp. 74284; Knoth to Gatica, July 18, 1842, p. 231.

pany engineer was waiting in the Verapaz, and Knoth was daily expecting Chaverría to arrive at Telemán with his cargo. When it became clear, however, that the Company agent in Belize was unable to supply the requested funds, these expectations immediately collapsed.

Meanwhile, the authorities at Guatemala City learned of the arrival of the bridge at Izabal. The government promptly relayed the information to Manuel Gatica, the corregidor of the Verapaz, and instructed him in late June to make such arrangements as were necessary to have the structure put in place over the Motagua. In execution of these orders Gatica requested Ampudia y Pulleiro to release the shipment for immediate transport to Telemán even though they might have to defer for some time collection from the Company of the freight charges he assumed they must hold against it. On July 14 the Corregidor informed Knoth of his commission from the government and of the action he had taken to carry it out.

Knoth in turn outlined to Gatica the current status of the measures taken by the Company for transport and erection of the bridge and the arrangements he had made for its shipment to Telemán. He promised to inform the Corregidor immediately when the bridge arrived at the river port and offered his own assistance at that time in facilitating overland transport and that of the Company engineer later in erecting the structure. He suggested that an escort be sent to maintain surveillance over the porters employed to carry the cargo to prevent them from mislaying their burdens, for loss of a single part might make it impossible to erect the bridge. He also relayed the engineer's warning that work to prepare the face of the cliff that was to serve as the bastion for the bridge on the north bank of the Motagua should be undertaken only under his own supervision. Gatica was so encouraged by these developments that he issued a public manifesto promising to have the bridge in place by September.[34]

The shipment, however, remained at Izabal. Impatient with the unexplained delay, the government at the end of July took direct action to start the bridge on its way to Telemán. On the assumption that the cargo was detained in Izabal as security that the Company would pay the charges against it, the Minister General proposed to Pulleiro that he release the bridge on the government's guarantee to

34. Juan José Aycinena, Minister of Government, to Gatica, June 25, 1842, ABVP, Notas del supremo govierno, Año de 1842, Junio, fol. 30; Knoth to Gatica, July 18, 1842, p. 231; Gatica to President, July 27, 1842, ANG, leg. 3361, exp. 74384.

pay the freight between Belize and Izabal and the transport costs to Telemán. Pulleiro corrected the official misconception that there were unpaid charges outstanding against the bridge, and he explained with some show of injured pride that the shipment had been held only for want of orders. On the basis of the government's request, he volunteered on August 6 to forward the shipment immediately and to prepay the freight charges, subject to reimbursement from customs receipts at Izabal. He apparently made good his offer, for he claimed repayment of 300 pesos advanced to the pirogue owners, José Rodríguez and Manuel Mena, for transport of the bridge. When after three weeks he had not been reimbursed for his outlay, he repeated his request that the government issue the appropriate orders to the customs officials and received the reassuring reply that the necessary instructions had already been issued.[35] It appears, therefore, that among the persons actively attempting to engage pirogue owners to carry the bridge upriver Pulleiro made the successful arrangements and that the government paid the cost.

On August 19 Gatica informed the government that the bridge had arrived at Telemán. He planned the following day to send four *mozos* to fetch the box containing a model of the structure lest prolonged detention in a humid climate result in its destruction by *comején*. He was gathering a force of 250 carriers whom he intended to dispatch four days later to the river port where he expected Knoth to deliver to the commissioner in charge of the operation 600 pesos from Company funds for the habilitation of the *mozos*. By these means Gatica hoped to bring half of the shipment to Salamá. Some eighteen days later, however, he apprised the government that the bridge was still at Telemán and that Knoth had not broken silence on the subject of the 600 pesos, probably because he was reported to be entirely without funds. On the basis of this evidence of Company penury, Gatica anticipated that shipment of the bridge to Salamá would be long delayed.[36]

The Corregidor's fears were well founded. The inability of either the Company or the government to defray the cost of transport for the bridge beyond Telemán left the shipment stranded half way to its destination. Finally, Guatemalan officials appear to have deter-

35. Draft letter to Cándido Pulleiro, July 30, 1842, ANG, leg. 1398, exp. 32685; Pulleiro to Minister General, Aug. 6, 1842, ANG, leg. 3224, exp. 66843; Pulleiro to Minister General, Aug. 26, 1842, and draft letter to Pulleiro, Sept. 2, 1842, both in ANG, leg. 3600, exp. 82824.

36. Gatica to Minister of Government, Aug. 19, 1842; Gatica to Minister General, Sept. 6, 1842; ANG, leg. 3361, exp. 74284.

mined to break the impasse by imposing a labor levy on the Indian towns of the Alta Verapaz. On October 29 Gatica instructed the alcalde of Cobán to have one hundred of his townsmen at Telemán on November 11 ready to carry the bridge parts to Salamá. In return for this service he promised free use of the completed structure to the residents of the town.

This labor levy encountered immediate resistance from the local authorities in Cobán. Sensing that execution of the order would draw upon him the recriminations of his confreres, the Indian alcalde took the issue to the Municipality. That body agreed that it would be difficult to find men to make the journey even if they were remunerated and that it would be impossible to persuade them to perform the service gratis. The right of free use of the bridge the Municipality acknowledged would be a valuable concession, but it believed that the residents would not think the ultimate advantage worth the immediate cost. On the basis of these considerations the corporate body appears, in its reply to the Corregidor on November 2, to have made a counterproposal which chance mutilation of the document has obliterated. The subsequent context implies, however, that the Municipality suggested payment for the service, but because it lacked power to impose a contribution to raise the necessary funds, it asked that the Corregidor authorize the action. It also suggested that the alcalde be excused from the commission because of his advanced age and infirmity and that he be replaced by the *alcalde segundo,* who was a young man and able to speak Spanish.

In view of the peculiar problems raised by the Corregidor's order, the Municipality determined, on second thought, to consult the Indian *principales* and *chimanes* of the town. This joint session, like the Municipality alone, believed that the men would refuse to go to Telemán, but the reasons it adduced to explain their reluctance were of a somewhat different order. The unhealthfulness of the river country was notorious in Cobán, the assembly averred, for several residents of the town had found it necessary to visit Telemán on business and all had died from diseases contracted there. On the basis of this experience the group confidently predicted that, if the levy were enforced, half of the men taken would perish. Furthermore, a short crop at the last harvest had left the residents of Cobán in want. They were currently engaged in performing the traditional ceremonies, neglected the previous year, that were expected to ensure a bountiful harvest the following season, and should they be interrupted by the departure of the required number of men, a second short crop would inevitably ensue. Given the current shortage of provisions, many families would be left destitute if the men were required to abandon their employment and absent themselves from their homes without pay. To avert the calamities threatened by execution of the Corregidor's order, the assembly agreed to offer a contribution of 150 pesos toward the cost of transporting the bridge, subject to the conditions that Cobán be excused from the obligation of providing the carriers, and that residents of the town be guaranteed free use of the structure when it was completed. This proposal was communicated to the Corregidor on November 3.[37]

Whether or not the Municipality of Cobán was forced to provide carriers, the bridge was promptly transported from Telemán to Salamá. In mid-December 1842 Gatica informed the central government that the entire shipment had been received in the departmental capital. His deprecatory reference to "a small amount" spent on transport suggests that he accepted the contribution from Cobán, and perhaps similar donations from other towns, and used public funds to complete the amount required to employ porters from the river towns. Assuming, however, that Cobán alone contributed and that the Corregidor's earlier estimate of 600 pesos was an accurate calculation of the cost of transporting half the bridge, the government's investment in freight over this leg of the route could have exceeded 1,000 pesos. A few days later Francisco Infiesta, the deputy of the Consulado de Comercio at Salamá, submitted an additional bill amounting to eighty pesos, two reales, covering transport of the bridge parts from the wharf to the warehouse in Telemán and storage charges which had accumulated on the shipment before it was removed. At the end of December Gatica consulted the central government on the mode of paying this charge, and when no response was received, he repeated his inquiry in mid-February of 1843.[38]

As soon as the entire bridge had been collected in Salamá, Gatica began to plan the next steps in the operation. He pointed out to the government that the parts would have to be transported to the Motagua and that a thatched shelter should be constructed near the site of the bridge for the protection of cargoes in transit between the capital and the Polochic. He requested authorization to proceed with

37. J. Tomás Riverro [sic], municipal secretary, to Gatica, Nov. 2, 1842, and ibid., Nov. 3, 1842, both in ABVP, Notas municipales de los pueblos de la Alta Verapaz, Año de 1842, No. 18.

38. Gatica to Minister of Government, Dec. 14, 1842; Francisco Infiesta to Gatica, Dec. 17, 1842; Gatica to Minister of Finance, Dec. 29, 1842, and Feb. 14, 1843; all in ANG, leg. 3361, exp. 74284.

these projects and to make the necessary expenditures from local revenues. He reported that he had already taken steps to begin work on the road between Salamá and the river crossing. This action the government had attempted to forestall. Two days before the Corregidor announced the arrival of the bridge in Salamá, the government, having learned of the event from private sources, instructed him to begin no work on a new road without prior notification to the central authorities. When the approaching completion of the span made a means of access essential, he was to submit a detailed plan of the most practicable route and await approval from the capital before he commenced the work.[39]

These instructions appear to mark a change of policy by the government of Guatemala. Early in 1843 it vacated the Company's title to the bridge, claimed it as property of the state, and assigned to the Consulado de Comercio, the agency traditionally responsible for major internal improvements, the task of erecting it. The merchant guild accepted the obligation and negotiated with the English engineer sent out by the Company to supervise the assembly of the structure a contract to perform the same function for the Consulado. The junta of the guild first calculated the cost of erecting the bridge at 1,500 pesos, then raised the estimate to slightly more than 3,000 pesos when it had received the plans of the engineer, and finally placed the figure at some 3,500 pesos. A commission named by the consular body was assigned to inspect the work as it progressed. At the end of October the government charged the Consulado with responsibility for maintenance and operation of the finished structure and authorized it to collect tolls from patrons according to a stipulated schedule.

During the next few months preparations were completed for erecting the bridge at La Canoa crossing of the Motagua. The bastion on the south bank had already been constructed, presumably during the government's abortive attempt to bridge the river in 1837, and the rocky ledge opposite was prepared to serve the equivalent function on the north bank. In mid-autumn the government ordered Gatica to move the bridge parts from Salamá to the river bank, and by early December transport was underway. Meanwhile the necessary timbers were cut on a neighboring mountain and dragged to the site by oxen whose profiteering owners took advantage of the "necessity and urgency" of the project to exact fees that doubled the estimated cost of transport. By mid-February all materials were assembled and

39. Gatica to Minister of Government, Dec. 14, 1842; draft letter to Gatica, Dec. 12, 1842; ANG, leg. 3361, exp. 74284.

the engineer was on the ground to supervise the actual construction.[40]

While the bridge was being erected, roads were opened to the crossing from Salamá and Guatemala City. The corregidor of the Department of Guatemala had a new route marked out from the capital via the town of Ayampuc, and a fresh track to avoid the steep grade on the south approach to the bridge was opened by the alcalde and residents of La Canoa. Gatica had at least two crews working on the northern segment of the road, one of them under the supervision of Knoth, who had evidently left Company employ. Although the construction was in charge of the corregidores of the departments of Verapaz and Guatemala, aid from the Consulado was solicited, and the guild paid at least a part of the cost.[41]

Actual assembly of the bridge was completed in some five months. Under any circumstance this speedy conclusion of the project would have been a notable accomplishment, but it was the more remarkable because it was achieved under what appears to have been a highly divided command. In addition to the engineer nominally in charge of construction, supervisory functions were assigned at different times to Francisco Infiesta, the consular deputy at Salamá; to Gatica; and to Manuel Francisco Pavón and José Domingo Dieguez, members of the Consulado's commission. The last three individuals were reported to have spent some time on the site on various occasions giving orders and instructions for the prosecution of the work. By late April 1844 temporary scaffolding was in place over the stream and workmen were assembling the iron pieces. At the end of July a special commission from the Consulado formally accepted the finished structure, and it went immediately into use. Despite the Consulado's promise of a full description of the work, information from that source was confined to the comment that the bridge was "magnificent" and that it was thirty varas long. Morelet, who crossed the span a few years later, described it as "a wooden bridge of a single arch suspended by

40. The preparations to erect the bridge were reported in a series of brief articles in the *Gaceta Oficial*, No. 114 (Aug. 4, 1843), p. 464; No. 122 (Sept. 22, 1843), p. 497; No. 124 (Oct. 6, 1843), p. 504; and No. 146 (Feb. 13, 1844), p. 594; and in the *Memoria . . . del Consulado . . . 19 de mayo de 1843* (Guatemala, 1843), p. 5, and *ibid., 20 de mayo de 1844* (Guatemala, 1844), n.p., paragraph 28, of which Dr. Ralph Lee Woodward, Jr., whose dissertation on the Consulado is cited elsewhere, furnished me transcripts. The decree charging the Consulado with responsibility for maintenance and repair of the bridge appears in the *Gaceta Oficial*, No. 133 (Nov. 28, 1843), p. 539.

41. *Gaceta Oficial*, No. 142 (Jan. 19, 1844), p. 579; No. 163 (July 19, 1844), p. 666; No. 169 (Sept. 7, 1844), p. 690; No. 177 (Nov. 2, 1844), p. 725.

chains, and solidly fastened to the ledges of rock which rise on either bank."[42]

For the construction of the bridge and related improvements the Consulado invested considerable sums. It spent 1,831½ pesos between May 1843 and the end of April 1844 and 3,210¾ pesos during the next twelve months, in addition to a contribution of 230 pesos toward the cost of opening the roads. During the next several years the merchant guild completed a number of auxiliary projects and maintained and operated the bridge. It continued with the aid of the corregidores to improve the road to the Verapaz in expectation that it would become a major route for commerce. In 1847 it constructed a building at one end of the bridge that served as a dwelling for the watchman and as a shelter for travelers, their merchandise, and their baggage. The structure measured twenty varas on the side paralleling the road and seven varas along the end facing the bridge. A roofed corridor ran the length of both faces of the building. For these construction projects, maintenance of the span, and the salary paid the watchman, the Consulado spent nearly 1,100 pesos between 1844 and 1847. To offset these costs, it had by October 1846 received bridge tolls to the total amount of 352 pesos 5¼ reales. Collection of the tolls had proved so difficult, however, that it abandoned direct exercise of its prerogative and with the approval of the government farmed out the privilege.[43]

For a decade the chain suspension bridge over the Motagua stood as the proudest exhibit of engineering achievement in Guatemala. During the *temporal* season of 1846 it withstood without damage one of the worst floods in the recorded history of the river, in the course of which it was twice completely submerged. In October 1852, however, the structure was carried away by flood waters, but the Consulado recovered the pieces from the river and rehung the bridge the following year at a cost of nearly 1,000 pesos. During the *temporal* season in the fall of 1855 the torrent of the Motagua again destroyed the bridge. When investigation revealed that a second recovery of the fallen pieces from the river was impracticable, the Consulado determined to replace the structure with a wooden span. With this de-

42. *Gaceta Oficial*, No. 124 (Oct. 6, 1843), p. 504; No. 155 (April 26, 1844), p. 632; No. 169 (Sept. 7, 1844), p. 690; Arthur Morelet, *Travels in Central America*, trans. Mrs. M. F. Squier (New York, 1871), p. 370.

43. *Memoria . . . del Consulado*, 1844, n.p. table of receipts and expenditures; *ibid., 19 de mayo de 1845* (Guatemala, 1845), p. 5 and table of receipts and expenditures; *ibid., 4 de agosto de 1847* (Guatemala, [1847]), p. 11, and Document No. 2.

cision the last visible monument of the Company's operations passed into oblivion.[44]

The history of the iron bridge epitomized the frustrated career of its owners. Its construction was symbolic both of the Company's expectation of restored status in Guatemala and of its hope of establishing commercial domination over the region through control of key transportation facilities. By the time the structure arrived in Central America, however, it was already an anachronism as a Company project, for the doom of the London speculators had been virtually sealed by the maneuvers of their erstwhile collaborators, the Belgian Colonization Company. The nascent settlement at Abbottsville was wasting away, and the authority of the directors, unsupported by either legal rights or by funds for local expenditure, existed only in fiction.

The inability of Company agents to assist materially in delivering the bridge to its destination forced Guatemalan agencies to assume responsibility for transport and erection. These circumstances enabled the government to assume the Company's title to the structure, guaranteed by its contract for twenty years, and to claim for itself the honor of inaugurating the improvement. "This is the kind of accomplishment that really reflects credit on a government," the *Gaceta Oficial* intoned in August 1842, while the bridge was in Izabal awaiting shipment to Telemán. "Deeds and not words are what the people want. . . ."[45] In similar vein, the Consulado's report on completion of the structure boasted that, despite a multitude of difficulties, "such a useful work has finally been accomplished and the state can take great pride in having it, for without doubt it will be a model and stimulus for constructing others like it."[46]

Some years later Morelet heard and recorded a folk history of similar tenor. The bridge, he recounted, was built by an English company "which ruined itself in some absurd scheme of colonization," was sold for debt, and was bought by the government of Guatemala. To his amused observation the extravagant pride manifested by the citizens of the country in possession of the work signified loss of all recollection "that it was built on the banks of the Thames."[47]

Perhaps better than in Morelet's recorded version of popular

44. *Memoria . . . del Consulado*, 1847, p. 11; *ibid.*, *19 de mayo de 1853* (Guatemala, 1853), p. 7; *ibid.*, *19 de mayo de 1854* (Guatemala, 1854), n.p.; *ibid.*, *19 de mayo de 1856* (Guatemala, 1856), p. 6. The data from the *Memorias* for 1853 and 1854 was furnished to me by Dr. Ralph Lee Woodward, Jr.

45. "Puente de fierro," *Gaceta Oficial*, No. 55 (Aug. 9, 1842), p. 237.

46. *Memoria . . . del Consulado*, 1844, n.p., paragraph 27.

47. Morelet, *Travels*, p. 370.

memory, the irony of the Company's role in Guatemalan development projects was exemplified in the career of Frederick Crowe. A deserter to Belize with an immigrant party destined for the Company's first colony at New Liverpool, he subsequently departed the Settlement aboard the steamer operated by the directors to join the second establishment at Abbottsville. When with his wife he fled that graveyard of the Company's expectations in the summer of 1844, these last colonists to abandon the decaying settlement were among the first travelers to find the journey from the Verapaz to the capital expedited by the bridge manufactured for the Company and erected by its engineer but assembled and operated through quirk of circumstance under the aegis of a Guatemalan rival, the Consulado de Comercio.[48]

48. Crowe, *Gospel*, p. 549.

XII

RETROSPECT

The Liberal leaders of the nascent Central American republic envisaged foreign colonization as a short cut to national development. Their hope to populate previously unoccupied territory with immigrant settlers who would apply imported capital, skill, and labor to hitherto unexploited resources was scarcely more than a restatement of a cherished colonial dream, but they believed that such projects, executed with vigor by an independent government, could overcome most of the major deficiencies their young nation inherited from the Spanish imperial regime. In this confidence they pushed through the National Constituent Assembly in 1824 a federal law that authorized the individual states of the Central American union under specified conditions to contract with either foreign or national *empresarios* to establish small-scale immigrant settlements on public lands within their territory.

The federal legislation produced little activity in any of the states until Dr. Mariano Gálvez became chief executive of Guatemala in 1831. He hoped to make extensive use of this device to attain the rapid economic, political, and social advancement of his state, but he cast his design for improvement on so grand a scale and he courted achievement with such impatience that he came to regard the conditions established by the federal law as too restrictive for his purpose. He conceived projects, therefore, which embodied the general Liberal view of development but to which he added dimensions of his own. First in the Verapaz colonization law approved by the Guatemalan Assembly in April 1834 and more comprehensively in the contracts negotiated during the following August, he combined the obligation to colonize with opportunity to undertake certain related public improvement projects for separate rewards and offered a monopoly of both to foreign contractors. He thought thus to induce foreign entrepreneurs to accept responsibility for massive developmental projects in return for proportionally vast concessions in unclaimed lands and natural resources and in special privileges and immunities. In this sense the contracts may be assumed to state the hope of Gálvez for Guatemalan development and the price his government believed it could expediently pay to achieve such ends.

The colonization charters approved by Gálvez fundamentally altered the traditional role of the *empresario*. No longer was he an agent who undertook to found a modest new settlement solely on the promise of land grants directly proportioned in area to the number of immigrant families he recruited abroad. Rather, he became a contractor to whom the government provisionally ceded for development the unassigned public lands within specified geographical limits; conceded certain monopolies, privileges, and immunities, some to be held in trust for colonists; and delegated full power to conduct a gigantic and momentous quasi-public enterprise which was expected, among other functions, to create important elements of the economic "infrastructure" needed by the country. This arrangement virtually removed the state from the operation, except to judge fulfillment or default of the contract.

Gálvez thus expected to make colonization projects an instrument for generalizing development—for directing large-scale foreign enterprise to attack a complex of problems in such manner as to achieve a broad national objective. His plan reveals no intent to create immediately an intricate economic structure in Guatemala. His principal hope was to diversify and modernize agricultural production so that it could sustain an increased population, supply a wider variety of commodities for commerce, and support some small-scale local industry. Rather than lack of imagination, these limited objectives may denote unusual insight into the essential role modernized agriculture must play in achieving the economic momentum required for development.[1]

In execution of his design, Gálvez expected the contractors to enlist foreign capital and foreign immigrants in sufficient volume to populate the empty lands of the north and to bring them into agricultural and industrial productivity. The fruits of the colonists' labor he believed would give new life to commerce and create for the state new sources of wealth. He anticipated that the improved transportation facilities the concessionaires were to provide would bind the new communities to existing centers of population and link both with the Gulf of Honduras and that the deepwater port to be opened at Santo Tomás would afford direct commercial access to Europe which

[1]. See the comments on this subject in Barbara Ward, *The Rich Nations and the Poor Nations* (New York, 1962), pp. 145-46.

would free Central America from economic dependence on the British Settlement of Belize. Successful execution of these plans would accomplish also a political purpose by establishing effective Guatemalan control over a sizeable area of former Spanish territory claimed by the Federation but threatened with incorporation into Belize by the expanding operations of British woodcutters.

Beyond the direct contribution to material development the foreign colonists were intended to make, Gálvez expected them to assume a tutorial role over the local population. By instruction and example they were to provide "technical assistance" and to serve as bearers of European "culture" and "civilization." Covertly, the select minority of European descent among the population expected the foreign colonies also to rectify in substantial measure the numerical imbalance between natives and whites and to reinforce the control of the latter over the indigenous residents and mixed bloods of the country. It is clear, therefore, that Europeanization of the country in institutions and culture, if not totally in blood, was one principal objective of the colonization scheme. Unlike Justo Rufino Barrios, his Liberal counterpart in the 1870's, Gálvez neither rejected the Indian as unfit material from which to build the new Guatemala nor denied his innate capacity to improve himself.[2] Rather, he intended the foreign colonizers to perform for the masses of the republic a function akin to that assigned to the secular office of the missions for the indigenous population of the Captaincy-General.

In the colonization ventures, as in no other single facet of his program, Gálvez consolidated the variety of constructive purposes to which he had committed his administration. Many of his measures stated idealistic aspirations for Guatemala and helped to provide what he believed to be proper institutions to foment the development he coveted. Others he intended as direct stimulation to some phase of material progress. The colonization projects, however, afforded a single device through which he expected to attain in some significant degree each of his important aspirations.

The moderate and Conservative regimes that succeeded Gálvez did not entirely concur in his objectives. They welcomed the promise of European dominance over the native population, and they showed some modest interest in promoting material development. They were perhaps willing even to allow the humbler classes opportunity to broaden their capabilities by contact with immigrants from more

2. For a characterization of the Barrios attitude toward the Indians see Chester Lloyd Jones, *Guatemala, Past and Present* (Minneapolis, 1940), p. 56.

advanced countries of Europe. But if the way to progress could be shown only under conditions that aroused nationals to internal conflict, they preferred to forego improvement. Overawed by the violence of the masses during the insurrection of the *montaña*, their principal concern was to maintain policies compatible with experience and precedent, respecting the limits of popular toleration of change, rather than to achieve distinction for material attainment or for uncompromising pursuit of perfection. In their scheme of values, cultural compatibility rated higher priority among desirable attributes of prospective colonists than ability to communicate useful knowledge or exemplary habits. Uniformity that conserved internal harmony, even at the cost of mediocrity, they believed preferable to stimulating diversity that might provoke discord.

Gálvez was aware that execution of his plan would require *empresarios* of extraordinary capacity, but as a negotiator he allowed eagerness to overwhelm wariness. He accepted postulants at their own evaluation without serious inquiry into their capabilities, yielded to their demands for wantonly generous subventions, and exacted from them no guarantees to insure that the subsidies granted from the public patrimony would be employed to secure the expected benefits for the state. By obtaining and exercising extraordinary powers to grant concessions under terms less exacting than those authorized by existing legislation, some of which the Assembly of Guatemala had just enacted on his own recommendation, he incurred the major share of responsibility for the hazards to which the contracts exposed the state.

However impetuous and injudicious he may have been, Gálvez can hardly be convicted of malfeasance. He was guilty of successive indiscretions that in sum approached negligence of his public responsibility, but there is no evidence to impugn his sincerity, his patriotism, or his integrity. Unfortunately, the same cannot be said of his more cautious successors in office who concluded the transaction with the Belgian Colonization Company.

It was a significant characteristic of the Gálvez contracts that the concessionaires were all of British nationality. This uniformity was circumstantial, but it coincided with the announced preference of the Chief of State. He recognized British pre-eminence in technology, industry, commerce, and finance, and he hoped the contractors would be able to draw upon these national capabilities for the development of Guatemala. He assumed also that the individual colonists would be predominately British and that they could be counted upon in external relations to provide an effective counterpoise to their kinsmen in Belize and domestically to exhibit for the improvement of his fellow countrymen the personal qualities characteristic of enlightened citizenship that had won for their nation the admiration of the world. Indeed, he may have identified British nationality so completely with competence and unimpeachable integrity that he omitted performance guarantees from the contracts as a needless formality.

These high expectations made the subsequent deceptions and failures of the concessionaires the more disastrous to British prestige in Central America. Even Gálvez based his high evaluation of British character on achievements in Europe rather than conduct in Central America, and Guatemalans who formed their opinions exclusively on local evidence found less to praise than to condemn. The colonization contracts lengthened the indictment against both the British and their domestic admirers. The favorable terms obtained by the contractors and the fraudulent use made of the concessions, particularly by Bennett and Meany, provided examples of what was popularly represented as characteristic British arrogance and rapacity, contemporaneously demonstrated also in Central America by Chatfield's overbearing conduct with local governments, by the commercial monopoly exercised by British merchants in Belize, and by aggressions from the British Settlement against the Bay Islands, San Juan del Norte, and especially the adjoining areas of Guatemala. These circumstances made the contracts equally vulnerable to attack on grounds that the provisions were misconceived or simply that the beneficiaries were British.

From the beginning the contracts were assailed by an important sector of popular opinion. In some cases the opposition may have been an expression of honest alarm that its eagerness to achieve economic growth had lured the government into unworkable and perhaps disastrous arrangements with foreign contractors. In one of its dimensions, however, the controversy was an episode in the recurring conflict between the intellectual and the common man. In another, it was probably an example of special pleading by domestic interests placed in jeopardy by the prospect of privileged foreign competition. Certainly, it demonstrated willingness by ambitious dissidents to employ disaffection of any sort as an instrument of partisan advantage in domestic politics.

The superior status and special privileges granted to foreigners by the contracts established one of the principal bases for objection. Many of the protesting municipal corporations of Chiquimula professed intellectually to accept the necessity of tutelage as a condition of growth and development. Emotionally, however, they found the implied debasement of nationals difficult to reconcile with the obligations they were expected to discharge as citizens and with the status to which they conceived themselves elevated as free men enjoying the fruits of liberty and independence. The conviction that only by emulating foreign mentors could ordinary Guatemalans rapidly divest themselves of the traditional characteristics of servilism made government officials unsympathetic to the overtones of wounded pride and outraged justice discernible in the petitions and, hence, insensitive to the possibility that the means they had adopted were incompatible with the qualities of mind and spirit they hoped to foster.

The reiterated evidence of the government's belief in their unfitness prepared the ordinary folk psychologically to accept the propaganda line that Gálvez intended to displace them with more capable citizens imported from abroad to possess the land. There was, indeed, some kernel of truth in the accusation. The restiveness evident among the masses confirmed the whites in their conviction that they could maintain their position of dominance against the rising popular tide only by an immediate influx of white settlers. However covertly they may have maintained this opinion, it was sensed by the masses or brought to their attention by their self-designated leaders. The humble classes were certainly deceived in their belief that the government plotted their wholesale extermination, but they were correct in principle, if not in detail, when they charged that the government wished to impose European culture and institutions on Guatemalan society and to people the country with foreigners. The desperate conviction that they and their accustomed way of life faced imminent destruction aligned the masses under Carrera's standard and gave his shabby operations the emotional intensity of a crusade. The insurrection afforded the simple folk an avenue of protest in action that deference to allegedly superior judgment inhibited them from seeking in writing.

If humility deterred ordinary citizens from public debate of their implied personal inferiority, they could argue the material aspects of privilege openly without sense of shame. Divergent views on the nature of the issue prevented a meeting of minds, however, and their protests were completely misunderstood by the authorities. The critics saw the contracts as vehicles for exploitation by concessionaires; the government could conceive of them only as instruments for national development by colonists. Hence, accusations that the patrimony of native sons had been squandered on undeserving foreign speculators were rebutted by disquisitions on the necessity and justice of offering peculiar advantages to foreign settlers. Reiterated complaints finally produced belated realization that the concessions could result in futile expenditure of the state's resources for the personal benefit of the contractors without accomplishing the larger objectives of the enterprise. Then the official attitude changed. What had been termed a selfish and provincial point of view was dignified by identity with the public interest and, as such, adopted as government policy.

The opponents of the contracts argued also that consequences harmful to Guatemala could result from establishment of a homogeneous immigrant population within the state. The distinct cultural heritage and the discrete interests of such a group could divide the inhabitants and lead to widespread internal strife. Moreover, the strategic situation of the colonies gave them a peculiar political and commercial significance to the remainder of the state.

A colony composed of Protestants, the critics alleged, would disastrously rend the mantle of religious uniformity traditionally worn by Guatemalan society. The dissidents in Chiquimula did not advance this argument, but it was used to generate an important part of the emotional thrust of the Carrera insurrection. The *montañeses* were persuaded that the colonists were heretics whose purpose was to extirpate the traditional religion of the masses and to profane their places of worship. The governments brought to power by the revolt nevertheless allowed the Company without interference to import Bibles into the Verapaz and permitted Frederick Crowe to preach without molestation in and about Abbottsville. Crowe even received some assistance from the local clergy in the distribution of Bibles among the native inhabitants. When the Company project had virtually disappeared, however, he began to encounter serious opposition from some priests of the area, and when he carried his crusade to the capital he incurred the enmity of the higher clergy and was finally expelled from the country.[3]

The situation of the projected colonies, the opponents warned, would give them strategic control of the country. A distinct population of common origin placed in possession of the Atlantic seacoast and of the routes of communication that connected it with the interior could reduce the state to abject economic vassalage to foreigners and threaten its political and territorial security. Distrust of British nationals and disbelief in the ability of the government to enforce

3. Frederick Crowe, *The Gospel in Central America* (London, 1850), pp. 551-86. There is an expediente on the subject in AMG, expedientes 1846.

the conditions of a limited concession led them freely to predict a repetition on the north coast of British usurpation in Belize. The timely example of successful revolution by immigrant settlers in the Mexican province of Texas they cited as further warning that cultural dissimilarity might induce foreign colonists to seek political independence.

The protests from Chiquimula against the material concessions made by the contracts gave the government early warning of abuses, unrevealed to the foresight of officials, which the contractors might intend to perpetrate. Events proved that the predictions, brushed aside by the government as the empty fears of self-seeking and unlettered yokels, were based on sound judgments of the *empresarios'* capacity for duplicity. Had the warnings been heeded when first given, a great deal of the frustration and disillusionment the contracts produced might have been averted. As it was, the popular disapprobation of the agreements both contributed to and was in part a result of a growing anti-British feeling among the masses to which the Carrera revolt gave overt expression. Thus, it may not be overstating the case to assert that resentment against the concessions and the slowness with which the government responded to popular warnings helped to weaken respect for both the state and national governments and to give strength to the forces that ultimately overthrew Gálvez and disrupted the Federation.

The criticism of the colonization grants during the mid-1830's centered in Chiquimula and was directed almost exclusively against the Bennett and Meany contracts. The Totonicapán and Verapaz concessions were included only in peripheral context. The insurrection of the *montaña*, however, tended to generalize the objections and to give them status as authentic public opinion. Thus arguments employed unsuccessfully in defense of local interests by the citizens of Chiquimula in 1835 provided, under the regimes brought to power by Carrera, an accepted rationale that allowed the re-established Consulado in its quasi-public capacity as advisor to the government to influence the Assembly in 1840 to reject the Santo Tomás agreement negotiated by Anderson. The same arguments restated two years later by opponents of the Belgian colonization project failed to dissuade a government corrupted by Belgian bribes from approving a similar contract, but they prevented the special commissioner sent to Guatemala to retrieve the fallen fortunes of the Eastern Coast Company from obtaining even a sympathetic hearing.

Dependence upon agents who assumed the incongruous role of

pressing against their home government the Central American claims on the Belize boundary question was yet another fateful consequence of employing British colonization contractors. Whether he expected the controversy to be settled by negotiation or by actual occupation of the territory in contention, Gálvez miscalculated. Perhaps because he reposed full confidence in the equality of states, he risked adding to the inherent difficulty of the projects, alone sufficient to make them a gamble under the most favorable conditions, the opposition of the most formidable military and maritime power on earth and the government under which all the *empresarios* expect Galindo would have to organize and conduct their colonizing efforts. Even had the contractors possessed vastly greater influence in London, they could scarcely have hoped to sway the Cabinet's decision on such an issue, and the patronage of Guatemala put them at a hopeless disadvantage.

His very objective of restricting the activity of British subjects resident in Belize might have warned Gálvez that London would not acquiesce in his attempted coup. Exclusion from the territory granted to the colonization contractors would deprive the British woodcutters of one area for expansion which they regarded as essential to their continued prosperity. Establishment of a deepwater port at Santo Tomás and development under hostile auspices of all practicable routes of communication by land and water between the Gulf of Honduras and the population centers of the republic could allow an upstart national rival to displace Belize as the entrepôt of Central American trade. Successful execution of the colonization enterprises, therefore, could bring the principal branches of the Settlement's economy to utter ruin. Required to choose between established interests in Belize exercising, however imprecisely, the treaty privileges conceded by Spain, and projected speculations under the patronage of the government of Guatemala undertaken by adventurers recently and casually arrived in the area, the British government unhesitatingly chose to support the interests of the existing Settlement against those of the prospective colonies.

The British policy was first stated in the Honduras settlement by authorities who probably considered no alternatives. There is no reason, however, to suppose that the decision would have been different had it been reached initially in London. The Cabinet took the position that the Central American claim was a belated and irrelevant republican challenge to territorial changes accomplished before 1821 at the expense of imperial Spain. It denied, therefore, the Central

American claims to sovereignty over, and even to a legitimate interest in, the disputed territory.

The British temper appeared in Central America to be voraciously expansionist, but had the Cabinet elected so to regard them the contracts offered a unique opportunity for even more extensive covert imperialism. Both Chatfield and the directors of the Eastern Coast Company pointed out that the concessions afforded means of extending British hegemony over Guatemala without necessarily assuming responsibility for its government. Had the Cabinet chosen to abandon its territorial claims and to support the colonization enterprises as Gálvez desired, the result could easily have been the execution of Chatfield's suggestion for the extension of overwhelming British influence over the greater part of the territory of the state and the gradual absorption of sovereignty over the remainder. Its refusal to countenance the manipulations suggested by Chatfield and the Eastern Coast Company may thus have helped to preserve the integrity of the major part of Guatemala. The decision to take this course, however, may not have been reached entirely on the basis of principle. Undissembled distrust of Galindo and of the Eastern Coast Company and the corollary doubt that either would be able to realize the possibilities offered by the grants may have made the Cabinet reluctant to relinquish its claim to a province already in British hands on the tenuous prospect of extended empire in the future.

On the issue of protecting the commercial interests of Belize against the threat of competition by the Guatemalan colonizers, the British government chose also to support the *status quo*. The Board of Trade consistently denied the right of officials at the Settlement to levy discriminatory duties against the steamer "Vera Paz," and the Colonial Office rejected as obviously immoral Chatfield's proposal that he be authorized to purchase clandestinely, and hold without improvement as a guarantee of the continued pre-eminence of Belize, the colonization grant that included the only harbor capable of development into a rival seaport. If the decision was made on the assumption that commercial advantages equal to those afforded by the colonization contracts could ultimately be attained through Belize, the judgment proved to be erroneous. Within a decade of the Company's failure the Settlement had lost its monopoly control of Central American commerce because direct trade with Europe had been established through Caribbean and, especially, Pacific ports.[4]

4. Robert Arthur Naylor, "British Commercial Relations with Central America, 1821-1851," (Unpubl. Diss., Tulane, 1958), pp. 205, 233.

The Central American authorities believed that the expanded British territorial claims challenged by the colonization agreements would engage the interest of the United States when the boundary issue erupted. The federal government argued that the extended boundaries claimed in Belize constituted a breach of the non-colonization principle stated by President Monroe, and on this basis it sought diplomatic support from Washington for its protest to Great Britain. The Department of State, however, appears to have accepted the British interpretation of the controversy, concluded that the doctrine stated in 1823 could not properly be invoked against a situation created prior to 1821, and declined on those grounds to become a party to the dispute.

Given public support, or even prosecuted energetically by private interests, the colonization projects themselves might have created circumstances to which the declaration of Monroe would have been applicable. The Central American authorities, of course, anticipated no such development, but there is some suggestion that Galindo may have pointed out the possibility to Washington in the hope that objection from that source would remove the London company as a competitor for his grant. Failure of the entrepreneurs to establish lasting colonies ended all probability that British control would be consolidated over the ceded territory either by subversion or by capitalizing on the prospect held out by the charters of forming a separate state from each colony. On the Mosquito Shore, however, the contracts indirectly produced such a result. Mahogany cutters from Belize who suffered competitive disadvantage as a result of Bennett's coup in Guatemala began a rush to obtain from the Mosquito "King" timber concessions that could be exploited under his authority. This revival of British interest in the Mosquito Shore was believed in the United States to have been undertaken with official sanction, and the resulting suspicion of British imperialistic designs exacerbated relations between the two countries until the Clayton-Bulwer settlement eased the tension.

The boundary crisis with Belize was the first fruit of the colonization contracts, and its taste was bitter in the mouth of Gálvez. The decision of the British Cabinet, backed by overwhelming power, reversed the result he had expected of the agreements and in effect permanently confirmed Great Britain in possession of the disputed territory. The nature of the British claims suggests that the outcome of the controversy would have been the same had it been brought less precipitously to a climax, but the impact under those circumstances might have been less shocking in Central America. The titillating sense of expectancy with which Gálvez awaited the denouement of his coup gave the British announcement when it came the dramatic quality of a lightning bolt. But instead of revealing with blinding clarity the trespass of British woodcutters on Central American territory, it obliterated the boundary markers Gálvez had attempted to erect and left only the blackened remains of Central American hopes for periodic examination by future diplomats. If before he had been in doubt, Gálvez now knew that the "revolution" of equality did not extend to states of disparate strength.

Ineffective though their efforts were, the support given by the contractors to the Central American claims on the Belize boundary question for a time won them the sympathetic appreciation of the Gálvez government. In every other respect, however, the challenge to proof of sovereignty, if indeed it influenced the result, was damaging to the colonization projects. The assertion of British jurisdiction over the disputed territory closed both to Galindo and to the Eastern Coast Company the most accessible portions of the grants which they believed they could most speedily and profitably occupy. Moreover, the reluctance of the British government to state its precise territorial claims obstructed colonization of any part of the grants lest such action provoke a collision with the authorities of Belize. The Eastern Coast Company, for example, delayed operations, in part for this reason, until the initial time period allowed by its contract had nearly expired and then sent out the first contingent of immigrant families to the Verapaz before it had been able to ascertain in what areas of its concession it could without threat of molestation establish settlements. The controversy thus tended to confine the operations of the concessionaires to areas remote from the sea and to retard initial activity until the contracts were jeopardized by failure to discharge the first set of obligations within the stipulated time periods.

If misconceived circumstances induced Gálvez to fix strategic objectives impossible of attainment for the colonization projects, similar miscalculations placed their developmental goals also in jeopardy. The contracts he approved proposed to accomplish national economic growth by offering opportunity for virtually unregulated private exploitation and to promote equality by conferring special privilege. Had he been more disposed to select his devices inductively, he might well have found means more compatible with the ends he pursued.

The Gálvez government deliberately chose to entrust its program of economic development to foreign private enterprise spurred by the incentive of profit. Furthermore, it conferred upon the contractors monopoly control, akin to that withdrawn a few years earlier from the local Consulado, over such new facilities as they provided within their concessions. This policy it adopted in the belief that private investment and monopolistic privilege were the most efficacious means of accomplishing improvements that would increase the productivity of the state by broadening the base of the economy. It revived monopoly, therefore, intending not to protect the *status quo,* in the interest of which the Consulado had exercised the privilege, but to stimulate economic growth. By these means Gálvez hoped to break the pattern of concentrated investment in existing industries and to create new branches of the economy.

Neither the government nor the contractors seems to have recognized that except for perhaps greater resources at their command foreign entrepreneurs would enjoy no appreciable advantages over domestic operators in overcoming Guatemala's inherent difficulties. Thus it could scarcely be expected that the contractors would find it more profitable than had the Consulado before them to provide "social overhead" capital in large amounts. Hence, they were unlikely to embark by choice upon socially productive but economically unrewarding ventures or if drawn by circumstances into such undertakings to command resources sufficient to sustain them adequately over long periods of time. Neither party to the contracts seems to have perceived the miscalculation in encouraging, as a field of investment promising immediate return, the employment of strictly limited private capital to build the economic "infrastructure" required by the underdeveloped state of the country.

In similar fashion the parties to the agreements seem to have had no realistic conception of the magnitude of the enterprise upon which they embarked. The contracts envisaged within a term of only a few years nothing less than a mass settlement of Europeans in newly-created towns freshly hewn from the virgin wilderness. To accomplish this result, the contractors had in some manner to find means to recruit and transport immigrants by the hundreds over sustained periods of time, to prepare in a scarcely inhabited tropical forest acceptable sites for European habitation, and to insure that the settlers they established were supplied with every requirement of existence, from elemental necessities to such auxiliary services as were indispensable to their way of life and means of livelihood.

The comprehensive array of improvements held in prospect by the contracts nevertheless encouraged the governments which signed them to believe that they had provided a solution to the nation's principal problems. Henceforward, they sought no more promising alternative but transferred to the contractors full responsibility for accomplishing the expected transformation. Without direct supervision, with little or no material aid, and often subjected to inadvertent or deliberate obstruction, foreign entrepreneurs and colonists were left to execute the contracts. The governments were quite ready to claim credit for accomplishment, but they accepted no share of responsibility for failure or abuses by the contractors. Rather, they found it easy to make a habit of the tendency, first manifested when they imputed to imperial Spain sole accountability for the post-independence imperfections of their country, to attribute domestic failure and deficiencies to foreign influence and external circumstance.

The grandiose proportions of the colonization projects also militated against achievement of the goals they set. The time intervals allowed were unrealistically brief for accomplishing the monumental tasks assigned, and the compensation offered was as readily convertible to speculation as to the purpose intended by the sponsoring government. Rather than responsible colonizers, therefore, the contracts tended to attract speculators and opportunists ready to exploit the concessions but incapable of honoring the obligations.

The imprecise terms of the agreements they signed and the relatively passive role thereafter assumed by the state allowed the contractors to resolve in their own interest the inherent conflict of objectives between themselves and the government. None of the contractors was primarily concerned with the developmental functions of the projects. Bennett and Meany made little pretense of fulfilling the obligation to colonize, and Galindo's feckless efforts to enlist settlers hardly progressed beyond the realm of fantasy. The Eastern Coast of Central America Commercial and Agricultural Company undertook more serious operations, but it originally intended only a ritual performance of its obligations. Nevertheless, it alone among the contractors of 1834 registered any substantial achievement toward discharging its obligations.

The basic deficiency of the Company as a colonizer was the attitude of speculation that dominated the enterprise. Conceived as a scheme to defraud English investors by manipulation of worthless Poyaisian securities, the Company opportunistically adjusted its course to the new circumstances created by its acquisition of a valuable new concession in Central America. The operation to which it found itself committed, however, required talents of a different order from those useful to the original enterprise. Nevertheless, it retained the same directors, and only superficially did it redirect its activities. Indeed, it intended to use its holdings in Guatemala, once its title was secure, principally to give some appearance of legitimacy to its operations in Poyaisian securities. As a bonus, it expected to exploit immediately the mahogany stands included within its Guatemalan concession and at somewhat greater leisure to capitalize on its commercial privileges and to realize a speculative profit from the sale of land.

A group of new directors attempted in 1837 to redirect the Company's effort toward realization of the more substantial and consistent revenues that they assumed would result from development of the nascent agricultural and commercial empire conferred by the Guatemalan contract. Although motivated by the expectation of profit, the operations projected by the new regime, had they been successfully executed, would probably have achieved many of the objectives sought by the Guatemalan government. The Company, however, was unable to remove from the minds of British officials the taint of its origin as a swindle and, probably for the same reason remembering the bubble mania of 1824, investors and prospective colonists were wary of its projects.

Although its competence progressively increased, the Company never achieved status commensurate with the task it assumed. It had neither sufficient personnel nor regular management capable of orderly planning and effective administration of the diverse operations it undertook simultaneously to conduct. Its financial resources were never adequate to the initial capital investments required to accomplish a massive development, and they were vastly inferior to the sustaining outlays necessary to bring its projects to the mature stage of yielding a return to the promoters. It possessed at first only a small store of miscellaneous and inapt information, hastily acquired from published sources, which it disseminated for the instruction of immigrants and used as its own guide for elaborating a project that required for success precise and expert knowledge. This deficiency it reduced but did not entirely eliminate by obtaining firsthand reports from Thomas Fletcher after the first group of colonists had been sent out and from Young Anderson before the second establishment was attempted. Both superintendents in the Verapaz appear to have been able men, but their freedom of action on many crucial issues was limited by prior decisions made by uninformed directors. The prime failure of the Company was in London, not in the Verapaz.

By decision of the directors Company settlements in the Verapaz were restricted to locations within reach of steamers operating inland from deepwater entrepôts on the Gulf of Honduras. This limitation confined the choice of sites to the Polochic Valley below Panzós. The Company, however, was unable to accomplish the development in anticipation of which its colonies had been situated. Despite the pretension of its name, New Liverpool was never connected by steam navigation with the sea nor was Abbottsville reached by steamer after loss of the "Polochiquito." Because the Company failed to provide a form of water transport superior to the native dugouts that had traditionally carried the commerce of the river, its settlements suffered the handicaps resulting from their isolation and their low-lying situation without reaping any of the benefits anticipated from their proximity to navigable water.

The Company colonies in the Verapaz were conceived principally as agricultural settlements offering opportunity for an independent livelihood to the economically depressed yeomanry of Europe. In accord with this concept the government of Guatemala transferred land and resources from the public domain to the private ownership of a single corporate proprietor, expecting that it would break up and assign the land to settlers in small, individually-owned plots. The Company policy of selling land to colonists obstructed the process of distribution because it made the colony less attractive to land-hungry Europeans than those competing areas where free land was offered. Even had the grant been managed as the government of Guatemala intended, however, it is doubtful that the environment would have proved appropriate to the success of small, individual cultivators.

In undeveloped resources the Verapaz was a region of great agricultural promise, but the potential could be realized only at the cost of arduous labor. Virtually every foot of land the Company chose to occupy had to be cleared before it could be tilled, and the local enviornment afforded nothing beyond raw resources to supply even the necessities, without regard for the amenities, of civilized life. Some of these deficiencies the Company might have corrected had it possessed capital, time, and disposition to undertake extensive preparation before it opened the area to settlement. It elected, however, to pass on most of these problems to the settlers. The demands of the environment were thus more appropriate to the skills and the personal qualities of tropical frontiersmen than to those of temperate-zone agriculturalists. Both the Guatemalan government and the Company disregarded the patent evidence that for at least a generation the pioneering immigrants in the Verapaz could aspire to nothing better than an extremely primitive existence; both acted on the romantic illusion that the forest could be immediately transformed into thriving cities and cultivated farms.

The quality of the colonists enlisted showed no realistic assessment of the demands made by the enterprise. The Company declared its intention to select only married colonists of industrious habits and unimpeachable character for its undertaking, but in practice it appears to have accepted all applicants without regard to fitness— occupational, physical, psychological, or ethical—for the work in prospect. This opportunistic procedure was apparently made necessary by the small number of colonists it could interest in the Verapaz. The failure of the Company to attract a larger proportion of the emigrants then leaving England each year may be explained in part by the relative obscurity of the area it sought to develop or by the competitive disadvantage of a colony offering land for purchase when free land was obtainable elsewhere. The sponsor's reputation for fraud appears to have been a more important consideration, however, for even the offer of employment on Company projects to emigrants who were unable to purchase land appears to have awakened but slight interest.

The consequences of their faulty conception of the venture the directors intensified by inept and tragic blunders in execution. Both of their colonies were established in haste in an attempt to avert the peril of default incurred by earlier procrastination. They transported a total of four shiploads of ill-assorted and misinformed immigrants, all of whom arrived during the season of most oppressive heat and heaviest rain, to a strange and forbidding environment in the tropical wilds of Guatemala. There they had them established in isolated, hastily erected encampments of primitive huts situated in raw forest clearings. From these rude outposts the settlers were expected to begin their conquest of the surrounding wilderness. With some justice a veteran of both experiments could charge that the policies of the directors were calculated to "make merchandise of their grant and of the people whom they deluded to emigrate for such ends."[5]

The Company establishments were apparently as well situated as the geographical scope allowed by the directors permitted, but they were entirely uncongenial to the new settlers. The agricultural settlement at New Liverpool could scarcely have been placed by deliberate

5. Crowe, *Gospel*, p. 138.

intent in an environment that to newly-arrived immigrants would appear less appropriate for residence and cultivation by Europeans and more unlike the New World Eden described in Company literature. The colonists who deserted to Santa Cruz thinking to improve their condition were hardly better installed. The commercial establishment at Abbottsville soon afforded living quarters superior to those provided at either of the earlier colonies, but for personal comfort and agricultural development it was only a slight improvement. The colonists at New Liverpool, and to a lesser degree those at Abbottsville, found the tiny forest clearings oppressive, the heat and the humidity ennervating, and the insect and animal life terrifying.

If climate made the region uncomfortable to arrivals from the temperate zone, endemic disease made it deadly as well. Guatemalans had shunned the area for centuries, and the government had been known to sentence offenders whom it wished to destroy to a term at the Castillo de San Felipe, at the entrance to Lake Izabal, in expectation that the mortiferous climate might execute on the victim a casual penalty that officials dared not formally impose. It was small wonder that disease struck the unacclimated Europeans and at Santa Cruz and Abbottsville at least took its toll of lives. Even if they escaped death or debility from disease, it was hardly to be expected that the settlers could maintain in that environment vigor for the heavy physical exertion required to hew farms from the forest and to defend them against encroachment by tropical vegetation.

These reckless agricultural ventures afforded opportunity neither for yeoman farmers to establish themselves nor for the Company to develop its projected plantations. Most of the available cleared land at the settlements seems to have been planted to subsistence crops by Company personnel. The scant harvests from this source, however, were insufficient to supply the needs of the colonists, and the problem of sustenance became acute. Illness and assignments to community tasks probably deprived the immigrants at New Liverpool of any opportunity to achieve self-sufficiency, and most of those at Abbottsville, after some initial effort to make individual clearings and establish rudimentary farms, ultimately succumbed to the easier life of dependence upon native suppliers. But for the timely purveyance of foodstuffs by the natives, the Europeans at both settlements must surely have perished. To the end of its existence the Abbottsville colony imported food.

The highly touted opportunities for plantation agriculture were entirely illusory under the circumstances. Company publications listed a wide variety of commercial productions alleged to be adapted to the general region, but neither for cultivation on its own projected plantations nor for the guidance of individual land purchasers did it identify a single recognized and established crop for the area. Beyond employment of former residents of the West Indies as its superintendents in the Verapaz it supplied no source of knowledge, experience, or skill in the cultivation of tropical plantation crops. Had the requirements for successful production been met, no adequate facilities were available for transport of bulky commodities from either settlement, and no thought appears to have been given to assuring a market, unless the merchants on the board planned to monopolize the production of the colony.

Aside from its agricultural function, the settlement at Abbottsville was better planned than its predecessors. It was appropriately situated to serve as a *point d'appui* on the upper Polochic River from which the purely agricultural colonies projected for the interior of the Verapaz could be serviced and the internal commerce of Guatemala laid under tribute. The dispatch of a work force to construct dwellings on the townsite for temporary occupancy by merchants expecting to establish permanent residences in the town and by land purchasers bound for the agricultural settlements in the interior, the provision of a river steamer for communication with the Gulf of Honduras, and the projected construction of a wharf at or near Panzós were all measures calculated to equip the settlement to serve its destined purpose. The loss of the river steamer "Polochiquito" and the failure of the Company to open any of the projected agricultural establishments, however, robbed the town of any significant function before it was well begun. Deprived of its reason for being and populated chiefly by workers who had been only temporarily employed, the settlement began to disintegrate before a year had passed.

The cancellation of its Santo Tomás concession and its inability to raise in Europe the funds necessary to develop its holdings in the Verapaz brought the Company by the end of 1840 to the brink of ruin. Its hopes of regaining solvency were rekindled briefly by a contracted sale of a part of its concession to the Belgian Colonization Company. Disappointed in its expectation of consummating the transaction with the Brussels speculators, however, the London enterprise collapsed when the Guatemalan government cancelled its Verapaz contract also.

The demise of the settlement at Abbottsville not only symbolized the ruin of the Gálvez grand design; it disappointed all expectation of corollary benefits from his colonization agreements. Chief among these was the improvement of the masses anticipated from contact with immigrants of superior attainments. Hope had remained so long as the colonies existed, even though circumstances at the settlements had not favored tutelage. The villages never achieved more than rudimentary organization, their isolation afforded contact with only a handful of local residents, and the European settlers were few in number. They therefore had little opportunity to make their influence widely felt.

Even had the establishments proved more durable, the relationship envisioned by the Company between immigrants and native inhabitants was not exactly what Gálvez had in mind. The Chief of State seems to have assumed that the universality among Europeans of the attributes he expected the colonists to possess made it unnecessary to forewarn Company representatives of the tutorial function he projected for the settlers. The recruiting efforts of the directors, in consequence, revealed no awareness of the intended responsibility, and such requirements as they established for prospective settlers were calculated only to assure success of their own operations. Nevertheless, had the Company adhered to its announced standards, it should have selected colonists to some degree capable of serving as preceptors for Guatemalan nationals. Young Anderson perhaps had some such relationship in mind when in 1839 he expressed to the directors the philanthropic hope that the Company "having the means of conferring lasting benefits upon the inhabitants of the country, will not neglect the opportunity. . . ."[6] The directors, however, were more inclined to think of the natives, in Thomas Fletcher's terms, as "both labourers for your fields and customers for your stores."[7] Anderson also recognized the potential usefulness of the Indians as a labor force for the colony, but he reversed the roles intended by Gálvez when he remarked: "Many of them are industrious to a degree, and might serve as an example to our settlers."[8]

Anderson's insight proved to be prophetic. Experience showed that Gálvez overestimated the quality of the immigrants who would be established in Guatemala and that he made no allowance for the deleterious effect a primitive environment could be expected to exert even on individuals of culture. The Europeans at Abbottsville at-

6. *Brief Statement, Supported by Original Documents, of the Important Grants Conceded to the Eastern Coast of Central America Commercial & Agricultural Company by the State of Guatemala* (2nd ed.; London, 1840), p. 91.

7. *Ibid.*, p. 146.

8. *Ibid.*, p. 147.

tempted no major improvements of the rude society but accommodated themselves to the conditions they found. If we may accept as trustworthy evidence Mora's testimony given to reassure a government distrustful of cultural diversity, immigrant males married native wives, and European women adopted the mode of dress, the customs, and the language of the country in preference to their own.[9] In short, rather than establishing European culture in the wilderness as Gálvez intended, the colonists went native.

As sources of technical skill and as examples of personal attainment worthy of emulation, the settlers were equally barren. They exhibited no store of useful knowledge, no ability to adapt European experience to the improvement of the primitive environment, and, even with due allowance made for disability resulting from disease or an ennervating climate, no habits of industry. Rather than Europeans introducing new crops and teaching new skills and better methods of cultivation to the natives, at both New Liverpool and Abbottsville the neighboring Indians supported the immigrants by indigenous agriculture, and their labor supplied deficiencies occasioned by the disability and indolence of their intended tutors.

Such influence as the colonists exerted on the natives appears to have been the reverse of that intended by Gálvez. By the almost unanimous testimony of observers, the Europeans gave themselves over to idleness and debauchery. Not all the witnesses were disinterested, but the fragmentary record of the colony, punctuated by instances of immorality, personal violence, and mistreatment of natives, gives no reason to question the veracity of their general description. It appears that intemperate consumption of alcoholic beverages was the preferred occupation of the Europeans and that sale of the commodity to natives was the only branch of commerce they cultivated. After observing the depraved state of the settlers, Remy de Puydt warned the directors of the Belgian company that unless all contact with residents of Abbottsville could be avoided the colonists they expected to send out would be hopelessly corrupted.[10] Crowe's Protestant missionary activity, a personal effort rather than a Company project, seems to have been the only force exerted for the improvement of personal conduct at the settlement. He made little

9. José María Mora to Minister General, Mar. 17, 1842, ANG, leg. 1395, exp. 32354, n.f.
10. Remy de Puydt to Comte de Hompesch, president of the Belgian Colonization Company, No. 1, Feb. 5, 1842, fol. 2, AMAE, 2027.

impression on the Europeans and the Ladinos, but his own account claims credit for some influence among the natives.[11]

At the official level, friendly and harmonious relations appear generally to have been maintained between Company personnel and nationals. The occasional misunderstandings were due to failure of governmental communications, as when the Corregidor of the Verapaz confessed ignorance of the special privileges accorded the Company, or to divergent emphasis on objectives, as in the dispute over contraband and the provisions trade on the Polochic, rather than to nationality. Perhaps the most serious issue arose when the absence of any regularly constituted police power at Abbottsville resulted in violence and injustice that more often victimized nationals than Europeans. Officials in the Verapaz occasionally expressed anti-British feeling, but in general the tendency to attribute unflattering national characteristics to the English colonizers was more prevalent among Guatemalans who had no contact with the colony than among those who were brought into firsthand relations with it.

The colonization projects achieved no greater success in providing public improvements than in accomplishing their other developmental objectives. They contributed temporarily some useful facilities for transport, but their failure to create a port on the Bay of Santo Tomás disappointed the expectation that internal improvements would re-route domestic commerce and expand its volume. The Gálvez plan cannot properly be said to have failed, however, because it was never fully carried out.

The Eastern Coast Company planned a series of innovations in transport that it expected to assist the development of its own settlements and to enable it to monopolize the internal carrying trade of Guatemala and adjacent states. It assumed that construction of a commercial center at Abbottsville, inauguration of steamer service on the Polochic and in the coastal waters of the Gulf of Honduras, and erection of an iron bridge over the Motagua would make the Verapaz route the principal artery of internal commerce. Until its projects were fully accomplished and its monopoly control over the route established, it anticipated that existing traffic would afford patronage of its isolated new facilities in sufficient volume to make their operation immediately profitable. Ultimately it expected the development of private agricultural holdings and Company plantations within its concession in the Verapaz to swell the flow of traffic to even more remunerative proportions.

11. Crowe, *Gospel*, p. 527.

These hypotheses were never fully tested. Miscalculation and mischance determined that each of the links in the Company's transportation chain should be forged in isolation, not simultaneously. For slightly more than two years the steamer "Vera Paz" was the solitary evidence in Guatemala of the Company's commitment to improve transport. Then the "Polochiquito" sported briefly on inland waters, but she disappeared before she inaugurated commercial service on the river. The iron bridge for the Motagua was delivered in Guatemala only after the "Vera Paz" had been withdrawn from service and when the Company's settlement at Abbottsville was moribund. Thus, only the steamer "Vera Paz" operated under Company control over a long enough period to have opportunity to affect the traditional flow of commerce.

Plying between Izabal and Belize in competition with sailing craft, the "Vera Paz" carried only a share of the existing trade. There is no evidence that the superior service she offered increased the total volume of commerce, and certainly she did not monopolize the traffic in either passengers or freight over her itinerary. Indeed, the returns on her operations appear to have disappointed the sanguine expectations of her sponsors. Her record might have been different had the Company been able simultaneously to supply all the projected units of its monopolistic transport system, but on the basis of isolated competition, operation of the "Vera Paz" appears not to have been a paying enterprise.

Similarly, the expectation that the bridge over the Motagua would be a remunerative investment seems to have been a miscalculation. The Company never had opportunity to levy tribute on the traffic that crossed the span, but the tolls collected by the Consulado produced a total revenue smaller than the cost of maintenance and repair during the same period. Granted the misfortunes that befell the structure, it seems improbable, even had the Company retained title to the work for the twenty years guaranteed by its contract, that it could have realized the cost of maintenance of the bridge, and certainly it could not have recovered its original investment.

The failure of the Company to erect a port at Santo Tomás likewise prevented a test of the value to the constructors and to the nation of a deepwater anchorage on the Atlantic. It seems probable, however, that Gálvez conceived the project too narrowly to attain the results he expected. Direct shipping connections with Europe, established relations between local merchants and foreign suppliers, and credit arrangements with merchandising firms abroad were requirements as important to establishment of a new entrepôt for the Central American trade as was the physical existence of port facilities within Guatemalan territory. The failure of the Belgian Colonization Company during the next decade to develop a functioning port at Santo Tomás seems to confirm this hypothesis.

Improved facilities actually provided by the Company did not fundamentally alter the nature of Guatemalan economic activity or significantly increase its tempo. The explanation is perhaps to be found in the circumstance that Guatemala needed new productivity to swell the volume of commerce before it desperately required such innovations in transport as the Company attempted to supply. Provision of the facilities in advance of need might ultimately have stimulated increased economic activity, but as self-liquidating investments the steamers and the bridge appear to have been anachronisms.

The demise of the Gálvez projects shackled again to unresponding earth the hopes sent soaring by the agreements of 1834. If Guatemalans were unable to accomplish the development of their country, so also, it seemed, were Englishmen. The Santo Tomás contract signed with the Belgian company in 1842 again quickened some expectations, but disillusionment with the results of the first experiment in colonization on a colossal scale was deeply rooted in the popular consciousness. The activities of the concessionaires had provided no security for the frontiers of the republic threatened from Belize, no significant increase in population, no augmentation of productivity or wealth, and no sudden flowering of liberated commerce. Except for the plundered mahogany stands that marked the concessions made to Bennett and Meany and the suspension bridge supplied by the Company that for a few years spanned the Motagua, Guatemala was superficially unchanged by the colonization enterprises. The scars left on sensibilities wounded by the controversies and pessimism consequent to the failure of the projects, however, remained as a less visible but more permanent heritage.

The governments dominated by Rafael Carrera reflected the popular disillusionment with the Gálvez projects. The resurgence of nationalistic emphasis, typefied by re-establishment of the Consulado, and the conviction that the contractors had demonstrated incapacity and bad faith brought the whole concept of foreign-sponsored colonization under hostile scrutiny. The new officials, however, believed that the defects of the projects lay in the specific arrangements concluded by Gálvez rather than in their underlying conception. They particularly deplored the provisions that ceded resources of enormous value to foreigners without cost, that granted in advance the rewards for successful colonization without the security of performance guarantees or of penalties to be exacted in case of default, that delegated important elements of sovereignty to be exercised by foreigners on Guatemalan soil, and that allowed the concentration of homogeneous colonists representing an alien culture in areas of strategic importance to the commercial life and the political integrity of the state.

The successors to Gálvez sought to remedy the deficiencies revealed in the original agreements by modification of the terms under which subsequent concessions were granted. The Guatemalan commissioners tried to correct the objectionable features in the Santo Tomás contract negotiated with Young Anderson in 1838, but the agent of the British company adamantly refused to yield the essential points. In consequence the Assembly, acting on the recommendation of the Consulado, disapproved the Santo Tomás agreement and later determined also to cancel the Verapaz concession and to entrust all future developmental endeavors to the local Consulado.

The opposition to foreign sponsorship of colonization was silenced in part by bribes when the Belgian contract was considered, but the approved agreement nevertheless bound the Brussels directors to terms that satisfied many of the Guatemalan objections. They were required to make token payment for the land ceded, to assent to penalties for non-performance of obligations, to agree that colonists must become Guatemalan citizens by the simple act of disembarkation, to restrict recruiting of immigrants to those who professed the Catholic faith, and to limit the proportion of colonists of any single nationality to a stipulated fraction of the total number of settlers. After some years of effort, the Belgian colony at Santo Tomás established under this agreement also failed.

During the remainder of the long Carrera regime the government sponsored no further colonization enterprises. The line of Liberal presidents inaugurated by the revolution of 1871 gave encouragement principally to individual immigration rather than to mass colonization, but they resumed their predecessor's practice of offering special inducements to individuals and to corporations to stimulate agricultural development. Had the new production which these measures helped to achieve been accompanied by arrangements to assure adequate saving for reinvestment in the economy, it might have provided a basis for a satisfactory first stage of capital formation for subsequent national development. Each period of agricultural advance, however, affected only a relatively small segment of the population and a

restricted geographical area of the country; never did one activate
an all-pervasive upsurge of the economy.

The results of these later Liberal efforts demonstrate that the
Gálvez plan of 1834 may have been premature and faulty in some
details, but it was not entirely visionary. Within the lifetime of many
an individual born while Abbottsville was still in existence, Europeans or foreigners of European descent occupied and developed in
whole or in part both the Verapaz and the district of Santo Tomás.
During the last quarter of the nineteenth century the advance guard
of a small stream of German settlers entered and began the transformation of the Verapaz. During the early part of the twentieth
century the corporate activities of the Guatemala Railroad Company
and the United Fruit Company accomplished a similar development
in the vicinity of Santo Tomás.

The German colonizers of the Verapaz enjoyed few inherent advantages not open to the Eastern Coast Company, but the two efforts
afford a sharp contrast. The German colonization was an informal
process, carried on by individuals without an intermediary *empresario*.
It was accomplished by a thin trickle of immigrants maintained over
a period of years rather than by a sudden mass transfer of population.
It was financed by individual capital or by loans obtained from German commercial firms in Guatemala or in Germany. It was assisted,
however, by policies of the Guatemalan government that bore marked
resemblance to those of Gálvez. Justo Rufino Barrios and his successors in the presidency encouraged enterprise by granting fiscal advantages and providing easily obtainable land and a subservient labor
force.

The contrast extended also to the locale selected for settlement
and to the sequence of steps by which economic exploitation was
undertaken. The Germans chose to establish themselves in the elevated and salubrious interior of the Verapaz where they could maintain their health and energy and where a dense native population
supplied in fact Fletcher's hypothetical customers for their stores and
laborers for their fields. The first arrivals set themselves up as merchants in Cobán supplying European goods to the local market. As
they accumulated capital, they gradually expanded their operations
to purchase and export of coffee produced by natives and then to
acquisition of land and direct cultivation of the trees. Their contacts
with commercial firms in Germany assured them of a market for their
crop. By this process, the Germans gradually extended their hold-

ings eastward from Cobán to the vicinity of Panzós on the Polochic.[12]

It is significant that the eastern boundary of the area thus success-fully occupied by the Germans coincided almost exactly with the western boundary of the territory chosen by the English company for initial occupation.[13] By electing to establish its settlements along the lower course of the Polochic, where they could be served by its river steamer, the Company committed its colonists to develop a virtually uninhabited wilderness, inhospitable to European constitutions, de-void of products that could be marketed immediately, and ill adapted to cultivation of any sort.

The Company directors were not entirely mistaken in recognizing the importance of adequate transportation to the success of their colonization venture. Their attempt, however, to reconcile their am-bition for commercial dominance with their plan to establish agri-cultural colonies seems to have resulted in giving undue priority to improved transport over production of a commodity that could employ such facilities. The German colonists chose to accept temporarily the handicap of deficient transport in order to secure the advantages afforded by the more inviting country of the interior, where they were able to exploit an already cultivated agricultural staple. Later, when the volume of the traffic warranted, steamer service was in-augurated between Panzós and Livingston, and they constructed the Verapaz Railway between Pancajché and Panzós to provide transport over the most treacherous segment of the land route from Cobán to the Polochic.[14] The Company expected to accomplish the same re-sults, but it planned the steps in reverse sequence. In this sense its project failed in conception as well as in execution.

The transformation wrought by the United Fruit Company in the Motagua Valley during the early years of the twentieth century more closely approximated the massive projects inaugurated by Gálvez. Al-though not concerned primarily with attracting foreign residents to uninhabited territory, it and companies with which it was closely affiliated developed virtually every aspect of the plan for colonization of the district of Santo Tomás proposed by Gálvez and his successors. These foreign entrepreneurs established new communities in the pre-

12. Guillermo Náñez Falcón, "German Contributions to the Economic Develop-ment of the Alta Vera Paz of Guatemala, 1865-1900" (Unpubl. Thesis, Tulane, 1961).

13. The "Karte der Alta Verapaz" and the "Liste der Grundstücke" published by Karl Sapper in "Die Alta Verapaz," *Mittheilungen der Geographischen Gesell-schaft in Hamburg,* XVIII (1901), 216-23, make this boundary graphically apparent.

14. Náñez Falcón, pp. 70-77.

viously uninhabited coastal areas, began the large-scale commercial production of bananas for export, operated a national deepwater port at Puerto Barrios on the Bay of Santo Tomás, and completed the Northern Railroad, which inaugurated rapid communication between the seacoast and the capital. Within its concession the enterprise inaugurated facilities that provided a variety of special services, and both formally and casually it exerted a tutorial influence over nationals in its area. In short, the United Fruit Company achieved in accord with the standards of its time essentially what both the Eastern Coast Company and the Belgian Colonization Company had been expected to accomplish for an earlier epoch.

The success of a twentieth-century corporation in executing a project on which the nineteenth-century contractors failed was undoubtedly due in part to more abundant resources, greater competence, and superior entrepreneurship. It may be attributed in part also to a difference in time and in technique. Discovery of the insect carriers of malaria and yellow fever made it possible by the early years of the twentieth century to control the endemic diseases that previously had scourged the tropical lowlands. Physical discomfort could perhaps not yet be eliminated, but health conditions tolerable to European constitutions could be created. Similarly, mechanization of agricultural operations and of transport reduced to a practicable level the human labor requirements for economic exploitation of the area. The facilities available during the first half of the nineteenth century probably made a similar accomplishment virtually impossible to the earlier contractors.

The successful foreign development of the Verapaz and the region of Santo Tomás in subsequent years evoked a local reaction strikingly similar to that of Chiquimula in 1835. Because the German colonization of the Verapaz was gradual and individual, however, and because the settlers established themselves among resident Guatemalans, it took some time for the realization to dawn that this development had produced results akin to those feared under the Gálvez contracts. The unitary nature of the United Fruit Company operation, in contrast, made its position immediately conspicuous. Its success demonstrated a principle that seems to have been clearly implicit in the colonization projects of the 1830's. The magnitude of the developmental program conceived by Gálvez, admittedly beyond the capabilities of the state, required for its execution such enormous resources that only a colossus could undertake it with hope of success. It followed, therefore, that a successful contractor could scarcely fail to rival the government itself in power. This probability Gálvez appears not to have forseen. It was sensed almost immediately, however, by the critics of the Bennett and Meany grant. It was also perceived by Pavón and Batres, whose *voto particular* on the Belgian contract argued that success of the colonization scheme could result only in calamity for Guatemala. With modifications appropriate to the disparity in time, their prophetic catalog of consequences to be anticipated from the successful execution of the Santo Tomás agreement in 1842 could well have served as a précis for the charges made by its enemies in Guatemala against the United Fruit Company in 1952.

The objectives he set for his colonization projects suggest that Gálvez clearly identified at least some of the fundamental requirements for development of his country. His touch was less certain, however, when he undertook to devise appropriate means by which to accomplish the necessary reforms or to choose suitable personnel to execute his plans. A scarcely better fate has been granted to most of the leaders who, since his time, have also endeavored to direct poor countries out of their poverty: the problem can be reasonably well defined, but an effective means of attacking it has rarely been discovered. The fundamental issues that the colonization projects were intended to resolve in Guatemala therefore remain tenaciously alive there and elsewhere in the underdeveloped world. The persistence of these basic problems and of the tensions that have arisen in consequence of the measures adopted during the intervening years in the hope of finding solutions has made the quest for acceptable and effective techniques of stimulating economic growth one of the crucial endeavors of our time. To an era thus critically concerned with finding avenues along which the poor nations of the world can be directed toward development, the mute populations and the unbuilt towns of the Guatemalan wilderness empires of the 1830's speak a vital, if silent, message.

ABBREVIATIONS

ABH	Archives of British Honduras. Belize.
ABVP	Archivo Departamental de Baja Verapaz. Salamá.
AMAE	Archives du Ministère des Affaires Étrangères, et du Commerce Extérieur. Brussels.
AMG	Archivo del Ministerio de Gobernación. Guatemala City.
AMRAHM	Archives du Musée Royal de l'Armée et d'Histoire Militaire. Brussels.
ANG	Archivo Nacional de Guatemala. Guatemala City.
CO	Colonial Office Papers, Public Record Office. London.
FO	Foreign Office Papers, Public Record Office. London.

GLOSSARY

acuerdo—An executive resolution.

alcalde—The principal executive and peace officer of a Municipality. Larger towns had more than one (designated *alcalde primero, alcalde segundo,* etc.) between (or among) whom the functions of the office were divided. For centers of population without municipal organization (such as Abbottsville) the Municipality within whose jurisdiction the territory fell designated an *alcalde auxiliar* from among the inhabitants who discharged the functions of *alcalde* under the supervision of the appointing Municipality.

arroba—A measure of weight equivalent to twenty-five pounds.

Bayman—The name assumed by the residents of British Honduras, situated on the Bay of Honduras.

bejuco—A tough, supple, slightly elastic vine or creeper.

bulto—A bundle or package. As applied to cargo, it often signified a bale made up in size and weight so that two or three would constitute a conventional mule-load—that is, about three hundred pounds.

chimán—A diviner, a native priest or shaman.

comeién—A kind of wood-borer.

corregidor—The chief administrative officer of a Guatemalan department after the law of October 2, 1839, re-created the office to supersede that of *jefe político.*

ejido—Village or town lands held in common ownership.

empresario—An entrepreneur or contractor, especially one who undertook to enlist abroad, import, and establish colonists in new settlements.

expediente—The file accumulated on a given subject.

hoja suelta—A handbill or flyer.

ingenio—A sugar mill and plantation.

jefe político—The chief administrative officer of a Guatemalan department prior to October 2, 1839.

Ladino—A culturally non-Indian individual. By extension, the term was sometimes used, perhaps only by the imprecisely informed, to mean a mixed-blood.

league—A term used popularly but imprecisely to express a distance usually of two and one-half to three miles. Great distances and large land areas were often expressed in leagues.

montaña—A mountain, hill country, or uplands. As used in the term "insurrection of the *montaña*," it carried the connotation of back country.

mozo—A porter, or man-of-all work.

nigua—A pest that embeds itself under the skin, especially under the toe nails, and as it grows to adulthood forms an itching blister that opens into a sore.

peso—The Spanish dollar which remained the principal coin of Central America and Guatemala after independence. It was equal in value to eight *reales,* to one Belgian franc, and to four English shillings or one-fifth of one pound sterling.

principal—One of the head men of an Indian town.

temporal—A seasonal storm of heavy rain accompanying the autumnal equinox.

vara—A linear measure equivalent to about 2.8 feet.

voto particular—A separate opinion often expressing a minority view.

zurrón (seroon)—The unit in which indigo and cochineal were customarily prepared for shipment from Guatemala. It was a bundle or bale usually weighing one hundred fifty pounds, two of which formed a mule-load.

BIBLIOGRAPHY

Contemporary Sources

Manuscript Collections

Belgium, Brussels.
Archives du Ministère des Affaires Étrangères, et du Commerce
Extérieur.
2027. Colonisation, Santo Thomas de Guatemala (jusqu'à
1852).
Archives du Musée Royal de l'Armée et d'Histoire Militaire.
Officier 1852 (Remy de Puydt).
British Honduras, Belize.
Registry. Government Archives.
Letters Inwards, 1826-1848, Records 10.
Letters Outwards, 1829-1838, Records 8.
El Salvador, San Salvador.
Biblioteca Nacional.
Libro de actos del Congreso Federal, 1835.
Great Britain, London.
British Museum.
Additional Manuscripts 38510, 40510.
Friends' House. Library of the Society of Friends.
A List of the Members of the Peel Monthly Meeting in
the County of Middlesex from 1st March 1837 to ——.
Luke Howard Collection.
Public Record Office.
Foreign Office 15 (Central America and Guatemala), 37
(Netherlands), 252 (Consulate in Central America and
Guatemala).
Colonial Office 123 (British Honduras).
Guatemala, Guatemala City.
Archivo Nacional (formerly Archivo General del Gobierno).
Archivo del Ministerio de Gobernación.
Comunicaciones 1835.
Expedientes 1837.

Guatemala, Salamá.
Archivo Departamental de Baja Verapaz.
United States, New Orleans.
Tulane University, Latin American Library.
Morazán Papers.

Published Documents and Collections

Arbitraje de límites entre Guatemala y Honduras: Anexos del alegato presentado por Guatemala ante el tribunal de arbitraje. . . . Washington, 1932.

Colección de los decretos de observancia general, expedidos por la Asamblea Constituyente del Estado de Guatemala, en los años de 1839 y 1840. Guatemala, 1840.

"Discurso del Presidente del Congreso Federal, Diputado J. Basilio Porras, pronunciado al cerrar sus sesiones ordinarias aquel cuerpo el 20 de julio de 1838," *Boletín* del Archivo General del Gobierno (Guatemala), III, No. 3 (April, 1938), 499-55.

Exposición que al comenzar la actual Legislatura ordinaria, hizo al Congreso federal de esta República el S[ecreta]rio de Estado y del despacho de Hacienda . . . leída . . . en . . . los días 20 y 23 de abril y 4 de mayo . . . de 1830 . . . . Guatemala, 1830.

Informe que presentó al Congreso federal, el Secretario de Estado y del despacho de Hacienda, al dar cuenta del negocio relativo à la apertura del canal de Nicaragua: en la sesión pública ordinaria del sábado 24 de julio de 1830. [Guatemala], n.d.

Informe que el Secretario de Relaciones hace a la nación de orden del Presidente de la República sobre la conducta del licenciado Nicolás Espinosa Gefe del Estado del Salvador [San Salvador?], 1836.

Manning, William Ray (ed.). *Diplomatic Correspondence of the United States. Inter-American Affairs, 1831-1860.* 12 vols. Washington, 1932-39.

Marure, Alejandro, and Andrés Fuentes Franco (comps.). *Catálogo razonado de las leyes de Guatemala.* Guatemala, 1856.

Memoria de la Secretaría Jeneral de Estado del supremo gobierno de Guatemala en la Federación de Centro-América, sobre todos los ramos de la administración pública presentada a la Legislatura de 1837 por el jeneral de división C. Carlos Salazar. Guatemala, [1837].

Memoria leída por el secretario del Consulado, al abrirse le sesión el 19 de mayo de 1843, en conformidad a lo que previene el art. 30 de la cédula de erección. Guatemala, 1843.

Memoria leída por el secretario del Consulado de Comercio del Estado de Guatemala al abrirse la sesión de 20 de mayo de 1844 en conformidad a lo que previene el artículo 30 de la cédula de erección; y mandada imprimir por acuerdo de la Junta de 4 de junio del mismo año. Guatemala, 1844.

Memoria leída por el secretario del Consulado de Comercio del Estado de Guatemala, al abrirse la sesión de 19 de mayo de 1845; mandada imprimir por acuerdo de la Junta; y en conformidad a lo que previene el artículo 30 de la cédula de erección. Guatemala, 1845.

Memoria leída por el secretario del Consulado de Comercio de la República de Guatemala, al abrirse la sesión el dia 4 de Agosto de 1847, en conformidad à lo que previene el artículo 30 de la cédula de erección. Guatemala, [1847].

Memoria leída por el secretario interino del Consulado de Comercio de la República de Guatemala, Lic. Don Vicente Zebadua, al abrirse la sesión el dia 19 de mayo de 1853, en conformidad à lo que previene el artículo de la cédula de erección. Guatemala, 1853.

Memoria leída por el secretario del Consulado de Comercio de la República de Guatemala, Lic. D. Jorge Menocal, al abrirse la sesión el dia 19 de mayo de 1854 en conformidad à lo que previene el artículo 30 de la cédula de erección. Guatemala, 1854.

Memoria leída por el secretario del Consulado de Comercio de la República de Guatemala, Lic. D. Jorge Menocal, al abrirse la sesión el dia 19 de mayo de 1856, en conformidad á lo que previene el art. 30 de la cédula de erección. Guatemala, 1856.

Memoria que el secretario general del Despacho presenta a la novena Legislatura del estado, leída el 12 de febrero de 1836. Guatemala, [1836].

"Mensaje del Jefe del Estado de Guatemala, Dr. Mariano Gálvez, al abrirse las sesiones ordinarias de la Asamblea Legislativa, en 1836," *Anales* de la Sociedad de geografía e historia de Guatemala, II, No. 3 (March, 1926), 310-17.

Noticia al Congreso Federal de la revolución de Guatemala. [Guatemala, 1838].

Pineda de Mont, Manuel (comp.). *Recopilación de las leyes de Guatemala.* 3 vols. Guatemala, 1869-72.

Newspapers

La Aurora (Guatemala City). Trim. 3, No. 17 (Aug. 15, 1845).

The Belize Advertiser (Belize, British Honduras). Supplement to Vol. I, No. 21 (Mar. 2, 1839).

Boletín Oficial (Guatemala City). 1834-36.
———, Segunda parte. 1833-36.
———, Tercera parte. 1837.
The Colonial Gazette (London). 1840.
Gaceta Oficial (Guatemala City). 1841-44.
Honduras Observer (Belize, British Honduras). 1841.
L'Indépendant (Brussels). 11e Année, No. 281 (Oct. 8, 1841).
Moniteur Belge (Brussels). 1841-42.
Morning Herald (London). 1833-40.
La Oposición (Guatemala City). 1837.
Semanario de Guatemala (Guatemala City). 1836.
El Siglo de Lafayette (Guatemala City). 1831.
Suffolk Chronicle (Ipswich). 1836.
El Tiempo (Guatemala City). 1839-40.
Times (London). 1833, 1841-42.
La Verdad (Guatemala City). Núm. 8 (Nov. 29, 1837).

Hojas Sueltas

Al Sr. Secretario del despacho de gobernación del Supremo Gobierno. [Guatemala, 1843].
Carlos Salazar Jeneral de la primera división, y Secretario del Supremo Gobierno del Estado. Guatemala, 1837.
Conciudadanos. Signed "Un Artezano." Antigua, Guatemala, 1837.
De la Municipalidad de Gualán al C. Gefe político del departamento. [Guatemala, 1834].
Documentos. El licenciado ciudadano José Antonio Azmitia, secretario del despacho de gobernación y justicia del Gobierno del Estado de Guatemala . . . á pedimiento del ciudadano Juan José Balcarsel. Guatemala, 1838.
Meany, Carlos A. *Pocas razones de un lego, á muchos desahogas elocuentes exornadas en textos eruditos y citas magistrales . . . formado por el Sr. Maestro y Dr. Andres Andreu, reclamando la nulidad de la venta de unas casas, ejecutada por ordenes de la Asamblea y Gobierno Supremo del Estado el año de 1829.* Guatemala, 1842.
Pequeño catecismo político sobre colonizaciones. Zacapa, 1835.
Privado de titulos y aptitudes. . . . Address without title attributed to José Antonio Azmitia. Guatemala, 1834.
Profesión de fe política. Guatemala, 1837.

Eastern Coast of Central America Commercial and Agricultural Company Publications

At a General Meeting of Proprietors Held at the Jamaica Coffeehouse on Monday [May] *the 25th inst., the Directors presented the following Report.* London, [1840].

Brief Statement, Supported by Original Documents, of the Important Grants Conceded to the Eastern Coast of Central America Commercial and Agricultural Company by the State of Guatemala. London, 1839.

Brief Statement, Supported by Original Documents, of the Important Grants Conceded to the Eastern Coast of Central America Commercial & Agricultural Company by the State of Guatemala. 2nd ed. London, 1840.

A Compendium of the Leading Points of the Charter Granted by the Government and Chief of State of Guatemala, to the Central America Commercial and Agricultural Company of London. [London, 1835].

Copy of Correspondence Relative to the Steam Boat "Vera Paz," Trading from Belize to the Ports of Omoa and Trujillo. New York, 1838.

Emigration to Central America. [London, 1840].

Emigration to Vera Paz. London, [1840].

Emigration to Vera Paz: Latest Intelligence from the Colony [London, 1840?].

Hints on Colonization, particularly with reference to the Valuable Grant made by the Supreme Government of Central America, to the "Eastern Coast of Central America Commercial and Agricultural Company." London, [1835?].

Information for Emigrants: or A Description of Guatemala, (One of the Federal States of Central America,) Including the British Colony of Verapaz. London, 1836.

Map of the Department of Vera-Paz, One of the States of Guatemala, Central America. London, 1835.

Mémoire contenant un aperçu statistique de l'Etat de Guatemala, ainsi que des renseignements précis sur son commerce, son industrie, son sol, sa température, son climat, et tout ce que est relatif a cet etat. . . . Brussels, 1840.

Mr. Anderson's Report. London, [1839].

Eastern Coast of Central America Commercial and Agricultural Company, Department of Vera Paz. One of the Principal States of Guatemala. Prospectus. [London, 1835].

Report of the Directors, to a General Meeting of Proprietors, 18th August, 1840. London, [1840].

To Respectable Emigrants of Small or Large Capital. London, [1836?].

Personal Memoirs and Travel Accounts

Crowe, Frederick. *The Gospel in Central America.* London, 1850.

Dunlop, Robert Glasgow. *Travels in Central America, being a journal of nearly three years' residence in the Country.* London, 1847.

Hastie, James. *Narrative of a Voyage in the Ship Kennersley Castle, from Leith Roads to Poyais.* Edinburgh, 1823.

Montgomery, George W. *Narrative of a Journey to Guatemala, in Central America, in 1838.* New York, 1839.

Morelet, Arthur. *Travels in Central America, including accounts of some regions unexplored since the conquest.* Translated by Mrs. M. F. Squier. Introduction and notes by E. Geo. Squier. New York, 1871.

Stephens, John Lloyd. *Incidents of Travel in Central America, Chiapas, and Yucatan.* 2 vols. London, 1842.

Thompson, George Alexander. *Narrative of an Official Visit to Guatemala from Mexico.* London, 1829.

Wood, James. *The Adventures, Sufferings, and Observations of James Wood, Containing Amongst Other Things, a Description of Various Places Lying Between the Gulfs of Darien and St. Lawrence . . . .* Ipswich, 1840.

Miscellaneous

Abbott, Peter Harris. *On the Public Debt, with a Plan for its Final Extinction.* London, 1839.

Hendriks, Herman. *A Plain Narrative of Facts.* London, 1824.

Lloyds *Register of Shipping* for 1836, information supplied from The Mariners Museum, Newport News, Virginia.

Parnell, Henry. *On Financial Reform.* London, 1830.

Pigot & Co.'s London Directory for 1834. London, 1834.

Pigot and Co.'s London & Provincial New Commercial Directory for 1828-29. London, 1829.

Post Office London Directory for 1833. London, 1833.

Post Office London Directory for 1834. London, 1834.

The Register of Persons Entitled to Vote in the Elections of Members of Parliament for the City of London. . . . London, 1833.

Robson's Court Guide with Analysis of Peerage for 1837. London, 1837.

Robson's London Directory for 1833. London, 1832.

Robson's London Directory for 1836. London, 1835.

Books, Monographs and Articles

Allen, Victor. "The Prince of Poyais," *History Today,* II (1952), 53-58.

Arriola, Jorge Luis. *Gálvez en la encrucijada. Ensayo crítico en torno al humanismo político de un gobernante.* Mexico, 1961.

Bancroft, Hubert Howe. *History of Central America.* 3 vols. San Francisco, 1886-87.

Batres Jáuregui, Antonio. *El Doctor Mariano Gálvez y su época.* Guatemala, 1925.

Díaz, Victor Miguel. *Boceto biográfico del Doctor Mariano Gálvez.* Guatemala, 1925.

Emden, Paul H. "The Brothers Goldsmid and the Financing of the Napoleonic Wars," *Transactions* (1935-39) of the Jewish Historical Society of England, XIV (1940), 225-46.

Fabri, Joseph. *Les Belges au Guatemala (1840-1845).* Brussels, 1955.

Graham, Ian. "Juan Galindo, Enthusiast," *Estudios de Cultura Maya,* III (1963), 11-35.

Griffith, William J. "Juan Galindo, Central American Chauvinist," *Hispanic American Historical Review,* XL (1960), 25-52.

Hasbrouck, Alfred. "Gregor MacGregor and the Colonization of Poyais Between 1820 and 1824," *Hispanic American Historical Review,* VII (1927), 438-59.

Humphreys, R. A. *The Diplomatic History of British Honduras, 1638-1901.* London, 1961.

Jones, Chester Lloyd. *Guatemala, Past and Present.* Minneapolis, 1940.

Marure, Alejandro. *Efemérides de los hechos notables acaecidos en la república de Centro-américa.* Guatemala, 1895.

Montúfar, Lorenzo. *Reseña histórica de Centro-América.* 7 vols. Guatemala, 1878-88.

Nañez Falcón, Guillermo. "German Contributions to the Economic Development of the Alta Vera Paz of Guatemala, 1865-1900." Unpublished Master's thesis, Tulane University, 1961.

Naylor, Robert Arthur. "British Commercial Relations with Central America, 1821-1851." Unpublished doctoral dissertation, Tulane University, 1958.

Naylor, Robert A. "The British Role in Central America Prior to the Clayton-Bulwer Treaty of 1850," *Hispanic American Historical Review,* XL (1960), 361-82.

Pérez Valenzuela, Pedro. *Santo Tomás de Castilla: Apuntes para la historia de las colonizaciones en la costa atlántica.* Guatemala, 1956.

Sapper, Karl. "Die Alta Verapaz," *Mittheilungen der Geographischen Gesellschaft in Hamburg,* XVIII (1901), 78-223.

Shepperson, W. S. *British Emigration to North America: Projects and Opinions in the Early Victorian Period.* Oxford, 1957.

Ward, Barbara. *The Rich Nations and the Poor Nations.* New York, 1962.

Williams, Mary Wilhelmine. *Anglo-American Isthmian Diplomacy,
    1815-1915*. Washington and London, 1916.
Woodward, Ralph Lee, Jr. "The Consulado de Comercio of Guate-
    mala, 1793-1871." Unpublished doctoral dissertation, Tulane Uni-
    versity, 1962.

INDEX

Note: To conserve space the Eastern Coast of Central America Commercial and Agricultural Company and the Compagnie belge de colonisation, except under their own headings, are referred to, respectively, as the Company and the Compagnie.

Abbott, Peter Harris, 69-71, 157-59, 162, 227
Abbottsville, settlement projected, 191-97; established, 200-3, 206-14, 219-22, 231-32; abandoned, 251-52; mentioned, 199, 216, 228-30, 237, 248, 269, 271-72, 280-81, 297-304, 307
Adhemar, Maurice d', 198-200
Agriculture, development needed in north, 8, 10; projected by Galindo, 121-22; planned by Company, 130-31, 136-38, 190-92, 194, 206-7, 215, 297 (attempted, 139-40, 146, 195, 201, 222; failed, 297-300). See also Development
Alberdi, Juan Bautista, 3
Alvarez, Miguel, 61, 63
Amatique Bay, 11, 13
Ampudia, Valentín, 139
Ampudia y Pulleiro, 261, 272-73
Anderson, John, 80, 145-48, 150
Anderson, Young, Company agent in Guatemala, 156, 162-63, 165; negotiates Verapaz and Santo Tomás contracts, 162, 166-81, 185, 206; manages "Vera Paz," 165-66, 256-68; relations with Chatfield, 181-85; returns to London, 187-88; reports to directors, 190-95; Company superintendent in Guatemala, 198-202, 206-14, 220-21; discredited and displaced, 218-19, 221, 229, 231, 251; mentioned, 230-32, 241, 252, 270-71, 289, 296, 301, 306
Andrew Kennedy & Company, 272
Animals, pack and saddle, 11-12; wild, 140, 150, 299; game, 142, 144. See also Livestock
Arce, Manuel José, 4-5
Arrivillaga, Manuel, 237
Aycinena, Juan José de, 245
Aycinena, Pedro, 169
Azmitia, José Antonio, 173

Bank, Anglo-Belgian, 217
Bank of Guatemala, 216-17
Bailey, Helen, 198, 213, 242
Balcarzel, Juan José, 10, 153, 168-69, 186, 230, 234, 244. See also Pulleiro associates
Baptist Missionary Society, 211, 251
Barnett, Captain, delegate of Superintendent at Abbottsville, 231-32
Barrett, Jeremiah, sketch, 24; mentioned, 49, 67-68, 126, 162
Barrett, Jonathan, 24
Barrios, Justo Rufino, 284, 307
Barrundia, José Francisco, 242
Batres, Luis, 203, 236, 246, 248, 310
Bay Islands, 151, 286
Bay of Honduras. See Honduras, Gulf (or Bay) of
Bay of Santo Tomás. See Santo Tomás, Bay of
Belgian Colonization Company. See Compagnie belge de colonisation
Belgian Exploratory Commission, 223-26, 228-52 passim
Belisario, J. M., 161
Belize, transit port of Central America, 8-9, 11, 37, 58, 182, 184; clearing port for mahogany, 80, 82, 160; port of "Vera Paz," 129, 165-66, 175, 191, 256-69 passim; Company colonists at, 144-48, 151-52; mentioned, 12, 20, 21n, 27-30, 37-45 passim, 51, 55-58, 63, 76-83, 90, 92, 122, 133, 135, 150, 153-54, 171, 182-85, 187, 200, 211, 220, 223, 228-29, 231, 235, 247-48, 250-51, 272-74, 281, 284, 290-91
Belize, Settlement of. See British Honduras
Belize River, 40, 57, 61, 76, 122
Bennett, Marshal, maneuvers colonization negotiations, 20, 30, 36-37; sketch,

28-30; conspires with Gould, 30; honorary director of Company, 37; dies, 90; mentioned, 10, 21n, 38, 51, 81-91 *passim*, 101-5, 113, 135, 137, 139, 142-45, 147, 150-52, 155, 160, 259, 292. *See also* Hall, Meany, and Bennett

Bennett and Meany, own San Jerónimo, 29; obtain colonization contracts, 32-38, 41-45 *passim;* mentioned, 39-40, 56, 58, 81-92, 94, 97-98, 100-7 *passim,* 120, 153, 164, 168, 203, 286, 295, 305. *See also* Colonization contracts

Bennett, Meany, and Rodríguez woodcutting company, 10, 30

Berghe de Binckum, J. van den, 226

Bingham, Parker Duckworth, 188, 218-21, 228, 266

Blount, Edward, 69

Boca Nueva River, 165, 187, 191, 194, 199-200, 271

Boletín Oficial (Guatemala), 106

Bourjot, Charles H., 70-71, 158-59, 162

Bridges, "la hamaca" at Polochic crossing described, 12; iron span for Motagua required of Company, 179-80 (constructed and shipped, 196, 214, 234, 249, 271-72; transported to site, 272-78; erected, 278-79; destroyed and replaced, 279-80; investment unprofitable, 304-5). *See also* Roads

"Britannia," 132-35, 144-48, 198, 256

British Honduras (Belize), woodcutters of, operate beyond treaty limits, 8-16 *passim,* 53, 68, 76, 290; tenure and boundary controversy, 8, 16, 37, 39-41, 52-78 *passim,* 84, 128-29, 154, 286, 290-92; Magistrates of, 28, 81, 145-46, 151, 165, 256-57, 260, 268-69; Public Meeting of, 28, 82, 269; mentioned, 8-9, 12, 25, 28, 30, 38, 45, 55, 76-83, 92, 103, 107, 109, 116, 121-29 *passim,* 138-39, 154, 183, 187, 202, 290, 293, 305. *See also* Belize, Concessions

Bugden, Thomas, 22, 27, 50

Cajabón River, 138, 148, 158, 174

Cajabón (town), 18, 131, 138, 141-43, 149

Camoyano, Francisco, 261

Canals, from Santo Tomás to Motagua, projected, 43; from Río San Francisco del Mar to Graciosa Bay allegedly built, 169; from Río San Francisco del Mar to Motagua, planned, 169

Canary Islanders, 87, 172, 177, 184

Canning, Charles John, Viscount, 250

Carette, Honoré Joseph, 226, 232

Caribs, 11-12, 139, 141, 222

Carrera, Rafael, 89-90, 152, 163-65, 185, 231-32, 240-41, 244, 266, 287, 289, 305-6

Castillo de San Felipe, 42, 265, 299

Central America, National Constituent Assembly of, 4, 282

Central America, United Provinces (Republic or Federation) of, fosters colonization, 3-4; declared, 4; torn by civil war, 4-5, 86, 112-13, 152, 163-65; dissolved, 185, 289; mentioned, 8, 26, 54, 63, 65, 68, 78, 81, 186, 282, 284

Chacón, C. J., 137

Chamiquín, 12, 143, 193, 202, 208-9

Chatfield, Frederick, prepares for post in Central America, 25-28; relations with Gould, 26-28, 34-35, 51, 66, 125, 149; comments on colonization grants, 38, 51-52, 54-56, 81; proposes purchase of Chiquimula, 58-59, 96, 291; on British tenure and limits of Belize, 59-61, 63, 66; to negotiate treaty of amity and commerce, 60; relations with Fletcher, 135, 137; relations with Anderson, 181-85; mentioned, 27, 39n, 64, 70, 77, 86, 93, 96, 116, 122-23, 136, 139, 152-53, 155, 158, 243, 286, 291

Chaverría, Basilio, 272-73

Chiantla, 252

Chiapas, 55

Chiquimula (city), 86, 113-14

Chiquimula, Department of, ceded to Bennett and Meany, 41; protests cession, 84-86, 87, 89, 94-108 *passim,* 112-19 *passim;* mentioned, 12, 43-44, 82-83, 88, 163, 193, 286, 288-89, 309

Chiquimula, Municipality of, 102-8 *passim,* 115

Chixoy (Negro) River, 41, 82, 180

Cholera, 148, 153-54, 163-64

Clayton-Bulwer Treaty, 292

Climate, and health debated, 8, 17, 26, 117-18, 136-37, 183-84, 195; suitability for Europeans considered, 138, 183, 298-99. *See also* Disease, Insects

Cobán, 275-76, 307-8

Cobb, Francis Riley, 162, 165, 255-56, 261

Cockburn, Francis, 38, 51-65 *passim,* 77, 81, 96

Colón, Antonio, 237

Colonies. *See* Abbottsville, New Liverpool, Santa Cruz

Colonists, special requirements for, 36,

43, 87, 116-17, 122, 174-75, 177; to be settled within concessions, 43, 87, 115, 120, 176-77; sent out by Company, 70, 72, 129, 132-35, 139-48 *passim*, 197 (named, 133-34, 198; mutiny of, 145-48); recruited by Bennett and Meany, 91, 121, 295 (by Galindo, 121-23, 295; by Company, 125-26, 129-32, 196-97, 214-16, 298, 301). *See also* Concessions, Development, Labor

Colonization, projected by Captaincy-General of Guatemala, 3 (by republic of Central America, 4; by state of Guatemala, 17); proposed to state of Guatemala, 4, 10, 14-16, 30, 34-36, 87, 167-73, 236. *See also* Woodcutting

Colonization contracts, made with Galindo for Petén, 5, 16, 32-34, 36, 37, 40-45 *passim* (modified, 123, 155, 166, 180; mentioned, 39, 53, 120); with Company for Verapaz, 5, 32-37, 40-45 *passim* (modified 69, 128, 154-56, 162, 166-67, 179-81; nullified, 228, 234-35, 238; mentioned, 39, 53, 56, 61, 120, 182, 187, 190, 213, 217, 224, 268, 289, 300, 306, 309); with Bennett and Meany for Chiquimula, 5, 32-33, 36-38, 41-45 *passim,* 84-85 (protested, 84-119 *passim;* modified, 84-86, 98, 114-15; nullified, 88-89, 119; mentioned, 39-40, 56, 58, 79, 82, 289, 310); with Bennett and Meany for Totonicapán, 5, 32-33, 36, 41-45 *passim* (mentioned, 39-40, 56, 82, 120, 289); with Bennett and Meany for Lake Izabal, 5, 32-33, 36, 41-45 *passim* (modified, 89-90; nullified, 91-92; mentioned, 39-40, 56, 79, 81-82, 120, 143, 186); with Pulleiro associates for Santo Tomás, 87-88, 153 (modified, 154, 172, 176; petition to reactivate, 186; rights sold to Compagnie, 230, 239); with Company for Santo Tomás, 173-79 (extended, 185; considered by Consulado, 186, 203-5; ratification denied, 205-6; restitution sought, 219, 228, 235, 237-38; refused, 219, 235, 238; mentioned, 180-90 *passim,* 203, 206, 217, 224, 227, 233, 237, 241, 289, 300, 306); with Compagnie for Santo Tomás, 236, 239 (mentioned, 229, 289, 305-6, 310); submitted for federal ratification, 39, 51, 88, 158; to be registered, 40. *See also* Concessions, Development

Colonization law, federal, 4, 14-15, 18, 44, 75, 105, 108-11, 169, 282; Verapaz, 15-20, 30, 32-33, 40, 282

Commerce of Central America, with Europe impeded by natural obstacles, 8; tributary to Belize, 8-9, 84, 284, 291; with Belize, 11, 95-96 (subject to punitive regulation, 37, 54, 63, 66, 84); Company plans to monopolize, 190-93, 253, 256, 280, 300, 303-4; disrupted by civil war, 163, 269. *See also* Development, Smuggling

Compagnie belge de colonisation (Compagnie), buys land and rights from Company, 218, 223-25, 228-32, 238-39, 248; organized, 225-26; obtains direct cession of Santo Tomás, 227, 230-31, 236-37, 239-41, 243-44; relations with Anderson, 229, 231, 248-49, 251; opinions on, 246; mentioned, 240, 248-51, 280, 285, 289, 300, 305-6, 309

Company. *See* Eastern Coast of Central America Commercial and Agricultural Company

Concessions to colonizers, of land and resources, offered, 18-19 (granted, 40-43, 81-83, 87-88, 174, 179-80, 282; infringed by Belize cutters, 57, 63, 68, 77-80, 187 [and by other grants, 88, 153, 162] exploited by concessionaires, 79-86, 88-92; criticized, 84-85, 95, 101, 104-6, 113, 163-64, 204, 289; Assembly requests report on, 186) (*see also* Agriculture, Woodcutting); of monopolies, offered, 18 (granted, 43-44, 126-27, 175-76, 179-81, 253) (*see also* Monopolies); of immunity from local monopolies, offered, 19 (granted, 45, 178); of privilege and special status, offered, 18-19 (granted, 45, 94, 177-79, 282; criticized, 100, 104-5, 107, 204, 286-87; defended, 109, 288); of options to construct public works, offered, 18 (granted, 43, 175; with monopoly control, offered, 18 [granted, 175, 180]) (*see also* Public works); of options to undertake further colonization, granted, 44

Conservatives, 96, 185, 284

Consulado de Comercio, development expected of, 9, 186, 306; re-established, 186; recommends disapprobation of Santo Tomás cession, 203-5; erects and maintains Motagua bridges, 277-79; mentioned, 3-4, 10, 206, 220, 242, 248, 276, 280-81, 289, 294, 304-5

Convento Viejo, 29
Córdova, Ignacio, 209
Costa Rica, 4
Cox, Leonard P., 261
Coxe, Leonard S., 50, 71, 156, 188
Croskey, José, 14, 75. *See also* Piñol and Croskey
Crowe, Frederick, sketch, 211; mentioned, 133-34, 151, 202, 211-12, 221, 251, 270, 281, 288, 302
Crozier, William, sketch, 25; mentioned, 24, 49, 126, 132, 162

Dawson, John, 188
Day, James, 21
Dechange, ship's doctor on "Louise-Marie," 226
Development, colonizers expected to promote, 4, 8, 117, 282 (but contradicted, 204, 247-48); by increasing laboring population, 4, 110; by applying technical knowledge and skill, 4, 17, 93, 282; by importing capital, 6, 17, 93, 111, 282-83 (but contradicted, 95, 101, 182); by securing frontiers of the state, 8, 9, 52-54, 84, 109-11, 184, 284, 286 (but contradicted, 95, 103-4, 107, 112-13, 204, 238, 246-47, 288-89, 292); by tutelage of nationals, 93, 103, 167, 284, 286-87 (but contradicted, 95, 104, 106, 287); by insuring white supremacy, 93, 167, 171, 240, 284 (but resisted, 164, 287); in commerce, 8, 190, 283 (but contradicted, 95-96, 104, 113, 246, 288); in transport, 11, 17, 110, 253, 303; in agriculture, 74, 109, 283 (but contradicted, 95, 101, 105-6, 182-83); in new industries, 110, 283 (but contradicted, 95, 106, 164). *See also* Agriculture, Commerce, Public works, Woodcutting
Devercy, Adrien Casimir Grosset, 226, 230, 232, 240, 243
Dieguez, José Domingo, 278
Disease, in Guatemalan northern lowlands, 8, 17, 26, 183, 202, 265, 275, 299; on immigrant ships, 134, 148; among Company colonists, 141-43, 148-49, 151-52, 201-2, 260, 299; in Belize, 148, 152, 184. *See also* Cholera, Climate
Domínguez, Vicente, 5, 12
Dorantes, José Mariano, 97-98
Dorantes, guerrilla leader in Chiquimula, 163
Dyer, John, 133, 152

Eastern Coast of Central America Commercial and Agricultural Company (Company), origins, 20-22; relations with Bennett, 20, 30, 36-37, 121, 135, 137, 142-45, 150, 259; officers, 22, 24-25, 37, 49-50, 69-71, 128, 158-59, 188-89, 227; offices, 22, 50, 189; finances, 23, 48-49, 159, 189, 196, 216, 218-20, 225-26, 280; opinions on, 25-27, 65, 187, 241; relations with Galindo, 34, 37, 66-67, 69-70, 128, 149, 166-67, 172, 180-82; relations with Meany, 34, 37, 155-56; reorganized, 47-48, 156-59, 188; publications, 50, 130, 189, 196, 215; price of shares, 51, 65, 126; involved in Belize boundary controversy, 64-79 *passim*, 92, 126, 128; interest in Guatemalan and Belgian bank projects, 216-18; relations with Compagnie, 227-45 *passim*, 248-50; commercial agents in Guatemala, 230, 261, 272 (in Belize, 259, 261, 272); mentioned, 5, 40-43, 56, 120, 123-87 *passim*, 246-47, 251-53, 280-81, 288-89, 291-93, 295-309. *See also* Anderson, Bingham, Colonies, Colonists, Colonization contracts, Fletcher, Gould, Mora, Murray, (Jr.), Poyaisian securities, Poyaisian Trust Office, Public works
El Mico, 169, 172
El Salvador, state of, 4-5, 28-29, 86, 112-14, 193
Empresarios, authorized by federal colonization law, 4; made agents for development in Guatemala, 15, 17, 120, 283; mentioned, 31-32, 37, 43, 52-53, 74, 84, 120, 282, 285, 289-90. *See also* Colonization contracts, Concessions, Development
England. *See* Great Britain
Espada y Piloña, 261
Espinosa, Nicolás, 86, 112-113, 163
Esquipulas, Municipality of, 102, 106. 115-16
Estanzuela, Municipality of, 102, 104

Fabri, Joseph, cited, 244
Fancourt, St. John, 269
Federal colonization law. *See* Colonization law, federal
Fenner, Rest, 50
Fletcher, Thomas, Company superintendent in Verapaz, 125-26, 128, 135-56 *passim*, 163, 165-66, 182-83, 254-56, 261, 296, 301, 307; agent in Guatemala

of London bankers, 216-17. *See also*
Bank of Guatemala
Flores, Juan José, 233, 241, 243-44
Flores, Plácido, 137, 139
Floripes, Angel, 14, 88, 168, 172, 174
Forsyth, John, 61, 63
France, consul of, in Central America, 96,
145; mentioned, 20, 67, 102, 247
Freedmen (from British West Indies),
to be enveigled into servitude, 22, 27;
unacceptable as colonists, 177, mentioned, 131, 179. *See also* Slavery

Gaceta Oficial (Guatemala), 280
Galindo, Juan, sketch, 15-16; obtains
colonization grant in Petén, 16, 32-34,
36-37, 40-45 *passim*, 155; relations
with Company, 30, 34, 37, 66-67, 69-
70, 121-23, 128, 149, 166-69, 172, 180-
82; tries in Belize to enforce grant,
51, 56-57, 63, 76-77, 122; involved in
Belize boundary controversy, 53, 59-
60, 63, 77-78, 92; mission to Washington and London, 60-61, 63-67, 69-70,
122; mentioned, 38, 53, 55, 290-93, 295.
See also Colonists, Colonization contracts
Galindo and Moscoso, obtain road contract, 168-69, 172, 175
Gálvez, Mariano, deputy to National
Constituent Assembly, 4; on development, 5-6, 8-10, 17, 93, 282-84; federal
Minister of Finance, 8-9; Chief of
State of Guatemala, 8, 99; submits
colonization proposals to Assembly, 8,
10, 14, 34-36, 75; role in contracts of
1834, 33-38, 285; relations with Company, 50, 128, 153-56; on Belize
boundary controversy, 60-61, 73, 116;
uprisings against, 86, 89, 96, 112-14,
163-65; overthrown, 163, 165, 289;
mentioned, 11-20 *passim*, 31, 40, 52-54,
66-67, 69, 76, 83-99 *passim*, 115-17, 123,
126, 128, 137, 167, 254-55, 282-87, 290-
94, 300-10
Garbutt's Falls, 57, 63, 77, 79, 122
Gardiner, Henry, 169
Gatica, Manuel, 273-78
German colonists, 91, 134, 198, 201, 307-9
Gillan, William Campbell, 216-17
Glenelg, Charles Grant, Baron, 65-71
passim
Glyn, Hallifax, Mills & Co., 189
Golfete, 42
Gough, Mr., colonist at New Liverpool,

133, 143-44, 146, 151
Gould, Thomas, relations with Chatfield, 26-28, 34-35, 51, 66, 125, 135, 149,
162; negotiates grant of Verapaz, 30,
32-37, 40-45 *passim;* mentioned, 20, 38,
46-47, 49-50, 64
Gower, R. F., 71
Graciosa Bay, 169
Great Britain, 16, 19, 53-55, 61-72 *passim*, 78, 81, 102, 122, 216, 245, 285-86,
289-93, 303. *See also* Chatfield,
O'Reilly
Grey, George, 72
Griffiths, Thomas, 263
Gualán, 11, 14, 83-84, 86, 94-96, 99-102,
174, 183, 232, 248
Guapinol River, 98
Guatemala, Captaincy-General (or Kingdom) of, 3-4, 9, 284
Guatemala, Department of, 41, 278
Guatemala, state of, 4; republic of, 185-
86
Guatemala City, 5, 11-12, 30, 45, 55, 83,
86, 96, 101, 114, 138, 151-52, 155, 166,
182, 185, 191, 210, 213-14, 219-20, 232-
33, 251-53, 261, 273, 278
Guatemala Railroad Company, 307
Guayavillas gold mine, 29
Gulf of Honduras. *See* Honduras, Gulf
(or Bay) of
Gutiérrez, José Dolores, 209
Guzmán, Ramón, 5, 12

Haefkens, J., 130
Hall, Meany, and Bennett, 29
Hall, William, 28, 90, 243
Hammond, J., 50
Havana, 191
Health. *See* Cholera, Climate, Disease
Hecht, Pierre-Emile van der, 224
Hedgecock, Thomas, 160-61
Henderson, Alexander, 211
Henry, Dr., Company doctor in Verapaz,
201
Hise, Elijah, 63
Hondo River, 40, 57, 71
Honduras, Gulf (or Bay) of, 8, 10-11, 18,
41, 44, 51, 79-82, 160, 163, 169, 180,
191, 230, 283, 297, 300, 303
Honduras, state of, 4, 27, 29, 41, 84, 102,
161, 181, 193
Honduras Observer (Belize), 260
Hood, William, 188
Hope, George W., 250-51
Housing, at New Liverpool, 140-41, 146,

298; at Abbottsville, 200-1, 222, 298-99
Huehuetenango, 252
Huggup, Captain, of the "St. Lawrence," 197
Hyde, James, 25, 27

Indians, of El Salvador revolt, 113; of Verapaz, establish towns near Abbottsville, 202-3 (object to service as carriers for Motagua bridge, 275-76; *principales* and *chimanes* consulted, 275; mentioned, 79, 138, 190, 212, 274, 301, 303). *See also* Labor, Mosquito Indians, Provisions
Industry. *See* Development
Infiesta, Francisco, 276, 278
Insects, 136, 140-41, 195, 299
Insurrection of the *montaña*, 89, 163, 254, 285, 287-89
Iturbide, Agustín, 4
Izabal, District of, created, 185; mentioned, 230, 252
Izabal, Lake, navigation by conventional craft, 11, 139; navigation by steam proposed, 14, 43, 126 (inaugurated, 156, 165, 175, 199, 254-55; planned, 191, 194-95; terminated, 270-71); mentioned, 11-12, 18, 32-33, 35, 37, 41-44, 75, 79, 81-83, 89-90, 95, 98, 129, 143, 147, 166, 168, 174, 257, 270, 299. *See also* "Polochiquito," "Vera Paz"
Izabal, port, fire at, 213, 242, 268; port of "Vera Paz," 254-55, 260-68; mentioned, 11, 13-14, 42, 45, 83-84, 90, 101, 128, 137, 139, 141, 143-44, 151, 156, 163, 165-66, 182-83, 199-200, 209-11, 218, 221, 223, 229-30, 232, 248, 254-55, 257, 271-74. *See also* Roads
Iztapa, port of, preferential duties for, 37

Jackson, Andrew, 63
Jamaica, 131, 147
John Oliver and Son, 254

Kelley, William, 263
Kennedy, Andrew, 259, 261, 265. *See also* Young & Kennedy, Andrew Kennedy & Company
King, Dr. W., 133, 201, 211
Klée, Carlos Rodolfo, 152, 155
Klée, Skinner and Company, request colonization grant, 35; said to promote Galindo grant, 37; mentioned, 155

Knoth, William, 251-52, 272-74, 278
Krause, E. Rudolph W., 198, 202, 211, 219-20, 222

La Canoa, 277-78
Ladbrokes, Kingscote & Company, 216
Ladino, 202, 222, 303
Labor, supply promised to colonists, 22, 131, 194, 301; Portuguese imported by Bennett, 121; performed by Indians at Company colonies, 139-44, 149, 200, 202, 222, 302; recruited by Bennett from Company colonists, 142-44, 147, 150-52; by Europeans, at New Liverpool, 138, 143-44, 146, 148-51 (at Abbottsville, 190, 196-97, 215, 302; regime, 197, 210); by Negroes (Caribs) at Abbottsville, 222
Land, offered for sale by Galindo, 76-77, 122; by Company, 79, 130-31, 190, 215, 297; by Bennett and Meany, 98; by Compagnie, 225
Leopold I, 225
Liberals, 4-6, 9, 29, 96, 185-86, 282, 284, 306-7
Livestock, slaughtered at New Liverpool, 143, 146, 148; raised at Abbottsville, 201, 222, 252. *See also* Animals
Livingston, District of, 12, 86
Livingston, port, created, 12-14; colonization proposed, 15, 17; mentioned, 135, 139, 145, 150-51, 230, 270, 308
Llano Grande, 191
Lockhorst, Bernard van, 226
Lockhorst, Dirck baron van, 224
London Tavern, 47
López, José Venancio, 233, 239, 241, 243-44
López, Juan, 263
"Lord Charles Spencer," 132-33, 142
Lord Mayor of London, 171
Los Altos, 165, 210
Los Encuentros, 11, 168, 172
"Louise-Marie," 226, 228, 233

Macdonald, Alexander, 187, 256-60, 269
MacDonnell, John, 71
MacGregor, Gregor, 20-21, 24, 27, 30-31, 46, 160, 269
MacKenney, John, 187, 195, 199, 208-10, 213-14, 220-22, 252
MacMinnis (or McManus), Mrs., passenger on "Britannia," 134, 144-45
Mahogany. *See* Woodcutting
Malta, 177, 184

Martínez, Juan Antonio, 169
Marure, Alejandro, 244
"Mary Ann and Arabella," 131-33, 139, 150
Meany, Carlos Antonio, 10, 28, 30, 34, 37, 98, 101, 114, 155-56, 188. *See also* Bennett and Meany; Bennett, Meany, and Rodríguez woodcutting company; Hall, Meany, and Bennett
Mena, Manuel, 274
Mexico, 4, 38, 41, 55, 61, 64-65, 67, 116, 191, 204, 247, 289
Mico Mountain, 11, 13, 248
Miller, Thomas, 56
Milward, Captain, of "Lord Charles Spencer," 132
Mocatta, Daniel, sketch, 24-25; mentioned, 49
Molina, Felipe, 14, 169
Molló, Felipe, 86, 261
Moniteur Belge (Brussels), 225, 249
Monopolies, justified, 127, 294. *See also* Concessions, Navigation, Roads, Woodcutting
Monroe, James, 3, 292
Monroe Doctrine, 3, 61, 292
Montgomery, Archibald, 268-69
Montgomery, George W., 154, 261-65 *passim*
Montúfar, Lorenzo, cited, 112
Mora, José María de, 228-43 *passim*, 248, 251, 272, 302
Morazán, Francisco, 5, 29, 82, 86, 89, 112, 161, 167, 181, 185
Morelet, Arthur, 278, 280
Morning Herald (London), 23-26, 47
Moscoso, Miguel, 168-69
Mosquito Indians, 27
Mosquito "King," 20, 21n, 27, 160, 292
Mosquito Shore (or Coast, or Kingdom), 20-21, 26, 28, 30, 80, 160-61, 181, 269, 292. *See also* Poyais
Motagua River, navigation, proposed, 3; by steam, 44, 191 (monopoly granted, 175); by conventional craft, 101; mentioned, 11-13, 41, 81-83, 94, 165, 168-69, 174, 183, 230, 239, 271-73, 276-77, 303, 308. *See also* Bridges, Roads
Mulard, John (or Joseph), 263
Murray, Adam, 159, 227
Murray, Adam, Jr., 218, 221-23, 229, 231-32, 238-39
Murphy, William S., 243
Mylord, Mr., explorer from Abbottsville, 198, 206

Navigation, obstacles to, 11, 191, 262, 270; improvements projected, 17-18, 126, 176; by steam, monopolies granted, 43-44, 174-75, 180-81, 253 (formalized, 126-27; practicality questioned, 183; inaugurated on Belize-Izabal route, 255-68, 271; on Lake Izabal-Polochic route, 199, 270-71; feared by Belize, 256). *See also* Canals, Izabal (Lake), Motagua River, Polochic River, Public works, Río Dulce, "Vera Paz," "Polochiquito"
Neal, Captain, of "Vera Paz," 261, 266
Netherlands (Dutch), 122-23, 134, 224, 232
New Liverpool, colony, 138-56 *passim*; mentioned, 187, 195, 200, 216, 254, 270, 281, 297-99, 302
Nicaragua, 4
Noller, Samuel, 132
Northern Railroad, 309
Nothomb, Baron Alphonse, 225

Obert, Louis Henri-Charles, 217-18, 224
Oliva, Pedro, 208
Omoa, 5, 12, 114, 183, 266-67
O'Reilly, John, 16, 53, 59-60

Paiz, Gerónimo, 209-11, 214
Palmerston, Henry John Temple, Viscount, 51, 56, 61, 63, 65-72, 78, 122
Pampá, 193
Pancajche, 308
Panzós, 187, 194, 199, 208-10, 214, 270, 297, 300, 308
Pasión River, 18, 180
Pasión (Usumacinta) River. *See* Usumacinta River
Pavón, Manuel Francisco, 169, 203, 246-48, 278, 310
Pearson, Captain, of "Turbot," 163, 269
Peel, Robert, 249
Pérez, Pedro, 208, 210, 214, 221
Petén, District of, contracts for colonization of, 16, 40-41; mentioned, 9, 15, 32, 34, 51, 55-56, 60, 67, 77, 122-23, 138, 184-85, 191, 193
Petit, P. L. N., 226, 229-30, 232
Philip, fireman of "Vera Paz," 263
Phillips, Thomas, 90
Piñol, Juan J., 186, 213
Piñol, Manuel J., 200, 213
Piñol and Croskey, 268

Pollock, David, 189, 227-28, 250
Polochic River, navigation by pirogue, 12, 79, 140-41, 143, 199, 207-10, 272-74, 297; navigation by steam, monopoly offered, 18 (granted, 43; formalized, 126; confirmed, 175; service, planned, 191, 195; inaugurated, 196, 199; terminated, 207, 270-71); mentioned, 41-42, 70, 79, 123, 136, 138-40, 151, 165, 174, 183, 194-95, 200, 203, 272, 276, 297, 300, 303, 308. *See also* Bridges, Roads
"Polochiquito," 196-97, 199, 207, 269-71, 297, 300, 304
Poptún, 191
Ports, construction of, entrusted to colonization *empresarios*, 42, 84-85, 87, 176; development by foreigners criticized, 104, 112, 183, 205, 246. *See also* Izabal, Iztapa, Livingston, Panzós, Public works, Refugio, Santo Tomás, Telemán
Poyais, swindle, 20-21, 24; mentioned, 25, 27, 65, 181
Poyaisian securities, held by Company, 21-26, 47-48, 161-62, 295-96; manipulated by other speculators, 160-61
Poyaisian Trust Office, 22, 161
Provisions, for Company colonies, supplied from natural sources, 142, 202; by import, 142, 148, 222, 251, 299; by Indians, 142, 201-2, 222, 299, 302; by purchase at neighboring towns, 142-43, 148, 209; by local production, 144, 201; trade on the Polochic, 209-10. *See also* Livestock
Public works, required for development, 8-10; navigation and road improvement opened to private capital, 11, 17 (offered under monopoly in Santo Tomás, Lake Izabal, Polochic area, 17-18; entrusted to colonization *empresarios*, 43-44; returned to Consulado, 186-87, 306); unprofitable as private investments, 294, 304-5. *See also* Consulado de Comercio, Navigation, Ports, Roads
Puerto Barrios, 309
Pulleiro, Cándido, 10, 230-31, 233, 240, 242, 274. *See also* Ampudia y Pulleiro
Pulleiro associates (Pulleiro, Balcarzel, Zerón), get woodcutting concession, 10, 87. *See also* Colonization contracts, Santo Tomás

Punta Lechuga, 98
Purulhá, 207
Puydt, Guillaume de, 226, 230, 232
Puydt, Remy de, 224-51 *passim*, 302

Recolección, 29
Refugio, 42-43, 166, 181
Religious freedom (toleration), guaranteed to colonists, 18, 45, 178; denied by populace, 96, 164, 251, 288; permitted, 211-12, 251, 288, 302
Río de la Plata, Republic of, 100
Río Dulce, bar to be opened, 17-18; monopoly of steam navigation granted, 43 (formalized, 126; confirmed, 175); mentioned, 9, 11, 41, 44, 58, 82, 87, 95, 133, 135, 139, 142, 144-45, 153, 165, 174-75, 183, 191, 198, 200, 262, 265-66, 270
Río Tinto Commercial and Agricultural Company, 21-22
Rivera Paz, Mariano, 90, 165-67, 171, 173, 180, 182, 185, 231, 233, 266
Roads, from Guatemala to Izabal, 11 (segment repaired, 11, 168; mentioned, 12, 13, 43, 172, 175); from Guatemala to Polochic, 12 (bridge at Motagua crossing begun, 13; colonization along proposed, 17, 193, 207; to be improved, 191, 207-8; transport over, 274-77; iron bridge erected at Motagua crossing, 278-79; but destroyed and replaced, 297-80; segment Guatemala to bridge built, 278-79; segment bridge to Salamá built, 278-79); from Santo Tomás to junction with Izabal road, traced, 14, 86 (option given to build, 43; allegedly built, 169, 172, 175); from Refugio to Salamá, option given to build, 43 (contracted, 166; repudiated, 180; contracted, 181-82); from Santo Tomás to Motagua, contracted, 168 (allegedly built, 169; monopoly granted, 175; planned, 191); from Santo Tomás to Río Dulce, projected, 175, 191; from Polochic to Petén, proposed, 191, 207 (colonization projected, 193, 206-7). *See also* Bridges
Rodríguez, José, 274
Rodríguez, Juan Manuel, 10, 30, 34, 37, 39. *See also* Bennett, Meany, and Rodríguez woodcutting company
Roper, H., 158
Rush, William, 199, 263

Sacasa, José, 10
Sacatepéquez, Department of, 41
St. John's Coffee House, 132
"St. Lawrence," 197-98, 200, 269
Salamá, 29, 45, 137, 139, 142, 166, 181, 183, 191, 200, 209, 251, 274-78
Salazar Carlos, 154, 185
San Francisco River, 98
San Francisco del Mar River, 169
San Jerónimo, purchased by Bennett and Meany, 29; operated as agricultural enterprise, 121; Portuguese laborers imported for, 121; Company colonists enlisted for, 121, 142-43, 150, 152; mentioned, 97, 115, 137
San Juan Chamelco, 202
San Juan del Norte, 286
San Luis, 55, 138
San Marcos River, 98
San Nicolás, Municipality of, 102, 106
San Pablo, 174
San Pedro Carchá, 202
San Salvador, 110, 182
Santa Cruz, Company colony at, 142-44, 148-50, 153, 254, 299; mentioned, 14, 101, 147
Santa Elena, Municipality of, 102
Santa Lucía, Municipality of, 102
Santa María, Andrés, 209, 220-21
Santo Tomás, Bay of, 3, 13, 41-43, 85, 87, 174, 191, 223, 228-30, 232-33, 265, 303, 309, See also Canals
Santo Tomás, development of port proposed by Captaincy-General, 3 (by state of Guatemala, 13-14, 85-88, 205); colonization proposed, 15, 17 (by Bennett and Meany, 84-86; by Pulleiro associates, 87; by Company, 153, 162, 165, 235, 237-38; by Compagnie, 236); colonization attempted by Pulleiro associates, 153-54 (halted, 168-69); colonization planned by Company, 191-92; colonized by Compagnie, 252; mentioned, 58, 115, 168, 182-84, 191, 239, 244, 250, 270, 283, 290, 303-4, 306. See also Roads
Santo Tomás, District of, ceded to Company, 167, 174 (to Compagnie, 236, 240); mentioned, 171, 196, 203, 206-7, 225, 236, 245-46, 307-8
Sarstoon River, 57, 64, 81, 190
Sears, Robert, sketch, 25; mentioned, 24, 49, 130
Senahú, 207
Shiel, Edward, 56, 76

Sibún River, 41, 57, 64, 67-68, 71, 78, 123, 190
Skinner, George, 155
Slavery, prohibited in colonies, 45, 179. See also Freedmen
Smuggling, 9, 13, 126, 208-10. See also Commerce
Snakes, 141-42
Society of Friends, 24
Soconusco, 5
Sotela, Antonino, 194-95, 202, 208-9, 221
Souper, Philip Dottin, 188-89
Spain, 4, 9, 55-71 passim, 78, 93, 102-3, 109, 177, 237, 245, 247, 290, 295
Spence, Captain, of "Mary Ann and Arabella," 132, 139, 150
Spurgin, John, 188, 196, 251, 271
Steamboats, exempted from port duties, 255. See also Navigation, "Polochiquito," "Vera Paz"
Stephen, James, 64-65, 71, 250
Stephens, John Lloyd, 264-66

Tabanco mine, 29
Taylor, Henry, 59, 64-65
Tegucigalpa, 29
Telemán, 12, 138, 142-43, 148, 165, 180, 183, 194, 208-9, 220, 272-76, 280
Texas, 116-17, 130, 204, 241, 246, 289
Thompson, George Alexander, 130
Thomson, W. Gordon, 70-71, 158
Times (London), 249
T'Kint de Roodenbeck, Auguste, 226, 232-34, 240-41
Totonicapán, Department of, ceded to Bennett and Meany, 32, 41; mentioned, 42-44, 82
Transport. See Bridges, Canals, Izabal (Lake), Motagua River, Navigation, Polochic River, Public works, Roads
Trece Aguas, 193, 206
Trujillo, 5, 12, 266
Tucurú, 202, 209
"Turbot," 80, 163, 254, 257, 269, 270
Tutelage. See Development

United Fruit Company, 307-10
United States, 61, 63, 67, 72, 100, 122, 129, 152, 154, 204, 222, 292. See also Hise, Montgomery (George W.), Murphy, Stephens
Usumacinta River, navigation by steam proposed, 44, 180; mentioned, 41, 82, 184, 191, 214

Vaughan, Charles R., 63

Velís, Manuel María, 86, 169
Verapaz, Department of, colonization
proposed, 15, 17-19; ceded to Company, 32, 41; Mexican designs on, 38,
55; Company colonies in, 70, 72, 132-
56 *passim*, 158, 198-224 *passim*, 231-32,
251-52; mentioned, 30, 50, 54, 65, 79-
80, 83, 125-26, 128-31, 135, 138, 164,
179-81, 187, 225-30 *passim*, 234-36,
248, 253, 273-81 *passim*, 288, 293, 296-
98, 300, 303, 307, 309
"Vera Paz," steamboat, purchased, 125-
26, 254; remains in London Dock, 126,
128-29, 131-32; plans for, 129; expected
in Verapaz, 141-43, 148, 153; sent out,
156, 162-63, 254; arrangements for at
Izabal, 165, 255 (at Belize, 166, 256-
60); operation, 175, 187, 198-99, 229,
257, 260-68; retired and lost, 268-69;
operation unprofitable, 304; mentioned, 191, 223, 230, 242, 270-71, 281,
291
Verapaz colonization law. *See* Colonization law
Verapaz Railway, 308
Vigil, Ramón, 29
Villa Nueva, 185

Walker, Joshua, 69
Wanks River, 80, 269
Ward, Barbara, cited, 5-6
Whattam, Captain, of "Britannia," 132,
135, 144-46
Winsor, James A., 189, 224, 228-29, 249-
51

Withers, John, 198, 213, 220
Wood, James, 133, 142, 150, 216
Woodcutting, grants to spur colonization, 10, 18-19, 37, 74-76 (policy
questioned, 15, 85-86, 117-19; clarified,
91, 111-12, 118-19); grants made to
Pulleiro associates, 10 (to Bennett,
Meany, and Rodríguez, 10, 30; to
Galindo and Moscoso, 168; to Floripes,
168, 172, 174); grants requested by
José Croskey, 14, 75 (by José Mariano
Dorantes, 97); monopoly grants in
Verapaz proposed, 18 (modified, 19);
grants revoked for revalidation, 40;
grants to be registered, 40; monopoly
grants made to Bennett and Meany,
44 (to Pulleiro associates, 87; to Company, 179); operations on Mosquito
Shore, promised by Hedgecock specula-
tors, 160 (conducted by Company,
269; by Belize cutters, 292). *See also*
Belize, Colonization, Concessions
Wright, John, 69
Wright, John Waldron, 40, 50, 83, 122,
126

Xenophobia, 96, 112-13, 163-64

Young & Kennedy, 261
Yucatán, 18, 55, 64, 101

Zacapa, 11, 86, 108; Municipality of,
102, 106, 109, 117-19
Zacualpa, 102
Zerón, Ignacio, 10. *See also* Pulleiro
associates